ELECTIONS IN INDIA
Nehru to Vajpayee

Arun Kumar

PRESS TRUST OF INDIA

in association with

GYAN

Published by

GYAN

Gyan Publishing House
5, Ansari Road
Daryaganj, New Delhi-110002
Phone: 011-47034999, 9811692060
E-mail: books@gyanbooks.com

Distribution Network
gyanbooks.com
India, USA, Canada, UK, Australia, France

ISBN: 978-81-212-0768-3 (HB)

Reprint in India, 2024
First Published, 2001

Printed at: Gyan Press, Delhi.

Elections in India: Nehru to Vajpayee
Author: Arun Kumar

CONTENTS

CONTENTS

DR. M. S. GILL

NIRVACHAN SADAN, ASHOKA ROAD,
NEW DELHI-110 001

FOREWORD

We Indians take pride in the fact, that this country of a billion people, with many contradictions, has functioned as the world's largest democracy for over a half century, even as other nations in the neighbourhood have often slipped in and out of autocratic rule.

Yet at times, faced with problems like growing criminalisation of politics, the accompanying violence and corruption in high places, people wonder whether India can afford to have democracy? My short answer is, that a country of India's size with such cultural diversity, cannot afford to be anything but democratic. And it's for us, the people to make it work. Over the last few years, the Election Commission has done its best to limit the role of money and muscle power to ensure a free and fair poll. Spreading the election schedule, posting election observers, keeping a strict watch on expenses and other malpractices, taking known criminal elements into "protective custody" before the polls, has helped in cleansing the election process. But cleansing the body politic of the country would require much more than such administrative measures.

Over the last four years, the Election Commission has made major system changes, and brought in technology to a large extent. We have computerised the national electoral rolls of 620 million, and put it in published books for each constituency of Parliament. We have further converted each book into a CD Rom disk. Three years back, we started a Website which today has 30,000 pages of material and carries election orders, directions and results, as and when they happen. Scholars worldwide are appreciative of this updated material. Electronic Voting Machines had been brought in 1989, and kept unused, barring a sample election or two. Over the last two years, the Commission has used them extensively in many state elections, and in the national parliamentary elections in 1999. The States of Goa and Pondicherry voted entirely electronically. Haryana substantially so. In 1999 Parliamentary elections,

60 million voters across 46 constituencies, used EVMs. We have given Photo Identity Cards to almost 450 million voters out of 620 million voters. We have used them for compulsory identification in the last elections to the Haryana Assembly along with EVMs. The Machines will be used extensively in the elections early next year to Kerala, Tamil Nadu, Pondicherry and West Bengal. The Commission has a powerful computer network across the country. The Commission believes that systems will last, while individuals will pass on.

Within its own regulations, the Commission has made many salutary improvements. Some limited reforms in the Electoral Law were made in 1966, on the Commission's recommendations. I am clear, that it is necessary to make many more in order to maintain a healthy, and clean democracy in the 21st century. For example, the first past the post system helps candidates win with a small minority vote. It appears that we should insist, as France does, on the winner getting 50% plus one vote. This will ensure a true mandate. More importantly, it will ensure that candidates of all parties, have to reach out to all voters, not concentrate on narrow religious, caste or ethnic support. This is what India needs. Incidentally, I may mention that it is not a problem for the Commission to have a run off election between the top two candidates.

In a 1996 historic judgement, the Election Commission has enforced the holding of regular party elections, as per their constitution, by all recognised political parties. This is the first step in inner party democracy, without which our democracy would be somewhat hollow. The Commission monitors and ensures regular compliance. I hope, that the churning and *manthan* going on within major political parties will strengthen internal democracy and, therefore, India's electoral system. I would like that our Parliamentarians study the German law for political parties. Their law regulates internal democracy, the choosing of the candidates, keeping of accounts etc. It is time, we did something in this direction.

The Commission, has in fact, urged electoral reforms, in repeated party meetings, and in regular letters from me to successive Prime Ministers. We have issued detailed books on our proposals. I have made Press propaganda to educate the people on the issues. I hope that India's powerful Press will support the Commission's endeavour in having better laws, better systems and, therefore, better elections.

I am happy to say that the PTI, which has for 50 years kept the nation informed with its balanced coverage of news and events, has again brought out a book on the 1999 parliamentary poll. As in the past, the book analyses the shifting pattern of votes and focuses on political issues that go beyond cold statistics. I wish to congratulate all those, who have worked on this magnificent publication, and I have no doubt that it will add to our documentation of Indian democracy.

Dr. M.S. Gill
Chief Election Commissioner of India

Preface

The phenomenon of 'hung Houses' and frequent elections in recent years left little time for a reflective look at the fascinating history of Indian elections until the poll of 1999. No sooner did one finish analysing the outcome of one general election that another loomed large on the horizon. With the third Vajpayee government offering hopes of a stable polity despite its make-up one could review the Indian election scene in a less hurried and more in-depth manner.

The result was this book tracing the eventful journey of a vibrant Indian democracy from the charismatic Jawaharlal Nehru to a more home-spun Atal Bihari Vajpayee. Looking back at how India has moved from a virtual single party monopoly in the Nehru days into a coalition era with regional players coming to the fore and contours of a truly federal structure taking shape, it encapsulates the story of Indian elections since the first one in 1952. Then picking up the thread from the 1998 Lok Sabha poll when changing political equations launched India on a coalition course, it provides a comprehensive analysis of the poll of 1999 which seem to have put India back on the road to electoral stability.

Not counting the Janata Party inerlude after Mrs Indira Gandhi's emergency rule in 1977, India saw its first true coalition in 1989 when Rajiv Gandhi was voted out. But the V.P. Singh-led Janata Dal government that then took office was backed from outside by the BJP and the Left. A rag-tag government that Chandra Shekhar formed after its fall, was propped up similarly by Rajiv Gandhi's Congress, until he chose to pull it down after just forty days.

Rajiv's assassination in the summer of 1991 in the midst of a poll brought the Congress back into power despite a split verdict. P.V. Narasimha Rao's minority government not only survived for five years, but also launched far-reaching economic reforms in a stable interlude. A third hung House in seven years, saw then President Shankar Dayal Sharma caught in a dilemma in 1996. Whom should he invite—the largest single party as copy book dictates or the one with greater support in the House. The nation witnessed the spectacle of two governments changing hands in less than two weeks as he chose BJP's Vajpayee over H.D. Deve Gowda at the head of a United Front of a motley group of parties.

The Congress stepped into the picture again and backed two UF goverments, one led by Gowda and the other by Inder Kumar Gujral from outside, until it chose to pull the plug on it over its alleged inaction on the Jain Commission report on Rajiv Gandhi's assassination.

If 1996 was a turning point in Indian politics signalling the end of single party dominance, the fractured verdict of 1998 brought more dramatic changes in the Indian polity with the emergence of a government with a somewhat different complexion. As President K.R. Narayanan looked for a Prime Minister "able and willing" to form a stable dispensation, the BJP as the single largest party itself led the coalition with all but one of the dozen odd supporting parties represented in the government. This was unlike 1996, when a large group like the Congress backed a United Front of smaller parties from outside. Again unlike last time, three broad formations were broadly in place before the elections even though these were more in the nature of seat adjustments rather than partnerships.

With Vajpayee embarking on a tight rope of consensual politics, the allies stuck together and went to the polls of 1999 as one when his second government fell after the withdrawal of support by Jayalalitha's AIADMK. If Chandrababu Naidu's TDP had saved the day for Vajpayee in 1998 with its dramatic switchover from the United Front after the poll, the DMK joining hands with the ruling National Democratic Alliance this time was indicative of the new ball game in the coalition era.

Relating the story of the last poll of the second millennium, this book also provides a flavour of the campaign, the contenders to power, and the issues that exercised the voters' mind, besides providing a comprehensive computer analysis of the shifting voting patterns. Charts showing how the elections went in what were to become three new states of Chhattisgarh, Jharkhand, and Uttranchal have been included to facilitate easy reference next time round.

This is the sixth in the series of books on Indian elections brought out by India's premier news agency, the Press Trust of India, since 1989. It goes without saying that it would not have been possible to put it together without the help and cooperation of PTI correspondents and editors across the country who gathered the basic data.

The painstaking work of Uday Shankar, who spent countless hours in translating cold statistics into charts and graphics that lucidly tell the election story at a glance, needs to be specially acknowledged. I must also thank Mr M.K. Razdan, General Manager of PTI, for his support to the project.

Arun Kumar

CHAPTER 1

TOWARDS A STABLE POLITY

When President K.R. Narayanan, ordered a fresh poll to the Lok Sabha after the fall of Atal Bihari Vajpayee's second government in April of 1999, only a year after it had taken office, India's tired voters heaved a collective sigh. Not again! They must have thought as the country headed for its third election in three years witnessing the change of four Prime Ministers.

Would India go the Italian way? Can stability ever return to the only oasis of democratic rule in the region? Was it the end of the road for the world's largest democracy? These were the questions that assailed the voter and constitutional pundits alike with the wags suggesting that the long run-up to the poll might provide the only interlude of stability to a country hit by the phenomenon of hung Houses since 1989.

The looming prospect of a fifth fractured verdict led to new alignments slowly turning the electoral battle of 1999 more and more into a duel between two formations, one led by the BJP and the other by the Congress with few giving a chance to the Third Front. Still the voters kept their fingers crossed.

The 13th round finally broke the jinx of a hung House putting India back on the road to stability even as it was firmly set on a coalition course with its inevitable pulls and pressures. The arithmetic of the House dictated that the new government would survive unless a group of allies gang up or the BJP itself split.

Thus as President Narayanan called upon Vajpayee to form his third government, criticism of the presidential role in foisting a totally unnecessary election on the nation, gave way to a sense of relief.

Several constitutional experts, among them former President R Venkataraman, suggested that it was not proper on the part of the head of the state to ask Vajpayee to seek a vote of confidence after the withdrawal of support by the AIADMK to his government. For as the budget session was on, the government, if it had lost majority, would have fallen on any financial bill. The Prime Minister, said the former President in a published interview, can be removed by the House and not by a letter containing the withdrawal of support.

And again after the fall of the Vajpayee government by a solitary vote, the President, going by the British convention, should have invited Sonia Gandhi as the leader of the opposition, to provide the alternative. She should have been called on the principle of being the leader of the second largest party, without going into the numbers, he suggested.

Venkataraman, who fancied himself as a "copybook president", still swears by the principle of the single largest party first. This was the principle he followed when he invited V.P. Singh to form the government in 1989, he says. The Congress was the largest single party, but the Congress Working Committee had announced that the party would not stake its claim. "I then called the second largest party of V.P. Singh... I did not insist on letters. I was going on the second largest party principle, and he had to prove his majority on the floor of the House," he says.

Chandra Shekhar, who had only 57 members with him, got a call on the fall of the V.P. Singh government in November 1990 only after the BJP and CPM, the second and third largest parties, declined and he staked his claim with a written assurance of support from Rajiv Gandhi.

However, Venkataraman now feels that after the bitter experience of the past, outside support should not be taken into account in the formation of coalition governments.

But Narayanan, who describes himself as a working president, does not subscribe to a mechanical application of principles and conventions. For in the final analysis it's the numbers that determine the fate of a government.

The 1998 presidential communique set out the constitutional position that it was the head of state's prerogative to choose the Prime Minister and then went on to give the rationale of his choice. While he did call Vajpayee first as the leader of the largest single party and pre-poll alliance, Narayanan suggested that it did not give him an inherent right to form the government. Vajpayee got the call only after he was convinced that he had the numbers with him.

The numbers held no dilemma for the President in 1999. But before the people settled the question with a clear verdict, constitutional experts started offering the President advice on what he should do in the event of a hung House. Who has the mandate to govern? The largest single party, the largest pre-poll alliance, or a larger grouping formed after the poll? Predictably the answers generally went along party lines. Constitutional pundits, as is their wont, too only agree to disagree. In fact the Constitution, running into 395 articles and 12 schedules, makes no reference to political parties, except in the Tenth Schedule—commonly known as the anti-defection law. This makes floor crossing by less than a third of party's strength in a legislature illegal. The only insight that the Constitution offers is that "the Prime Minister shall be appointed by the President, and the council of ministers shall be collectively responsible to the House of the People (Lok Sabha)."

Questioning the single largest party first principle, a few experts suggest that the convention is based on the presumption that it is more likely to command a majority in the house—as responsibility to the House implies. The President should follow the convention "if he wants to be above controversy, but there are no absolutes in this," according to constitutional expert Fali S. Nariman. In his view "...the overriding factor is who, in the mature judgement and opinion of the President, will be able to command a majority."

Coalitions, experts say, are not incompatible with political stability going by the European experience with countries like Italy practically going without single party rule. India too has had its share of coalitions, successful ones at that, in Kerala and West Bengal, with the Jyoti Basu-led Left Front government starting its fifth successive term in 1996. At the Centre too, Indira Gandhi ran a minority government for two years after the Congress split in 1969. The 1977 Janata government that overthrew her emergency regime too was essentially a grand coalition of four major opposition groups—Bhartiya Lok Dal, Congress (O), Jana Sangh and Socialist Party—which came apart due to their internal contradictions within two years. Charan Singh's minority regime that followed was backed briefly by the Congress in 1979 in Indira Gandhi's quest for a return to power. Her son, Rajiv Gandhi, deployed the same tactic in backing Chandra Shekhar in 1991.

Back in power, the NDA government decided to go ahead with a constitutional review even as critics suggested that it may be used as a

First Lok Sabha : Congress Government

Prime Minister : Jawaharlal Nehru, 1952-57

Seats Won and Vote Share in % (in brackets), State-wise

State (Total Seats)	INC	BJS	CPI	SP	KMPP	Others @	Ind.
All-India (489) *	364 (45.0)	3 (3.1)	16 (3.3)	12 (10.6)	9 (5.8)	47 (16.3)	38 (15.9)
Assam (12)	11 (45.7)	0 (3.6)	-	1 (19.2)	0 (10.0)	0 (7.8)	0 (13.7)
Bihar (55)	45 (45.8)	0 (0.4)	0 (0.4)	3 (21.3)	0 (3.4)	6 (15.9)	1 (12.8)
Bombay (45)	40 (50.1)	-	0 (1.3)	0 (14.6)	0 (5.6)	2 (16.4)	3 (12.0)
Madhya Bharat(29)	27 (51.6)	0 (4.9)	0 (0.4)	0 (12.2)	0 (6.3)	0 (12.7)	2 (11.9)
Madras (75)	35 (36.4)	-	8 (8.9)	2 (5.3)	6 (9.8)	9 (16.5)	15 (23.1)
Orissa (20)	11 (42.5)	-	1 (5.8)	1 (15.4)	0 (1.4)	5 (26.2)	2 (8.7)
Punjab (18)	16 (42.8)	0 (5.6)	0 (5.0)	0 (2.2)	-	2 (25.8)	0 (18.6)
Uttar Pradesh (86)	81 (53.0)	0 (7.3)	0 (0.3)	2 (12.9)	0 (4.9)	1 (10.3)	2 (11.3)
West Bengal (34)	24 (42.1)	2 (5.9)	5 (9.5)	0 (2.0)	0 (8.9)	3 (13.1)	0 (18.5)
Hyderabad (25)	14 (40.1	-	-	1 (13.4)	-	9 (38.5)	1 (8.0)
Madhya Bharat (11)	9 (50.8)	0 (9.7)	0 (1.3)	0 (13.7)	0 (0.2)	2 (20.6)	0 (3.7)
Mysore (11)	10 (53.4)	0 (4.2)	0 (2.6)	0 (6.4)	1 (23.0)	-	0 (10.4)
Pepsu (5)	2 (33.4)	0 (2.9)	-	0 (2.6)	0 (2.7)	2 (37.3)	1 (21.1)
Rajasthan (20)	9 (41.4)	1 (3.0)	0 (0.2)	0 (3.4)	0 (0.9)	4 (21.9)	6 (29.2)
Saurashtra (6)	6 (66.4)	-	-	0 (4.8)	0 (4.2)	0 (17.0)	0 (7.6)
Travancore-Cochin (12)	6 (35.1)	-	-	0 (13.2)	-	2 (15.5)	4 (36.2)
Ajmer (2)	2 (50.1)	0 (16.2)	0 (14.0)	-	-	0 (13.7)	0 (6.0)
Bhopal (2)	2 (57.4)	-	-	0 (2.0)	-	0 (25.7)	0 (14.9)
Bilaspur (1) (Unopposed)	-	-	-	-	-	-	1
Coorg (1)	1 (59.6)	-	-	-	-	-	0 (40.4)
Delhi (4)	3 (49.4)	0 (25.9)	-	-	1 (7.3)	0 (4.7)	0 (12.7)
Himachal Pradesh (3)	3 (52.4)	0 (10.7)	-	0 (7.5)	0 (12.3)	0 (8.5)	0 (8.6)
Kutch (2)	2 (65.9)	-	-	0 (5.0)	-	-	0 (29.1)
Manipur (2)	1 (23.8)	-	0 (8.6)	1 (19.3)	-	0 (39.3)	0 (9.0)
Tripura (2)	0 (25.6)	0 (6.1)	2 (61.3)	-	-	-	0 (7.0)
Vindhya Pradesh (6)	4 (33.7)	0 (12.7)	-	1 (17.8)	1 (15.0)	0 (7.4)	0 (13.4)

* including 10 unopposed (INC 7, KMPP 1, Independents 2).

@ ***Break-up for Others***:- **Bihar**: JHP 3(7.5), JPB 1(2.4), LSS 2(3.1); **Bombay**: ASCF 1(4.4), PWP 1(7.0); **Madras:** TNTP 4(4.5), FBL 1(1.7), MUL 1(0.4), CWP 3(1.6); **Orissa:** GP 5(26.2); **Punjab:** SAD 2(11.4); **UP:** ABHM 1(1.9); **West Bengal:** ABHM 1(4.3), RSP 2(2.4); **Hyderabad:** PDF 7(28.2), PWP 1(3.8), ASCF 1(6.4); **Madhya Bharat:** ABHM 2(6.3); **Pepsu:** SAD 2(32.4); **Rajasthan:** KLP 1(10.1), RRP 3(9.4); **Travancore-Cochin:** RSP 1(6.3), TTNC 1(3.3).

Second Lok Sabha : Congress Government
Prime Minister : Jawaharlal Nehru, 1957-1962
Seats Won and Vote Share in % (in brackets), State-wise

State (Total Seats)	INC	CPI	PSP	BJS	Others @	Ind.
All-India (494) *	371 (47.8)	27 (8.9)	19 (10.4)	4 (5.9)	31 (7.6)	42 (19.4)
Andhra Pradesh (43)	37 (51.5)	2 (12.0)	0 (3.6)	0 (0.1)	2 (13.5)	2 (19.3)
Assam (12)	9 (51.7)	0 (10.2)	2 (20.0)	-	-	1 (18.1)
Bihar (53)	41 (44.5)	0 (5.1)	2 (21.6)	0 (0.1)	9 (12.4)	1 (16.3)
Bombay (66)	38 (48.7)	4 (6.3)	5 (8.7)	2 (3.4)	9 (14.3)	8 (18.6)
Kerala (18)	6 (34.8)	9 (37.5)	1 (7.2)	-	0 (5.1)	2 (15.4)
Madhya Pradesh (36)	35 (52.1)	0 (0.4)	0 (16.1)	0 (14.0)	1 (9.4)	0 (8.0)
Madras (41)	31 (46.5)	2 (10.1)	0 (3.6)	-	-	8 (39.8)
Mysore (26)	23 (55.5)	0 (1.5)	1 (18.7)	0 (2.5)	1 (2.0)	1 (19.8)
Orissa (20)	7 (40.0)	1 (4.8)	2 (15.4)	-	7 (29.1)	3 (10.7)
Punjab (22)	21 (51.3)	1 (16.8)	0 (0.6)	0 (16.0)	0 (4.1)	0 (11.2)
Rajasthan (22)	19 (53.6)	0 (4.8)	0 (1.3)	0 (11.1)	0 (1.6)	3 (27.6)
Uttar Pradesh (86)	70 (46.3)	1 (1.7)	4 (15.3)	2 (14.8)	0 (0.4)	9 (21.5)
West Bengal (36)	23 (48.2)	6 (19.0)	2 (5.7)	0 (1.4)	2 (11.8)	3 (13.9)
Delhi (5)	5 (54.3)	0 (4.7)	0 (3.5)	0 (19.7)	0 (4.8)	0 (13.0)
Himachal Pradesh (4)	4 (47.3)	0 (2.7)	0 (11.8)	-	0 (8.6)	0 (29.6)
Manipur (2)	1 (28.0)	0 (11.1)	0 (7.3)	-	-	1 (53.6)
Tripura (2)	1 (46.0)	1 (45.2)	-	-	-	0 (8.8)

* including 12 INC unopposed.

@ ***Break-up for Others***:- **AP**: PDF 2(11.0); **Bihar**: JHP 6(7.5), CSPJ 3(5.0); **Bombay**: ASCF 5(8.1), PWP 4(5.5); **MP**: ABHM 1(4.9); **Mysore**: ASCF 1(2.0); **Orissa**: GP 7(29.1); **West Bengal**: FBL 2(6.4).

Third Lok Sabha : Congress Government

Prime Minister : Jawaharlal Nehru, 1962 - 27/5/1964

Seats Won and Vote Share in % (in brackets), State-wise

State (Total Seats)	INC	CPI	Swatantra	BJS	PSP	Others @	Ind.
All-India (494) *	361 (44.7)	29 (9.9)	18 (7.9)	14 (6.4)	12 (6.8)	40 (13.2)	20 (11.1)
Andhra Pradesh (43)	34 (48.0)	7 (21.0)	1 (14.9)	0 (1.2)	0 (0.1)	0 (0.9)	1 (13.9)
Assam (12)	9 (45.1)	0 (7.1)	-	-	2 (19.1)	1 (8.0)	0 (20.7)
Bihar (53)	39 (43.9)	1 (6.4)	7 (18.2)	0 (2.3)	2 (12.7)	4 (11.3)	0 (5.2)
Gujarat (22)	16 (52.6)	-	4 (25.0)	0 (1.4)	1 (7.1)	1 (5.0)	0 (8.9)
Kerala (18)	6 (34.3)	6 (35.5)	0 (0.2)	0 (0.7)	0 (9.9)	3 (8.0)	3 (11.4)
Madhya Pradesh (36)	24 (39.6)	0 (0.9)	0 (0.7)	3 (17.9)	3 (12.3)	2 (16.2)	4 (12.4)
Madras (41)	31 (45.3)	2 (10.2)	0 (10.5)	0 (0.1)	0 (1.7)	8 (24.7)	0 (7.5)
Maharashtra (44)	41 (52.9)	0 (4.1)	0 (0.3)	0 (4.4)	1 (5.4)	0 (18.7)	2 (14.2)
Mysore (26)	25 (52.7)	0 (1.5)	0 (7.8)	0 (2.7)	0 (14.5)	1 (7.2)	0 (13.6)
Orissa (20)	14 (55.5)	0 (5.1)	0 (1.2)	-	1 (15.5)	5 (20.1)	0 (2.6)
Punjab (22)	14 (41.3)	0 (4.7)	0 (4.3)	3 (15.2)	-	5 (22.7)	0 (1.8)
Rajasthan (22)	14 (37.6)	0 (3.0)	3 (18.1)	1 (9.3)	-	1 (7.6)	3 (24.4)
Uttar Pradesh (86)	62 (38.2)	2 (3.6)	3 (5.0)	7 (17.6)	2 (10.4)	5 (15.0)	5 (10.2)
West Bengal (36)	22 (46.8)	9 (29.4)	0 (1.0)	0 (1.1)	0 (4.5)	3 (11.1)	2 (6.1)
Delhi (5)	5 (50.7)	0 (2.1)	-	0 (32.7)	0 (0.1)	0 (3.6)	0 (10.8)
Himachal Pradesh (4)	4 (68.7)	-	0 (12.8)	0 (4.5)	-	0 (6.5)	0 (7.5)
Manipur (2)	1 (30.9)	0 (8.1)	-	-	0 (4.1)	1 (26.3)	0 (30.6)
Tripura (2)	0 (42.8)	2 (51.3)	-	-	0 (2.0)	0 (3.9)	-

* including 3 INC unopposed.

@ ***Break-up for Others***:- **All-India**: SP 6(2.7); **Assam**: APHLC 1(3.7); **Bihar**: JHP 3(4.7), SP 1(6.1); **Gujarat**: NMGJ 1(3.7); **Kerala**: MUL 2(4.5), RSP 1(3.6); **MP**: SP 1(5.3), RRP 1(4.8); **Madras**: DMK 7(18.6), FBL 1(1.4); **Mysore**: LSS 1(3.3); **Orissa**: GP 4(17.4); SP 1(2.7); **Punjab**: SAD 3(12.2), SP 1(2.3), HLS 1(1.8); **Rajasthan**: RRP 1(3.7); **UP**: RPI 3(4.3), SP 1(8.6), ABHM 1(1.4); **West Bengal**: FBL 1(6.3), RSP 1(2.6), LSS 1(0.7); **Manipur**: SP 1(26.3).

Third Lok Sabha : Congress Government
Prime Minister : Lal Bahadur Shastri 9/6/1964 - 11/1/1966
Seats Won and Vote Share in % (in brackets), State-wise

State (Total Seats)	INC	CPI	Swatantra	BJS	PSP	Others @	Ind.
All-India (494) *	361 (44.7)	29 (9.9)	18 (7.9)	14 (6.4)	12 (6.8)	40 (13.2)	20 (11.1)
Andhra Pradesh (43)	34 (48.0)	7 (21.0)	1 (14.9)	0 (1.2)	0 (0.1)	0 (0.9)	1 (13.9)
Assam (12)	9 (45.1)	0 (7.1)	-	-	2 (19.1)	1 (8.0)	0 (20.7)
Bihar (53)	39 (43.9)	1 (6.4)	7 (18.2)	0 (2.3)	2 (12.7)	4 (11.3)	0 (5.2)
Gujarat (22)	16 (52.6)	-	4 (25.0)	0 (1.4)	1 (7.1)	1 (5.0)	0 (8.9)
Kerala (18)	6 (34.3)	6 (35.5)	0 (0.2)	0 (0.7)	0 (9.9)	3 (8.0)	3 (11.4)
Madhya Pradesh (36)	24 (39.6)	0 (0.9)	0 (0.7)	3 (17.9)	3 (12.3)	2 (16.2)	4 (12.4)
Madras (41)	31 (45.3)	2 (10.2)	0 (10.5)	0 (0.1)	0 (1.7)	8 (24.7)	0 (7.5)
Maharashtra (44)	41 (52.9)	0 (4.1)	0 (0.3)	0 (4.4)	1 (5.4)	0 (18.7)	2 (14.2)
Mysore (26)	25 (52.7)	0 (1.5)	0 (7.8)	0 (2.7)	0 (14.5)	1 (7.2)	0 (13.6)
Orissa (20)	14 (55.5)	0 (5.1)	0 (1.2)	-	1 (15.5)	5 (20.1)	0 (2.6)
Punjab (22)	14 (41.3)	0 (4.7)	0 (4.3)	3 (15.2)	-	5 (22.7)	0 (1.8)
Rajasthan (22)	14 (37.6)	0 (3.0)	3 (18.1)	1 (9.3)	-	1 (7.6)	3 (24.4)
Uttar Pradesh (86)	62 (38.2)	2 (3.6)	3 (5.0)	7 (17.6)	2 (10.4)	5 (15.0)	5 (10.2)
West Bengal (36)	22 (46.8)	9 (29.4)	0 (1.0)	0 (1.1)	0 (4.5)	3 (11.1)	2 (6.1)
Delhi (5)	5 (50.7)	0 (2.1)	-	0 (32.7)	0 (0.1)	0 (3.6)	0 (10.8)
Himachal Pradesh (4)	4 (68.7)	-	0 (12.8)	0 (4.5)	-	0 (6.5)	0 (7.5)
Manipur (2)	1 (30.9)	0 (8.1)	-	-	0 (4.1)	1 (26.3)	0 (30.6)
Tripura (2)	0 (42.8)	2 (51.3)	-	-	0 (2.0)	0 (3.9)	-

* including 3 INC unopposed.

@ ***Break-up for Others***:- **All-India**: SP 6(2.7); **Assam**: APHLC 1(3.7); **Bihar**: JHP 3(4.7), SP 1(6.1); **Gujarat**: NMGJ 1(3.7); **Kerala**: MUL 2(4.5), RSP 1(3.6); **MP**: SP 1(5.3), RRP 1(4.8); **Madras**: DMK 7(18.6), FBL 1(1.4); **Mysore**: LSS 1(3.3); **Orissa**: GP 4(17.4); SP 1(2.7); **Punjab**: SAD 3(12.2), SP 1(2.3), HLS 1(1.8); **Rajasthan**: RRP 1(3.7); **UP**: RPI 3(4.3), SP 1(8.6), ABHM 1(1.4); **West Bengal**: FBL 1(6.3), RSP 1(2.6), LSS 1(0.7); **Manipur**: SP 1(26.3).

tool to carry out BJP's own hidden agenda which it had put on the backburner due to compulsions of coalition politics. The President himself cautioned against tinkering with the basic features of the Constitution. But a few others like the former Lok Sabha secretary general, Subhash Kashyap saw no harm in a review provided it was done with an open mind.

One could look at all the available choices and pick the US model, where the President is the chief executive or opt for the French model where there is a Prime Minister too, but appointed by the President. Then there is the German model where the Chancellor, or the head of the government cannot be removed unless his successor has been selected in a constructive vote of confidence, to which Vajpayee alluded after losing out by just one vote in April.

As India looks for the right recipe for stability, let us look at how the parliamentary system inherited from the British has fared in this country since independence.

A Stable Start

The fifties and the sixties were a period of stability with the Congress under charismatic Nehru scoring facile victories in three elections even as the first Prime Minister sought to give India strong democratic foundations after centuries of colonial rule. The Congress, which has formed seven governments after 13 elections to date, never got a majority of the popular vote, even in the heydays of Nehru, but won a majority in the Lok Sabha six times thanks to the first-past-the-post electoral system.

In the first Lok Sabha, it secured 74.44% seats with only 45% of the popular vote, increasing its share to 75.1% in the second with 47.8% votes. Its seat share dipped marginally to 73.08% in the third as its votes dropped to 44.7%.

1969-The Great Divide

In 1967, the first election without Nehru at the helm, the Congress saw its seat share plunge by nearly 20 points from 73.08% to 54.42% with a near four point erosion in its popular vote that reduced its share to 40.8%, marking a seven-point downslide in ten years.

But India's oldest political party, which had managed to corner nearly three fourths of the Lok Sabha seats in the first three general elections polling an average of 45.83 % votes, still commanded an absolute majority with 283 seats in a house of 520.

Third Lok Sabha : Congress Government

Prime Minister : Indira Gandhi, 24/1/1966 - 13/3/1967

Seats Won and Vote Share in % (in brackets), State-wise

State (Total Seats)	INC	CPI	Swatantra	BJS	PSP	Others @	Ind.
All-India (494) *	361 (44.7)	29 (9.9)	18 (7.9)	14 (6.4)	12 (6.8)	40 (13.2)	20 (11.1)
Andhra Pradesh (43)	34 (48.0)	7 (21.0)	1 (14.9)	0 (1.2)	0 (0.1)	0 (0.9)	1 (13.9)
Assam (12)	9 (45.1)	0 (7.1)	-	-	2 (19.1)	1 (8.0)	0 (20.7)
Bihar (53)	39 (43.9)	1 (6.4)	7 (18.2)	0 (2.3)	2 (12.7)	4 (11.3)	0 (5.2)
Gujarat (22)	16 (52.6)	-	4 (25.0)	0 (1.4)	1 (7.1)	1 (5.0)	0 (8.9)
Kerala (18)	6 (34.3)	6 (35.5)	0 (0.2)	0 (0.7)	0 (9.9)	3 (8.0)	3 (11.4)
Madhya Pradesh (36)	24 (39.6)	0 (0.9)	0 (0.7)	3 (17.9)	3 (12.3)	2 (16.2)	4 (12.4)
Madras (41)	31 (45.3)	2 (10.2)	0 (10.5)	0 (0.1)	0 (1.7)	8 (24.7)	0 (7.5)
Maharashtra (44)	41 (52.9)	0 (4.1)	0 (0.3)	0 (4.4)	1 (5.4)	0 (18.7)	2 (14.2)
Mysore (26)	25 (52.7)	0 (1.5)	0 (7.8)	0 (2.7)	0 (14.5)	1 (7.2)	0 (13.6)
Orissa (20)	14 (55.5)	0 (5.1)	0 (1.2)	-	1 (15.5)	5 (20.1)	0 (2.6)
Punjab (22)	14 (41.3)	0 (4.7)	0 (4.3)	3 (15.2)	-	5 (22.7)	0 (1.8)
Rajasthan (22)	14 (37.6)	0 (3.0)	3 (18.1)	1 (9.3)	-	1 (7.6)	3 (24.4)
Uttar Pradesh (86)	62 (38.2)	2 (3.6)	3 (5.0)	7 (17.6)	2 (10.4)	5 (15.0)	5 (10.2)
West Bengal (36)	22 (46.8)	9 (29.4)	0 (1.0)	0 (1.1)	0 (4.5)	3 (11.1)	2 (6.1)
Delhi (5)	5 (50.7)	0 (2.1)	-	0 (32.7)	0 (0.1)	0 (3.6)	0 (10.8)
Himachal Pradesh (4)	4 (68.7)	-	0 (12.8)	0 (4.5)	-	0 (6.5)	0 (7.5)
Manipur (2)	1 (30.9)	0 (8.1)	-	-	0 (4.1)	1 (26.3)	0 (30.6)
Tripura (2)	0 (42.8)	2 (51.3)	-	-	0 (2.0)	0 (3.9)	-

* including 3 INC unopposed.

@ ***Break-up for Others***:- **All-India**: SP 6(2.7); **Assam**: APHLC 1(3.7); **Bihar**: JHP 3(4.7), SP 1(6.1); **Gujarat**: NMGJ 1(3.7); **Kerala**: MUL 2(4.5), RSP 1(3.6); **MP**: SP 1(5.3), RRP 1(4.8); **Madras**: DMK 7(18.6), FBL 1(1.4); **Mysore**: LSS 1(3.3); **Orissa**: GP 4(17.4); SP 1(2.7); **Punjab**: SAD 3(12.2), SP 1(2.3), HLS 1(1.8); **Rajasthan**: RRP 1(3.7); **UP**: RPI 3(4.3), SP 1(8.6), ABHM 1(1.4); **West Bengal**: FBL 1(6.3), RSP 1(2.6), LSS 1(0.7); **Manipur**: SP 1(26.3).

Fourth Lok Sabha : Congress Government

Prime Minister : Indira Gandhi, 13/3/1967 - 18/3/1971

Seats Won and Vote Share in % (in brackets), State-wise

State (Total Seats)	INC	BJS	Swatantra	CPI	SSP	Others @	Ind.
All-India (520) *	283 (40.8)	35 (9.4)	44 (8.7)	23 (5.0)	23 (4.9)	77 (17.5)	35 (13.7)
Andhra Pradesh (41)	35 (45.8)	0 (1.4)	3 (13.8)	1 (11.4)	0 (0.4)	0 (8.1)	2 (18.1)
Assam (14)	10 (45.8)	0 (5.5)	0 (1.0)	1 (8.3)	0 (3.8)	3 (16.6)	0 (19.0)
Bihar (53)	34 (34.8)	1 (11.1)	0 (3.4)	5 (9.9)	7917.8)	2 (9.0)	4 (14.0)
Gujarat (24)	11 (46.9)	-	12 (39.9)	-	0 (0.2)	0 (3.5)	1 (9.5)
Haryana (9)	7 (44.1)	1 (19.9)	0 (5.6)	0 (1.7)	0 (5.5)	0 (3.4)	1 (19.8)
Jammu & Kashmir (6)	5 (50.5)	0 (20.3)	-	-	-	1 (28.6)	0 (0.6)
Kerala (19)	1 (36.2)	0 (1.4)	0 (2.3)	3 (8.0)	3 (8.2)	11 (36.5)	1 (7.4)
Madhya Pradesh(37)	24 (40.8)	10 (29.6)	1 (2.7)	0 (1.4)	0 (3.7)	0 (8.1)	2 (13.7)
Madras (39)	3 (41.7)	0 (0.2)	6 (9.2)	0 (1.9)	-	29 (42.9)	1 (4.1)
Maharashtra (45)	37 (48.5)	0 (7.4)	0 (1.0)	2 (5.1)	2 (3.7)	3 (22.8)	1 (11.5)
Mysore (27)	18 (49.0)	0 (2.3)	5 (14.3)	-	1 (2.6)	2 (9.8)	1 (22.0)
Nagaland (1) (Unopposed)	-	-	-	-	-	1	-
Orissa (20)	6 (33.3)	0 (0.6)	8 (30.9)	0 (3.9)	1 (4.5)	4 (16.0)	1 (10.8)
Punjab (13)	9 (37.3)	1 (12.5)	0 (4.7)	0 (4.3)	0 (0.4)	3 (31.5)	0 (9.3)
Rajasthan (23)	10 (40.0)	3 (10.3)	8 (27.0)	0 (0.7)	0 (2.6)	0 (2.3)	2 (17.1)
Uttar Pradesh (85)	47 (33.4)	12 (22.2)	1 (4.8)	5 (3.3)	8 (10.3)	4 (9.0)	8 (17.0)
West Bengal (40)	14 (39.7)	0 (1.4)	0 (0.8)	5 (9.1)	1 (1.5)	13 (32.2)	7 (15.3)
A & N Islands (1)	1 (52.6)	-	0 (4.7)	-	-	0 (13.3)	0 (29.4)
Chandigarh (1)	0 (23.0)	1 (48.7)	0 (20.9)	-	-	0 (3.2)	0 (4.2)
Dadra & N. Haveli (1)	1 (50.1)	0 (4.1)	0 (9.2)	-	-	0 (36.6)	-
Delhi (7)	1 (38.8)	6 (46.7)	-	-	0 (0.2)	0 (5.7)	0 (8.6)
Goa, Daman & Diu (2)	0 (5.5)	-	-	0 (2.1)	-	1 (38.5)	1 (53.9)
Himachal Pradesh (6)	6 (48.4)	0 (19.1)	0 (4.4)	0 (2.1)	-	0 (3.5)	0 (22.5)
Laccadive, M & A Islands (1)	-	-	-	-	-	-	1 (100.0)
Manipur (2)	0 (32.7)	-	-	1 (28.9)	0 (5.8)	-	1 (32.6)
Pondicherry (1)	1 (39.8)	-	-	-	-	0 (26.9)	0 (33.3)
Tripura (2)	2 (58.3)	-	-	-	-	0 (41.7)	-

* including 4 INC unopposed.

@ ***Break-up for Others***:- **All-India**: CPM 19(4.4), PSP 13(3.1); **Assam**: PSP 2(12.8), APHLC 1(3.8); **Bihar**: PSP 1(7.4), JKD 1(1.3); **J&K**: NC 1(24.9); **Kerala**: CPM 9(24.6), MUL 2(6.6); **Maharashtra**: PSP 1(2.6), PWP 2(7.5); **Mysore**: PSP 2(5.1);; **Nagaland**: NNO 1 (Unopposed); **Orissa**: PSP 4(16.0); **Punjab**: ADSF 3(22.6); **Tamil Nadu**: DMK 25(35.8), CPM 4(6.9); **UP**: CPM 1(1.2); PSP 2(3.7), RPI 1 (4.1); **West Bengal**: CPM 5(15.7), PSP 1(1.7), BC 5(9.4), FBL 2(4.9); **Goa, Daman & Diu**: UGSG 1(36.0); **Pondicherry**: PF 0(26.9); **Tripura**: CPM 0(41.7).

Fifth Lok Sabha : Congress Government

Prime Minister : Indira Gandhi, 18/3/1971 - 24/3/1977

Seats Won and Vote Share in % (in brackets), State-wise

State (Total Seats)	INC	INCO	CPM	BJS	CPI	Others @	Ind.
All-India(518) *	352 (43.7)	16 (10.4)	25 (5.1)	22 (7.4)	23 (4.7)	66 (20.3)	14 (8.4)
Andhra Pradesh (41)	28 (55.7)	0 (5.6)	1 (2.8)	0 (1.6)	1 (6.0)	10 (20.1)	1 (8.2)
Assam (14)	13 (57.0)	0 (2.9)	0 (1.4)	0 (2.5)	0 (5.7)	1 (12.6)	0 (17.9)
Bihar (53)	39 (40.1)	3 (11.5)	0 (0.8)	2 (12.1)	5 (9.9)	3 (16.5)	1 (9.1)
Gujarat (24)	11 (44.9)	11939.7)	-	0 (2.2)	-	2 (7.6)	0 (5.6)
Haryana (9)	7 (52.6)	0 (11.3)	0 (0.1)	1 (11.2)	-	1 (15.0)	0 (9.8)
Himachal Pradesh (4)	4 (75.8)	0 (3.0)	-	0 (10.6)	0 (1.7)	0 (5.8)	0 (3.1)
Jammu & Kashmir (6)	5 (54.1)	-	-	0 (12.2)	-	0 (1.5)	1 (32.2)
Kerala (19)	6 (19.8)	0 (1.4)	2 (26.2)	0 (1.4)	3 (9.1)	7 (24.1)	1 (18.0)
Madhya Pradesh(37)	21 (45.6)	0 (2.3)	0 (0.1)	11 (33.6)	0 (1.0)	1 (3.5)	4 (13.9)
Maharashtra (45)	42 (63.1)	0 (2.7)	0 (0.5)	0 (5.2)	0 (1.9)	3 (18.3)	0 (8.3)
Mysore (27)	27 (70.9)	0 (16.4)	0 (0.5)	0 (1.9)	0 (0.1)	0 (6.1)	0 (4.2)
Nagaland (1)	-	-	-	-	-	1 (100.0)	-
Orissa (20)	15 (38.5)	0 (2.3)	0 (1.0)	0 (0.2)	1 (4.3)	4 (51.3)	0 (2.4)
Punjab (13)	10 (46.0)	0 (4.6)	0 (2.2)	0 (4.5)	2 (6.2)	1 (32.0)	0 (4.5)
Rajasthan (23)	14 (50.4)	0 (1.7)	0 (0.7)	4 (12.4)	0 (0.4)	3 (22.1)	2 (12.3)
Tamil Nadu (39)	9 (12.5)	1 (30.4)	0 (1.6)	0 (0.1)	4 (5.4)	24 (46.8)	1 (3.2)
Uttar Pradesh (85)	73 (48.6)	1 (8.60	0 (0.2)	4 (12.3)	4 (3.7)	1 (18.2)	2 (8.4)
West Bengal (40)	13 (28.2)	0 (7.0)	20 (34.3)	0 (0.9)	3 (10.6)	3 (13.2)	1 (5.8)
A & N Islands (1)	1 (61.5)	-	-	-	-	-	0 (38.5)
Chandigarh (1)	1 (66.9)	-	-	0 (23.3)	-	0 (0.2)	0 (9.6)
Dadra & Nagar Haveli (1)	1 (39.2)	0 (33.0)	0 (27.8)	-	-	-	-
Delhi (7)	7 (64.4)	0 (1.7)	-	0 (29.6)	-	0 (2.4)	0 (1.9)
Goa, Daman & Diu (2)	1 (24.4)	0 (0.7)	-	-	-	1 (47.9)	0 (27.0)
L, M & A Islands (1) (Unopposed)	1						
Manipur (2)	2 (30.0)	0 (9.0)	-	-	0 (15.0)	0 (17.0)	0 (29.0)
Pondicherry (1)	1 (66.3)	0 (28.0)	-	-	-	-	0 (5.7)
Tripura (2)	0 (36.3)		2 (43.5)	0 (0.5)	0 (6.8)	-	0 (12.9)

* including one INC unopposed.

@ ***Break-up for Others***:- **All-India**: Swatantra 8(3.1), SSP 3(2.4); PSP 2(1.0); **AP:** TPS 10(14.3); **Assam:** APHLC 1(3.0); **Bihar**: SSP 2(9.5), JHP 1(0.9); **Gujarat:** Swatantra 2(5.5); **Haryana:** VHP 1(9.2); **Kerala**: MUL 2(5.6), KC 3(8.3), RSP 2(6.4); **Nagaland**: UFN 1(63.9), NNO 0(36.1); **Orissa:** Swatantra 3(15.9), UC 1(23.6); **Punjab**: SAD 1(30.9); **Rajasthan:** Swatantra 3(14.6); **Tamil Nadu**: DMK 23(35.2), FBL 1(1.3); **UP**: BKD 1(12.7); **West Bengal**: BC 1(4.0), PSP 1(1.3), RSP 1(2.0); **Goa**: UGSG 1(24.8).

Even as Congress dominated the electoral scene, two political formations emerged. The first was the Bhartiya Jana Sangh, forerunner of the present day Bhartiya Janata Party, founded in 1951 by Dr Shyama Prasad Mookerji, who quit the Nehru government for its alleged weak handling of problems with Pakistan.

The second was the Swatantra Party formed in 1959 by veteran freedom struggle leaders like C. Rajagopalachari, Prof. N.G. Ranga and M.R. Masani to fight the 'control-licence-permit-raj' in the garb of socialism.

Contesting the elections in 1962, 1967 and 1971, the Swatantra Party did win a fair share of the popular vote in the feudal belt and some other pockets of support, but soon went into oblivion.

In contrast, the Jana Sangh gradually raised its seats in the Lok Sabha nearly 12 fold from three to 35 seats between 1952 to 1967 as its vote share went up three times from 3.1% to 9.4%.

Two years after the 1967 poll, the Congress underwent a major split when defying a 'syndicate' of old Congress leaders, Mrs Gandhi called for a 'conscience vote' to get V.V. Giri elected President over the official Congress nominee Neelam Sanjiva Reddy after the death in office of Dr Zakir Hussain.

While Mrs Gandhi accused her opponents of hobnobbing with the right wing Jana Sangh party in the run-up to the presidential poll, the 'syndicate' struck back by expelling her from the party.

The resultant split reduced the Congress to a minority in the Lok Sabha, but Mrs Gandhi continued to rule for two more years with the backing of Communists. Then calling a mid-term poll on a Garibi Hatao (banish poverty) call, Mrs Indira Gandhi regained the lost ground winning 353 seats—257 of them with a more than 15% margin of win—as the vote share of her Congress (I) Party rose to 43.7 per cent.

1977—The Great Fall

Four years later, when the Allahabad High Court overturned her 1971 election to the Lok Sabha for using government machinery, Mrs Gandhi stifled all opposition by imposing an internal emergency on June 26, 1975. Then going to the polls after her 21-month Emergency rule in 1977, Mrs Gandhi lost about 200 seats in the face of a virtually united opposition and an adverse 9.2% swing. A high IOU of 0.898 ensured

Sixth Lok Sabha : Janata Party Government

Prime Minister : Moraji Desai, 24/3/1977 - 28/7/1979

Seats Won and Vote Share in % (in brackets), State-wise

State (Total Seats)	JP #	INC	CPM	CPI	Others @	Ind.
All-India(542) *	**298 (45.0)**	154 (34.5)	22 (4.3)	7 (2.8)	52 (9.9)	9 (5.5)
Andhra Pradesh (42)	**1 (32.3)**	41 (57.4)	0 (4.7)	0 (2.7)	0 (0.1)	0 (2.8)
Assam (14)	**3 (35.8)**	10 (50.6)	0 (2.9)	0 (1.4)	0 (1.7)	1 (7.6)
Bihar (54)	**52 (65.0)**	0 (22.9)	0 (0.2)	0 (5.6)	1 (1.7)	1 (4.6)
Gujarat (26)	**16 (49.5)**	10 (46.9)	-	-	-	0 (3.6)
Haryana (10)	**10 (70.4)**	0 (18.0)	0 (0.1)	0 (0.6)	0 (4.7)	0 (6.2)
Himachal Pradesh (4)	**4 (57.2)**	0 (38.6)	0 (0.7)	0 (1.4)	-	0 (2.1)
Jammu & Kashmir (6)	**0 (8.2)**	3 (16.4)	-	-	2 (33.9)	1 (41.5)
Karnataka (28)	**2 (39.9)**	26 (56.8)	-	0 (0.4)	0 (0.3)	0 (2.6)
Kerala (20)	**0 (7.2)**	11 (29.1)	0 (20.3)	4 (10.4)	5 (24.3)	0 (8.7)
Madhya Pradesh(40)	**37 (57.9)**	1 (32.5)	-	0 (0.5)	1 (1.3)	1 (7.8)
Maharashtra (48)	**19 (31.4)**	20 (47.0)	3 (3.6)	0 (0.7)	6 (11.2)	0 (6.1)
Manipur (2)	**0 (8.6)**	2 (45.3)	-	0 (11.5)	0 (23.5)	0 (11.1)
Meghalaya(2)	-	1 (35.9)	-	-	-	1 (64.1)
Nagaland (1)	-	0 (48.3)	-	-	1 (51.7)	-
Orissa (21)	**15 (51.8)**	4 (38.2)	1 (2.0)	0 (3.2)	0 (0.7)	1 (4.1)
Punjab (13)	**3 (12.5)**	0 (34.9)	1 (4.9)	0 (1.7)	9 (42.8)	0 (3.2)
Rajasthan (25)	**24 (65.2)**	1 (30.6)	0 (0.4)	0 (0.5)	0 (0.4)	0 (2.9)
Sikkim (1) (Unopposed)	**1**					
Tamil Nadu (39)	**3 (17.7)**	14 (22.3)	0 (1.6)	3 (4.6)	19 (48.6)	0 (5.2)
Tripura (2)	**1 (17.8)**	1 (39.7)	0 (34.1)	0 (2.2)	0 (6.2)	-
Uttar Pradesh (85)	**85 (68.1)**	0 (25.0)	0 (0.1)	0 (1.1)	0 (0.3)	0 (5.4)
West Bengal (42)	**15 (21.5)**	3 (29.4)	17 (26.2)	0 (6.5)	6 (9.6)	1 (6.8)
A & N Islands (1)	-	1 (58.5)	-	-	-	0 (41.5)
Arunachal Pradesh (2)	-	1 (41.3)	-	-	-	1 (58.7)
Chandigarh (1)	**1 (66.1)**	0 (28.4)	-	0 (2.3)	-	0 (3.2)
Dadra & N. Haveli (1)	**0 (31.8)**	1 (46.9)	-	-	-	0 (21.3)
Delhi (7)	**7 (68.2)**	0 (30.2)	-	0 (0.4)	0 (0.2)	0 (1.0)
Goa, Daman & Diu (2)	**0 (14.7)**	1 (40.0)	-	-	1 (40.5)	0 (4.8)
Lakshadweep (1)	-	1 (58.6)	-	-	-	0 (41.4)
Mizoram (1)	-	0 (37.1)	-	-	-	1 (62.9)
Pondicherry (1)	**0 (44.4)**	-	-	-	1 (53.3)	0 (2.3)

* including 2 INC unopposed.

\# contested in Tamil Nadu and Pondicherry under the Indian National Congress (Organisation) symbol and in other states and union territories under Bharatiya Lok Dal symbol.

@ ***Break-up for Others***:- **Bihar**: ALJP 1 (0.6); **J&K:** NC 2(33.9); **Kerala**: MUL 2(6.0), KC 2(5.6), RSP1(3.1); **MP:** RPIK 1(1.3); **Maharashtra:** RPIK 1(4.3), PWP 5(6.1); **Manipur:** MPP 0(23.5); **Nagaland**: UDF 1(51.7); **Punjab**: SAD 9(42.3); **Tamil Nadu**: ADMK 18(30.6), DMK 1(18.1); **West Bengal**: RSP 3 (3.8), FBL 3(4.3); **Goa, Daman & Diu**: MGP 1(40.5); **Pondicherry**: ADMK 1(53.3).

Sixth Lok Sabha : Janata Party (Secular) Government

Prime Minister : Charan Singh, 28/7/1979 - 14/1/1980

Seats Won and Vote Share in % (in brackets), State-wise

State (Total Seats)	JPS #	INC $	JP *	CPM	Others @	Ind.
All-India (542)	76	154 (34.5)	222 (43.0)	22 (4.3)	59 (12.7)	9 (5.5)
Andhra Pradesh (42)		41 (57.4)	1 (32.3)	0 (4.7)	0 (2.8)	0 (2.8)
Assam (14)		10 (50.6)	3 (35.8)	0 (2.9)	0 (3.1)	1 (7.6)
Bihar (54)		0 (22.9)	52 (65.0)	0 (0.2)	1 (7.3)	1 (4.6)
Gujarat (26)		10 (46.9)	16 (49.5)	-	-	0 (3.6)
Haryana (10)		0 (18.0)	10 (70.4)	0 (0.1)	0 (5.3)	0 (6.2)
Himachal Pradesh (4)		0 (38.6)	4 (57.2)	0 (0.7)	0 (1.4)	0 (2.1)
Jammu & Kashmir (6)		3 (16.4)	0 (8.2)	-	2 (33.9)	1 (41.5)
Karnataka (28)		26 (56.8)	2 (39.9)	-	0 (0.7)	0 (2.6)
Kerala (20)		11 (29.1)	0 (7.2)	0 (20.3)	9 (34.7)	0 (8.7)
Madhya Pradesh (40)		1 (32.5)	37 (57.9)	-	1 (1.8)	1 (7.8)
Maharashtra (48)		20 (47.0)	19 (31.4)	3 (3.6)	6 (11.9)	0 (6.1)
Manipur (2)		2 (45.3)	0 (8.6)	-	0 (34.0)	0 (11.1)
Meghalaya (2)		1 (35.9)	-	-	-	1 (64.1)
Nagaland (1)		0 (48.3)	-	-	1 (51.7)	-
Orissa (21)		4 (38.2)	15 (51.8)	1 (2.0)	0 (3.9)	1 (4.1)
Punjab (13)		0 (34.9)	3 (12.5)	1 (4.9)	9 (44.5)	0 (3.2)
Rajasthan (25)		1 (30.6)	24 (65.2)	0 (0.4)	0 (0.9)	0 (2.9)
Sikkim (1) (Unopposed)		1				
Tamil Nadu (39)		14 (22.3)	3 (17.7)	0 (1.6)	19 (53.2)	0 (5.2)
Tripura (2)		1 (39.7)	1 (17.8)	0 (34.1)	0 (8.4)	-
Uttar Pradesh (85)		0 (25.0)	85 (68.1)	0 (0.1)	0 (1.4)	0 (5.4)
West Bengal (42)		3 (29.4)	15 (21.5)	17 (26.2)	6 (16.1)	1 (6.8)
A & N Islands (1)		1 (58.5)	-	-	-	0 (41.5)
Arunachal Pradesh (2)		1 (41.3)	-	-	-	1 (58.7)
Chandigarh (1)		0 (28.4)	1 (66.1)	-	(2.3)	0 (3.2)
Dadra & N. Haveli (1)		1 (46.9)	0 (31.8)	-	-	0 (21.3)
Delhi (7)		0 (30.2)	7 (68.2)	-	0 (0.6)	0 (1.0)
Goa, Daman & Diu (2)		1 (40.0)	0 (14.7)	-	1 (40.5)	0 (4.8)
Lakshadweep (1)		1 (58.6)	-	-	-	0 (41.4)
Mizoram (1)		0 (37.1)	-	-	-	1 (62.9)
Pondicherry (1)		-	0 (44.4)	-	1 (53.3)	0 (2.3)

Being a post-poll breakaway party, no vote share; statewise seat position not available.

$ Party position as in 1977, though in 1979 INC was two parties with one party part of the Charan Singh government and the other supporting it from outside.

* contested in Tamil Nadu and Pondicherry under the Indian National Congress (Organisation) symbol and in other states and union territories under Bharatiya Lok Dal symbol.. Vote % and state-wise seat position here is as per the 1977 position.

@ ***Break-up for Others:*-** **Bihar:** AIJP 1(0.6); **J&K:** NC 2(33.9); **Kerala:** MUL 2(6.0), KC 2(5.6), RSP1(3.1); **MP:** RPIK 1(1.3); **Maharashtra:** RPIK 1(4.3), PWP 5(6.1); **Manipur:** MPP 0(23.5); **Nagaland:** UDF 1(51.7); **Punjab:** SAD 9(42.3); **Tamil Nadu:** ADMK 18(30.6), DMK 1(18.1); **West Bengal:** RSP 3 (3.8), FBL 3(4.3); **Goa, Daman & Diu:** MGP 1(40.5); **Pondicherry:** ADMK 1(53.3).

practically straight contests over most of the country as the number of candidates put up by national parties fell to an all-time low of 1.9 per seat.

Almost completely decimated in the north, Congress won 92 seats in the south to keep a tally of 154 with an all-time low voter support of 34.5% in its worst defeat as power at the Centre slipped out of its hands for the first time since Independence.

Winning 54.43% seats with only 41.3% of the votes, Janata Party formed at the initiative of "Total Revolution" leader Jayaprakash Narayan, dislodged Indira Gandhi's emergency regime and veteran Congress leader, Morarji Desai, now on the other side of the political divide, became India's fourth Prime Minister.

1980—Return of the Congress

Essentially a coalition of disparate groups, the Janata Party dispensation did not make for stability despite the numbers. With some Janata leaders making an issue out of dual membership of a few Jana Sangh leaders in the Rashtriya Swayamsevak Sangh (RSS), the Morarji Desai government fell in mid-1979. As the successor Charan Singh government failed to face the Lok Sabha since it lacked a majority, fresh elections were called in January 1980 to form the seventh Lok Sabha.

Mrs Gandhi then led her party back to power with swing and split factors helping it in a big way. An 8.2% swing combined with a low IOU of 0.651 raised the Congress (I) tally by 200 to 353 seats won with 42.7% voter support.

On the other hand, the 0.247 drop in IOU as the number of candidates put up by national parties per seat went up to 2.9, cost the combined opposition dearly as it lost 212 seats bringing down its strength from 388 to 176.

Mrs Gandhi's return to power in a poll less than three years after her emergency regime was thrown out, was widely seen as an expression of voters' desire for stability at the centre.

While Charan Singh and Raj Narain's breakaway Janata (Secular) converted itself into the Lok Dal, Jana Sangh left the Janata Party led by Chandra Shekhar after the 1980 poll to emerge as the Bhartiya Janata Party.

Seventh Lok Sabha : Congress Government

Prime Minister : Indira Gandhi, 14/1/1980 -31/10/1984

Seats Won and Vote Share in % (in brackets), State-wise

State (Total Seats)	INCI	JP	JPS	CPM	INCU	Others @	Ind.
All-India(542) (Poll in 529 *)	**353 (42.7)**	31 (18.9)	41 (9.4)	36 (6.2)	13 (5.3)	46 (11.1)	9 (6.4)
Andhra Pradesh (42)	**41 (56.2)**	0 (15.2)	0 (6.4)	0 (3.6)	1 (7.2)	0 (3.8)	0 (7.6)
Assam (14) (Poll in 2)	**2 (51.0)**	0 (8.0)	-	0 (9.2)	0 (31.8)	-	-
Bihar (54)	**30 (36.4)**	8 (23.6)	5 (16.6)	0 (0.9)	4 (6.8)	5 (8.3)	2 (7.4)
Gujarat (26)	**25 (54.8)**	1 (36.9)	0 (2.9)	-	0 (1.7)	0 (0.2)	0 (3.4)
Haryana (10)	**5 (32.6)**	1 (28.1)	4 (33.5)	-	0 (0.1)	0 (0.3)	0 (5.4)
Himachal Pradesh (4)	**4 (52.1)**	0 (36.4)	0 (5.3)	-	0 (0.3)	0 (1.9)	0 (4.0)
Jammu & Kashmir (6)	**1 (18.7)**	0 (8.6)	-	-	1 (14.5)	3 (36.9)	1 (21.3)
Karnataka (28)	**27 (56.3)**	1 (22.9)	0 (1.2)	0 (0.2)	0 (16.7)	0 (0.3)	0 (2.4)
Kerala (20)	**5 (26.3)**	0 (6.7)	-	6 (19.1)	3 (15.9)	5 (21.3)	1 (10.8)
Madhya Pradesh(40)	**35 (47.2)**	4 (31.3)	0 (7.8)	0 (0.1)	0 (1.3)	0 (1.0)	1 (11.3)
Maharashtra (48)	**39 (53.3)**	8 (20.4)	0 (1.1)	0 (1.4)	1 (11.8)	0 (7.1)	0 (5.0)
Manipur (2)	**1 (23.0)**	0 (17.60	-	-	0 (16.6)	1 (16.6)	0 (26.2)
Meghalaya(2) (Poll in 1)	**1 (74.3)**	-	-	-	-	0 (18.1)	0 (7.6)
Nagaland (1)	-	-	-	-	-	0 (49.0)	1 (51.0)
Orissa (21)	**20 (56.1)**	0 (14.1)	1 (19.6)	0 (0.9)	0 (2.1)	0 (2.5)	0 (4.7)
Punjab (13)	**12 (52.5)**	0 (10.0)	0 (2.2)	0 (2.5)	0 (2.6)	1 (25.0)	0 (5.3)
Rajasthan (25)	**18 (42.6)**	4 (31.7)	2 (12.0)	0 (0.2)	1 (6.0)	0 (0.7)	0 (6.8)
Sikkim (1)	-	-	-	-	0 (1.8)	1 (94.2)	0 (4.0)
Tamil Nadu (39)	**20 (31.6)**	0 (8.0)	0 (.5)	0 (3.2)	0 (0.2)	18 (52.0)	1 (4.4)
Tripura (2)	**0 (22.6)**	0 (1.0)	-	2 (47.5)	0 (0.60	0 (13.5)	0 (14.9)
Uttar Pradesh (85)	**51 (35.9)**	3 (22.6)	29 (29.0)	0 (0.1)	0 (1.5)	1 (2.3)	1 (8.7)
West Bengal (42)	**4 (36.5)**	0 (4.5)	0 (0.5)	28 (39.9)	0 (1.2)	10 (15.7)	0 (1.6)
A & N Islands (1)	**1 (53.3)**	0 (2.6)	0 (0.9)	0 (20.3)	-	-	0 (22.9)
Arunachal Pradesh (2)	**2 (44.1)**	-	-	-	0 (10.9)	0 (40.2)	0 (4.8)
Chandigarh (1)	**1 (49.7)**	0 (9.3)	0 (0.8)	-	0 (7.2)	-	0 (33.0)
Dadra & N. Haveli (1)	**1 (61.9)**	0 (18.3)	-	-	0 (5.7)	-	0 (14.1)
Delhi (7)	**6 (50.4)**	1 (37.9)	0 (6.9)	-	0 (0.8)	0 (0.6)	0 (3.4)
Goa, Daman & Diu (2)	**0 (12.2)**	0 (6.9)	0 (3.4)	-	1 (27.6)	1 (36.0)	0 (13.8)
Lakshadweep (1)	**0 (3.9)**	0 (39.8)	-	-	1 (56.4)	-	-
Mizoram (1)	-	-	-	-	-	0 (42.0)	1 (58.0)
Pondicherry (1)	**1 (66.5)**	0 (26.7)	0 (6.9)	-	-	-	-

* All India vote % is for 527 seats.

@ ***Break-up for Others***:- **All-India**: CPI 11(2.6), ADMK 2(2.4), DMK 16(2.2); **Bihar**: CPI 4(7.3), JHP 1(0.7); **J&K**: NC 3(36.9) incl. Srinagar unopposed; **Kerala**: CPI 2(6.5), MUL 2(5.6), KC 1(4.4); **Manipur**: CPI 1(9.7); **Meghalaya**: CPI 0(6.3), APHLC 0(11.8); **Nagaland**: UDF 0(49.0); **Punjab**: SAD 1(23.4); **Sikkim**: Sikkim Janata Parishad 1(61.7), SCR 0(22.6); **Tamil Nadu**: DMK 16(23.0), ADMK 2(25.4); **UP**: CPI 1(1.6); **Tripura**: TUJS 0(13.5); **West Bengal**: CPI 3(4.3), RSP 4(5.2), FBL 3(4.6); **Arunachal Pradesh**: PPA 0(40.2); **Goa, Daman & Diu**: MGP 1(36.0); **Mizoram**: PPC 0(42.0).

Seventh Lok Sabha : Congress Government

Prime Minister : Rajiv Gandhi, 31/10/1984 - 31/12/1984

Seats Won and Vote Share in % (in brackets), State-wise

State (Total Seats)	INCI	JP	JPS	CPM	INCU	Others @	Ind.
All-India(542) (Poll in 529 *)	**353 (42.7)**	31 (18.9)	41 (9.4)	36 (6.2)	13 (5.3)	46 (11.1)	9 (6.4)
Andhra Pradesh (42)	**41 (56.2)**	0 (15.2)	0 (6.4)	0 (3.6)	1 (7.2)	0 (3.8)	0 (7.6)
Assam (14) (Poll in 2)	**2 (51.0)**	0 (8.0)	-	0 (9.2)	0 (31.8)	-	-
Bihar (54)	**30 (36.4)**	8 (23.6)	5 (16.6)	0 (0.9)	4 (6.8)	5 (8.3)	2 (7.4)
Gujarat (26)	**25 (54.8)**	1 (36.9)	0 (2.9)	-	0 (1.7)	0 (0.2)	0 (3.4)
Haryana (10)	**5 (32.6)**	1 (28.1)	4 (33.5)	-	0 (0.1)	0 (0.3)	0 (5.4)
Himachal Pradesh (4)	**4 (52.1)**	0 (36.4)	0 (5.3)	-	0 (0.3)	0 (1.9)	0 (4.0)
Jammu & Kashmir (6)	**1 (18.7)**	0 (8.6)	-	-	1 (14.5)	3 (36.9)	1 (21.3)
Karnataka (28)	**27 (56.3)**	1 (22.9)	0 (1.2)	0 (0.2)	0 (16.7)	0 (0.3)	0 (2.4)
Kerala (20)	**5 (26.3)**	0 (6.7)	-	6 (19.1)	3 (15.9)	5 (21.3)	1 (10.8)
Madhya Pradesh(40)	**35 (47.2)**	4 (31.3)	0 (7.8)	0 (0.1)	0 (1.3)	0 (1.0)	1 (11.3)
Maharashtra (48)	**39 (53.3)**	8 (20.4)	0 (1.1)	0 (1.4)	1 (11.8)	0 (7.1)	0 (5.0)
Manipur (2)	**1 (23.0)**	0 (17.60	-	-	0 (16.6)	1 (16.6)	0 (26.2)
Meghalaya(2)(Poll in 1)	**1 (74.3)**	-	-	-	-	0 (18.1)	0 (7.6)
Nagaland (1)	-	-	-	-	-	0 (49.0)	1 (51.0)
Orissa (21)	**20 (56.1)**	0 (14.1)	1 (19.6)	0 (0.9)	0 (2.1)	0 (2.5)	0 (4.7)
Punjab (13)	**12 (52.5)**	0 (10.0)	0 (2.2)	0 (2.5)	0 (2.6)	1 (25.0)	0 (5.3)
Rajasthan (25)	**18 (42.6)**	4 (31.7)	2 (12.0)	0 (0.2)	1 (6.0)	0 (0.7)	0 (6.8)
Sikkim (1)	-	-	-	-	0 (1.8)	1 (94.2)	0 (4.0)
Tamil Nadu (39)	**20 (31.6)**	0 (8.0)	0 (.5)	0 (3.2)	0 (0.2)	18 (52.0)	1 (4.4)
Tripura (2)	**0 (22.6)**	0 (1.0)	-	2 (47.5)	0 (0.60	0 (13.5)	0 (14.9)
Uttar Pradesh (85)	**51 (35.9)**	3 (22.6)	29 (29.0)	0 (0.1)	0 (1.5)	1 (2.3)	1 (8.7)
West Bengal (42)	**4 (36.5)**	0 (4.5)	0 (0.5)	28 (39.9)	0 (1.2)	10 (15.7)	0 (1.6)
A & N Islands (1)	**1 (53.3)**	0 (2.6)	0 (0.9)	0 (20.3)	-	-	0 (22.9)
Arunachal Pradesh (2)	**2 (44.1)**	-	-	-	0 (10.9)	0 (40.2)	0 (4.8)
Chandigarh (1)	1 (49.7)	0 (9.3)	0 (0.8)	-	0 (7.2)	-	0 (33.0)
Dadra & N. Haveli (1)	1 (61.9)	0 (18.3)	-	-	0 (5.7)	-	0 (14.1)
Delhi (7)	6 (50.4)	1 (37.9)	0 (6.9)	-	0 (0.8)	0 (0.6)	0 (3.4)
Goa, Daman & Diu (2)	0 (12.2)	0 (6.9)	0 (3.4)	-	1 (27.6)	1 (36.0)	0 (13.8)
Lakshadweep (1)	0 (3.9)	0 (39.8)	-	-	1 (56.4)	-	-
Mizoram (1)	-	-	-	-	-	0 (42.0)	1 (58.0)
Pondicherry (1)	1 (66.5)	0 (26.7)	0 (6.9)	-	-	-	-

* All India vote % is for 527 seats.

@ ***Break-up for Others***:- **All-India**: CPI 11(2.6), ADMK 2(2.4), DMK 16(2.2); **Bihar**: CPI 4(7.3), JHP 1(0.7); **J&K**: NC 3(36.9) incl. Srinagar unopposed; **Kerala**: CPI 2(6.5), MUL 2(5.6), KC 1(4.4); **Manipur**: CPI 1(9.7); **Meghalaya**: CPI 0(6.3), APHLC 0(11.8); **Nagaland**: UDF 0(49.0); **Punjab**: SAD 1(23.4); **Sikkim**: Sikkim Janata Parishad 1(61.7), SCR 0(22.6); **Tamil Nadu**: DMK 16(23.0), ADMK 2(25.4); **UP**: CPI 1(1.6); **Tripura**: TUJS 0(13.5); **West Bengal**: CPI 3(4.3), RSP 4(5.2), FBL 3(4.6); **Arunachal Pradesh**: PPA 0(40.2); **Goa, Daman & Diu**: MGP 1(36.0); **Mizoram**: PPC 0(42.0).

Eighth Lok Sabha : Congress Government

Prime Minister : Rajiv Gandhi, 31/12/1984 - 2/12/1989

Seats Won and Vote Share in % (in brackets), State-wise

State (Total Seats)	INC	JP	CPM	CPI	BJP	Others @	Ind.
All-India(542) *	**415 (49.1)**	10 (6.9)	22 (5.9)	6 (2.7)	2 (7.7)	82 (19.9)	5 (7.9)
Andhra Pradesh (42)	**6 (41.8)**	1 (1.2)	1 (1.8)	1 (1.9)	1 (2.2)	31 (45.8)	1 (5.3))
Assam (14) (Poll held in 1985)	**4 (23.6)**	0 (3.5)	0 (3.6)	0 (1.4)	0 (0.4)	10 (56.6)	0 (10.2)
Bihar (54)	**48 (51.8)**	1 (6.7)	0 (1.1)	2 (8.2)	0 (6.9)	2 (16.8)	1 (8.4)
Gujarat (26)	**24 (53.2)**	1 (16 6)	0 (0.1)	0 (0.1)	1 (18.6)	0 (3.1)	0 (8.2)
Haryana (10)	**10 (55.0)**	0 (1.4)	-	0 (0.9)	0 (7.5)	0 (29.6)	0 (5.6)
Himachal Pradesh (4)	**4 (67.6)**	0 (3.6)	-	0 (0.9)	0 (23.3)	0 (1.3)	0 (3.3)
Jammu & Kashmir (6)	**3 (30.2)**	-	-	-	0 (1.7)	3 (50.7)	0 (17.4)
Karnataka (28)	**24 (51.6)**	4 (35.1)	0 (0.1)	0 (1.0)	0 (4.7)	0 (0.5)	0 (7.0)
Kerala (20)	**13 (33.3)**	1 (2.1)	1 (22.3)	0 (7.4)	0 (1.8)	5 (21.3)	0911.9)
Madhya Pradesh(40)	**40 (57.1)**	0 (2.7)	-	0 (0.9)	0 (30.0)	0 (1.1)	0 (8.2)
Maharashtra (48)	**43 (51.2)**	1 (7.6)	0 (1.5)	0 (1.0)	0 (10.1)	3 (15.4)	1 (13.2)
Manipur (2)	**2 (35.0)**	-	-	0 (9.5)	0 (7.0)	0 (22.6)	0 (25.9)
Meghalaya(2)	**2 (62.4)**	-	-	0 (3.7)	-	-	0 (33.9)
Mizoram (1) (Unopposed)	**1**						
Nagaland (1)	**1 (64.6)**	-	-	-	-	0 (29.3)	0 (6.0)
Orissa (21)	**20 (57.5)**	1 (32.0)	0 (1.8)	0 (1.5)	0 (1.2)	0 (1.2)	0 (4.8)
Punjab (13) (Poll held in 1985)	**6 (41.5)**	0 (2.2)	0 (3.0)	0 (3.8)	0 (3.4)	7 (37.2)	0 (8.9)
Rajasthan (25)	**25 (52.7)**	0 (3.9)	0 (0.2)	0 (0.3)	0 (23.7)	0 12.4)	0 (6.8)
Sikkim (1)	**0 (25.8)**	0 (0.7)	-	0 (1.0)	-	-	1 (72.4)
Tamil Nadu (39)	**25 (40.5)**	0 (4.2)	0 (2.8)	0 (3.4)	0 (0.1)	14 (46.2)	0 (2.8)
Tripura (2)	**0 (45.6)**	-	2 (50.5)	-	0 (0.8)	-	0 (3.2)
Uttar Pradesh (85)	**83 (51.0)**	0 (3.6)	-	0 (1.7)	0 (6.4)	2 (24.5)	0 (12.8)
West Bengal (42)	**16 (48.2)**	0 (0.0)	18 (35.9)	3 (3.8)	0 (0.4)	5 (9.8)	0 (1.9)
A & N Islands (1)	**1 (52.9)**	-	0 (12.5)	-	-	0 (31.3)	0 (3.4)
Arunachal Pradesh (2)	**2 (43.3)**	0 (4.2)	-	-	-	0 (34.6)	0 (17.8)
Chandigarh (1)	**1 (66.0)**	0 (23.6)	-	-	0 (5.6)	-	0 (4.8)
Dadra & N. Haveli (1)	**0 (40.3)**	0 (3.7)	-	-	-	-	1 (56.0)
Delhi (7)	**7 (68.7)**	0 (3.3)	-	-	0 (18.9)	0 (5.5)	0 (3.7)
Goa, Daman & Diu (2)	**2 (46.2)**	0 (3.1)	0 (0.4)	0 (1.5)	0 (3.0)	0 (21.7)	0 (24.1)
Lakshadweep (1)	**1 (54.5)**	-	-	-	-	-	0 (45.5)
Pondicherry (1)	**1 (58.9)**	-	-	-	-	0 (36.7)	0 (4.4)

* All-India Vote % is for 515 seats, excluding Punjab & Assam which went to poll in 1985.

@ ***Break-up for Others*:-** **All-India:** LKD 3(6.0), ICS 4(1.5), TDP 30(4.3), ADMK 12(1.7), DMK 2(2.4); **AP:** ICS 1(1.0), TDP 30(44.8); **Assam:** AGP 7(33.4), ICS 1(6.1), UMF 1(13.0), PTCA 1(4.1); **Bihar:** LKD 1(13.7), ICJ 1(1.1); **Haryana:** LKD 0(19.1), ICJ 0(10.5); **J&K:** NC 3(46.2); **Kerala:** ICS 1(4.4), MUL 2(5.3), KCJ 2(5.5); **Maharashtra:** ICS 2(12.1), PWP 1(2.1); **Manipur:** MPP 0(17.7); **Nagaland:** NNDP 0(29.3); **Punjab:** SAD 7(37.2); **Rajasthan:** LKD 0(11.2); **Tamil Nadu:** ADMK 12(18.4), DMK 2(25.9); **UP:** LKD 2(21.6); **West Bengal:** RSP 3(4.6), FBL 2(4.1); **Andaman & Nicobar Islands:** LKD 0(31.3); **Arunachal Pradesh:** PPA 0(34.6), **Goa, Daman & Diu:** MGP 0(20.3).

1984—Sympathy Sweep

After the assassination of Mrs Gandhi on October 31, 1984, her son Rajiv Gandhi, sworn in as Prime Minister by President Zail Singh, called the elections for the eighth Lok Sabha a month ahead of schedule.

Riding on the crest of a "sympathy wave," Rajiv Gandhi gave the Congress its biggest victory-415 seats or 76.57% seats with 48.1% votes, nearly two points less than half—in December 1984.

A higher voter turn out had generally spelt a drop in Congress votes, but 1984 proved an exception to the rule with sympathy factor overriding everything else to build up a 5.4% swing in its favour.

The voters' honeymoon with the youthful former Indian Airlines pilot, however, did not last long. Vishwanath Pratap Singh from the former princely family of Manda in Uttar Pradesh, soon became the rallying point of dissidents within the Congress. Quitting as Rajiv Gandhi's Defence Minister on January 24, 1987 after launching probes into some controversial defence deals, Singh forged a broad National Front. Besides his own Jan Morcha, it included three powerful regional parties—Dravida Munnetra Kazhagam in Tamil Nadu, the Telugu Desam in Andhra Pradesh and the Asom Gana Parishad in Assam.

Formally launched in Madras on September 17, 1988, the centrist National Front made seat adjustments with both BJP on the right and the two Communist parties on the left in the run up to the 1989 elections to the ninth Lok Sabha.

1989—Bofors and After

They had no shared policies or programmes, but only a common goal-to dislodge Rajiv Gandhi by avoiding a split in the opposition vote. While the Bofors gun deal emerged as a focal issue for the opposition, it was the high degree of opposition unity that brought about Congress' second worst defeat in 12 years in November 1989 as it had in 1977.

The opposition strategy had clearly worked. A drop in voter participation also did not help Congress much in November 1989 when seat adjustments and understanding among various anti-Congress parties raised the IOU to 0.851, practically ensuring virtual straight contests in nine out of ten seats.

On the other hand, a decline of less than nine percentage points in its popular vote slashed the Congress tally of 415 by more than half. Polling 39.33% votes, the Congress did emerge as the single largest

Ninth Lok Sabha : Janata Dal Government

Prime Minister : V P Singh, 2/12/1989 -10/11/1990

Seats Won and Vote Share in % (in brackets), State-wise

State (Total Seats)	JD	BJP	CPM	CPI	INC	Others @	Ind.
All-India(543) (Poll in 529)	142 (17.7)	86 (11.5)	33 (6.6)	12 (2.6)	197 (39.5)	47 (16.8)	12 (5.3)
Andhra Pradesh (42)	0 (1.6)	0 (2.0)	0 (2.4)	0 (2.0)	39 (51.0)	3 (38.4)	0 (2.6)
Arunachal Pradesh (2)	-	-	-	-	2 (50.0)	0 (35.2)	0 (14.8)
Assam (14) (No Poll)							
Bihar (54)	31 (36.4)	9 (13.0)	1 (1.4)	4 (7.9)	4 (28.1)	5 (8.9)	0 (4.3)
Goa (2)	0 (18.1)	0 (0.7)	-	0 (0.9)	1 (47.4)	1 (29.7)	0 (3.2)
Gujarat (26)	11 (27.8)	12 (30.5)	-	-	3 (37.2)	0 (1.6)	0 (2.9)
Haryana (10)	6 (38.9)	0 (8.3)	-	0 (0.3)	4 (46.2)	0 (2.7)	0 (3.6)
Himachal Pradesh (4)	0 (7.2)	3 (45.3)	0 (0.5)	0 (1.3)	1 (42.0)	0 (3.1)	0 (0.7)
Jammu & Kashmir (6)	0 (30.1)	0 (7.2)	-	-	2 (39.0)	3 (14.2)	1 (9.6)
Karnataka (28)	1 (28.3)	0 (2.60	-	0 (0.8)	27 (48.9)	0 (14.9)	0 (4.5)
Kerala (20)	0 (1.9)	0 (4.5)	2 (22.9)	0 (6.20	14 (41.7)	4 (13.3)	0 (9.5)
Madhya Pradesh(40)	4 (8.3)	27 (39.7)	0 (0.1)	0 (0.6)	8 (37.7)	0 (6.1)	1 (7.6)
Maharashtra (48)	5 (11.0)	10 (23.7)	0 (1.20	1 (1.9)	28 (45.4)	1 (8.6)	3 (8.2)
Manipur (2)	0 (1.5)	0 (2.3)	-	0 (5.6)	2 (45.0)	0 (33.4)	0 (12.2)
Meghalaya(2)	-	-	-	0 (4.8)	2 (55.4)	-	0 (39.8)
Mizoram (1)	-	-	-	-	1 (48.5)	0 (50.6)	0 (1.0)
Nagaland (1)	-	-	-	-	1 (60.3)	0 (39.7)	-
Orissa (21)	16 (49.5)	0 (1.3)	1 (3.0)	1 (3.70	3 (38.4)	0 (2.1)	0 (2.1)
Punjab (13)	1 (5.5)	0 (4.2)	0 (3.9)	0 (2.1)	2 (26.5)	7 (45.1)	3 (12.7)
Rajasthan (25)	11 (25.7)	13 (29.6)	1 (2.1)	0 (0.2)	0 (37.0)	0 (1.9)	0 (3.5)
Sikkim (1)	-	-	-	-	0 (21.6)	1 (78.1)	0 (0.3)
Tamil Nadu (39)	0 (1.4)	0 (0.3)	0 (3.7)	1 (2.0)	27 (39.9)	11 (50.5)	0 (2.30
Tripura (2)	-	0 (0.6)	0 (41.7)	-	2 (55.5)	0 (1.1)	0 (1.1)
Uttar Pradesh (85)	54 (35.9)	8 (7.6)	1 (0.5)	2 (1.4)	15 (31.8)	3 (14.6)	2 (8.4)
West Bengal (42)	0 (0.50	0 (1.7)	27 (38.4)	3 (3.9)	4 (41.4)	8 (12.0)	0 (2.1)
A & N Islands (1)	-	-	0 (30.5)	-	1 (47.2)	0 (17.0)	0 (5.3)
Chandigarh (1)	1 (42.1)	0 (12.3)	-	-	0 (40.2)	0 (2.1)	0 (3.3)
Dadra & Nagar Haveli (1)	-	-	0 (10.8)	-	0 (28.6)	0 (1.4)	1 (59.3)
Daman & Diu (1)	0 (18.4)	-	-	-	0 (37.8)	-	1 (43.8)
Delhi (7)	1 (16.3)	4 (26.2)	-	-	2 (43.4)	0 (4.8)	0 (9.4)
Lakshadweep (1)	-	-	-	-	1 (52.3)	-	0 (47.7)
Pondicherry (1)	-	-	-	-	1 (50.5)	0 (48.8)	0 (0.8)

@ ***Break-up for Others***:- **All-India**: ADMK 11(1.5), BSP 3(2.1), DMK 0(2.4), SADM 6(0.8), TDP 2(3.3); **AP**: TDP 2(34.5), MIM 1(2.1); **Arunachal Pradesh:** PPA 0(35.2); **Bihar**: JMM 3(3.2), IPF 1(2.3), MCOR 1(0.8); **Goa:** MGP 1(27.9); **J&K:** NC 3(6.8) incl. Srinagar unopposed; **Karnataka:** JP 0(10.6); **Kerala**: ICS-SCS 1(2.5), MUL 2(5.2), KCM 1(2.4); **Maharashtra**: SHS 1(1.2); **Manipur**: MPP 0(17.1), KNA 0(12.6); **Mizoram:** MNF 0(31.3), DP 0(19.3); **Nagaland**: NPC 0(39.7); **Punjab**: BSP 1(8.6), SADM 6(29.2), SADB 0(5.4); **Sikkim:** SSP 1(68.5), RIS 0(9.6); **Tamil Nadu**: ADMK 11(17.1), DMK 0(26.7); **UP**: BSP 2(9.9), ABHM 1(0.6); **West Bengal**: RSP 4(4.7), FBL 3(4.0), GNLF 1(1.4); **A&N Islands**: ICS-SCS 0(17.0); **Pondicherry**: DMK 0(41.7), PMK 0(6.6).

party with 194 or 37.02% seats, but Janata Dal finished second with 142 or 27.1% seats with 17.73% or less than half the Congress vote. BJP turned in its most impressive performance raising its tally from two in 1984 to 86 with only 11.56% votes.

Compared with 1967, Congrees(I) had only polled 1.47 % fewer votes, but its seat share had gone down by as much as 17.4%. But if the Congress was routed in the north, Janata Dal's partners in the National Front were rejected in the south where Congress won record 104 seats in 1989, topping the 100 mark for the first time.

Faced with India's first 'hung' Lok Sabha, where no party commanded a majority and the anti-Congress parties unable to form a coalition because of their ideological differences, President R. Venkataraman again turned to Rajiv Gandhi to form a government as the leader of the single largest party.

It was only when Gandhi declined that V.P. Singh as the leader of the second largest Janata Dal was invited to cobble together the country's second non-Congress government, not counting Charan Singh's short-lived caretaker dispensation, with the Left and the BJP support it from the outside. Questions about the longevity of the new regime began to be raised even before V.P. Singh was sworn in on December 3,1989 with BJP offering only "general but critical support" to the National Front government.

In the event, hopping from one crisis to another, it lasted just 11 months and five days. V.P. Singh was defeated on the floor of the Lok Sabha by 142 to 364 votes on November 7, 1990 after BJP withdrew its support following the arrest of party president L.K. Advani leading his Ayodhya Rath in Bihar, ruled by Janata Dal chief minister, Laloo Prasad Yadav.

Invited by President R. Venkataraman to form the government as leader of the opposition, Rajiv Gandhi chose to pass up the opportunity and instead backed a rag-tag group of 54 MPs led by Chandra Shekhar, who had broken away from the Janata Dal.

Thanks to Congress support, Chandra Shekhar's government won a vote of confidence in the Lok Sabha by 280 votes to 214 a week later, but the strange bedfellows could not remain partners for long.

Accusing his government of keeping an eye on the Gandhis' 10 Janpath residence, Congress members stayed away from the Lok Sabha as it met to discuss a motion of thanks to the President's address in

Ninth Lok Sabha : JDS Government

Prime Minister : Chandra Shekhar, 10/11/1990 - 21/6/1991

Seats Won and Vote Share in % (in brackets), State-wise

State (Total Seats)	JDS *	INC	JD #	BJP	CPM	Others @	Ind.
All-India(543) (Poll in 529)	54	197 (39.5)	88 (17.7)	86 (11.5)	33 (6.6)	59 (19.4)	12 (5.3)
Andhra Pradesh (42)		39 (51.0)	0 (1.6)	0 (2.0)	0 (2.4)	3 (40.4)	0 (2.6)
Arunachal Pradesh (2)		2 (50.0)	-	-	-	0 (35.2)	0 (14.8)
Assam (14) (No Poll)							
Bihar (54)		4 (28.1)	31 (36.4)	9 (13.0)	1 (1.4)	9 (16.8)	0 (4.3)
Goa (2)		1 (47.4)	0 (18.1)	0 (0.7)	-	1 (30.6)	0 (3.2)
Gujarat (26)		3 (37.2)	11 (27.8)	12 (30.5)	-	0 (1.6)	0 (2.9)
Haryana (10)		4 (46.2)	6 (38.9)	0 (8.3)	-	0 (3.0)	0 (3.6)
Himachal Pradesh (4)		1 (42.0)	0 (7.2)	3 (45.3)	0 (0.5)	0 (4.4)	0 (0.7)
Jammu & Kashmir (6)		2 (39.0)	0 (30.1)	0 (7.2)	-	3 (14.2)	1 (9.6)
Karnataka (28)		27 (48.9)	1 (28.3)	0 (2.60	-	0 (15.7)	0 (4.5)
Kerala (20)		14 (41.7)	0 (1.9)	0 (4.5)	2 (22.9)	4 (19.5)	0 (9.5)
Madhya Pradesh(40)		8 (37.7)	4 (8.3)	27 (39.7)	0 (0.1)	0 (6.7)	1 (7.6)
Maharashtra (48)		28 (45.4)	5 (11.0)	10 (23.7)	0 (1.20	2 (10.5)	3 (8.2)
Manipur (2)		2 (45.0)	0 (1.5)	0 (2.3)	-	0 (39.0)	0 (12.2)
Meghalaya(2)		2 (55.4)	-	-	-	0 (4.8)	0 (39.8)
Mizoram (1)		1 (48.5)		-	-	0 (50.6)	0 (1.0)
Nagaland (1)		1 (60.3)		-	-	0 (39.7)	-
Orissa (21)		3 (38.4)	16 (49.5)	0 (1.3)	1 (3.0)	1 (5.8)	0 (2.1)
Punjab (13)		2 (26.5)	1 (5.5)	0 (4.2)	0 (3.9)	7 (47.2)	3 (12.7)
Rajasthan (25)		0 (37.0)	11 (25.7)	13 (29.6)	1 (2.1)	0 (2.1)	0 (3.5)
Sikkim (1)		0 (21.6)	-	-	-	1 (78.1)	0 (0.3)
Tamil Nadu (39)		27 (39.9)	0 (1.4)	0 (0.3)	0 (3.7)	12 (52.5)	0 (2.3)
Tripura (2)		2 (55.5)	-	0 (0.6)	0 (41.7)	0 (1.1)	0 (1.1)
Uttar Pradesh (85)		15 (31.8)	54 (35.9)	8 (7.6)	1 (0.5)	5 (16.0)	2 (8.4)
West Bengal (42)		4 (41.4)	0 (0.5)	0 (1.7)	27 (38.4)	11 (15.9)	0 (2.1)
A & N Islands (1)		1 (47.2)	-	-	0 (30.5)	0 (17.0)	0 (5.3)
Chandigarh (1)		0 (40.2)	1 (42.1)	0 (12.3)	-	0 (2.1)	0 (3.3)
Dadra & Nagar Haveli (1)		0 (28.6)	-	-	0 (10.8)	0 (1.4)	1 (59.3)
Daman & Diu (1)		0 (37.8)	0 (18.4)	-	-	-	1 (43.8)
Delhi (7)		2 (43.4)	1 (16.3)	4 (26.2)	-	0 (4.8)	0 (9.4)
Lakshadweep (1)		1 (52.3)	-	-	-	-	0 (47.7)
Pondicherry (1)		1 (50.5)	-	-	-	0 (48.8)	0 (0.8)

* Being a post-poll breakaway party, no vote share; statewise seat position not available.

\# Vote % and state-wise seat position here is as per the 1989 position.

@ ***Break-up for Others***:- **All-India**: ADMK 11(1.5),BSP 3(2.1), CPI 12(2.6), DMK 0(2.4), SADM 6(0.8), TDP 2(3.3); **AP**: TDP 2(34.5), MIM 1(2.1); **Arunachal Pradesh:** PPA 0(35.2); **Bihar**: CPI 4(7.9), JMM 3(3.2), IPF 1(2.3), MCOR 1(0.8); **Goa:** MGP 1(27.9); **J&K**: NC 3(6.8) incl. Srinagar uncontested; **Karnataka:** JP 0(10.6); **Kerala**: ICS-SCS 1(2.5), MUL 2(5.2), KCM 1(2.4), CPI 0(6.2); **Maharashtra**: CPI 1(1.9), SHS 1(1.2); **Manipur**: MPP 0(17.1), KNA 0(12.6); **Mizoram:** MNF 0(31.3), DP 0(19.3); **Nagaland**: NPC 0(39.7); **Orissa:** CPI 1(3.7); **Punjab**: BSP 1(8.6), SADM 6(29.2), SADB 0 (5.4); **Sikkim:** SSP 1(68.5), RIS 0(9.6); **Tamil Nadu:** ADMK 11(17.1), DMK 0(26.7), CPI 1(2.0); **UP**: BSP 2(9.9), CPI 2(1.4), ABHM 1(0.6); **West Bengal**: RSP 4(4.7), FBL 3(4.0), CPI 3(3.9), GNLF 1(1.4); **A&N Islands**: ICS-SCS 0(17.0); **Pondicherry:** DMK 0(41.7), PMK 0(6.6).

February. Rather than face defeat on the floor of the House, Chandra Shekhar resigned on March 6, 1991 and the President called for fresh elections in May.

1991—Gift of the Dead

It was a three-horse race with Congress making a comeback bid on the stability plank, BJP riding the Ayodhya Rath and Janata-Dal led National Front banking on the Mandal magic of caste-based reservations.

The Congress failed to repeat its feat of 1980, when the Indian voter, disenchanted with the squabbles of the Janata years, had brought back Mrs Indira Gandhi. But in his death, Rajiv Gandhi appeared to have given another chance to the Congress. Had he lived, his party might have won even fewer seats than it did in 1989 considering its poor (25%) success rate in the first phase of the poll before his assassination on May 21.

The 1991 poll threw up a second hung House in 18 months with Congress(I) again emerging as the single largest party with 227 members, 28 short of an absolute majority in a House with an effective strength of 508. But this time, there was none of the uncertainty associated with a fractured verdict.

Rajiv Gandhi's death had touched off a power struggle within the Congress (I), but in the end, the party managed to forge a consensus around P.V Narasimha Rao after Rajiv's Italian born widow Sonia refused to take up the mantle of leadership.

No one questioned Congress' right to form a government, as President Venkataraman swore Rao in on June 21, 1991 at the head of the nation's third minority government in a row, with little hesitation.

Rao won a vote of confidence 24 days later, on July 15, by 241 votes to 111 with 112 members of the National Front-Left combine abstaining. He went on to rule for another five years, despite several scams, by means fair or foul.

For once it was not a fight between the Congress and others. Nor did the voter response to the three major contenders conform to the usual North-South divide witnessed in the past. The second hung House that emerged in 1991 was split three ways among the Congress (I) and its allies, the National Front-Left combine and the Bhartiya Janata Party and Shiv Sena partnership.

If 'sympathy' gave the Congress (I) a lead in the south, it was not of

Tenth Lok Sabha : Congress Government

Prime Minister : P. V. Narasimha Rao, 21/6/1991-16/5/1996

Seats Won and Vote Share in % (in brackets), State-wise

State (Total Seats)	INC	JD	CPM	CPI	BJP	Others @	Ind.
All-India(543 *)	244 (36.5)	61 (11.9)	35 (6.2)	14 (2.5)	120 (20.1)	61 (18.9)	2 (3.9)
Andhra Pradesh (42)	25 (45.6)	0 (0.6)	1 (2.4)	1 (1.9)	1 (9.6)	14 (35.9)	0 (4.1)
Arunachal Pradesh (2)	2 (68.9)	0 (24.7)	-	-	0 (6.1)	-	0 (0.3)
Assam (14)	8 (28.5)	0 (5.2)	1 (4.7)	0 (2.2)	2 (9.6)	2 (35.6)	1 (14.2)
Bihar (54) $	1 (24.2)	32 (34.1)	1 (1.4)	8 (7.6)	5 (16.0)	6 (13.9)	1 (2.8)
Goa (2)	2 (57.7)	0 (1.0)	-	0 (1.5)	0 (15.6)	0 (22.1)	0 (2.1)
Gujarat (26)	5 (29.0)	0 (3.4)	-	-	20 (50.4)	1 (14.3)	0 (2.9)
Haryana (10)	9 (37.2)	0 (12.5)	-	-	0 (10.2)	1 (34.6)	0 (5.5)
Himachal Pradesh (4)	2 (46.2)	0 (7.0)	-	0 (0.7)	2 (42.8)	0 (1.9)	0 (1.5)
Jammu & Kashmir (6) *							
Karnataka (28)	23 (42.1)	0 (18.5)	0 (0.2)	0 (0.6)	4 (28.8)	1 (7.0)	0 (2.8)
Kerala (20)	13 (38.8)	0 (4.5)	3 (20.7)	0 (8.1)	0 (4.6)	4 (15.5)	0 (7.7)
Madhya Pradesh(40)	27 (45.3)	0 (4.2)	0 (0.0)	0 (0.4)	12 (41.9)	1 (4.8)	0 (3.3)
Maharashtra (48)	38 (48.4)	0 (9.9)	1 (1.3)	0 (1.0)	5 (20.2)	4 (15.1)	0 (4.2)
Manipur (2)	1 (38.4)	0 (18.6)	-	-	0 (8.1)	1 (31.9)	0 (3.1)
Meghalaya(2)	2 (56.6)	-	-	0 (1.3)	0 (6.9)	-	0 (35.3)
Mizoram (1)	1 (38.1)	0 (23.5)	-	-	-	0 (34.1)	0 (4.4)
Nagaland (1)	0 (44.3)	-	-	-	0 (3.0)	1 (52.7)	-
Orissa (21)	13 (44.1)	6 (34.6)	1 (2.1)	1 (3.1)	0 (9.5)	0 (4.5)	0 (2.2)
Punjab (13)	12 (49.7)	0 (1.3)	0 (4.0)	0 (1.6)	0 (15.9)	1 (23.6)	0 (4.0)
Rajasthan (25)	13 (44.0)	0 (6.2)	0 (0.7)	0 (0.1)	12 (40.9)	0 (4.4)	0 (3.8)
Sikkim (1)	-	-	0 (2.9)	-	-	1 (90.1)	0 (7.0)
Tamil Nadu (39)	28 (42.6)	0 (2.9)	0 (2.5)	0 (2.0)	0 (1.7)	11 (46.9)	0 (1.4)
Tripura (2)	2 (82.8)	-	0 (6.5)	-	0 (3.0)	0 (3.7)	0 (3.9)
Uttar Pradesh (85) +	5 (18.3)	23 (21.6)	0 (0.70	1 (1.0)	51 (32.8)	5 (20.3)	0 (5.2)
West Bengal (42)	5 (36.2)	0 (1.1)	27 (35.2)	3 (3.7)	0 (11.7)	7 (10.3)	0 (1.9)
A & N Islands (1)	1 (50.4)	-	0 (44.1)	-	0 (4.9)	-	0 (0.6)
Chandigarh (1)	1 (35.9)	0 (2.8)	-	-	0 (28.8)	0 (28.4)	0 (4.1)
Dadra & Nagar Haveli (1)	1 (61.7)	-	-	-	0 (35.4)	0 (2.0)	0 (0.9)
Daman & Diu (1)	0 (22.7)	0 (2.7)	-	-	1 (31.9)	0 (0.1)	0 (42.5)
Delhi (7)	2 (39.6)	0 (14.2)	-	0 (0.1)	5 (40.2)	0 (3.4)	0 (2.6)
Lakshadweep (1)	1 (50.6)	0 (49.5)	-	-	-	-	-
Pondicherry (1)	1 (53.1)	-	-	-	0 (2.0)	0 (42.4)	0 (2.6)

* No poll in J&K. Total 537 resuits but vote % for 521 seats (excluding Punjab which went to poll in 1992, Purnea and Patna seats of Bihar and Meerut of UP which went to poll later).

$ Vote share excluding Patna and Purnea.

+ Vote share excluding Meerut result.

@ ***Break-up for Others***:- **All-India**: ADMK 11(1.6),BSP 3(1.6), DMK 0(2.1), JMM 6(0.5), JP: 5(3.3), RSP 4(0.6), SHS 4(0.8), TDP 13(3.0); **AP**: TDP 13(32.3), MIM 1(1.8); **Assam:** AGP 1(17.6), ASDC 1(1.7); **Bihar**: JMM 6(4.5); **Goa:** MGP 0(20.6); **Gujarat**: JD(G) 1 (13.1); **Haryana:** HVP 1 (5.4), JP 0(25.4); **Karnataka:** JP 1(3.8); **Kerala**: ICS(SCS) 1(2.8), MUL 2(5.0), KC(M) 1(2.7); **MP:** BSP 1(3.5); **Maharashtra**: SHS 4(9.5); **Manipur**: MPP 0 (20.0), KNA 0(12.6), ICS(SCS) 0(10.9); MNF 0(34.1), DP 0(19.3); **Nagaland**: NPC 1(52.7); **Punjab**: BSP 1(8.6), SADM 6 (29.2); **Sikkim:** SSP 1(90.1); **Tamil Nadu**: ADMK 11(18.1), DMK 0(22.7); **UP**: BSP 1(8.7), ABHM 1(0.6); **West Bengal**: RSP 4(4.5), FBL 3(3.7), GNLF 1(1.4); **Andaman & Nicobar Islands**: ICS-SCS 0(17.0); **Pondicherry**: DMK 0(35.8).

much help to it in the Hindi heartland of Uttar Pradesh and Bihar. And if Ram propelled BJP into power in UP, it could not withstand the Mandal magic in Bihar, but it made unexpected gains in Karnataka and Andhra.

There were no uniform sweeps or swings, yet in almost every state two dominant parties emerged. The Congress, for one, faced an adverse 6.63% swing to begin with, but the pendulum swung its way in the second phase after the Rajiv assassination. Stirred by the tragedy, six to seven per cent more people turned out to vote, resulting in a swing in favour of Congress ranging from 1.8% in Bihar to a massive 14% in Rajasthan.

Even as the Congress (I) vote dropped from 39.33% in 1989 to its second lowest figure of 37.57%, it went on to win 32 more seats—227 instead of 195—thanks to the absence of one-to-one contests. But despite a sympathy wave, the Congress vote share dropped from 31.77% to a dismal 19.94% in Uttar Pradesh with almost half of its candidates losing their deposits.

Going it alone, BJP, on the other hand, nearly doubled its vote share from 11.5% to 20.95% in toting up 119 seats as it added 36 seats to its tally, making deep inroads—in terms of votes, if not seats—in states where it had no presence earlier.

Spearheading the National Front, Janata Dal turned out to be the biggest loser—surrendering 77 seats to finish with only 56 as its vote share went down by over six percentage points on an average, ranging from four points in Bihar to over 15 in Orissa.

Voters completely rejected Chandra Shekhar's rival Samajwadi Janata Party with only five of its candidates making it—down from 54 it had started with when it broke away from JD.

The Left lost Kerala, but retained West Bengal, with the two communist parties, now again working in tandem, raising their tally by four seats to 49, while their combined vote share remained practically the same at a little over nine per cent.

1996—Return of Uncertainty

The short spell of stability was broken again in 1996 as a hung house emerged for the third time in as many general elections with three major national combines headed by the Congress, BJP and JD falling far short of a simple majority.

Following the example of his predecessor, R. Venkataraman, President Dr Shankar Dayal Sharma invited Atal Bihari Vajpayee to

Eleventh Lok Sabha : BJP-led Government

Prime Minister : Atal Bihari Vajpayee, 16/5/1996 - 1/6/1996

Seats Won and Vote Share in % (in brackets), State-wise

State (Total Seats)	BJP	SAP	Supporters #	INC	JD	Others @	Ind.
All-India (543)	161 (20.3)	8 (2.2)	26 (2.6)	140 (28.8)	46 (8.1)	153 (31.7)	9 (6.3)
Andhra Pradesh (42)	0 (5.7)	0 (0.0)	-	22 (39.7)	-	20 (50.8)	0 (3.8)
Arunachal Pradesh (2)	0 (17.4)	-	-	0 (28.8)	-	-	2 (53.8)
Assam (14)	1 (15.9)	-	-	5 (31.6)	0 (0.7)	7 (40.1)	1 (11.7)
Bihar (54)	18 (20.5)	6 (14.5)	-	2 (13.0)	22 (31.9)	5 (14.7)	1 (5.4)
Goa (2)	0 (13.8)	-	-	0 (34.4)	-	2 (50.3)	0 (1.5)
Gujarat (26)	16 (48.5)	0 (0.1)	-	10 (38.7)	0 (0.4)	0 (4.8))	0 (7.5)
Haryana (10)	4 (19.7)	0 (19.0)	3 (15.2)	2 (22.6)	0 (1.5)	0 (11.7)	1 (10.3)
Himachal Pradesh (4)	0 (39.6)	-	-	4 (54.3)	0 (0.2)	0 (4.4)	0 (1.5)
Jammu & Kashmir (6)	1 (19.0)	-	-	4 (27.5)	1 (17.6)	0 (11.6)	0 (24.3)
Karnataka (28)	6 (24.9)	-	-	5 (30.3)	16 (34.9)	1 (5.3)	0 (4.6)
Kerala (20)	0 (5.6)	0 (0.0)	-	7 (38.0)	1 (4.4)	11 (55.0)	1 (7.0)
Madhya Pradesh(40)	27 (41.3)	0 (0.1)	-	2 (40.2)	0 (1.8)	0 (27.9)	1 (9.6)
Maharashtra (48)	18 (21.8)	0 (0.1)	15 (16.8)	15 (34.8)	0 (3.3)	0 (13.5)	0 (9.7)
Manipur (2)	0 (5.3)	0 (1.7)	-	2 (40.2)	0 (1.8)	0 (27.9)	0 (23.1)
Meghalaya (2)	0 (9.1)	-	-	1 (53.6)	-	0 (1.5)	1 (35.8)
Mizoram (1)	-	-	-	1 (42.5)	-	0 (37.6)	0 (19.9)
Nagaland (1)	-	-	-	1 (62.3)	-	-	0 (37.7)
Orissa (21)	0 (13.4)	1 (1.6)	-	16 (44.9)	4 (30.1)	0 (4.3)	0 (5.7)
Punjab (13)	0 (6.5)	-	8 (28.7)	2 (35.1)	0 (2.7)	3 (19.5)	0 (7.5)
Rajasthan (25)	12 (42.4)	0 (0.9)	-	12 (40.5)	0 (2.6)	1 (6.4)	0 (7.2)
Sikkim (1)	-	-	-	-	-	1 (96.7)	0 (3.4)
Tamil Nadu (39)	0 (2.9)	0 (0.0)	-	0 (18.3)	0 (1.5)	39 (74.3)	0 (3.0)
Tripura (2)	0 (6.5)	-	-	0 (34.1)	0 (0.3)	2 (58.2)	0 (0.9)
Uttar Pradesh (85)	52 (33.4)	1 (0.9)	-	5 (8.1)	2 (4.3)	24 (46.8)	1 (6.5)
West Bengal (42)	0 (6.7)	0 (0.0)	-	9 (40.1)	0 (0.4)	33 (52.6)	0 (0.2)
A & N Islands (1)	0 (24.3)	-	-	1 (58.2)	-	0 (14.7)	0 (2.8)
Chandigarh (1)	1 (39.1)	0 (17.6)	-	0 (29.8)	0 (0.9)	0 (9.5)	0 (3.1)
Dadra & NH (1)	0 (42.4)	-	-	1 (55.6)	-	0 (0.6)	0 (1.4)
Daman & Diu (1)	0 (40.5)	-	-	1 (50.6)	-	-	0 (8.9)
Delhi (7)	5 (49.6)	0 (0.1)	-	2 (37.3)	0 (4.2)	0 (4.9)	0 (3.9)
Lakshadweep (1)	-	-	-	1 (51.7)	0 (48.3)	-	-
Pondicherry (1)	0 (4.4)	-	-	1 (40.0)	-	0 (49.2)	0 (6.4)

*# **Break-up for BJP Supporters**:-* **All India**: HVP 3(0.4), SAD 8(0.8), SHS 15(1.5); **Haryana**: HVP 3(15.2); **Maharashtra**: SHS 15(16.8); **Punjab**: SAD 8(28.7).

@ ***Break-up for Others***:- **All-India**: AGP 5(0.8), AIICT 4(1.5), BSP 11(3.6), CPI 12(2.0), CPM 32(6.1), DMK 17(2.2), FBL 3(0.4), RSP 5(0.6), SP 17(3.3), TDP 16(3.0), TMC 20(2.2), Others 11(1.8); **AP**: MIM 1(1.1), CPI 2(2.4), CPM 1(2.9), TDP 16(32.6); **Assam**: AGP 5(27.8), ASDC 1(1.9), CPM 1(3.9); **Bihar**: CPI 3(5.1), JMM 1(3.0), SP 1(1.3); **Goa**: MGP 1(26.8), UGDP 1(22.7); **Karnataka**: KCP 1(3.1); **Kerala**: CPI 2(8.2), CPM 5(21.2), KCM 1(2.7), MUL 2(5.1), RSP 1(2.5); **MP**: AIICT 1(4.7), BSP 2(8.2), MPVC 1(1.5); **Punjab**: BSP 3(9.4); **Rajasthan**: AIICT 1(4.7); **Tamil Nadu**: CPI 2(2.3), DMK 17(25.8), TMC 20(27.0); **Tripura**: CPM 2(52.4); **UP**: AIICT 2(3.0), BSP 6(20.6), SP 16(20.8); **West Bengal**: CPI 3(3.8), CPM 23(36.7), FBL 3(3.4), RSP 4(4.8).

form a government as the leader of the single largest party, BJP with 161 seats in the 543 member house amidst protests from a rival United Front backed by the Congress.

In the event, the BJP government lasted for an all too brief an interlude of 13 days when Vajpayee chose to resign on May 28, 1996 rather than face sure defeat in the house. Accusing the UF partners of ganging up just to "keep us out" and making an "opportunistic" alliance with the Congress for a price—going slow on corruption probes against its leaders.

As the balance of power shifted towards regional players, a relatively unknown Janata leader from Karnataka, Haradanahalli Doddegowda Deve Gowda took the office of the Prime Minister on June 1, 1996 after cobbling together a 13-party coalition supported from outside by the Congress.

The four regional parties—Chandrababu Naidu's Telugu Desam Party (TDP) in Andhra, Karunanidhi's DMK and breakaway Tamil Maanila Congress (TMC) in Tamil Nadu and the Asom Gana Parishad in Assam—with 58 MPs joined the Gowda government only after being allowed to form a pressure group within.

Releasing a "unanimously accepted" document, Gowda declared providing a stable government based on political, administrative and economic federalism would be on the top of United Front's agenda as it strove for "growth and social justice".

But that was not to be. Not before long, Congress started getting restless and pulled the plug on the UF government in early 1998 after first forcing it to replace Gowda with Inder Kumar Gujral as Prime Minister in April 1997.

The third uncertain verdict in 1996 marked a clear continuation of the shift towards regional players since 1989 with only the Congress and BJP among the national parties winning 301 seats between them. Five other national parties including the Janata Dal and CPI (M) picked up another 102 seats. The remaining 140 seats were shared by regional and smaller parties besides three independents.

After the elections in Jammu and Kashmir, BJP and its allies finished with 195 seats, 71 more than 1991, The United Front 14 behind with 181 also gained 52. But the Congress dropped 92 seats to end up as the biggest loser with a tally of 140. With ally AIADMK ceding all its eleven seats, their combined losses topped 100.

Eleventh Lok Sabha : United Front Government

Prime Minister : H.D. Deve Gowda, 1/6/1996 - 21/4/1997

Seats Won and Vote Share in % (in brackets), State-wise

State (Total Seats)	JD	UF Parties *	CPM	INC	BJP	Others #	Ind.
All-India (489)	46 (8.1)	102 (16.5)	32 (6.1)	140 (28.8)	161 (20.3)	53 (13.9)	9 (6.3)
Andhra Pradesh (42)		18 (35.5)	1 (2.9)	22 (39.7)	0 (5.7)	1 (12.4)	0 (3.8)
Arunachal Pradesh (2)	-	-	-	0 (28.8)	0 (17.4)	-	2 (53.8)
Assam (14)	0 (0.7)	5 (30.9)	1 (3.9)	5 (31.6)	1 (15.9)	1 (5.3)	1 (11.7)
Bihar (54)	22 (31.9)	4 (6.7)	0 (0.8)	2 (13.0)	18 (20.5)	7 (21.6)	1 (5.4)
Goa (2)	-	1 (27.8)	-	0 (34.4)	0 (13.8)	1 (22.7)	0 (1.5)
Gujarat (26)	0 (0.4)	0 (2.2)	0 (0.0)	10 (38.7)	16 (48.5)	0 (2.7)	0 (7.5)
Haryana (10)	0 (1.5)	0 (3.8)	-	2 (22.6)	4 (19.7)	3 (41.9)	1 (10.3)
Himachal Pradesh (4)	0 (0.2)	0 (1.3)	0 (1.0)	4 (54.3)	0 (39.6)	0 (2.0)	0 (1.5)
Jammu & Kashmir (6)	1 (17.6)	0 (0.8)	-	4 (27.5)	1 (19.0)	0 (10.8)	0 (24.3)
Karnataka (28)	16 (34.9)	1 (4.4)	0 (0.4)	5 (30.3)	6 (24.9)	0 (0.6)	0 (4.6)
Kerala (20)	1 (4.4)	3 (12.9)	5 (21.2)	7 (38.0)	0 (5.6)	3 (11.0)	1 (7.0)
Madhya Pradesh(40)	0 (1.1)	2 (7.0)	0 (0.1)	8 (31.0)	27 (41.3)	2 (10.0)	1 (9.6)
Maharashtra (48)	0 (3.3)	0 (3.0)	0 (1.1)	15 (34.8)	18 (21.8)	15 (25.1)	0 (9.7)
Manipur (2)	0 (1.8)	0 (7.9)	-	2 (40.2)	0 (5.3)	0 (21.8)	0 (23.1)
Meghalaya (2)	-	0 (1.4)	-	1 (53.6)	0 (9.1)	-	1 (35.8)
Mizoram (1)	-	-	-	1 (42.5)	-	0 (37.6)	0 (19.9)
Nagaland (1)	-	-	-	1 (62.3)	-	-	0 (37.7)
Orissa (21)	4 (30.1)	0 (0.7)	0 (1.7)	16 (44.9)	0 (13.4)	1 (3.5)	0 (5.7)
Punjab (13)	0 (2.7)	0 (2.2)	0 (2.7)	2 (35.1)	0 (6.5)	11 (43.4)	0 (7.5)
Rajasthan (25)	0 (2.6)	1 (4.1)	0 (0.4)	12 (40.5)	12 (42.4)	0 (2.7)	0 (7.2)
Sikkim (1)	-	-	-	-	-	1 (96.6)	0 (3.4)
Tamil Nadu (39)	0 (1.5)	39 (57.3)	0 (1.8)	0 (18.3)	0 (2.9)	0 (15.2)	0 (3.0)
Tripura (2)	0 (0.3)	0 (0.4)	2 (52.4)	0 (34.1)	0 (6.5)	0 (5.4)	0 (0.9)
Uttar Pradesh (85)	2 (4.3)	18 (24.2)	0 (0.7)	5 (8.1)	52 (33.4)	7 (22.7)	1 (6.5)
West Bengal (42)	0 (0.4)	10 (12.1)	23 (36.7)	9 (40.1)	0 (6.9)	0 (1.9)	0 (2.0)
A & N Islands (1)	-	-	0 (14.3)	1 (58.2)	0 (24.3)	0 (0.4)	0 (2.8)
Chandigarh (1)	0 (0.9)	0 (0.2)	0 (2.3)	0 (29.8)	1 (39.1)	0 (24.6)	0 (3.1)
Dadra & NH (1)	-	0 (0.6)	-	1 (55.6)	0 (42.4)	-	0 (1.4)
Daman & Diu (1)	-	-	-	1 (50.6)	0 (40.5)	-	0 (8.9)
Delhi (7)	0 (4.2)	0 (2.7)	0 (0.3)	2 (37.3)	5 (49.6)	0 (2.0)	0 (3.9)
Lakshadweep (1)	0 (48.3)	-	-	1 (51.7)	-	-	-
Pondicherry (1)	-	0 (39.9)	-	1 (40.0)	0 (4.4)	0 (9.2)	0 (6.4)

Break-up for UF Parties:- **All-India:** AGP 5(0.8), CPI 12(2.0), DMK 17(2.2), SP 17(3.3), TDP 16(3.0), TMC 20(2.2); **AP:** TDP 16(32.6), CPI 2(2.4); **Assam:** AGP 5(27.2); **Bihar:** CPI 3(5.1), SP 1(1.3); **Goa:** MGP 1(26.8); **Karnataka:** KCP 1(3.1); **Kerala:** CPI 2(8.2), RSP 1(2.5); **MP:** AIICT 1(4.7), MPVC 1(1.5); **Manipur:** CPI 0(4.0), AIICT 0(3.9); **Rajasthan:** AIICT 1(3.6); **Tamil Nadu:** TMC 20(27.0), DMK 17(25.8), CPI 2(2.3); **UP:** SP 16(20.8), AIICT 2(3.0); **West Bengal:** RSP 4(4.8), CPI 3(3.8), FBL 3(3.4).

Break-up for Others:- **All-India:** BSP 11(3.6), SAP 8(2.2), SHS 15(1.5), SAD 8(0.8); **AP:** MIM 1(1.1); **Assam:** ASDC 1(1.9); **Bihar:** SAP 6(14.5), JMM 1(3.0); **Goa:** UGDP 1(22.7); **Haryana:** HVP 3(15.2), SAP 0(19.0), BSP 0(6.6); **J&K:** BSP 0(6.0); **Kerala:** MUL 2(5.1), KCM 1(2.7); **MP:** BSP 2(8.2); **Maharashtra:** SHS 15(16.8), RPI 0(4.9); **Manipur:** FPM 0(12.6), MPP 0(6.7); **Mizoram:** MNF 0(37.6); **Orissa:** SAP 1(1.6); **Punjab:** SAD 8(28.7), BSP 3(9.4), SADM 0(3.9); **Sikkim:** SDF 1(72.2); SSP 0(24.5); **Tamil Nadu:** ADMK 0(7.8); **UP:** BSP 6(20.6), SAP 1(0.9); **Chandigarh:** SAP 0(17.6); **Pondicherry:** PMK 0(4.3).

Eleventh Lok Sabha : United Front Government

Prime Minister : Inder Kumar Gujral, 21/4/1997 - 19/3/1998

Seats Won and Vote Share in % (in brackets), State-wise

State (Total Seats)	JD	UF Parties *	CPM	INC	BJP	Others #	Ind.
All-India (489)	46 (8.1)	102 (16.5)	32 (6.1)	140 (28.8)	161 (20.3)	53 (13.9)	9 (6.3)
Andhra Pradesh (42)		18 (35.5)	1 (2.9)	22 (39.7)	0 (5.7)	1 (12.4)	0 (3.8)
Arunachal Pradesh (2)	-	-	-	0 (28.8)	0 (17.4)	-	2 (53.8)
Assam (14)	0 (0.7)	5 (30.9)	1 (3.9)	5 (31.6)	1 (15.9)	1 (5.3)	1 (11.7)
Bihar (54)	22 (31.9)	4 (6.7)	0 (0.8)	2 (13.0)	18 (20.5)	7 (21.6)	1 (5.4)
Goa (2)	-	1 (27.8)	-	0 (34.4)	0 (13.8)	1 (22.7)	0 (1.5)
Gujarat (26)	0 (0.4)	0 (2.2)	0 (0.0)	10 (38.7)	16 (48.5)	0 (2.7)	0 (7.5)
Haryana (10)	0 (1.5)	0 (3.8)	-	2 (22.6)	4 (19.7)	3 (41.9)	1 (10.3)
Himachal Pradesh (4)	0 (0.2)	0 (1.3)	0 (1.0)	4 (54.3)	0 (39.6)	0 (2.0)	0 (1.5)
Jammu & Kashmir (6)	1 (17.6)	0 (0.8)	-	4 (27.5)	1 (19.0)	0 (10.8)	0 (24.3)
Karnataka (28)	16 (34.9)	1 (4.4)	0 (0.4)	5 (30.3)	6 (24.9)	0 (0.6)	0 (4.6)
Kerala (20)	1 (4.4)	3 (12.9)	5 (21.2)	7 (38.0)	0 (5.6)	3 (11.0)	1 (7.0)
Madhya Pradesh(40)	0 (1.1)	2 (7.0)	0 (0.1)	8 (31.0)	27 (41.3)	2 (10.0)	1 (9.6)
Maharashtra (48)	0 (3.3)	0 (3.0)	0 (1.1)	15 (34.8)	18 (21.8)	15 (25.1)	0 (9.7)
Manipur (2)	0 (1.8)	0 (7.9)	-	2 (40.2)	0 (5.3)	0 (21.8)	0 (23.1)
Meghalaya (2)	-	0 (1.4)	-	1 (53.6)	0 (9.1)	-	1 (35.8)
Mizoram (1)	-	-	-	1 (42.5)	-	0 (37.6)	0 (19.9)
Nagaland (1)	-	-	-	1 (62.3)	-	-	0 (37.7)
Orissa (21)	4 (30.1)	0 (0.7)	0 (1.7)	16 (44.9)	0 (13.4)	1 (3.5)	0 (5.7)
Punjab (13)	0 (2.7)	0 (2.2)	0 (2.7)	2 (35.1)	0 (6.5)	11 (43.4)	0 (7.5)
Rajasthan (25)	0 (2.6)	1 (4.1)	0 (0.4)	12 (40.5)	12 (42.4)	0 (2.7)	0 (7.2)
Sikkim (1)	-	-	-	-	-	1 (96.6)	0 (3.4)
Tamil Nadu (39)	0 (1.5)	39 (57.3)	0 (1.8)	0 (18.3)	0 (2.9)	0 (15.2)	0 (3.0)
Tripura (2)	0 (0.3)	0 (0.4)	2 (52.4)	0 (34.1)	0 (6.5)	0 (5.4)	0 (0.9)
Uttar Pradesh (85)	2 (4.3)	18 (24.2)	0 (0.7)	5 (8.1)	52 (33.4)	7 (22.7)	1 (6.5)
West Bengal (42)	0 (0.4)	10 (12.1)	23 (36.7)	9 (40.1)	0 (6.9)	0 (1.9)	0 (2.0)
A & N Islands (1)	-	-	0 (14.3)	1 (58.2)	0 (24.3)	0 (0.4)	0 (2.8)
Chandigarh (1)	0 (0.9)	0 (0.2)	0 (2.3)	0 (29.8)	1 (39.1)	0 (24.6)	0 (3.1)
Dadra & NH (1)	-	0 (0.6)	-	1 (55.6)	0 (42.4)	-	0 (1.4)
Daman & Diu (1)	-	-	-	1 (50.6)	0 (40.5)	-	0 (8.9)
Delhi (7)	0 (4.2)	0 (2.7)	0 (0.3)	2 (37.3)	5 (49.6)	0 (2.0)	0 (3.9)
Lakshadweep (1)	0 (48.3)	-	-	1 (51.7)	-	-	-
Pondicherry (1)	-	0 (39.9)	-	1 (40.0)	0 (4.4)	0 (9.2)	0 (6.4)

Break-up for UF Parties:- **All-India:** AGP 5(0.8), CPI 12(2.0), DMK 17(2.2), SP 17(3.3), TDP 16(3.0), TMC 20(2.2); **AP**: TDP 16(32.6), CPI 2(2.4); **Assam**: AGP 5(27.2); **Bihar**: CPI 3(5.1), SP 1(1.3); **Goa**: MGP 1(26.8); **Karnataka**: KCP 1(3.1); **Kerala:** CPI 2(8.2), RSP 1(2.5); **MP:** AIICT 1(4.7), MPVC 1(1.5); **Manipur:** CPI 0(4.0), AIICT 0(3.9); **Rajasthan**: AIICT 1(3.6); **Tamil Nadu**: TMC 20(27.0), DMK 17(25.8), CPI 2(2.3); **UP**: SP 16(20.8), AIICT 2(3.0); **West Bengal**: RSP 4(4.8), CPI 3(3.8), FBL 3(3.4).

Break-up for Others:- **All-India:** BSP 11(3.6), SAP 8(2.2), SHS 15(1.5), SAD 8(0.8); **AP:** MIM 1(1.1); **Assam:** ASDC 1(1.9); **Bihar:** SAP 6(14.5), JMM 1(3.0); **Goa:** UGDP 1(22.7); **Haryana:** HVP 3(15.2), SAP 0(19.0), BSP 0(6.6); **J&K:** BSP 0(6.0); **Kerala:** MUL 2(5.1), KCM 1(2.7); **MP:** BSP 2(8.2); **Maharashtra:** SHS 15(16.8), RPI 0(4.9); **Manipur:** FPM 0(12.6), MPP 0(6.7); **Mizoram:** MNF 0(37.6); **Orissa:** SAP 1(1.6); **Punjab:** SAD 8(28.7), BSP 3(9.4), SADM 0(3.9); **Sikkim:** SDF 1(72.2); SSP 0(24.5); **Tamil Nadu:** ADMK 0(7.8); **UP:** BSP 6(20.6), SAP 1(0.9); **Chandigarh:** SAP 0(17.6); **Pondicherry:** PMK 0(4.3).

In terms of votes, an all India adverse swing of a little less than eight per cent reduced the Congress vote share to an all time low of 28.76%—7.74 points less than the 36.5% it polled in 1991. This translated into heavy losses for the party all over except in Andhra, Orissa and West Bengal.

With negative swings ranging from 10% in Uttar Pradesh to a massive 24% per cent in Tamil Nadu, the Congress position worsened in UP and Bihar, while it suffered a reversal of fortunes in Assam, Haryana and Karnatka. While lack of opposition unity failed to help it anywhere except in Andhra Pradesh, Congress losses were largely attributed to a thinning out of its pretty evenly spread out support base.

BJP too ran into a minor negative swing of less than a quarter per cent, but at 161 finished with 41 more seats with only 20.13 % votes—8.45% less than its nearest rival Congress. This was essentially due to two factors. One, its alliances in various states produced a combined swing of 3.5% at the national level. Second, most of BJP seats came from a support belt extending from Bihar to Karnataka with an average 36% vote share—a good 13 points more than the Congress.

The Third Front remained practically where it was before the poll in terms of seats with gains in the south offsetting major losses in the east. Among the original constituents of the National Front-Left Front, Janata Dal lost the most with its popular support declining from 11.9 to 8.1%—marking a negative swing of 3.8 points. A marginal adverse swing of 0.66% reduced the Left parties vote share to about 9%, TDP managed to broadly hang on to its near three per cent votes, while the AGP raised its support from 0.54 to 0.77%.

It were the 'others' who gained the most at the cost of Congress with a dozen small parties ranging from BSP to DMK raising their combined strength from 27 in 1989 to 43 in 1991 and doubling it in 1996.

1998—The Saffron Surge

As the poll of 1998 threw up India's fourth hung House in as many elections since 1989, President K.R. Narayanan did his own bit to ensure a modicum of stability for the new dispensation that was to replace the 13-party "united dalliance" as a wag described the outgoing government.

Unlike his predecessor Dr Shankar Dyal Sharma, who, following convention had invited Vajpayee to form the government in 1996, Narayanan merely asked if he was "able and willing to do so". And

Twelfth Lok Sabha : BJP-led Government

Prime Minister : Atal Bihari Vajpayee, 19/3/1998 - 13/10/1999

Seats Won and Vote Share in % (in brackets), State-wise

State (Total Seats)	BJP	Allies *	INC	CPM	JD	Others @	Ind.
All-India(543)	182 (25.6)	95 (15.1)	141 (25.8)	32 (5.2)	6 (3.2)	81 (22.7)	6 (2.4)
Andhra Pradesh (42)	4 (18.3)	12 (32.0)	22 (38.5)	0 (2.9)	1 (0.9)	3 (5.7)	0 (1.7)
Arunachal Pradesh (2)	0 (21.8)	2 (52.5)	0 (23.9)	-	0 (1.9)	-	-
Assam (14)	1 (24.5)	-	10 (39.0)	0 (3.3)	0 (0.1)	2 (23.6)	1 (9.5)
Bihar (52)	20 (24.0)	10 (15.7)	5 (7.3)	0 (0.4)	1 (8.7)	18 (41.9)	0 (2.0)
Goa (2)	0 (30.0)	-	2 (31.6)	-	-	0 (38.1)	0 (0.3)
Gujarat (26)	19 (48.3)	-	7 (36.5)	-	0 (2.9)	0 (11.2)	0 (1.1)
Haryana (10)	1 (18.9)	5 (37.5)	3 (26.0)	0 (0.3)	0 (0.4)	1 (15.7)	0 (1.2)
Himachal Pradesh (4)	3 (51.4)	-	1 (41.9)	-	0 (0.9)	0 (5.7)	0 (0.1)
Jammu & Kashmir (6)	2 (28.6)	3 (36.4)	1 (19.2)	-	0 (0.5)	0 (8.1)	0 (7.2)
Karnataka (28)	13 (27.0)	3 (11.5)	9 (36.2)	0 (0.0)	3 (21.7)	0 (2.8)	0 (0.8)
Kerala (20)	0 (8.0)	-	8 (38.7)	6 (21.0)	0 (3.9)	6 (28.8)	0 (6.8)
Madhya Pradesh(40)	30 (45.7)	-	10 (39.4)	0 (0.1)	0 (1.2)	0 (12.3)	0 (1.3)
Maharashtra (48)	4 (22.5)	6 (19.7)	33 (43 6)	0 (0.6)	0 (1.7)	5 (9.5)	0 (2.4)
Manipur (2)	0 (12.6)	1 (25.4)	0 (18.6)	-	-	1 (42.8)	0 (0.6)
Meghalaya(2)	0 (9.0)	-	2 (47.6)	-	-	0 (42.8)	0 (0.6)
Mizoram (1)	0 (2.9)	-	0 (34.9)	-	-	0 (27.2)	1 (35.0)
Nagaland (1)	-	0 (13.3)	1 (86.7)				
Orissa (21)	7 (21.2)	9 (27.5)	5 (41.0)	0 (0.4)	0 (4.9)	0 (4.6)	0 (0.4)
Punjab (13)	3 (11.7)	8 (32.9)	0 (25.9)	0 (1.1)	1 (4.2)	0 (19.3)	1 (4.9)
Rajasthan (25)	5 (41.7)	-	18 (44.5)	0 (1.3)	0 (2.3)	1 (6.4)	1 (3.8)
Sikkim (1)	-	1 (65.7)	0 (33.1)	-	-	-	0 (1.2)
Tamil Nadu (39)	3 (6.9)	26 (39.3)	0 (4.8)	0 (0.6)	-	9 (45.9)	1 (2.5)
Tripura (2)	0 (8.2)	-	0 (42.1)	2 (48.8)	-	0 (0.6)	0 (0.3)
Uttar Pradesh (85)	57 (36.5)	2 (0.8)	0 (6.0)	0 (0.2)	0 (0.5)	25 (53.2)	1 (2.8)
West Bengal (42)	1 (10.2)	7 (24.4)	1 (15.2)	24 (35.4)	-	9 (13.8)	0 (1.0)
A & N Islands (1)	0 (35.5)	-	1 (35.9)	0 (5.7)	-	0 (20.4)	0 (2.5)
Chandigarh (1)	1 (42.4)	-	0 (38.7)	-	-	0 (17.3)	0 (1.6)
Dadra & N. Haveli (1)	1 (53.7)	0 (41.7)	0 (4.1)	-	-	-	0 (0.4)
Delhi (7)	6 (50.7)	-	1 (42.6)	-	0 (2.5)	0 (3.7)	0 (0.5)
Daman & Diu (1)	1 (42.0)	-	0 (2.0)	-	-	-	0 (56.1)
Lakshadweep (1)	-	-	1 (51.6)	-	0 (48.5)	-	-
Pondicherry (1)	-	0 (25.1)	0 (32.1)	-	-	1 (42.6)	0 (0.2)

* ***Break-up for BJP Allies:-*** **All-India:** SAP 12(1.8), ADMK 18(1.8), BJD 9(1.0), SAD 8(0.8), SHS 6(1.8), TC 7(2.4), TDP (post poll) 12(2.8); **Arunachal Pradesh:** ANC (post poll) 2(52.5); **AP:** TDP 12(32.0); **Bihar:** SAP 10(15.7); **Haryana:** HVP 1(11.6), HLDR (post poll) 4(25.9); **J&K:** NC (post poll) 3(36.4); **Karnataka:** LS 3(11.5); **Manipur:** MSCP (post poll) 1(25.4); **Maharashtra:** SHS 6(19.7); **Nagaland:** LS 0(13.3); **Orissa:** BJD 9(27.5); **Punjab:** SAD 8(32.9); **Sikkim:** SDF (post poll) 1(65.7); **Tamil Nadu:** ADMK 18(25.9), JP 1(1.0), MDMK 3(6.3), PMK 4(6.1).

@ ***Break-up for Others:-*** **All-India:** BSP 5(4.7), CPI 9(1.8), DMK 6(1.4), RJD 17(2.8), SP 20(4.9); **AP:** CPI 2(2.6), MIM 1(1.5); **Assam:** ASDC 1(2.2), UMFA 1(4.3), AGP 0(12.7); **Bihar:** RJD 17(26.6), RJP 0(1.0); **Haryana:** BSP 1(7.7); **Kerala:** CPI 2(8.3), MUL 2(5.0), KCM 1(2.4), RSP 1(2.7); **Maharashtra:** RPI 4(4.1), PWP 1(0.9); **Manipur:** CPI 1(20.5), MPP 0(18.6); **Mizoram:** MNF 0(26.9); **Meghalaya:** UDP 0(25.5), HSPDP 0(7.4), PDP 0(6.0); **Punjab:** BSP 0(12.7), SADM 0(2.7); **Rajasthan:** AIICS 1(1.9), BSP 0(2.1); **Tamil Nadu:** DMK 5(20.1), TMC 3(20.2), CPI 1(2.5); **UP:** BSP 4(20.9), SP 20(28.7), SJPR 1(0.5); **West Bengal:** CPI 3(3.6), FBL 2(3.3), RSP 4(4.5); **Chandigarh:** SJPR 0(14.6); **Pondicherry:** DMK 1(41.1).

when Vajpayee asserted that he was indeed willing, the President insisted on proof that he had the necessary numbers to be able to do so.

Back as Prime Minister at the head of another shaky coalition, the pulls and pressures that Vajpayee was to face, became all too evident even before his government took office on March 19, 1998 as AIADMK leader J. Jayalalitha threw up a tantrum before sending in her letter of support.

The government that Vajpayee cobbled together after a great deal of haggling and hard bargaining with 253 pre-and 11 post-poll allies, still fell eight short of the magic figure of 272 in a house of 543 before the United Front convenor Chandrababu Naidu came to his rescue.

Taking umbrage at UF's "unprincipled, unilateral" decision to back the Congress nominee Purno Agitok Sangma for the Lok Sabha speakership, Naidu threw the weight of his 12 TDP MPs behind the government in return for the speaker's job for his nominee, Ganti Mohan Singh Balayogi.

Four days after Balayogi's election as the speaker, Vajpayee won the confidence vote on March 28, 1998 by 13 votes with 264 "ayes" and 261 "noes" as three members of Farooq Abdullah's National Conference too broke ranks with the UF to abstain from the vote.

Embarking on a tightrope walk of consensual politics, Vajpayee told a party forum that running the coalition was a great experiment and having "got this chance after 50 years of toil and sacrifice," BJP would ensure its success.

Finally, Jayalalitha proved the undoing of the second Vajpayee government even as he made efforts to evolve a coalition culture and broaden the BJP-led alliance to give stability to the Indian polity.

Like 1996, three major formations led by the Congress, BJP and the United Front spearheaed by the Janata Dal emerged to fight out the battle of 1998 after the Congress pulled the plug on the Gujral government over the Jain Commission issue.

The fractured verdict of 1998 brought little cheer to BJP, for even as it finally got a chance to set up a government at the centre, it found itself a virtual prisoner to its 18 disparate pre- and post-poll allies. For the first time polling almost as many votes as the Congress, BJP won 182 seats, a gain of 21, with 25.59% votes to retain its status as the largest single party in the 12th Lok Sabha. Its 14 pre-poll partners added another 11.69% to the vote pie and brought in 73 seats, 39 more, to give it 255 seats with 37.28% votes, a clear gain of 60 thanks to a ten per cent swing.

Largely going it alone, except in Maharashtra, Bihar and Kerala, Congress won 141 seats, just three more than in 1996, even as a near three per cent downswing brought its vote share down to a historic low of 25.82%. It also managed with a whisker to stay as the single party with most votes.

An understanding with Laloo Prasad Yadav's RJD in Bihar and a strategic alliance with RPI and SP in Maharashtra, however, did help the Congress combine to pile up 166 seats, 25 more than last time, with 29.77 per cent votes, just about the same as the smaller alliance polled in 1996.

Cobbled together after the 1996 poll threw up a hung house, the United Front generally stuck together during its 20-month rule under two Prime Ministers of the Janata Dal. But it turned out to be the worst loser in the poll of 1998 with its tally reduced to 99 won with 22.18% votes in the face of a 6.33% downswing. Losing 40 seats across the board, JD was left holding on to only six seats as the four left parties—CPM, CPI, Forward Bloc and RSP -took the lead position with 48 wins. Among the regional partners, AGP was completely wiped out in Assam, DMK-TMC combine was cut down from 37 to nine in Tamil Nadu. Only SP won 20 seats in Uttar Pradesh and TDP won 12 in Andhra only to switch sides after the poll.

1999-Millennium's Last Poll

Prospects of uncertainty loomed large as Vajpayee's second government fell and India headed for its fifth mid-term poll in 28 years. The arithmetic of the 13th house, however, dictated that the poet-premier's third coming would be a stable affair.

But one year down the line there have been rumblings among the disparate partners of the National Democratic Alliance over issues like Ayodhya. How long would parties like Naidu's Telugu Desam, Karunanidhi's DMK and Mamata Banerjee's Trinamool, anxious to retain their secular credentials, would remain sitting uneasily within, only the morrow would tell.

Thirteenth Lok Sabha : NDA Government

Prime Minister : Atal Bihari Vajpayee, 13/10/ 1999 -

Seats Won and Vote Share in % (in brackets), State-wise

State (Total Seats)	BJP	Allies *	INC	CPM	BSP	Others @	Ind.
All-India(543)	182 (23.7)	121 (17.0)	114 (28.3)	33 (5.4)	14 (4.2)	73 (18.7)	6 (2.7)
Andhra Pradesh (42)	7 (9.1)	29 (40.7)	5 (42.8)	0 (1.4)	-	1 (4.6)	0 (1.4)
Arunachal Pradesh (2)	0 (16.3)	0 (16.6)	2 (56.9)	-	-	0 (10.2)	-
Assam (14)	2 (29.8)	-	10 (38.4)	0 (1.9)	-	1 (20.6)	1 (9.4)
Bihar (52)	23 (23.0)	18 (20.8)	4 (8.8)	1 (1.0)	0 (1.3)	7 (41.1)	1 (4.0)
Goa (2)	2 (51.5)	-	0 (39.0)	-	-	0 (8.0)	0 (1.5)
Gujarat (26)	20 (52.5)	-	6 (45.4)	-	0 (0.1)	0 (1.3)	0 (0.7)
Haryana (10)	5 (29.2)	5 (28.7)	0 (34.9)	0 (0.2)	0 (1.9)	0 (3.5)	0 (1.6)
Himachal Pradesh (4)	3 (46.3)	1 (12.4)	0 (39.5)	-	0 (0.3)	0 (1.6)	0 (0.5)
Jammu & Kashmir (6)	2 (31.6)	4 (28.9)	0 (17.8)	0 (1.0)	0 (4.8)	0 (6.3)	0 (9.6)
Karnataka (28)	7 (27.2)	3 (13.3)	18 (45.4)	0 (0.1)	0 (0.7)	0 (11.5)	0 (1.8)
Kerala (20)	0 (6.6)	0 (1.4)	8 (39.4)	8 (27.9)	0 (0.1)	4 (19.8)	0 (4.8)
Madhya Pradesh(40)	29 (46.6)	-	11 (43.9)	0 (0.1)	0 (5.2)	0 (3.1)	0 (1.1)
Maharashtra (48)	13 (21.2)	15 (16.9)	10 (29.7)	0 (0.5)	0 (0.3)	9 (28.1)	1 (3.3)
Manipur (2)	0 (1.0)	1 (24.9)	0 (25.3)	-	-	1 (42.2)	0 (6.6)
Meghalaya(2)	0 (9.5)	-	1 (32.8)	-	-	1 (56.9)	0 (0.8)
Mizoram (1)	-	-	-	-	-	0 (4.4)	1 (95.6)
Nagaland (1)	0 (5.1)	-	1 (71.2)	-	-	0 (0.8)	0 (22.9)
Orissa (21)	9 (24.6)	10 (33.0)	2 (36.9)	0 (0.2)	0 (0.3)	0 (3.7)	0 (1.3)
Punjab (13)	1 (9.2)	2 (31.3)	8 (38.4)	0 (2.2)	0 (3.8)	2 (12.6)	0 (2.5)
Rajasthan (25)	16 (47.2)	-	9 (45.1)	0 (0.5)	0 (2.8)	0 (3.0)	0 (1.4)
Sikkim (1)	-	1 (52.6)	0 (4.8)	-	-	0 (42.2)	0 (0.5)
Tamil Nadu (39)	4 (7.1)	22 (40.0)	2 (11.1)	1 (2.4)	-	10 (38.2)	0 (1.2)
Tripura (2)	0 (12.8)	0 (14.5)	0 (13.9)	2 (56.2)	-	0 (1.2)	0 (1.4)
Uttar Pradesh (85)	29 (27.6)	2 (1.5)	10 (14.8)	0 (0.0)	14 (22.1)	29 (30.4)	1 (3.6)
West Bengal (42)	2 (11.1)	8 (26.0)	3 (13.3)	21 (35.6)	0 (0.2)	8 (11.9)	0 (1.9)
A & N Islands (1)	1 (52.7)	-	0 (43.2)	-	-	0 (0.7)	0 (3.4)
Chandigarh (1)	0 (45.1)	-	1 (47.0)	-	0 (2.8)	0 (2.0)	0 (3.2)
Dadra & N. Haveli (1)	0 (20.8)	0 (19.5)	0 (14.7)	-	-	-	1 (44.9)
Delhi (7)	7 (51.8)	-	0 (42.0)	-	0 (2.2)	0 (2.3)	0 (1.7)
Daman & Diu (1)	0 (43.1)	0 (0.7)	1 (49.5)	-	-	-	0 (6.7)
Lakshadweep (1)	-	0 (43.3)	1 (54.0)	-	-	0 (1.8)	0 (0.9)
Pondicherry (1)	-	0 (31.7)	1 (37.2)	-	-	0 (25.2)	0 (5.9)

* ***Break-up for other National Democratic Alliance (NDA) Partners*:- All-India:** BJD 10(1.2), DMK 12(1.7), INLD 5(0.6), JDU 21(3.1), PMK 5(0.7), SHS 15(1.6), TC 8(2.6), TDP 29(3.7); **AP:** TDP 29(40.7); **Arunachal Pradesh:** ANC 0(16.6); **Bihar:** JDU 18(20.9); **Haryana:** INLD 5(28.7); **HP:** HVC 1(12.4); **J&K:** NC (post poll) 4(28.9); **Karnataka:** JDU 3(13.3); **Kerala:** JDU 0(1.4); **Manipur:** MSCP 1(24.9); **Maharashtra:** SHS 15(16.9); **Orissa:** BJD 10(33.0); **Punjab :** SAD 2(28.6), DBSM 0(2.7); **Sikkim:** SDF 1(52.6); **Tamil Nadu:** DMK 12(23.1), MDMK 4(6.0), PMK 5(8.2), MADMK 1(1.5), TRC 0(1.2); **Tripura:** TC 0(14.5); **UP:** LCP 2(1.5); **West Bengal:** TC 8(26.0); **Dadra & Nagar Haveli :** SHS 0(19.5); **Lakshadweep:** JDU 0(43.3); **Pondicherry:** PMK 0(31.7).

@ ***Break-up for Others*:- All-India:** ADMK 10(1.9), CPI 4(1.5), JDS 1(0.9), NCP 8(2.2), RJD 7(2.8), SP 26(3.8); **AP:** MIM 1(1.4); **Arunachal Pradesh:** NCP 0(7.7); **Assam:** AGP 0 (11.9), CPML 1(2.3); **Bihar:** RJD 7(28.3), CPI 0(2.7), CPML 0(2.5), JMM 0(2.0); **Goa:** NCP 0(3.8), CPI 0(2.9); **Haryana:** HVP 0(2.7); **Karnataka:** JDS 0(10.9); **Kerala:** CPI 0(7.6), JDS 0(2.2), KEC 1(2.4), KCM 1(2.3), MUL 2(5.3),; **Maharashtra:** BBM 1(2.1), JDS 1(0.9), NCP 6(21.3), PWP 1(0.9); **Manipur:** CPI 1(4.0), MPP 0(16.3), NCP 1(13.5); **Meghalaya:** NCP 1(28.0), UDP 0(16.4), HSPDP 0(6.2); **Punjab:** CPI 1(3.7), SADM 1(3.4), SHSAD 0(4.6); **Tamil Nadu:** ADMK 10(25.7), TMC 0(7.2), CPI 0(2.6), PT 0(2.1); **UP:** RLD 2(2.5), SP 26(24.0), SJPR 1(0.5); **West Bengal:** CPI 3(3.5), FBL 2(3.5), RSP 3(4.3); **Chandigarh:** SJPR 0(14.6); **Pondicherry:** TMC 0(25.2).

CHAPTER 2

LUCKY 13!

His first government lasted all of 13 days. The second fell after 13 months with a single vote in a vertically divided house. Now when the fifth poll in a decade broke the jinx of a fractured verdict in the 13th Lok Sabha, he chose the sunny morning of October 13 to get his band of 70 sworn in the forecourt of Rashtrapati Bhavan. Back in the Prime Minister's chair in South Block atop Raisina Hill overlooking Lutyens' New Delhi, without the 'caretaker' tag, was Atal Bihari Vajpayee, being superstitious or cautious or both. As he surveyed the office once occupied by his hero, Pt. Jawaharlal Nehru, "the man India awaits," as BJP publicists hailed him last time or the soft "mask" of the hardline saffron brigade as critics would have it, did Vajpayee wonder again how long would it last this time?

If the arithmetic of the 12th house, which at 412 days was the shortest in Indian history, was a recipe for instability, the numbers this time only added up to spell stability, pundits suggested. But Vajpayee was not taking any chances as he put together his third government in three years. It was another balancing act to ensure that his government gives the nation a stable polity and does not crumble again under the weight of its own contradictions as coalitions in the past have.

Deciding to induct all his ministers at one go to avoid any anger or heartburn of those who missed the bus, Vajpayee asked his alliance partners to name their own people under a six-for-one formula for a berth in the cabinet with fractions adjusted as ministers of state. Thus, if Shiv Sena with members got two cabinet berths and an MoS, Biju Janata Dal with ten and Trinamool Congress with eight got a cabinet berth and an MoS each. PMK and MDMK, with five and four were each given an MoS post with independent charge though MDMK leader Vaiko himself was offered a cabinet berth, but he declined. They got two additional posts of MoS too, while Jammu and Kashmir Chief Minister Farooq Abdullah's son Omer got in on behalf of National Conference with four MPs.

Arithmetic dictated that Janata Dal (United) with twenty MPs get three cabinet berths and a couple of MoS, but with five heavyweights waiting in the wings—George Fernandes, Nitish Kumar, Ram Vilas Paswan, Sharad Yadav and Rama Krishna Hegde—Hegde was dumped unceremoniously, but Fernandes got in as Vajpayee's trouble-shooter. Not only did it cause a rumpus within JDU with a fuming Hegde giving a mouthful to friend George, other allies like BJD and Trinamool Congress too demanded more. Shiv Sena ministers also shunned office for a couple of days over troubles in Maharashtra, but there was no visible tussle for office within BJP, which naturally took the lion's share of 46 ministerial berths, 15 of them of cabinet rank.

All the major states were given representation by BJP with O. Rajagopal, a Rajya Sabha member from Madhya Pradesh, getting in for Kerala, where the saffron party is yet to score a win. With Telugu Desam again opting for the speakership, BJP nominated four MoS from Andhra Pradesh. Orissa BJP president too found a cabinet berth. And besides the JDU ministers. BJP named a cabinet minister and five MoS of its own from Bihar.

Overall, Bihar with five cabinet members and six MoS and Maharashtra with as many cabinet and three junior ministers, bagged a quarter of the posts leaving the country's most populous state, Uttar Pradesh under-represented with only two cabinet ministers and four MoS. Tamil Nadu got eight berths, three of them in the cabinet. Madhya Pradesh got two cabinet and five MoS, while Orissa and Gujarat got two cabinet and two MoS each. Himachal Pradesh and Delhi were given a cabinet post each with the capital getting an MoS too. West Bengal, Karnataka and Rajasthan also got a cabinet minister with two MoS each. Andhra Pradwsh was represented by four MoS, Jammu and Kashmir with two, while Assam, Manipur, Haryana and all others together got one apiece.

Vajpayee also chose to pick up younger members for government responsibility with only nine, six of them from BJP, above 66. Though among 25 cabinet members only seven were below fifty, as many as 15 of the ministers were aged 45 or less. Of the seven MoS holding independent charge, only two were above 50. In all 17 ministers, including 11 BJP, were between 60 and 65, while 18, again with 11 BJP, were between 51 and 59. Twenty, 14 of them BJP, were below 50. Of the six under 40, four came from the saffron ranks.

Later, on November 22, in a bid to attract fresh talent and contain dissidence, Vajpayee inducted four more ministers, all but one of cabinet rank, making his 73-member council of ministers the largest that India has ever had. Akali Dal's S S Dhindsa came in to represent Punjab, BJP's own C P Thakur to push its chances in the upcoming assembly poll in Bihar and Rajnath Singh to placate ousted chief minister Kalyan Singh in Uttar Pradesh, though it did not work in the end. Only journalist Arun Shourie's appointment did not seem dictated by hard politics. But the reshuffle and expansion, raising the cabinet strength to 28 with seven ministers of state with independent charge and 38 other junior ministers, only ended up ruffling more feathers among the allies and the *Sangh Parivar* alike. For none would settle for anything less than a cabinet post.

Many an ally saw red with some alluding that the BJP was acting like the big brother in placing BJP ministers of state under cabinet ministers from other NDA partners. For instance, BJP's Hiren Pathak was placed under Defence Minister George Fernandes (JDU), BJP Vice President Bangaru Laxman was asked to assist Railway Minister Mamata Banerjee (Trinamool) and Ramesh Bais and Vallabhbhai Kathiriya were sent in to help Shiv Sena's Suresh Prabhu and Manohar Joshi. Again Chaman Lal Gupta was paired with Sharad Yadav (JDU) in civil aviation, Tapan Sikdar with Ramvilas Paswan (JDU) in communications, Rita Verma with Naveen Patnaik (BJD) in mines and minerals and Babulal Marandi with DMK's T R Baalu in environment and forests.

There was also resentment among allies over BJP keeping key portfolios like Home, Finance, Urban Affairs, Human Resources Development, Power, Information Technology, Tribal Affairs, Water Resources and Tourism exclusively to itself. Within BJP too many claimants like film star Shatrughan Sinha and former Delhi Chief Minister Sahib Singh Verma were miffed at being left out. BJP women were upset that not even one of them was elevated to the cabinet rank though at least three, Uma Bharati, Vasundhara Raje and Maneka Gandhi, who won with BJP support, are serving their fifth term in the Lok Sabha since 1989.

But despite the pulls and pressures, political pundits were in agreement that the third Vajpayee government may last much longer because of that very arithmetic. With the NDA, including post poll ally National Conference, crossing the 300 mark, Vajpayee is placed in what the poll pundits call the "comfort zone". If *Puratchi Thalaivi* or "revolutionary leader" as AIADMK chief, J Jayalalitha is called by her supporters, held the second Vajpayee government to ransom right from day one with her 18 MPs, even Chandrababu Naidu's TDP with its 29 is not in a position to bring down the government on its own. Unless a group of allies gang up or the BJP itself splits, there is little danger of the government falling despite its internal contradictions. The fact that the allies stood together before the confidence vote and fought the poll as one also lends it stability as a much weakened Congress was in no position to offer an alternative, howsoever elusive, as it did in 1998.

Chandrababu Naidu, it appears, may be the least of BJP's headaches. As convenor of the United Front, he played a key role in keeping the Deve Gowda and Gujral governments afloat, and after switching sides he never asked for his pound of flesh from Vajpayee during his 13-month second rule. The biggest problem may stem from the Janata Dal (U), whose 21 members speak in as many voices. The exclusion of Ramakrishna Hegde has already caused bad blood and delayed the formal merger of his Lokshakti with JDU. The split prone party could break again, but its limited numbers prevent it from taking a reckless course.

Stridently anti-Left firebrand Trinamool leader Mamata Banerjee too is mercurial and could walk out on a trivial issue. Chautala with his five MPs could also be a problem with his insistence on populist profarmer measures, but his dependence on BJP for survival as Haryana chief minister could hold him back.

Unlike Jayalalitha's 18, the DMK's dozen members may be more reliable as it wants a friendly centre and there is no love lost between it and AIADMK and the Congress. There is also little danger from old ally Shiv Sena with 15 MPs, though its leader Bal Thackeray may act difficult if Maharashtra politics so dictates. Naveen Patnaik's ten BJD MPs may be considered a safe bet as it needs BJP as an ally in Orissa, but he himself has some problems with the local unit there. But at the end of the day no one has the numbers to make a fatal strike.

Similarly, choices for the fringe elements within the *Parivar* opposed to the government line on issues like WTO/liberalisation, CTBT and *Ram Mandir*, too are very limited. For none can hope for an embrace from the Congress. Thus BJP's shelving of contentious issues from its agenda in a bid to become a "party of governance" too spells longevity for the new dispensation under a moderate Vajpayee.

CHAPTER 3

INTO THE BATTLE

The fall of the Vajpayee led coalition by one vote amid high drama on April 17, 1999 after only thirteen months in power had the seeds of bipolarisation in it. Despite differences all the 17 allies of BJP stood behind the Prime Minister after AIADMK leader Jayalalitha withdrew support from him in a huff. Except Saifuddin Soz of National Conference who chose to break ranks with his party to vote against the government, there was little movement across the political divide before Samajwadi Party leader Mulayam Singh Yadav declined to back the Congress' thus scuttling its Italian born president Sonia Gandhi's bid for power.

In the long run-up to the battle of 1999, fears of yet another hung parliament spawned several marriages of convenience. But unlike 1998 when three major formations led by BJP, Congress and the United Front emerged to fight it out, it appeared more like a two-horse race with few takers for a third force.

As rival AIADMK ditched the Vajpayee-led alliance, Tamil Nadu chief minister M Karunanidhi's DMK came in to bring it southern comfort. Janata Dal broke again with one faction choosing to join BJP allies, Samata Party of Defence Minister George Fernandes and Lok Shakti of Commerce Minister Ramakrishna Hegde to form Janata Dal (United) — and create ripples within the saffron ranks.

Congress too found a few regional allies in Laloo Prasad Yadav's RJD in Bihar, Ajit Singh's Rashtriya Lok Dal in UP and two factions of Republican Party in Maharashtra besides its long time partners Kerala Congress (Mani) and the Muslim League in the United Democratic Front in Kerala.

Failing to install a Congress government at the Centre, Left took up an anti- BJP position with a limited understanding with RJD in Bihar and the Gandhi party elsewhere. Miffed at being given only three seats by Laloo, CPI decided to go it alone with Forward Bloc carrying the banner of equidistance from Congress and BJP both.

Janata Dal (Secular) led by former UF Prime Minister H D Deve Gowda chose to stay non-aligned like the Bahujan Samaj Party of Kanshi Ram. So did Maratha strongman Sharad Pawar and former Lok Sabha speaker Purno Agitok Sangma after trying to cause a mighty split in India's oldest political party.

The Nationalist Congress Party that they formed, with little appeal beyond Maharashtra tied up with Yadav's SP, equally allergic to see a foreign born lady in the nation's highest political office. Jammu and Kashmir Chief Minister Farooq Abdullah of the National Conference decided to plough his lonely furrow, but was all too ready to plump for the winning side after the polls. As the battlelines were drawn and the campaign carnival got rolling, it became more like an American-style presidential poll between veteran Atal Behari Vajpayee leading the National Democratic Alliance and a greenhorn Sonia Gandhi at the apex of a divided opposition though on paper 170 parties with 4,648 candidates were in the fray.

That either leading formation did not present a picture of perfect unity becomes evident from the fact that various constituents of NDA put up 595 candidates for the 543 seats up for grabs with BJP itself contesting 339 seats. The rival Congress combine had only 24 less with the Gandhi party fielding 453. The Left had 202, including 72 of spearhead CPM, 54 of CPI and 56 of new entrant CPML. The other big four—BSP, SP, NCP and JDS—entered another 604 with BSP alone putting up 225.

NDA: A Big Joint Family

Placed as the forerunner by most opinion polls, in the North, BJP broke up with Bansi Lal's Haryana Vikas Party to align with Om Prakash Chautala's Indian National Lok Dal, kept up its alliance with Parkash Singh Badal's Akali Dal in Punjab, gave four seats to Loktantrik Congress in Uttar Pradesh and a seat to Sukh Ram's Himachal Vikas Congress.

In the South, it attracted besides DMK, MDMK, PMK and MADMK in Tamil Nadu after Jayalalitha's AIADMK switched over to Congress side. It entered into a shotgun wedding with JDU in Karnataka as the merger of chief minister J H Patel's Janata Dal and Hegde's Lok Shakti turned adversaries in to allies. And in Andhra, it went along with TDP of chief minister Chandrababu Naidu, who had played no mean part in keeping it in power for 13 months, instead of with NTR's widow Lakshmi Parvathi.

To further consolidate its position in the East, it embraced Sharad Yadav's faction of Janata Dal following its merger with George Fernandes'

Samata Party in Bihar, while continuing its ties with Mamata Banerjee's Trinamool Congress and Naveen Patnaik's Biju Janata Dal in Orissa.

The arrangement with Bal Thackeray's Shiv Sena held in Maharashtra, but elsewhere in the west, BJP was essentially on its own even as Shiv Sena put up 41 candidates against it all over the rest of the country.

Congress: Reluctant Partners

At 114, India's oldest party, the Congress too made a few tie-ups to stem the downslide since 1996. In the North an arrangement with the Bahujan Samaj Party did not hold in Punjab, but an understanding was reached there with the left parties and an arrangement of sorts again made with Ajit Singh's party in its new Rashtriya Lok Dal incarnation in UP.

In the South, Congress agreeing to play the junior partner in Tamil Nadu became friends again with AIADMK, while in Kerala the United Democratic Front comprising the Congress, Muslim League and the Kerala Congress (Mani) continued.

In the East, it accepted the 15 seats offered by Laloo Prasad Yadav's Rashtriya Janata Dal in Bihar despite an uproar in the state unit. At loggerheads with Samajwadi Party now, it again gave a few seats to two factions of RPI in Maharashtra, while in Gujarat, BJP rebel Shankersinh Vaghela's Rashtriya Janata Party had by now merged with the Congress.

With the 13-party United Front as it emerged after the 1996 poll now in tatters after more than a year out of power, Mulayam Singh Yadav's Samajwadi Party put up candidates in 84 seats in UP while forging a front with Pawar's NCP in Maharashtra, where a similar arrangement with the Congress had helped the latter in 1998.

Except for the understanding between RJD and CPM in Bihar, the Left Front made up of the CPM, CPI, Forward Bloc and Revolutionary Socialist Party (RSP) did battle alone with CPM taking the lead in West Bengal and Tripura. Prafulla Kumar Mohanta's Asom Gana Parishad too was left to fight a lone battle in Assam.

CHAPTER 4

PROMISES TO KEEP

As the day of reckoning drew near, promises came aplenty with parties across the political divide calling each other names and blaming them for the election that nobody wanted with stability first and Kargil later emerging as key issues. Branding the 1999 election as an "unnecessary imposition", the NDA manifesto alleged that it had been thrust upon the country by a motley combination that put political negativism, personal interests and greed for power way above the national weal.

The Vajpayee government, it recalled, had lost the vote of confidence in the Lok Sabha by just one and that too a questionable one, a reference to the vote cast by Orissa chief minister Giridhar Gamang, who had held on to his seat in the lower house even after taking up the state post.

Despite promising a new government "in five minutes", it said quoting RJD chief Laloo Prasad Yadav, a "negative coalition led by the Congress" had failed to come up with any alternative arrangement, forcing the dissolution of the Lok Sabha and fresh elections. Neverthless, the election allowed the country a great opportunity of finally putting an end to the era of political negativism, uncertainty and dynasticism, it said and offered the NDA as the response to a "historic need" claiming it was representative of both national interests and regional aspirations. "After all the NDA is nothing but the mirror-image of our unity in multifaceted diversity, rich pluralism and federalism."

The Congress, in turn, dubbed NDA as the "National Disaster Alliance" saying it had become a mockery with all principles and ideologies abandoned in its quest for new partners. The 18-party coalition government, it alleged, had demonstrated the essence of unprincipled and opportunistic politics. Experience had shown that the coalitions had never worked at the centre, it said suggesting that choice before the electorate was between "a coalition that has failed miserably and a cohesive Congress alternative"

Spearheading the Left, the CPM put the responsibility for India being forced to elect a new Lok Sabha squarely on the BJP. The Vajpayee led government had made an ignominous exit after 13 months of mind-boggling misrule, because the BJP had put together a rag-tag coalition including in it even parties that had fought the election against it.

Yet the CPM did not see the Congress as the alternative. On questions of economic policies, the BJP and the Congress had no basic differences, it said suggesting that it is the effective intervention of the Left, which would enable all the democratic and secular forces to work for an effective third alternative. It made a three-point call: defeat the BJP and its allies, strengthen the CPM and Left, and support the Left democratic and secular forces for a secular government. In plain words, it was suggesting that the Congress was the lesser evil than BJP in places where the Left itself was not strong.

While the 24-party NDA banking on the charisma of "tried, tested and trusted" Atal Bihari Vajpayee, projected him clearly as the future Prime Minister, the Congress again chose not to suggest anyone for the top job after Pawar made Sonia Gandhi's foreign origin an election issue. But with media focusing on its star campaigner, the voter clearly saw Gandhi as the Congress alternative, though the party said it was for the people to decide and the Congress parliamentary party would choose its leader after the poll. Everyone promised *Roti, Kapda aur Makan* for all besides education and health, but such bread and butter matters took the back seat behind stability, Kargil and Sonia Gandhi's foreign origin as the main campaign themes of major contenders to power. Here is what each formation had on offer:

Stability

Promising "a stable, honest, transparent, and efficient government capable of accomplishing all-round development," the NDA steered clear of contentious issues—*Mandir*, uniform civil code and scrapping of Art 370 providing special status to Kashmir—to paint a picture of a stable polity, vibrant economy, federal harmony and a strong India.

Asserting that a nation of a billion people representing a sixth of humanity could not be run on the arithmetic of majority and minority alone, it promised to strive to develop national consensus on major issues confronting the nation. It would also try for a consensual mode of governance as far as practicable.

Harping on its past glory as "a central part of Indian life for the past 114 years", the Congress said political stability is the biggest challenge that India faced today. Every Congress government had completed its term under five prime ministers in the last 52 years, while in just five years, non-Congress governments had given seven of them.

Stability, it said does not come from numbers alone, but from a clarity of vision and dedication to national goals. It was born out of the knowledge of and expertise in running of government. The Congress alone could give stability, it claimed as it had the experience of 45 years of governance and all its governments had a clear agenda.

Kargil

Though the Election Commission had asked the political parties to refrain from politicising Kargil, all of them did so with the Vajpayee government taking credit for its handling of the situation in the high Himalayas after Pakistani soldiers crossed the Line of Control in May 1999 and the opposition accusing it of negligence.

"The government rose to the challenge and acted decisively. Faced by this aggression in Kargil, the response of the Government was swift, though measured," the NDA claimed.

Kargil was a tragedy brought about by the cavalier functioning of the BJP government and its criminal negligence, countered the Congress suggesting the BJP had cost the nation heavily. CPM too voiced the same sentiment accusing the government of ignoring or not taking seriously early reports of intrusion in its anxiety to project the Lahore bus trip as a great achievement of the Prime Minister.

Constitutional Reforms

NDA also announced its intention to appoint a commission to review the constitution not only in the light of experiences and developments since 1996—an allusion to fall of four coalition governments since then, but indeed of the entire post-Independence period.

A National Judicial Commission would be set up to recommend judicial appointments to High Courts and Supreme Court and draw up a code of ethics for the judiciary, it said.

The Congress proposed to set up a new administrative reforms commission to prepare a detailed blueprint for a public administration system that can become a more effective instrument of change and transformation. It also was for a National Judicial Reforms Commission to suggest radical improvements in the judicial system. Similarly, CPM wanted such reforms to provide speedy relief at affordable cost to the common people. It also wanted a proper balance in the relations between the legislature, judiciary and the executive.

Electoral Reforms

NDA promised electoral reforms to deal with the malaise of defections, corruption and criminalisation of politics and prevent electoral malpractice.

The Congress said it was fully committed to radical electoral reforms to reduce the influence of money and muscle power and check the criminalisation of politics at all levels.

But CPM went the farthest of them all. It sought proportional representation with a partial list system, state funding in the form of material for recognised political parties, amendment of anti-defection law to make it obligatory for a party hopper to vacate one's seat and amendment in the electoral laws to bring all election expenses including those by parties and friends under the candidate's ceiling.

Economic Reforms

Another common theme running through the agenda of the three main alliances was economic reforms with NDA and Congress promising to continue the liberalisation process, but the Left branding it as a recipe for disaster.

Declaring its intention to continue with the reform process, NDA said it would be given a strong swadeshi thrust to ensure that the national economy grows on the principle that "India shall be built by Indians." It would reappraise and revitalise reforms through giving primacy to removal of unemployment and to an accelerated development of infrastructure, particularly energy and power production. Swadeshi, it asserted was not reinventing the wheel and only meant that NDA would facilitate the domestic industry to gain flourish and acquire a trans-national status.

Resolving to relegate poverty "to history like slavery, colonialism, small pox and cholera", NDA said it would do so by restructuring priorities and mainstreaming them into new programmes of pro-poor growth and redistribution towards poverty eradication.

The Congress, which initiated the economic reforms in 1991 under P V Narasimha Rao, said every time there has been a non-Congress government in Delhi, the first and the immediate casualty has been the economy. Twice in the past two decades, it has had to rebuild and recostruct. Only it can do so a third time. Reiterating its firm commitment to faster economic reforms with a human face, the Congress said higher growth was possible only if India invested more productively in physical and social infrastructure and only if the pattern of public expenditures at all levels reflect pressing socio-economic priorities.

Describing eradication of poverty as the single most important objective of national development, the party committed itself to doubling the expenditure on poverty alleviation and social development programmes over the next five years. A sustained 4-5 per cent annual rate of growth in agriculture is the essential prerequisite for the time-bound eradication of rural poverty, it said.

The CPM, on its part, proposed a "comprehensive platform of economic policies" in place of the policies of liberalisation since 1991, which it said had benefited the affluent ten per cent of the upper strata while subjecting the rest to acute deprivation.

Trade and Commerce

NDA said it would focus on specific products in specific growth areas for exports. It intended to strongly support attempts to build a system of trade and economic cooperation through expanded global system for trade preferences (GSTP) among developing countries. The Congress promised immediate steps to revive the export momentum in the economy that was so much in evidence in the latter half of the eighties and the mid-1990s saying India's exports must grow by at least 15-20 per cent per year on a sustained basis. Seeking to use the WTO to gain additional market access for products and services of interest to India, Congress said it would proactively encourage investment from foreign companies and overseas Indians. It set a target of at least 8-10 billion dollars of foreign direct investment inflows early in the next decade. The Left wanted a renewal of power and telecom policies in tune with interests of national development, strengthening of public sector in the core and strategic areas, protection of domestic industry from indiscriminate lowering of import duties and takeover of existing Indian companies by foreign companies. It also sought a critical review of the agreements made during the Uruguay Round at the WTO review, opposed entry of private and foreign companies in the insurance sector and suggested a broadening of the direct taxes base.

Education

NDA said it was committed to a total eradication of illiteracy and planned to gradually raise the spending on education up to six per cent of the GDP, and make primary education free and compulsory up to the fifth standard.

Congress was for investing at least 6 per cent of the nation's GDP in education and earmarking 50 per cent of this expenditure on elementary education. The party said it would strive to attain this target by the end of the Ninth Plan.

The CPM said it would strive for allocation of ten per cent of the Union budget for education, introduction of compulsory primary and free universal education for children under 14 and support mass literacy programmes.

Health

NDA said it would spare no efforts to ensure that potable drinking water was made available to all villages in the next five years, but did not elaborate on its plans in the health sector.

The Congress said it would aim to reach the quality of life indicators already achieved in some southern states of India by 2010. A network of super-speciality hospitals will be set up all over the country and every district hospital upgraded to a minimum level of standards and facilities. The Left proposed reversal of the trend towards privatisation of health services and increasing the expenditure on public health to five per cent of the GDP.

Employment

Recognising the right to work of every citizen, the main thrust of the new NDA government will be 'Berozgaari Hatao'. Its new investment and institutional thrust to agriculture, the self-employed, the unincorporated sector, infrastructure development and housing will act as the vehicles for massive employment creation at all levels.

Saying accelerated employment creation will be the cornerstone of all the Congress' economic policies and programmes, it noted ten million jobs a year would have to be created aimed at every family having at least one of its members in regular employment.

The Left wanted guaranteed right to work as a fundamental right, provide food-for-work programme to generate employment, ensure adequate credit for self-employment schemes and ending the freeze in government jobs.

Rural Development

Promising to ensure food security for all to create a hunger free India in the next five years, the NDA said no efforts would be spared to ensure that potable drinking water is available to all villages in the same period.

The Congress said all possible measures would be taken to step up the momentum of public investment in agriculture especially in the backward and poor regions. The Rural Infrastructure Development Fund (RIDF) launched by the Congress government in 1995 would be expanded. It also promised to give top priority to supplying drinking water to the people in the villages, towns and cities. In the next five years, universal coverage of drinking water supply will be assured in villages and a safe water source provided within a kilometre of each habitation.

The Left proposed land reforms, non-dilution of land ceilings, takeover and distribution of surplus land, increased public investment in agriculture and infrastructure. It also wanted a national water policy, a role to community/ panchayats in management of water resources and provision of potable drinking water to all villages on a priority basis.

Housing

Promising to evolve a national housing and habitat policy, NDA said it would facilitate construction of two million additional housing units annually. The Congress said the Indira Awas Yojna launched by its earlier governments to build houses for the poor and the disadvantaged would be expanded and consolidated and high priority accorded to innovative schemes for the housing of the urban poor and the slum dwellers. The Left wanted housing to be accorded the status of a basic right and housing schemes for urban and rural poor to be stepped up.

Corruption

To deal with corruption in high places, NDA proposed to enact a Lok Pal Bill with adequate powers to deal with charges against anyone including the Prime Minister.

The Congress said it attached high priority to the passage of a Lok Pal Bill without indicating whether the Prime Minister too would be under its purview. It supported the bill to make the CVC statutory as per the directions of the Supreme Court. The party would also launch a multi-pronged crusade against corruption.

The Left too wanted a Lok Pal to provide for investigation and binding recommendation of prosecution of public servants, including the Prime Minister. It also wanted functional autonomy for CBI and other investigating agencies and passage of a Right to Information Act to make the system of governance more accountable.

National Security

Promising to correct the imbalance of budgetary neglect of defence needs and ensure adequate budgetary allocations, NDA said in today's unipolar world it was of paramount importance that India constantly maintains and strengthens the state of preparedness, morale and combat effectiveness of the armed forces.

NDA said the National Security Council would advise the government in this regard as also on the establishment of a credible nuclear deterrence—calling these the minimum requirements in the new era of global inequality and increased vulnerability.

Pledging never to allow Kargil-type incidents and Bhagwat-type episodes, the Congress proposed appointment of a high level Defence Reforms Committee to suggest a detailed operational plan for the reorganisation of the defence establishment following the nuclear tests and Kargil. The National Security Council would be made a purposeful, forward-looking, analysis-based organisation that represents a wider cross-section of intellectual opinion. It proposed to appoint a full-time National Security Advisor unlike the NDA dispensation, where the Prime Minister's Principal secretary Brajesh Mishra has been doubling as such. The Left advocated halting nuclear weaponisation, reversion to nuclear policy of developing India's independent technological potential while not signing any international treaty, including CTBT, which is discriminatory and creation of a national security apparatus which will work within the framework of parliamentary democratic system.

International Relations

NDA said the government had demonstrated its capability to secure for India a place, role and position in the global arena, commensurate with its size and importance. It would develop an engagement process to improve India's standing in the international community.

Accusing the BJP of wilfully destroying the national consensus on nuclear matters, the Congress said it would be meticulously rebuilt. India's approach to CTBT, FMCT, and other global regimes of nuclear non-proliferation must be integrally linked to the over-arching goal of time-bound elimination of nuclear weapons, it said.

Suggesting that it was essential to reverse the "harmful foreign policy positions of the Vajpayee government", CPM said it would work for a foreign policy which is independent, non-aligned and defends India from imperialist pressures.

Centre-State Relations

Noting that there was a clear case for devolution of more financial and administrative powers and functions to the States, NDA promised to take steps to ensure harmonious Centre-State relations in the light of Sarkaria Commission recommendations. It also promised to create Uttaranchal, Vananchal, and Chhattisgarh as new states besides giving full statehood to the national capital of Delhi, but the reference to Vidarbha in the 1998 manifesto was dropped.

The Congress too promised to create Uttarakhand, Chhattisgarh and Jharkhand without any further delay while representative and elected forums in the nature of mini-assemblies will be established in all union territories. To give a better deal to the states, the Congress proposed strengthening of bodies like the National Development Council and the Inter-State Council, and make their functioning business-like and purposive. It may even consider enshrining this role in the Constitution itself so that the decisions of these bodies become binding on both the Centre and the states.

CPM said it would work for greater powers to the states in economic and political spheres, institutionalisation of the federal system by activating the Inter-State Council and replacement of Article 356 to curb the draconian powers of the Centre to dismiss state governments.

Kashmir

Unlike 1998 when BJP was forthright in demanding abrogation of Article 370 giving a special status to Jammu and Kashmir, NDA made no reference to the contentious issue.

Congress, which was silent on the subject then, declared this time that it stood committed to respecting Article 370 in letter and spirit. While cross-border terrorism and militancy will continue to be fought relentlessly, the Congress was open to dialogue and discussions with any group within the framework of the Constitution.

CPM wanted maximum autonomy to be given to the state by revising Article 370 and regional autonomy to be provided to Jammu and Ladakh regions.

Minorities

Promising genuine secularism, NDA said it would genuinely and truly uphold and practise the concept of secularism consistent with the Indian tradition of *Sarva Pantha Samadara* (equal respect for all faiths). It also promised effective steps for economic, social and educational development of the minorities. Reservation for SC/STs would be extended for another ten years and reservations above 50 per cent as followed by certain states would be sanctified through law, it said.

The Congress promised to vigorously pursue its seven point intensified programme for the protection and promotion of the minorities. Measures will be taken to increase the representation of minorities in all public, police and para-military services both in the central and state governments.

The Constitution, it said, would be amended to establish a commission for minority educational institutions and to provide direct affiliation for minority professional institutions to central universities. The Congress will examine demands to declare Urdu as an official language in states where a substantial number of people speak it. The party would also not initiate and support amendments in the personal laws of the minorities.

CPM advocated special measures for Muslims and some other minorities suffering from deprivation and discrimination, to remove their social and economic backwardness, provision for equal opportunities for employment and protection and encouragement of Urdu language.

Media

Promising a review of the Prasar Bharati Act, NDA said a comprehensive broadcasting bill would be enacted to regulate private broadcasting and protect Indian interests. Foreign equity holding in private television broadcasting would be restricted to 20 per cent to avoid emergence of monopolies in the media.

The Congress did not come out with a clear media policy, but CPM wanted the Prasar Bharati Corporation to be strengthened so that it becomes a genuine public broadcasting service. It also sought legislation to prevent growth of monopolies in the print and electronic media, called for a media code for satellite broadcasters and opposed foreign ownership of print media.

Women

All the three combinations sought to woo the fair sex with promises of one-third reservation in all elected bodies. For the empowerment of women, NDA also promised to institute plans for providing free education for girls upto college level and set up a development bank for women entrepreneurs in the small scale and tiny sectors.

Besides reservation in parliament and state assemblies, the Congress proposed to increase across the board the number of women in government services inclusive of primary school teachers, in the police force and in the judiciary at all levels.

Similarly, CPM sought equal legal rights for women of all communities, compulsory registration of marriages, equal property and inheritance rights for women and joint matrimonial property rights.

CHAPTER 5

THE CAMPAIGN CARNIVAL

It was dubbed as a presidential poll, a great contest between a son of the soil and a daughter-in-law from foreign shores, all dignified and correct. But at the end of the day it resembled more like a street brawl, a free-for-all muck raking exercise. To be sure there were the traditional buttons, buntings and banners to TV shows and the internet, but what made the headlines was the mudslinging in an election devoid of any issues worth the name.

Notwithstanding the model code of conduct, hitting below the belt was the name of the game. If Information and Broadcasting Minister, Pramod Mahajan chose to compare Sonia Gandhi with Monica Lewinsky—a charge he later denied and blamed on the usual "misreporting"—Congress spokesman Kapil Sibal called Prime Minister Atal Bihari Vajpayee a "habitual liar" who was "not only sleeping when the enemy came but also actively connived and consorted with the enemy."

Again when Defence Minister George Fernandes joined the battle of Bellary with a rhetorical: "What is Sonia Gandhi's contribution to the nation?—the two children she gave birth to!" Congress General Secretary, Ghulam Nabi Azad wondered: "How does the PM have a son-in-law without being married?"

BJP campaigners teased Sonia with a song sung to the tune of a popular Altaf Raja number: *"Tum to thehre pardesi sath kya nibhaogi, subah pehli flight se Italy bhag jaogi.* (You are a foreigner, you can't be trusted. You'll catch the first flight to Italy.)" Congress' former screen hero Rajesh Khanna retorted in true Bollywood style: *"Aulad nahin lekin damaad hai. Yeh public hai, sab janti hai.* (He's got no children but has a son-in-law. The people know everything.)"

The AICC office even distributed extracts from The *Morarji Papers* where the former Prime Minister cited rumours that his Foreign Minister "spent more time imbibing alcohol and flirting with women than in the administration of his ministry" and ally AIADMK chief Jayalalitha turned to her theatrical skills to tease him with a song: "*Yeamathi poittingale ayya, Vajpayee ayya* (Oh Vajpayee Sir, you have cheated us.)"

In another Tamil song Jayalalitha told the Prime Minister: "*Nanga onnum kavukkale, cherai pudichi izhukkale, Neengalaga kavunthutteengale, Ayya Vajpayee, Ayya.* (We haven't pulled you down, we haven't grabbed your chair, you have fallen on your own, Oh Vajpayee Sir.)"

Rival DMK chief minister, M Karunanidhi, a one time film scriptwriter could not resist the temptation of suggestively quipping: "If a woman says a man has cheated her, what conclusion can one draw?" At this rate, suggested Karunanidhi, Jayalalitha may end up dancing in her next campaign inviting a caustic comment from the lady: "Karunanidhi is a rotten egg. The foul smell is now crossing all limits and becoming intolerable."

The lesser mortals were not spared such personal attacks either. It was again Mahajan who likened Nationalist Congress leader Sharad Pawar to Elizabeth Taylor: "He marries, divorces, remarries and again divorces." West Bengal chief minister Jyoti Basu called Trinamool Congress leader Mamata Banerjee a "lunatic", an Orissa Congress leader, Suresh Kumar Routray branded BJD leader Naveen Patnaik "neither man nor woman" and when BJP fielded the small screen Krishna, Nitish Bhardwaj against Madhya Pradesh Chief Minister Digvijay Singh's brother Laxman Singh, he suggested an actress could have entertained his brother better.

Shiv Sena chief 'tiger' Bal Thackeray targeted Sonia Gandhi's son, campaigning with his mother, asking: "Where was Rahul Gandhi when soldiers were dying at Kargil? At Wimbledon with his *firangi* girlfriend?" With media turning it into a contest of two personalities, Vajpayee and Sonia Gandhi flew from state to state in a relentless campaign that ended for both on October 1, in the city of Lucknow with each addressing rallies within a few minutes drive from the other.

Sonia Gandhi may have lost the battle of the ballot, but she won the high flyers' race hands down addressing 160 rallies way ahead of Vajpayee with 108. It was film star Shatrughan Sinha who came second with 134 rallies for BJP followed by Home Minister L K Advani with 110.

Samajwadi Party leader Mulayam Singh Yadav, having foiled Sonia Gandhi's bid for power after Vajpayee's fall, ran an aggressive campaign in Uttar Pradesh covering all the 85 constituencies in the state with rallies, *dharnas* and demonstrations to project BJP's failures. Twice chief minister, BSP leader Mayawati too played the anti-incumbency card as she made fiery speeches all over the state targeting both the BJP and the Congress.

In the epic battle of Bellary, Sushma Swaraj making it a contest between a *desi beti* and a *videshi bahu* launched an emotional campaign in Hindi mixed with Kannada asking applauding crowds: "What does Sonia have?" Then she would answer herself, "*Sonne, sonne, sonne* (zero, zero, zero)." She seemed to be making a dent before petite Priyanka Gandhi came to win the day for her mother with an equally emotional appeal to take care of her

Former Haryana chief minister Bhajan Lal roped in the state's only eunuch municipal councillor, Shobha. Sporting a tricolour sari, tricolour nose-ring and tricolour hair band, Shobha campaigned for him in Karnal, while her dance companion Geeta rooted for Congress' Birender Singh. In neighbouring Punjab eunuch municipal councillor Santosh Mahant backed the Akalis in Bhatinda. But it didn't help any as all the three lost. Support of everyone from writer Khushwant Singh to Bollywood's Javed Akhtar in South Delhi too could not save former Finance Minister, Manmohan Singh, the architect of the 1991 economic reforms, dubbed as "the man with the Midas touch". Taking on Advani in Gandhinagar, former Chief Election Commissioner T N Seshan launched a barefoot campaign. Struggling with his Hindi, the retired Tamil bureaucrat often turned to Hindi films to make his point. "*Hum to dil de chuke sanam* (I've given my heart)," or "*Hum dulhaniya lene aye hain*" (I've come to take the bride)," he would tell amused farmers or morning joggers in Ahmedabad. But it was Advani who took the bride.

After playing the revolutionary in films like *Lal Salaam* and *Rakthasakshikal Zindabad*, top Malayalam actor, Murali picked up the CPM banner in the backwaters areas of Alappuzha. There were several 'retakes' as crowds greeted him with cries of "*Saghavu DK* (Comrade DK)", a role played by him in *Lal Salaam*.

And in Tamil Nadu, controversial judge Ramaswamy, who barely escaped impeachment in 1993, hit the campaign trail in a Tempo Traveller in Sivakasi with the blessings of Amma Jayalalitha. Back in Punjab

Maharani Parneet Kaur of Patiala, wife of state Congress chief Amrinder Singh, campaigned in her airconditioned Cielo with a sleek cell-phone in hand. She defeated Prem Singh Chandumajra of the Akali Dal despite Akali propaganda that electronic voting machines used there and in Tarn Taran and Faridkot would give an electric shock on pressing the Congress 'hand' symbol, while their 'scales' would bring lilting music.

Elsewhere in Punjab to attract crowds in the summer heat, candidates resorted to having themselves weighed against *laddoos* instead of coins. Days before the weighing in ceremony the message would go round the villages, "*Aao, aao, ladoo khao.*" BJP *sanyasin* Uma Bharati, shifted from the erotic temple town of Khajuraho to Bhopal on health grounds and won using her USP, "A *sanyasin* belongs to the whole universe."

And in Maharashtra, the Election Commission turned to the age-old method of *davandi* to relay news about two phase simultaneous poll to the Lok Sabha and the state assembly with davandi exponents going round villages beating drums and metal utensils to do the needful.

For an estimated three million netizens of India, about 369 poll-related web sites were available with several parties following the BJP and CPM in setting up their own home pages. Latecomers like the Congress, SP and the AIADMK displayed "under construction" pages for days as the leaders hit the campaign trail to woo voters in more traditional ways.

With several TV channels starting election specials, the Indian politician never '. d it so good with television bringing them home to voters in every nook and corner of the country. State-owned Doordarshan itself doled out more than hundred hours to various political parties for free. Politicians of all hues put on make-up, donned colourful clothes and many a time changed kurtas and jackets in their cars as they hopped from channel to channel to appear on the talk shows by the dozen.

The war of words did not stop here as major contenders pulled all the plugs as the campaign carnival got rolling. Advertising agencies and image builders made a beeline to the party offices to tell politicians how to sell their election soaps. The and war too was not always straight with some front organisations on either side taking up surrogate campaigns.

In hard hitting press campaigns, if the Congress chose to attack Vajpayee over Kargil and his "13 months of bungling", BJP focused on

Sonia Gandhi's foreign origin. "Don't vote for him because HE was born in India. Vote for him because YOU were," said one adding "he doesn't have to go around saying that this is his country. And that he loves his country." Another one suggested, "As a friend he can travel far to shake a hand. When betrayed he can crush it with a Kargil." The Congress hit back suggesting, "The Lahore bus ride was just a gimmick" and that "Sugar imports allowed by the Vajpayee government paid for Pakistani weapons in Kargil." Another one wondered, "If Pokhran II was a deterrent, why was there a Kargil war?"

Surrogate ads were no less pungent. A Congress look-alike Lok Abhiyan ad demanded: "What can we expect of a party that needs to import its own leader?" and another admonished: "A responsible opposition does not play political games while the nation is at war."

Similarly, an ad by Communalism Combat, a small Mumbai journal, released on the day Congress publicised a 1948 letter from India's iron man to the RSS, asked, "Who do we believe—the RSS or Sardar Patel?" Another rejoinder to BJP's ad line, "The leader you can trust In War. In Peace," suggested Vajpayee "knew of the intrusions in Kargil on May 6th. Yet he ordered action only on May 16th—a good ten days later" and asked "Can you really trust him? In War." Then again it alleged that "He shunted out his own Minister of Telecommunications to benefit some multinationals" with the poser, "Can you really trust him? In Peace," to wonder aloud: "Can you trust him at all?"

Lok Abhiyan, run by a BJP Delhi MP Vijay Goel, went into the battle soon after the fall of Vajpayee government with ads asking "What wrong did this man do?" Another proxy ad by Purva Sainik Sewa Parishad (PSSP) alleged "the Congress is ready to allow soldiers to die for the country. But not ready to allow them to vote for the country."—an allusion to Congress' disinclination to readily agree to proxy voting for the armed forces.

Shortly after former Delhi Chief Minister Sushma Swaraj of BJP followed Sonia Gandhi to Bellary in Karnataka on her 'secret' mission to file her nomination papers, BJP in another cloak and dagger operation prepared a rejoinder to a Congress ad on the Kargil war for publication on the same day with a cheeky PS: "After Bellary and this ad, should they not start looking amongst themselves for an intelligence failure?"

But the Congress apparently got wind of it and withdrew its ad and published another four days later forcing the BJP to hold back its reply. In the age of satellites and computers, it looked like a long-drawn-out poll, but at 54 days it was far from the longest in India. The first one lasted all of 120 days from October 25, 1951 to February 21, 1952. The second in 1957 lasted 106 days and the third five years later 111 days.

Come polling day, some 4.5 million polling staff manned 773,708 polling booths to begin the massive exercise that among other things would consume 2,000 tonnes of paper and cost the nation close to Rs 845 crore, Rs 178.78 crore more than the poll of '98. Despite the intense wooing, only 60.02 per cent of the 618,107,559 electorate turned out to pick 543 representatives from 4,648 candidates, including 1,299 of seven national parties, 750 of state and 654 of other registered parties besides 1,945 independents, making for an average of 8.56 per constituency. At 277, the number of women was three more than the last time.

CHAPTER 6

HOW INDIA VOTED

For the first time in five elections in a decade, the Indian voter gave a clear verdict breaking the jinx of hung houses since 1989. But it was not a mandate for a bipolar polity either. If the verdict appeared less fractured than in the last four polls, it was more so because changed political equations had turned friends into foes and enemies into long lost pals than by people's design.

Although after a few missed heartbeats, the NDA did attain a clear majority, its spearhead the BJP found itself stuck at the same 182 members with two dozen allies holding the balance of power. Rival Congress got the worst drubbing in its history making its return to power after its longest exile still more distant.

Maratha strongman Sharad Pawar's pretentious NCP, the Left, Kanshi Ram's Bahujan Samaj Party, former Defence Minister, Mulayam Singh Yadav's Samajwadi Party, and a few others, who chose not to ally with the big two, met varying degrees of success, but the idea of yet another third front remained stillborn. The days of grand sweeps and single party majorities seemed to be over as India set course on another coalition experiment.

Yet if the verdict did not pose a dilemma to the President, it was not because of any greater polarisation in favour of the two leading contenders—BJP and Congress—themselves. For although BJP-led National Democratic Alliance sought a mandate on the stability plank under an able leader, Atal Bihari Vajpayee, his own party again won 182 seats, exactly the same number as last time.

Still if his new government appeared to start on a firmer footing, it was because six more parties had jumped on to the NDA bandwagon to make it a grand coalition of two dozen small parties together contributing 122 seats in its tally of 304 in the 543-member Lok sabha. And if mercurial

Outcome in a Nutshell

Electorate: 61,81,07,559 Turnout: 60.02% Valid Votes: 36,35,04,742

Party	Seats Contested	Seats Won	Lost Deposit	1999 Vote%	1998 Vote%	Vote Swing %
BJP + Allies	**601**	**303**	**93**	**40.68**	**37.20**	**+3.48**
BJP	339	182	25	23.70	25.59	-1.89
TDP	34	29	0	3.66	2.77	+0.89
JD(U)	60	21	24	3.10	-	+3.10
SHS	63	15	41	1.56	1.77	-0.21
DMK	19	12	0	1.73	1.44	+0.29
BJD	12	10	0	1.20	1.00	+0.20
TC	29	8	2	2.58	2.42	+0.16
PMK	8	5	0	0.65	0.42	+0.23
INLD	5	5	0	0.55	-	+0.55
MDMK	5	4	0	0.45	0.44	+0.01
SAD	9	2	0	0.69	0.81	-0.12
LCP	4	2	0	0.23	-	+0.23
MADMK	1	1	0	0.11	0.08	+0.03
HVC	1	1	0	0.07	0.02	+0.05
MSCP	2	1	1	0.06	0.05	+0.01
SDF	1	1	0	0.03	0.03	0.00
TRC	1	0	0	0.09	0.10	-0.01
DBSM	1	0	0	0.07	-	+0.07
ANC	1	0	0	0.02	0.05	-0.03
NC (post poll)	6	4	0	0.13	0.21	-0.08
INC + Allies	**571**	**136**	**139**	**33.73**	**30.67**	**+3.06**
INC	453	114	88	28.29	25.82	+2.47
ADMK	29	10	5	1.94	1.83	+0.11
RJD	61	7	26	2.79	2.70	+0.09
RLD	15	2	10	0.38	-	+0.38
MUL	12	2	10	0.23	0.22	+0.01
KEC(M)	1	1	0	0.10	0.10	0.00
RPI	14	0	12	0.14	0.37	-0.23
BSP	225	14	153	4.19	4.67	-0.48
CPI	54	4	39	1.48	1.75	-0.27
CPM	72	33	20	5.42	5.16	+0.26
JD(S)	96	1	88	0.92	-	+0.92
NCP	132	8	98	2.24	-	+2.24
AGP	8	0	3	0.32	0.29	+0.03
AIMIM	1	1	0	0.12	0.13	-0.01
BBM	4	1	0	0.19	-	+0.19
BPSP	2	0	0	0.17	-	+0.17
CPML	56	1	53	0.34	0.25	+0.09
FBL	15	2	12	0.35	0.33	+0.02
HVP	2	0	1	0.05	0.24	-0.19
JMM	23	0	20	0.27	0.36	-0.09
JP	26	0	26	0.05	0.12	-0.07
KEC	1	1	0	0.10	0.09	+0.01
PT	10	0	8	0.16	0.12	+0.04
PWP	2	1	1	0.08	0.07	+0.01
RSP	5	3	1	0.41	0.55	-0.14
SADM	1	1	0	0.08	0.07	+0.01
SHAD	7	0	7	0.11	-	+0.11
SJPR	14	1	13	0.08	0.32	-0.24
SP	151	26	90	3.75	4.93	-1.18
TMC	28	0	21	0.57	1.40	-0.83
Others	582	0	575	1.28	8.64	-7.36
Independents	1945	6	1928	2.73	2.27	+0.46
Total	**4648**	**543**	**3401**	**100.00**	**100.00**	**0.00**

Jayalalitha with her 18-member AIADMK held the key to power in 1998, it was Chandrababu Naidu's TDP with 29 that gave it a modicum of stability this time, though it again preferred to stay out of the government.

With the process of political realignments continuing as it has through the nineties, the balance of power shifted further towards regional players. Seven national parties together picked up 369 seats, 18 fewer and 0.88 per cent less than their 67.98 per cent share last time. Leading contenders BJP and Congress between them accounted for 296 instead of 323 seats, or 54.51 compared with 59.48 per cent in 1998. While five other national parties could win only 73 or 13.44 per cent seats, 40 state and 122 unrecognised parties cornered nearly a third of the seats bagging 168 with only six of the 1,945 independents making it.

If strategic alliances helped BJP to break out of its moorings in north and central India into the south and the east last time, it was the allies who seemed to have made more of the Vajpayee charisma this time to gain 54 seats for themselves even as they helped NDA gain the support of nearly 56 per cent of the Lok Sabha.

The rival Congress-led alliance was left with only the backing of a quarter of the lower house in winning 136 seats as Congress turned out to be the biggest loser. While Sonia Gandhi and daughter Priyanka did help Congress to storm Karnataka and regain a foothold in Punjab and Uttar Pradesh, they could not undo the damage caused by Sharad Pawar going his separate way in Maharashtra. Nor could ally Laloo Yadav hold back a Janata Dal United in Bihar as Jayalalitha lost almost half her support. Together the allies lost 45 seats.

With the United Front in tatters, the Left too lost a little of support in West Bengal finishing with a national tally of 43 instead of 48 as earlier. But SP going it alone made half a dozen gains, though only in Uttar Pradesh. BSP, which had won recognition as a national party in 1996, again ploughed a lonely furrow and gained nine seats to give the 'fourth front' sixty seats-a little over 11 per cent of the total.

Anti-incumbency swings did not affect the fortunes of parties in power in states alone, but also in individual constituencies with nearly half (263 instead of 275) of the 543 seats changing hands. Even as they made new conquests, they lost ground in old strongholds. While NDA gained 60 seats across the board, BJP itself lost 67 and gained as many for a zero net deficit. Rival Congress, on the other hand, losing 89 could

PARTY POSITION

Abbreviation	Party	No. of Seats
BJP	Bharatiya Janata Party	182
INC	Indian National Congress	114
CPM	Communist Party of India (Marxist)	33
TDP	Telugu Desam Party	29
SP	Samajwadi Party	26
JDU	Janata Dal (United)	21
SHS	Shivsena	15
BSP	Bahujan Samaj Party	14
DMK	Dravida Munnetra Kazhagam	12
ADMK	All India Anna Dravida Munnetra Kazhagam (AIADMK)	10
BJD	Biju Janata Dal	10
TC	All India Trinamool Congress	8
NCP	Nationalist Congress Party	8
RJD	Rashtriya Janata Dal	7
INLD	Indian National Lok Dal	5
PMK	Pattali Makkal Katchi	5
CPI	Communist Party of India	4
MDMK	Marumalarchi Dravida Munnetra Kazhagam	4
NC	Jammu & Kashmir National Conference	4
RSP	Revolutionary Socialist Party	3
SAD	Shiromani Akali Dal	2
FBL	All India Forward Bloc	2
MUL	Muslim League	2
LCP	Loktantrik Congress Party	2
RLD	Rashtriya Lok Dal	2
HVC	Himachal Vikas Congress	1
JDS	Janata Dal (Secular)	1
SJPR	Samajwadi Janata Party (Rashtriya)	1
AIMIM	All India Majlis-e-Ittehadul Muslimeen	1
BBM	Bharipa Bahujan Mahasangh	1
CPML	Communist Party of India (Marxist-Leninist) (Liberation)	1
KEC	Kerala Congress	1
KECM	Kerala Congress (M)	1
MADMK	MGR Anna Dravida Munnetra Kazhagam (MGRADMK)	1
MSCP	Manipur State Congress Party	1
PWP	Peasants and Workers Party of India	1
SAD(M)	Shiromani Akali Dal (Simranjit Singh Mann)	1
SDF	Sikkim Democratic Front	1
Ind.	Independent	6

OTHER PARTIES

Abbreviation	Party
AD	Apna Dal
ASDC	Autonomous State Demand Committee (1998)
AGP	Asom Gana Parishad
ANC	Arunachal Congress
AIICS	All India Indira Congress (Secular) (1998)
AJBP	Ajeya Bharat Party
AMB	Amra Bangalee
ATDP	Anna Telugu Desam Party
BPSP	Bihar People's Socialist Party
BSP(A)	Bahujan Samaj Party (Ambedkar)
DBSM	Democratic Bahujan Samaj Morcha
EU	Ephraim Union
FPM	Federal Party of Manipur
GGP	Gondvana Ganatantra Party
GNC	Garo National Council
HLD(R)	Haryana Lok Dal (Rashtriya)
HSPDP	Hill State People's Democratic Party
HVP	Haryana Vikas Party
JD	Janata Dal (1998)
JP	Janata Party
JKAL	J&K Awami League
JKNPP	J&K National Panthers Party
JMM	Jharkhand Mukti Morcha
LS	Lok Shakti
HLD(R)	Haryana Lok Dal (Rashtriya) (1998)
MCO	Marxist Coordination
MDF	Maraland Democratic Front
MPP	Manipur People's Party
NTRTDP(LP)	NTR Telugu Desam Party (Lakshmi Parvathi)
PDF	People's Democratic Front
PDM	People's Democratic Movement
RJP	Rashtriya Janata Party (1998)
RPI	Republican Party of India
SAP	Samata Party (1998)
SHAD	Sarb Hind Shiromani Akali Dal
SSP	Sikkim Sangram Parishad
UDP	United Democratic Party
UMF	United Minorities Forum
URMCA	United Reservation Movement Council of Assam
Oth.	Others

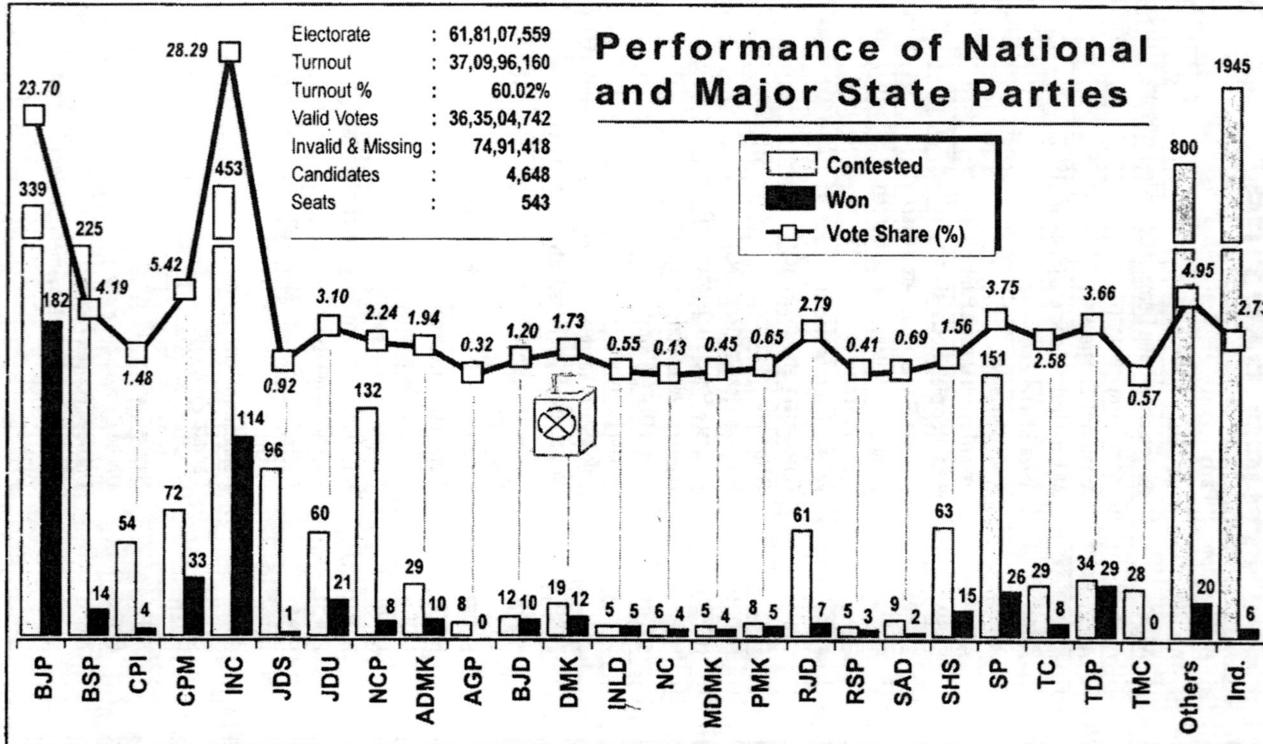
Performance of National
and Major State Parties
Electorate : 61,81,07,559
Turnout : 37,09,96,160
Turnout % : 60.02%
Valid Votes : 36,35,04,742
Invalid & Missing : 74,91,418
Candidates : 4,648
Seats : 543
Contested
Won
Vote Share (%)
23.70
339
182
225
4.19
14
1.48
54
4
5.42
72
33
28.29
453
114
0.92
96
1
3.10
60
21
2.24
132
8
1.94
29
10
0.32
8
0
1.20
12
10
1.73
19
12
0.55
5
5
0.13
6
4
0.45
5
4
0.65
8
5
2.79
61
7
0.41
5
3
0.69
9
2
1.56
63
15
3.75
151
26
2.58
29
8
3.66
34
29
0.57
28
0
4.95
800
20
2.73
1945
6
BJP
BSP
CPI
CPM
INC
JDS
JDU
NCP
ADMK
AGP
BJD
DMK
INLD
NC
MDMK
PMK
RJD
RSP
SAD
SHS
SP
TC
TDP
TMC
Others
Ind.

recoup only 62 to finish with a net deficit of 27. Allies RJD (ten) and AIADMK (eight) added another 18 to the losses. Only others like BSP, SP and new entrant NCP, not choosing to align with either of the big two, gained 28 seats.

It was yet another election that no one wanted coming as it had all too soon without any promise of a stable polity that everyone craved. If at nearly 62 per cent, more people came out to vote in 1998 than in any mid-term poll before, only 60.02 per cent of the 618,107,559 electorate turned out this time.

An *Insight* post-poll survey for *India Today* news weekly suggested that in keeping with its reputation as the favoured party of the entrenched sections of society, more than half the upper caste and many more men than women voted for the BJP. Though OBC support for BJP had come down four per cent since the last poll, 38 per cent still favoured it as against 23 per cent for Congress and 29 per cent for others. Not only has the party succeeded with its "social engineering", but made considerable inroads into rural India from its traditional urban base, while emerging as the favoured party of the young.

While 42 per cent urban voters favoured BJP as against 28 per cent for the Congress, 35 per cent backed it in the villages compared to about one-fourth for India's oldest party. Others appealed to 21 per cent urban and 29 per cent rural voters. Again 41 per cent men and 32 per cent women preferred BJP as against a quarter of either sex for the Congress, while 26 per cent male and 28 per cent female voters chose others.

Among the Hindus, 41 per cent favoured BJP, while 23 per cent opted for the Congress and 26 per cent others. But Congress may take heart from the fact that it has again become more popular among the Muslims with 45 per cent of them preferring it, indicating a six-point upswing, as against a mere ten per cent for the BJP and 31 per cent others.

Besides 39 per cent youth under 25, BJP was backed by 37 per cent of those between 25 and 45, and 35 per cent older ones. In the case of Congress only 24 per cent of youth under 25 favoured it while 26 per cent of the higher age groups chose it. Others were favoured by 28 per cent youth, 27 per cent in 25-44 group and 26 older ones.

Party Performance

Bharatiya Janata Party

State/UT/Region	Total Seats	Seats Fought	Seats Won	Lost Deposit	1999 Vote%	1998 Vote%	Vote Swing %
All-India	**543**	**339**	**182**	**25**	**23.70**	**25.59**	**-1.89**
North	**151**	**126**	**63**	**5**	**30.99**	**34.59**	**-3.60**
Haryana	10	5	5	0	29.21	18.89	+10.32
Himachal Pradesh	4	3	3	0	46.27	51.43	-5.16
Jammu & Kashmir	6	6	2	4	31.56	28.64	+2.92
Punjab	13	3	1	0	9.16	11.67	-2.51
Rajasthan	25	24	16	0	47.23	41.65	+5.58
Uttar Pradesh	85	77	29	1	27.62	36.49	-8.87
Chandigarh	1	1	0	0	45.07	42.36	+2.71
Delhi	7	7	7	0	51.76	50.73	+1.03
South	**132**	**48**	**19**	**14**	**12.29**	**15.44**	**-3.15**
Andhra Pradesh	42	8	7	0	9.10	18.30	-9.20
Karnataka	28	19	7	1	27.18	26.95	+0.23
Kerala	20	14	0	13	6.56	8.02	-1.46
Tamil Nadu	39	6	4	0	7.14	6.86	+0.28
A & N Islands	1	1	1	0	52.74	35.53	+17.21
Lakshadweep	1	-	-	-	-	-	-
Pondicherry	1	-	-	-	-	-	-
East	**142**	**69**	**36**	**5**	**18.97**	**17.99**	**+0.98**
Arunachal Pradesh	2	1	0	0	16.30	21.75	-5.45
Assam	14	12	2	0	29.82	24.47	+5.35
Bihar	54	29	23	0	23.01	24.03	-1.02
Manipur	2	1	0	1	1.02	12.61	-11.59
Meghalaya	2	2	0	2	9.45	9.01	+0.44
Mizoram	1	-	-	-	-	2.94	-2.94
Nagaland	1	1	0	1	5.12	-	+5.12
Orissa	21	9	9	0	24.63	21.19	+3.44
Sikkim	1	-	-	-	-	-	-
Tripura	2	1	0	0	12.82	8.19	+4.63
West Bengal	42	13	2	1	11.13	10.20	+0.93
West	**118**	**96**	**64**	**1**	**36.12**	**36.46**	**-0.34**
Goa	2	2	2	0	51.49	30.04	+21.45
Gujarat	26	26	20	0	52.48	48.28	+4.20
Madhya Pradesh	40	40	29	0	46.58	45.73	+0.85
Maharashtra	48	26	13	1	21.18	22.49	-1.31
Dadra & Nagar Haveli	1	1	0	0	20.83	53.73	-32.90
Daman & Diu	1	1	0	0	43.13	41.96	+1.17

BJP: Winning Friends and Influencing People

Leading the NDA, spearheaded by BJP, in what was dubbed as a presidential style poll, Atal Bihari Vajpayee may have become the first non-Congress Prime Minister to win a second term, but BJP had little to cheer about its own score. Although it had swept Delhi clean, the debacle in the Hindi heartland of UP was a cause of concern ahead of the Assembly poll in 2001. But it did consolidate its spread in the south thanks to alliances with TDP and DMK in Andhra and Tamil Nadu even as it faced losses in Karnataka due to a forced alliance with Janata Dal United. It also broke new ground in Assam, but the loss of power in Maharashtra was sobering.

Although a few new allies helped BJP-led NDA return to power, with the backing of 304 members among its two dozen supporting parties, BJP itself could not add a single seat to its tally. While still finishing at the top with 182 seats, its own support base suffered a near two point erosion. It was the allies, riding piggyback on the Vajpayee charisma, who with 40.68 per cent of the national vote brought in 49 more seats than the 255 won by BJP's 14 pre-poll partners last time with 37.28 per cent votes. BJP, which had after replacing Congress as the largest party in 1996 nearly caught up with India's oldest party in terms of votes too two years later, again dropped behind Congress, still the leader with 28.29 per cent.

While an adverse 1.89 point swing brought down the BJP share from 25.59 to 23.70 per cent, the allies with their 122 seats added another 16.98 per cent to the NDA vote pie, though they too had fought each other in quite a few places. Except for Parkash Singh Badal's Shiromani Akali Dal, Arunachal Congress and Tamizhaga Rajiv Congress, who together lost nine seats, the alliance with BJP helped them all.

Janata Dal United, formed with the merger of Sharad Yadav's Janata Dal, George Fernandes' Samata and Rama Krishna Hegde's Lok Shakti, gained the most—21 seats, but considering that the three separately had won as many seats last time, it had only broken even. It was Chandrababu Naidu's TDP which really made the most of it in increasing its tally from 12 to 29 with 17 gains to emerge as the second largest partner.

Old ally Shiv Sena in Maharashtra gained nine seats, while new ally DMK won half a dozen extra in Tamil Nadu. Foresaken by BJP, Haryana Vikas Party of Bansi Lal lost its lone seat, while Om Prakash

Chautala's INLD in its new incarnation added a seat to win five. In Andhra too, Lakshmi Parvathi's TDP again came a cropper without it.

In the north, with a combined vote share of 38.29 per cent—down 0.67 points from the 38.96 per cent polled by the old alliance in 1998—the new BJP alliance won 77 of the 151 seats, a dozen less. Anti-incumbency vote took a heavy toll in Uttar Pradesh and Punjab even as BJP swept Haryana and Delhi clean while upsetting the Congress applecart in Rajasthan.

BJP itself lost 15 seats, mostly in UP, as it won 63 for 30.99 per cent—a 3.60 point downswing—instead of 78 for 34.59 per cent. Capturing all the seven seats in Delhi, it shared five seats each with Chautala's INLD, polling 2.13 per cent, in Haryana. But Badal's Shiromani Akali Dal could bring in only two instead of eight as its vote share dropped from about three to 2.66 per cent.

New ally Loktantrik Congress with 0.87 per cent added two in UP while JDU unable to retain the two won by Samata last time came a cropper. Sukh Ram's Himachal Vikas Congress Party brought in one, while four National Conference winners extended their support to the new government after opposing BJP candidates in all the six constituencies in Kashmir.

In the south, which sends 132 MPs to the Lok Sabha, the new alliance won 73, a gain of 23 seats, with 40.28 per cent of the popular vote. The largest share of 29 was contributed by Chandrababu Naidu's TDP with 13.53 per cent. BJP itself picked up 19, one less, with only 12.29 per cent of the popular vote. Led by DMK, which won a dozen for 6.41 per cent, BJP's new allies in Tamil Nadu brought in 22 instead of the 27 by estranged Jayalalitha's own Tamil grouping last time with almost the same 11.22 per cent votes. JDU, like Hegde's Lok Shakti last time, could take only three in Karnataka with 3.24 per cent. The allies thus brought 54 seats for 28 per cent, almost thrice as many as BJP with a little over double its vote.

In the east too, BJP and allies picked up 74 of the 142 seats, a net gain of 19, with 40.87 per cent—4.24 points more than the 36.63 polled by the old alliance last time. Winning 36 seats, seven more, BJP again was the main vote-getter polling 18.97 per cent—an upswing of 0.98 points. New ally JDU brought in 18 in Bihar instead of ten by Samata as it added 7.55 per cent to NDA's regional vote share. But Naveen Patnaik's

Party Performance

Janata Dal (United)

State/UT/Region	Total Seats	Seats Fought	Seats Won	Lost Deposit	1999 Vote%	1998 Vote%	Vote Swing %
All-India	**543**	**60**	**21**	**24**	**3.10**	**-**	**+3.10**
North	**151**	**7**	**0**	**4**	**0.63**	**-**	**+0.63**
Haryana	10	-	-	-	-	-	-
Himachal Pradesh	4	-	-	-	-	-	-
Jammu & Kashmir	6	1	0	1	0.14	-	+0.14
Punjab	13	2	0	2	0.10	-	+0.10
Rajasthan	25	2	0	1	1.60	-	+1.60
Uttar Pradesh	85	2	0	0	0.59	-	+0.59
Chandigarh	1	-	-	-	-	-	-
Delhi	7	-	-	-	-	-	-
South	**132**	**16**	**3**	**5**	**3.24**	**-**	**+3.24**
Andhra Pradesh	42	-	-	-	-	-	-
Karnataka	28	10	3	0	13.28	-	+13.28
Kerala	20	5	0	5	1.35	-	+1.35
Tamil Nadu	39	-	-	-	-	-	-
A & N Islands	1	-	-	-	-	-	-
Lakshadweep	1	1	0	0	43.28	-	+43.28
Pondicherry	1	-	-	-	-	-	-
East	**142**	**26**	**18**	**4**	**7.55**	**-**	**+7.55**
Arunachal Pradesh	2	-	-	-	-	-	-
Assam	14	-	-	-	-	-	-
Bihar	54	23	18	1	20.77	-	+20.77
Manipur	2	1	0	1	3.19	-	+3.19
Meghalaya	2	-	-	-	-	-	-
Mizoram	1	-	-	-	-	-	-
Nagaland	1	-	-	-	-	-	-
Orissa	21	2	0	2	0.03	-	+0.03
Sikkim	1	-	-	-	-	-	-
Tripura	2	-	-	-	-	-	-
West Bengal	42	-	-	-	-	-	-
West	**118**	**11**	**0**	**11**	**0.08**	**-**	**+0.08**
Goa	2	-	-	-	-	-	-
Gujarat	26	9	0	9	0.40	-	+0.40
Madhya Pradesh	40	2	0	2	0.02	-	+0.02
Maharashtra	48	-	-	-	-	-	-
Dadra & Nagar Haveli	1	-	-	-	-	-	-
Daman & Diu	1	-	-	-	-	-	-

Biju Janata Dal won ten instead of nine with 4.44 per cent, up 0.75 points, in Orissa, while Mamata Banerjee's Trinamool with eight also contributed an extra seat, with a 9.50 per cent vote share, up 0.56 points, in West Bengal.

West with 118 seats again brought mixed cheer with the Shiv Sena-BJP combine losing power in the parallel assembly poll in Maharashtra, but gaining seats in the Lok Sabha with another good show in Gujarat and Madhya Pradesh, where the BJP went alone. The two together won 79 seats with a combined vote share of 43.84 per cent—a gain of 18 despite a 0.92 point downswing—with BJP contributing 64 for 36.12 per cent. Ally Sena won 15 seats, nine extra, all in Maharashtra to add 7.72 per cent to the alliance kitty. Both Sena and JDU put up 23 candidates in opposition to BJP in the region, but while Sena could not win a seat outside Maharashtra, JDU earned just a handful of votes.

NDA gains in the southern and eastern coastal belts, coupled with the recovery in the west, far outweighed the ups and downs in BJP's traditional northern stronghold to give it the winning edge. While only 53.69 per cent of BJP's 339 candidates came through, TDP registered the best success ratio (85.29 per cent), closely followed by BJD (83.33 per cent) among the bigger partners. Only 35 per cent of JDU's 60 candidates made it, as did 23.81 per cent of Shiv Sena's 63 candidates.

BJP did its best in Madhya Pradesh with 29 wins for 46.58 per cent, but its highest support came in the Andaman and Nicobar Islands, where aided by a 17.21 point swing it polled 52.74 per cent, followed by Gujarat with 52.48 per cent and Delhi with 51.76 per cent. Its worst was in Kerala where all but one of its 14 candidates lost their deposits even as it polled 6.56 per cent, while in Nagaland it got the least votes—5.12 per cent. Swings for the BJP ranged from a negative 32.9 per cent in Dadra and Nagar Haveli to a favourable 21.45 per cent in Goa.

Among the allies, JDU did its best in Bihar winning 18 seats for 20.77 per cent vote followed by three for 13.28 per cent in Karnataka. None of its candidates in nine other states succeeded with 24 (40 per cent) losing deposits.

Overall, not only did the BJP alliance win more general seats—232 out of 423 or 54.85 per cent, but surprisingly also 72 of the 120 or 60 per cent of the reserved seats. With 49 seats, 25 of BJP itself, the alliance won 62 per cent of the 79 SC seats with 41.80 per cent votes. While BJP polled 21.48 per cent, eleven other allies won 24 seats with 20.32 per cent votes.

In tribal areas too, it overtook the Congress to win 23, or 56.10 per cent of the 41 ST seats with 35.88 per cent votes. BJP alone took 21 for a third of the ST vote, while ally TDP won the other two for 2.60 per cent.

Congress: Another Failed Gamble

Going along with Jayalalitha to pull down the BJP government without an alternative in sight was a gamble that did not work for the Congress despite the euphoria over its success in the November 1998 assembly poll after the once reclusive Sonia Gandhi finally took her political plunge.

If pulling the plug on the Gujral government had brought it only one more seat with a near three per cent downswing slashing its vote share to a historic low of 25.82 per cent in 1998, bringing down Vajpayee proved an even greater disaster. Finishing with only 114 seats, 27 less than the last time, its sole consolation was that it managed to hang onto its position as the single party with most votes thanks to a little 2.47 point swing that raised its national share to 28.29 per cent.

But then with 453 candidates, it had contested 114 more seats than the second placed BJP with 23.70 per cent. With old ally Laloo's RJD and new old ally Jayalalitha's AIADMK, both losing another 18 seats in Bihar and Tamil Nadu, and Pawar's breakaway NCP playing the spoilsport in Maharashtra, the Congress-led combine finished with 136 seats. Its tally was 30 less than last time, with 33.70 per cent votes, four per cent more than the smaller alliance did without AIADMK in 1998.

Largely going it alone, except in Bihar, Kerala, Maharashtra, Punjab, Tamil Nadu and Uttar Pradesh, the Congress made a few gains in UP, retained its position in Assam, lost much ground in Maharashtra and Rajasthan, and failed to make any headway in West Bengal or Tamil Nadu. Anti-incumbency factor further eroded its base in Orissa and Madhya Pradesh, where Chief Minister Digvijay Singh's government had returned to power only last year defying all odds.

In the north, Priyanka's charm worked in Uttar Pradesh, where Congress was completely wiped out last time, to win it ten seats. Sonia Gandhi regained husband Rajiv Gandhi's Amethi constitutency with a

Party Performance

Indian National Congress

State/UT/Region	Total Seats	Seats Fought	Seats Won	Lost Deposit	1999 Vote%	1998 Vote%	Vote Swing %
All-India	**543**	**453**	**114**	**88**	**28.29**	**25.82**	**+2.47**
North	**151**	**139**	**28**	**48**	**25.61**	**19.01**	**+6.60**
Haryana	10	10	0	0	34.93	26.02	+8.91
Himachal Pradesh	4	4	0	0	39.52	41.90	-2.38
Jammu & Kashmir	6	5	0	1	17.83	19.24	-1.41
Punjab	13	11	8	0	38.44	25.85	+12.59
Rajasthan	25	25	9	0	45.12	44.45	+0.67
Uttar Pradesh	85	76	10	47	14.77	6.02	+8.75
Chandigarh	1	1	1	0	47.00	38.70	+8.30
Delhi	7	7	0	0	41.95	42.64	-0.69
South	**132**	**101**	**35**	**0**	**34.05**	**28.79**	**+5.26**
Andhra Pradesh	42	42	5	0	42.81	38.46	+4.35
Karnataka	28	28	18	0	45.41	36.22	+9.19
Kerala	20	17	8	0	39.35	38.67	+0.68
Tamil Nadu	39	11	2	0	11.10	4.78	+6.32
A & N Islands	1	1	0	0	43.17	35.91	+7.26
Lakshadweep	1	1	1	0	53.96	51.55	+2.41
Pondicherry	1	1	1	0	37.17	32.12	+5.05
East	**142**	**101**	**23**	**36**	**18.19**	**18.75**	**-0.56**
Arunachal Pradesh	2	2	2	0	56.92	23.90	+33.02
Assam	14	14	10	1	38.44	38.97	-0.53
Bihar	54	16	4	1	8.81	7.27	+1.54
Manipur	2	2	0	0	25.30	18.60	+6.70
Meghalaya	2	2	1	0	32.75	47.62	-14.87
Mizoram	1	-	-	-	-	34.86	-34.86
Nagaland	1	1	1	0	71.18	86.70	-15.52
Orissa	21	20	2	0	36.94	41.04	-4.10
Sikkim	1	1	0	1	4.76	33.11	-28.35
Tripura	2	2	0	2	13.88	42.12	-28.24
West Bengal	42	41	3	31	13.29	15.20	-1.91
West	**118**	**112**	**28**	**4**	**37.68**	**40.43**	**-2.75**
Goa	2	2	0	0	39.01	31.59	+7.42
Gujarat	26	26	6	0	45.44	36.49	+8.95
Madhya Pradesh	40	40	11	0	43.91	39.40	+4.51
Maharashtra	48	42	10	3	29.71	43.64	-13.93
Dadra & Nagar Haveli	1	1	0	1	14.74	4.13	+10.61
Daman & Diu	1	1	1	0	49.48	1.98	+47.50

record three lakh-vote margin and Congress again emerged as a force to reckon with in Punjab. But the national capital was a disaster with even former finance minister Manmohan Singh, seen as a Prime Ministerial alternative, failing to win his first Lok Sabha election. Thanks to an over six per cent regional swing, Congress gained four seats to finish with 28 seats in its kitty for 25.61 per cent as against 24 for 19 per cent last time.

Down south, despite a good show in Karnataka, where it wrested power, Congress lost six seats to finish with 35 seats for 34.05 per cent despite a 5.26 point regional upswing. In Tamil Nadu AIADMK won ten seats and in Kerala, long standing United Democratic Front (UDF) partners Muslim League and Kerala Congress hung on to their two and one seats respectively, to give the alliance 48 seats with a 42.40 per cent regional vote share, 2.12 points higher than the rival BJP alliance.

In the east, Congress itself lost only one seat with a poor showing in Orissa to finish with 23 for 18.19 per cent. But with ally Laloo's RJD losing ten in Bihar, the combine could win only 30 seats for 28.45 per cent of the votes instead of 42 seats with 29.21 per cent of the vote share last time.

But in the west, where a strategic alliance with RPI and Mulayam Singh Yadav's SP in Maharashtra, had helped Congress put up a good show, Sharad Pawar played spoilsport. The split cost the Congress heavy with its share almost halved to 28 for 37.68 per cent from 52 for 40.43 per cent.

Although NCP itself could win only half a dozen seats, it sliced away ten per cent of the vote to spell defeat for Congress in many a seat. With RPI split too, it also lost the four seats it had won in alliance with Congress last time. In fact at 47.69 per cent, Congress and NCP together polled 3.85 per cent more votes than the BJP-Shiv Sena combine but won less than half the seats won by them.

In all the Congress lost 89 seats across the board, 48 of them to BJP alone, but recovered 62 seats to finish with a net loss of 27. Besides BJP, it lost 15 seats to TDP, nine to Shiv Sena, seven to NCP, two to BJD and one each to CPM, JDS, JDU, INLD, HVC, NC, KEC and an independent. In turn, it wrested 36 seats from BJP, four from Akali Dal, three from JD, two each form CPI, Lok Shakti, ANC, TMC and independents and nine more from as many parties.

Only a little over one fourth of the Congress' 453 candidates emerged successful. In terms of votes, Congress again did its best in Nagaland to win 71.18 per cent support even as it dropped 15.52 per cent votes there. Its worst was in Sikkim where a massive 28.35 point erosion reduced its vote share to 4.76 per cent. A 33 per cent swing gave it both the seats in Arunachal Pradesh.

Congress could win only seven of the 79 SC seats with 22.58 per cent vote while rival BJP took 25 for 21.48 per cent, 1.10 points less. In tribal seats too, Congress fell behind BJP in winning nine of the 41 ST seats with 36.69 per cent votes with the saffron party getting 21 for 33.28 per cent or 3.41 points fewer votes.

In the general category, Congress with 28.71 per cent polled about 5.25 points more than BJP but won fewer seats. Allies ADMK and RJD brought in two and one more SC seats for 2.61 and 4.19 per cent votes respectively to give the alliance ten for 29.59 per cent, but none of them joined battle in ST areas.

Third Front: Nothing but Left

The United Front that ruled India for twenty months under two Janata Dal Prime Ministers had come unstuck with the verdict of 1998 with its spearhead JD nearly wiped out and a leading driving force, Telugu Desam switching support to the rival BJP headed coalition. The smell of power briefly brought them together when Jayalalitha pulled the plug on Vajpayee in April 1999, but with Mulayam Singh Yadav's SP unwilling to accept a Congress government under Sonia Gandhi, the break-up was complete.

Then with DMK and a major section of Janata Dal crossing over, it fell on the Left to take up the "secular" cause with the Congress. But Pawar's NCP, which had broken with the Congress on the Sonia issue, Yadav's SP, which had declined to back a government headed by her, and Kanshi Ram's BSP, which unabashedly favoured an unstable government, declined to join either camp.

In the event, five Left parties—CPM, CPI, Forward Bloc, RSP and CPML—took the lead position with 43 wins even as they dropped five seats. SP and BSP, separately taking on the BJP upset the saffron applecart in Uttar Pradesh with 15 gains. Pawar's ambition to offer an alterative to the once mighty Congress fell flat with his NCP winning only eight seats, all but two of them in Pawar's home state of Maharashtra.

Party Performance

Communist Party of India (Marxist)

State/UT/Region	Total Seats	Seats Fought	Seats Won	Lost Deposit	1999 Vote%	1998 Vote%	Vote Swing %
All-India	**543**	**72**	**33**	**20**	**5.42**	**5.16**	**+0.26**
North	**151**	**6**	**0**	**5**	**0.33**	**0.48**	**-0.15**
Haryana	10	1	0	1	0.15	0.34	-0.19
Himachal Pradesh	4	-	-	-	-	-	-
Jammu & Kashmir	6	1	0	1	1.00	-	+1.00
Punjab	13	1	0	0	2.18	1.06	+1.12
Rajasthan	25	1	0	1	0.49	1.28	-0.79
Uttar Pradesh	85	2	0	2	0.03	0.23	-0.20
Chandigarh	1	-	-	-	-	-	-
Delhi	7	-	-	-	-	-	-
South	**132**	**22**	**9**	**7**	**5.51**	**4.49**	**+1.02**
Andhra Pradesh	42	7	0	6	1.43	2.89	-1.46
Karnataka	28	1	0	1	0.08	0.04	+0.04
Kerala	20	12	8	0	27.90	21.00	+6.90
Tamil Nadu	39	2	1	0	2.35	0.63	+1.72
A & N Islands	1	-	-	-	-	5.67	-5.67
Lakshadweep	1	-	-	-	-	-	-
Pondicherry	1	-	-	-	-	-	-
East	**142**	**40**	**24**	**4**	**13.99**	**14.11**	**-0.12**
Arunachal Pradesh	2	-	-	-	-	-	-
Assam	14	2	0	1	1.77	3.27	-1.50
Bihar	54	2	1	1	0.98	0.40	+0.58
Manipur	2	-	-	-	-	-	-
Meghalaya	2	-	-	-	-	-	-
Mizoram	1	-	-	-	-	-	-
Nagaland	1	-	-	-	-	-	-
Orissa	21	2	0	2	0.20	0.41	-0.21
Sikkim	1	-	-	-	-	-	-
Tripura	2	2	2	0	56.24	48.80	+7.44
West Bengal	42	32	21	0	35.57	35.41	+0.16
West	**118**	**4**	**0**	**4**	**0.25**	**0.29**	**-0.04**
Goa	2	-	-	-	-	-	-
Gujarat	26	-	-	-	-	-	-
Madhya Pradesh	40	1	0	1	0.05	0.11	-0.06
Maharashtra	48	3	0	3	0.52	0.61	-0.09
Dadra & Nagar Haveli	1	-	-	-	-	-	-
Daman & Diu	1	-	-	-	-	-	-

Party Performance

Communist Party of India

State/UT/Region	Total Seats	Seats Fought	Seats Won	Lost Deposit	1999 Vote%	1998 Vote%	Vote Swing %
All-India	**543**	**54**	**4**	**39**	**1.48**	**1.75**	**-0.27**
North	**151**	**17**	**1**	**16**	**0.59**	**0.55**	**+0.04**
Haryana	10	-	-	-	-	0.15	-0.15
Himachal Pradesh	4	1	0	1	0.46	0.56	-0.10
Jammu & Kashmir	6	-	-	-	-	-	-
Punjab	13	1	1	0	3.74	3.40	+0.34
Rajasthan	25	4	0	4	0.42	0.62	-0.20
Uttar Pradesh	85	11	0	11	0.28	0.18	+0.10
Chandigarh	1	-	-	-	-	-	-
Delhi	7	-	-	-	-	-	-
South	**132**	**12**	**0**	**4**	**2.34**	**2.86**	**-0.52**
Andhra Pradesh	42	6	0	4	1.36	2.56	-1.20
Karnataka	28	-	-	-	-	0.06	-0.06
Kerala	20	4	0	0	7.57	8.32	-0.75
Tamil Nadu	39	2	0	0	2.56	2.45	+0.11
A & N Islands	1	-	-	-	-	-	-
Lakshadweep	1	-	-	-	-	-	-
Pondicherry	1	-	-	-	-	-	-
East	**142**	**19**	**3**	**13**	**2.47**	**2.98**	**-0.51**
Arunachal Pradesh	2	-	-	-	-	-	-
Assam	14	1	0	1	0.58	0.95	-0.37
Bihar	54	9	0	7	2.69	3.40	-0.71
Manipur	2	1	0	1	3.95	20.47	-16.52
Meghalaya	2	2	0	2	0.68	1.44	-0.76
Mizoram	1	-	-	-	-	-	-
Nagaland	1	-	-	-	-	-	-
Orissa	21	3	0	2	1.18	0.99	+0.19
Sikkim	1	-	-	-	-	-	-
Tripura	2	-	-	-	-	-	-
West Bengal	42	3	3	0	3.47	3.64	-0.17
West	**118**	**6**	**0**	**6**	**0.13**	**0.29**	**-0.16**
Goa	2	2	0	2	2.93	-	+2.93
Gujarat	26	1	0	1	0.04	0.09	-0.05
Madhya Pradesh	40	1	0	1	0.23	0.66	-0.43
Maharashtra	48	2	0	2	0.06	0.07	-0.01
Dadra & Nagar Haveli	1	-	-	-	-	-	-
Daman & Diu	1	-	-	-	-	-	-

Among the regional parties, ruling AGP wiped out in Assam last time, again failed to win a seat. A divided RPI lost all its four seats in Maharashtra. With DMK crossing over to NDA, TMC dropped its three seats in Tamil Nadu. And Bansi Lal's HVP yielded its lone seat in Haryana after breaking with BJP. The National Conference alone, choosing to fight both BJP and Congress all over Jammu and Kashmir, wrested a seat from Congress, only to extend its backing to the Vajpayee government after the poll. In the bargain, it got a berth for Chief Minister Farooq Abdullah's son, Omer in the Union Council of Ministers.

In the Left, CPI lost five and RSP two, but CPM and CPML won an extra seat each to limit their losses to five. The Left's 43 seats were won with a combined vote share of eight per cent. CPM alone contributed 33, one more than last time, with 5.42 per cent votes indicating a 0.26 point upswing. CPM lost two seats to Trinamool and one each to BJP and Congress, but gained five, one apiece from BJP, Congress, Trinamool, Janata Party and ally RSP.

In terms of votes, CPM's best again came in Tripura where it won both the seats with 56.24 per cent, up 7.44 points. Next came West Bengal with success in 21 of the 32 seats with 35.57 per cent, up 0.16 points, and Kerala with eight wins out of 12 with 27.9 per cent, up 6.9 points. But a poor show in Andhra Pradesh, where six of its seven candidates lost deposits in the face of an adverse 1.46 point swing, put CPM's national status in jeopardy.

CPI was the worst Left loser as it yielded half a dozen seats, two each to TDP and Congress and one apiece to NCP and DMK, but it wrested one from the Akali Dal in Punjab. CPI did its best in West Bengal where it won all the three seats it contested with 3.47 per cent votes, but it lost both its seats in Kerala as its vote share dropped by 0.75 points to 7.57 per cent.

Forward Bloc won two of the three seats it contested in West Bengal with 3.45 per cent votes, but its 12 other candidates lost their deposits in Tamil Nadu (eight), Bihar (three), Punjab (one). RSP won three of the four seats it contested in West Bengal with 4.25 per cent votes, while its lone candidate in Bihar lost his deposit polling 164 votes. Besides conceding a seat to ally CPM in Kerala, it lost one to Congress in West Bengal.

New entrant CPML won a seat in Assam with 2.25 per cent votes as

Party Performance

Bahujan Samaj Party

State/UT/Region	Total Seats	Seats Fought	Seats Won	Lost Deposit	1999 Vote%	1998 Vote%	Vote Swing %
All-India	**543**	**225**	**14**	**153**	**4.19**	**4.67**	**-0.48**
North	**151**	**114**	**14**	**48**	**13.84**	**14.13**	**-0.29**
Haryana	10	3	0	3	1.93	7.68	-5.75
Himachal Pradesh	4	1	0	1	0.31	1.15	-0.84
Jammu & Kashmir	6	2	0	2	4.83	4.97	-0.14
Punjab	13	3	0	2	3.84	12.65	-8.81
Rajasthan	25	16	0	15	2.76	2.12	+0.64
Uttar Pradesh	85	85	14	21	22.06	20.90	+1.16
Chandigarh	1	1	0	1	2.75	-	+2.75
Delhi	7	3	0	3	2.24	2.34	-0.10
South	**132**	**11**	**0**	**11**	**0.16**	**0.28**	**-0.12**
Andhra Pradesh	42	-	-	-	-	0.21	-0.21
Karnataka	28	6	0	6	0.65	0.56	+0.09
Kerala	20	5	0	5	0.09	0.13	-0.04
Tamil Nadu	39	-	-	-	-	0.23	-0.23
A & N Islands	1	-	-	-	-	-	-
Lakshadweep	1	-	-	-	-	-	-
Pondicherry	1	-	-	-	-	-0.63	-0.63
East	**142**	**53**	**0**	**52**	**0.61**	**0.33**	**+0.28**
Arunachal Pradesh	2	-	-	-	-	-	-
Assam	14	-	-	-	-	-	-
Bihar	54	30	0	29	1.34	0.53	+0.81
Manipur	2	-	-	-	-	-	-
Meghalaya	2	-	-	-	-	-	-
Mizoram	1	-	-	-	-	-	-
Nagaland	1	-	-	-	-	-	-
Orissa	21	4	0	4	0.33	0.32	+0.01
Sikkim	1	-	-	-	-	-	-
Tripura	2	-	-	-	-	-	-
West Bengal	42	19	0	19	0.24	0.24	0.00
West	**118**	**47**	**0**	**42**	**1.99**	**3.42**	**-1.43**
Goa	2	-	-	-	-	-	-
Gujarat	26	4	0	4	0.07	-	+0.07
Madhya Pradesh	40	27	0	22	5.23	8.70	-3.47
Maharashtra	48	16	0	16	0.32	0.75	-0.43
Dadra & Nagar Haveli	1	-	-	-	-	-	-
Daman & Diu	1	-	-	-	-	-	-

Party Performance

Nationalist Congress Party

State/UT/Region	Total Seats	Seats Fought	Seats Won	Lost Deposit	1999 Vote%	1998 Vote%	Vote Swing %
All-India	**543**	**132**	**8**	**98**	**2.24**	**-**	**+2.24**
North	**151**	**23**	**0**	**23**	**0.07**	**-**	**+0.07**
Haryana	10	2	0	2	0.06	-	+0.06
Himachal Pradesh	4	3	0	3	0.31	-	+0.31
Jammu & Kashmir	6	2	0	2	0.29	-	+0.29
Punjab	13	3	0	3	0.08	-	+0.08
Rajasthan	25	7	0	7	0.20	-	+020
Uttar Pradesh	85	-	-	-	-	-	-
Chandigarh	1	-	-	-	-	-	-
Delhi	7	6	0	6	0.17	-	+0.17
South	**132**	**8**	**0**	**8**	**0.03**	**-**	**+0.03**
Andhra Pradesh	42	4	0	4	0.01	-	+0.01
Karnataka	28	2	0	2	0.10	-	+0.10
Kerala	20	-	-	-	-	-	-
Tamil Nadu	39	1	0	1	0.01	-	+0.01
A & N Islands	1	1	0	1	0.70	-	0.70
Lakshadweep	1	-	-	-	-	-	-
Pondicherry	1	-	-	-	-	-	-
East	**142**	**44**	**2**	**41**	**0.82**	**-**	**+0.82**
Arunachal Pradesh	2	1	0	1	7.77	-	+7.77
Assam	14	8	0	8	0.50	-	+0.50
Bihar	54	19	0	18	1.07	-	+1.07
Manipur	2	1	1	0	13.50	-	+13.50
Meghalaya	2	1	1	0	27.95	-	+27.95
Mizoram	1	-	-	-	-	-	-
Nagaland	1	-	-	-	-	-	-
Orissa	21	3	0	3	0.13	-	+0.13
Sikkim	1	-	-	-	-	-	-
Tripura	2	1	0	1	0.16	-	+0.16
West Bengal	42	10	0	10	0.06	-	+0.06
West	**118**	**57**	**6**	**26**	**10.01**	**-**	**+10.01**
Goa	2	2	0	2	3.79	-	+3.79
Gujarat	26	7	0	7	0.52	-	+0.52
Madhya Pradesh	40	10	0	10	0.18	-	+0.18
Maharashtra	48	38	6	7	21.58	-	+21.58
Dadra & Nagar Haveli	1	-	-	-	-	-	-
Daman & Diu	1	-	-	-	-	-	-

all but three of its 56 candidates in 12 states lost their deposits. Of them 21 were in Bihar, where it collected 2.47 per cent votes. The left won nine SC and four ST seats with 9.26 and 8.14 per cent vote with CPM taking five of the former with 4.80 per cent and two of the latter with 4.06 per cent. RSP won two SC and one ST seat with 1.44 and 1.97 per cent votes. CPI won a SC seat for 2.06 per cent but could not get any ST seat with 1.14 per cent. While Forward Bloc took one SC seat for 0.82 per cent, CPML took a tribal seat in Assam with 0.97 per cent of the national ST vote.

Yadav's SP put up 151 candidates in 13 states. Of them 90 lost deposits. All its 26 victories came from UP where it polled 24.03 per cent as its national vote share dropped by 1.18 points to 3.75 per cent. SP gained 16 seats in UP, 14 from BJP and two from BSP, but conceded six to BJP, two each to BSP and Loktantrik Congress. SP won five SC seats with 5.63 per cent vote, but had no luck in Tribal areas where it polled a minuscule 0.16 per cent.

Kanshi Ram's BSP hoping to play the king-maker again chose to stay non-aligned and raised its tally from five to 14 even as its vote share dropped by half a point to 4.19 per cent. While 154 of its 225 candidates in 16 states, lost their deposits, it won ten more seats in UP alone, yielding its lone seat in Haryana to BJP. In all BSP gained 13 seats, nine from BJP and two each from SP and Samata, all in UP. In turn, it lost two apiece to BJP, one in UP and another in Haryana, and SP, both in UP. Five of its seats came from SC areas with 6.93 per cent votes as against three for 8.49 per cent last time, but no seat came its way in tribal areas.

In terms of votes, BSP still did its best in UP with 22.06 per cent votes, an upswing of 1.16 points. But it lost 8.81 points in Punjab to finish with 3.84 per cent, while its share in Madhya Pradesh slipped by 3.47 points to 5.23 per cent. In Haryana too its share dropped by 5.75 points to 1.93 per cent as it lost its only seat outside UP.

Pawar's NCP put up 132 candidates in 22 states, but it could win only eight seats, with 2.24 of the national vote pie. All but one of its seats were won at the cost of Congress, six in Maharashtra and one in Meghalaya. The eighth seat was wrested from the CPI in Manipur. In all 98 of its candidates lost their deposits. It won a tribal seat in Meghalaya with 3.08 per cent vote, but 0.75 per cent SC vote could not bring it any.

Party Performance

Janata Dal (Secular)

State/UT/Region	Total Seats	Seats Fought	Seats Won	Lost Deposit	1999 Vote%	1998 Vote%	Vote Swing %
All-India	**543**	**96**	**1**	**88**	**0.92**	**-**	**+0.92**
North	**151**	**33**	**0**	**32**	**0.14**	**-**	**+0.14**
Haryana	10	1	0	1	0.02	-	+0.02
Himachal Pradesh	4	2	0	2	0.19	-	+0.19
Jammu & Kashmir	6	5	0	5	0.92	-	+0.92
Punjab	13	2	0	2	0.03	-	+0.03
Rajasthan	25	4	0	4	0.06	-	+0.06
Uttar Pradesh	85	18	0	18	0.09	-	+0.09
Chandigarh	1	-	-	-	-	-	-
Delhi	7	1	0	0	1.39	-	+1.39
South	**132**	**36**	**0**	**31**	**2.87**	**-**	**+2.87**
Andhra Pradesh	42	4	0	4	0.05	-	+0.05
Karnataka	28	27	0	23	10.85	-	+10.85
Kerala	20	1	0	0	2.17	-	+2.17
Tamil Nadu	39	3	0	3	0.15	-	+0.15
A & N Islands	1	-	-	-	-	-	-
Lakshadweep	1	1	0	1	1.82	-	+1.82
Pondicherry	1	-	-	-	-	-	-
East	**142**	**18**	**0**	**18**	**0.06**	**-**	**+0.06**
Arunachal Pradesh	2	-	-	-	-	-	-
Assam	14	1	0	1	0.01	-	+0.01
Bihar	54	13	0	13	0.14	-	+0.14
Manipur	2	-	-	-	-	-	-
Meghalaya	2	-	-	-	-	-	-
Mizoram	1	-	-	-	-	-	-
Nagaland	1	-	-	-	-	-	-
Orissa	21	-	-	-	-	-	-
Sikkim	1	-	-	-	-	-	-
Tripura	2	-	-	-	-	-	-
West Bengal	42	4	0	4	0.02	-	+0.02
West	**118**	**9**	**1**	**7**	**0.45**	**-**	**+0.45**
Goa	2	-	-	-	-	-	-
Gujarat	26	3	0	3	0.06	-	+0.06
Madhya Pradesh	40	4	0	4	0.07	-	+0.07
Maharashtra	48	2	1	0	0.91	-	+0.91
Dadra & Nagar Haveli	1	-	-	-	-	-	-
Daman & Diu	1	-	-	-	-	-	-

Party Performance

Major State Parties

State/UT/Region (Total Seats)	Party	Seats Fought	Seats Won	Lost Deposit	1999 Vote%	1998 Vote%	Vote Swing %
Andhra Pradesh (42)	TDP	34	29	0	40.66	31.97	+8.69
Arunachal Pradesh (2)	ANC	1	0	0	16.62	52.47	-35.85
Assam (14)	AGP	8	0	3	11.91	12.72	-0.81
Bihar (54)	RJD	36	7	1	28.29	26.58	+1.71
	JMM	13	0	10	2.04	2.45	-0.41
Dadra & Nagar Haveli (1)	SHS	1	0	0	19.51	41.71	-22.20
Haryana (10)	INLD	5	5	0	28.72	-	+28.72
	HVP	2	0	1	2.71	11.60	-8.89
Himachal Pradesh (4)	HVC	1	1	0	12.37	3.57	+8.80
Jammu & Kashmir (6)	NC	6	4	0	28.93	36.35	-7.42
Kerala (20)	KEC	1	1	0	2.38	2.20	+0.18
	KECM	1	1	0	2.32	2.40	-0.08
	MUL	2	2	0	5.27	5.01	+0.26
Maharashtra (48)	BBM	4	1	0	2.10	-	+2.10
	SHS	22	15	1	16.86	19.66	-2.80
Manipur (2)	FPM	2	0	2	3.36	-	+3.36
	MPP	1	0	0	16.25	15.44	+0.81
	MSCP	2	1	1	24.89	25.39	-0.50
Meghalaya (2)	HSPDP	1	0	1	6.16	7.41	-1.25
	PDM	1	0	1	5.07	-	+5.07
	UDP	1	0	0	16.38	25.49	-9.11
Mizoram (1)	MDF	1	0	1	2.89	-	+2.89
Orissa (21)	BJD	12	10	0	33.00	27.50	+5.50
Pondicherry (1)	PMK	1	0	0	31.73	-	+31.73
	TMC	1	0	0	25.16	-	+25.16
Punjab (13)	SAD	9	2	0	28.59	32.93	-4.34
	SHAD	7	0	7	4.64	-	+4.64
	SADM	1	1	0	3.41	2.73	+0.68
Sikkim (1)	SDF	1	1	0	52.56	65.72	-13.16
	SSP	1	0	0	42.15	-	+42.15
Tamil Nadu (39)	ADMK	24	10	0	25.68	25.89	-0.21
	DMK	19	12	0	23.13	20.08	+3.05
	MDMK	5	4	0	5.95	6.26	-0.31
	PMK	7	5	0	8.21	6.05	+2.16
	TMC	27	0	21	7.15	20.19	-13.04
Tripura (2)	TC	1	0	0	14.46	-	+14.46
Uttar Pradesh (85)	LCP	4	2	0	1.51	-	+1.51
	RLD	7	2	2	2.50	-	+2.50
	SP	84	26	24	24.03	28.70	-4.67
West Bengal (42)	FBL	3	2	0	3.45	3.30	+0.15
	RSP	4	3	0	4.25	4.48	-0.23
	TC	28	8	2	26.04	24.43	+1.61

With the Left taking 43 and BSP, SP, NCP and JDS cornering 49 seats for a combined vote share of 19.10 per cent, the remaining 12 seats were evenly shared by independents and small parties together polling 6.49 per cent. A total of 1945 independents polled 2.73 per cent votes and won three tribal and one SC seat with 4.22 and 2.33 per cent vote respectively. As many as 1928 independents failed to even save their deposits.

NORTH

Seats: 151	Candidates: 1,825

Electorate	:	17,89,45,324
Turnout	:	9,55,36,837
Turnout %	:	53.39%
Valid Votes	:	9,41,71,018
Invalid & Missing	:	13,65,819

Party	Seats Contested	Seats Won	Lost Deposit	1999 Vote%	1998 Vote%	Vote Swing %
BJP + Allies	**159**	**77**	**9**	**38.29**	**38.49**	**-0.20**
BJP	126	63	5	30.99	34.59	-3.60
JD(U)	7	0	4	0.63	-	+0.63
HVC	1	1	0	0.28	0.08	+0.20
INLD	5	5	0	2.13	-	+2.13
SAD	9	2	0	2.66	3.03	-0.37
LCP	4	2	0	0.87	-	+0.87
DBSM	1	0	0	0.25	-	+0.25
NC (post poll)	6	4	0	0.48	0.79	-0.31
INC + Allies	**148**	**30**	**52**	**27.05**	**19.01**	**+8.04**
INC	139	28	48	25.61	19.01	+6.60
RLD	9	2	4	1.44	-	+1.44
BSP	114	14	48	13.84	14.13	-0.29
CPI	17	1	16	0.59	0.55	+0.04
CPM	6	0	5	0.33	0.48	-0.15
JD(S)	33	0	32	0.14	-	+0.14
NCP	23	0	23	0.07	-	+0.07
HVP	2	0	1	0.20	0.88	-0.68
SJP(R)	6	1	5	0.28	0.73	-0.45
SP	110	26	50	13.92	16.27	-2.35
AD	45	0	44	0.89	0.53	+0.36
SAD(M)	1	1	0	0.32	0.25	+0.07
SHAD	7	0	7	0.43	-	+0.43
Others	273	0	273	0.90	5.70	-4.80
Ind.	881	1	876	2.91	2.98	-0.07
Total	**1825**	**151**	**1441**	**100.00**	**100.00**	**0.00**

CHAPTER 7

THE NORTH: SWEET AND SOUR

Despite major setbacks in India's most populous state, Uttar Pradesh and Punjab, BJP alliance retained its pre-eminent position in the north winning 77 of the 151 seats up for grabs thanks to a change in fortunes in Rajasthan and Haryana even as it lost a dozen seats across the board. Congress and its allies with 31 made a net gain of five with good performances in UP and Punjab making up for a poor show in the desert state and Haryana. But it was Mulayam Singh Yadav's SP and a resurgent BSP which made the most of the turning tide in UP picking up between them 40 seats, 15 more than last time, as they separately took on the saffron challenge. Former Prime Minister Chandra Shekhar winning Ballia for his SJPR and Simranjit Singh Mann taking one for the rival Akali Dal raised the 'non-aligned' total to 42, while Maneka Gandhi, the lone independent to taste victory in the region, again backed Vajpayee led NDA.

BJP and allies polled 38.29 per cent of the region's votes, 0.67 points less than the 1998 combine's share of 38.96 per cent, to drop a dozen seats, with the saffron party itself winning 63 of the 77 for 30.99 per cent as against 78 seats for 34.59 per cent. Losing 39 seats and holding on to an equal number, BJP recouped 24 new seats from its rivals to limit its losses to 15. If infighting did BJP in despite a divided opposition in UP and a split in Badal's Shiromani Akali Dal lost the alliance Punjab, an anti-incumbency wave in Rajasthan and a switch in allies in Haryana evened the odds for it somewhat. Among its allies, Shiromani Akali Dal lost six seats to bring in only two for 2.66 per cent instead of eight for 3.03 per cent of the regional vote. New ally Indian National Lok Dal of Haryana chief minister, Om Prakash Chautala, brought in five gains with 2.13 per cent, Loktantrik Congress added two for 0.87 per cent, while Samata Party lost two seats as the JDU in which it had merged failed to win a single seat while contributing 0.63 per cent. Sukh Ram's

Himachal Vikas Congress gained one for the alliance with 0.28 per cent, while Farooq Abdullah's National Conference again backed the NDA with its four winners with 0.48 per cent though BJP had opposed it in all the six seats in Jammu and Kashmir. Shiv Sena too put up 18 candidates against alliance partners, but all lost deposits polling a miserable 0.03 per cent of the regional vote.

As many as 15 of BJP's 24 gains in the north were from the Congress, a dozen of them in Rajasthan alone, two in Haryana and one in Delhi. Congress in turn took back all but one. BJP gained six from SP, all in UP, and two from BSP, one in UP and another in Haryana besides one from Chautala's old party HLDR, but gave away 14 and nine to SP and BSP in UP, where it lost two more to Ajit Singh's Rashtriya Lok Dal. Swings for BJP ranged from 1.03 per cent in Delhi to 5.58 per cent in Rajasthan and 10.32 per cent in Haryana. It faced adverse swings of 5.16 per cent in Himachal and 2.51 per cent in Punjab. Overall, BJP lost 3.60 points in the north as its vote share dropped from 34.59 to 30.99 per cent.

Less than a year after winning back power in Rajasthan and Delhi in the November 1998 assembly poll, the Congress was completely wiped out in Haryana, Himachal, Jammu and Kashmir and Delhi besides losing heavily in Rajasthan. But with major gains in UP and Punjab, Congress picked up 28 seats, four more than last time as it raised its regional vote share by 6.60 points from 19.01 to 25.61 per cent. Apart from losing 15 to BJP, 12 in Rajasthan, two in Haryana and one in Delhi, it conceded one each to INLD in Haryana, HVC in Himachal and NC in Kashmir. Winning back 14 from BJP, ten in UP, two in Punjab and one in Rajasthan besides Chandigarh Congress gained four from Akali Dal, one from an independent as also former Prime Minister Inder Kumar Gujral's Janata Dal seat in Punjab. The homecoming of Buta Singh and Sis Ram Ola in Rajasthan gave it two more seats. Ally RLD wrested two seats from BJP with 1.44 per cent votes. CPI with 0.59 per cent won its only seat from Akali Dal in Punjab, but all six CPM candidates lost leaving the Left with a tally of one for a regional vote share of 0.92 per cent.

Among the 'non-aligned', SP finished third in the popularity stakes with 26 seats, all in UP, to add six to its kitty even as its regional share slid 2.35 points from 16.27 to 13.92 per cent. In all it gained 16 seats, 14 from BJP and two from BSP, but returned six to BJP and two each to

BSP and Loktantrik Congress. Former Prime Minister Chandra Shekhar won again by a reduced margin in Ballia with the backing of SP, his SJPR polling 0.28 per cent.

BSP polling just a little less, 13.84 instead of 14.13 per cent gained nine seats. It snatched 13 seats, nine from BJP and two each from Samata and SP in UP but returned two to SP and one to BJP. It lost another seat to BJP in Haryana.

All the 23 candidates of the newly formed Nationalist Congress Party of Sharad Pawar lost their deposits. So did 40 candidates of either faction of Janata Dal together polling 0.77 per cent compared to 1.23 per cent by the united party to win its only seat in the north in 1998. Seven national parties cornered 72.13 per cent of the regional vote, while 20.14 per cent went to state parties with Samajwadi Party taking the lion's share of 13.92 per cent. Of the rest, smaller parties took 4.82 per cent with 2.91 per cent going to 881 independents among a total of 1825 candidates. BJP and allies won 15 of the 29 SC seats for 35.30 per cent with the saffron party itself taking a dozen for 26.34 per cent. INLD, LCP and HVC took one seat each polling 2.39, 2.01 and 1.52 per cent respectively. Badal's Akali Dal polled nearly three per cent SC votes but could not win a single seat. Congress polling 20.80 per cent won three, while ally RLD failed to win a seat with nearly half a per cent vote and CPI took one for 2.34 per cent. BSP and SP equally shared the remaining ten with 17.82 and 16.89 per cent votes as 122 independents gathering 1.68 per cent came a cropper. Congress took two of the three ST seats with 51.65 per cent vote with BJP taking the third for 30.22 per cent. JDS too polled 15.38 per cent but without success. BSP and CPI gathered an identical 1.1 per cent and SP half as much, but again in vain.

Electorate	:	1,10,38,691
Turnout	:	70,29,065
Turnout %	:	63.68%
Valid Votes	:	69,73,039
Invalid & Missing	:	56,026
Candidates	:	114

HARYANA

Seats: 10 (General: 8; SC: 2)

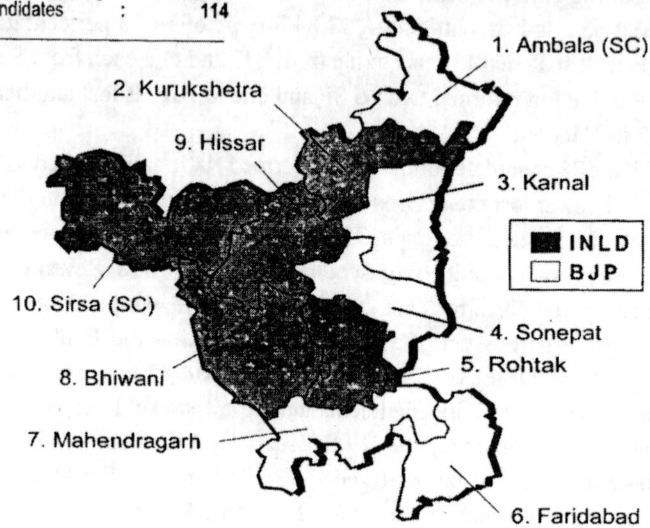

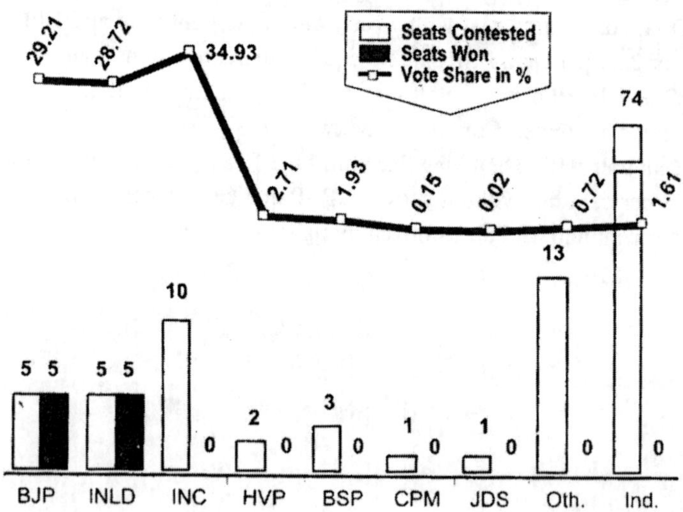

HARYANA

History: Tracing its history to Vedic times, Haryana was formed on November 1,1966 out of the Hindi-speaking areas of composite Punjab. Kurukshetra, the scene of the epic Mahabharata battle, is located in Haryana. Sub-Himalayan terrain and the Indo-Gangetic plain form its two natural areas.

Communities: Muslims 4%, Sikhs 7%, Scheduled Castes 20%. Communities include Jats, Sainis, Aroras/Khatris, Vaishyas/Banias and Gujjars. Balmikis, Chamars and Dhanuks are the principal scheduled castes.

Population (1991)	:	16,463,618
Area	:	44,212 sq km
Languages	:	Hindi, Punjabi
Capital	:	Chandigarh
Lok Sabha Seats	:	10 (SC 2)

Election 1999: BJP-INLD Combine Makes A Clean Sweep

BJP and its new found ally Om Prakash Chautala's Indian National Lok Dal (INLD) made a clean sweep of Haryana's ten seats thanks to Congress's flip-flop policy of first backing former chief minister Bansi Lal after BJP withdrew support to his government and then ditching him within a month. Thus, instead of gaining from the anti-incumbency factor, Congress even lost the three seats it had, two to BJP and one to INLD. This was despite a near nine per cent swing that raised its vote share from 26.02 to 34.93 per cent, 23 points lower than the BJP-INLD combine's total of 57.93 per cent.

Bansi Lal's Haryana Vikas Party, which had run a coalition with BJP for over two years before the saffron party switched sides in return for Chautala's backing at the Centre after HVP lost its clout in the 1998 Lok Sabha poll, yielded its lone seat to INLD. Its vote share dropped 8.89 points from 11.6 to 2.71 per cent.

HVP ally BSP too lost its only seat to BJP as its support fell 5.75 points from 7.68 to 1.93 per cent. Two candidates of CPM and JDS polled a minuscule 0.15 and 0.02 per cent, while 13 'others' and 74 independents shared 2.33 per cent. Winning five seats with 29.21 per cent, over ten points higher than the 18.89 it got last time, BJP gained four seats, two from Congress and one each from BSP and Chautala's

Haryana

Vote Share (in %)

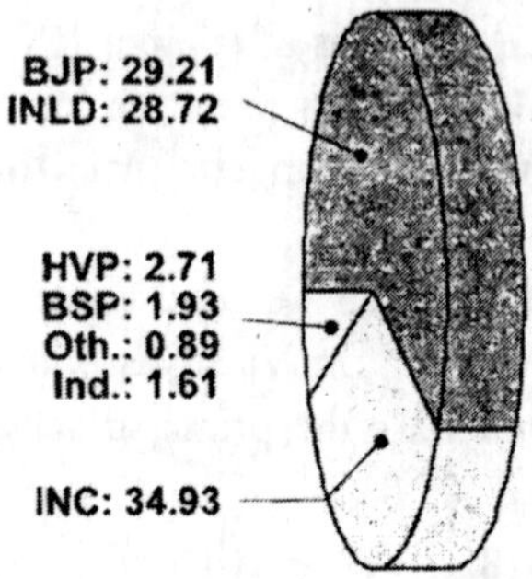

Seat Share (in %)

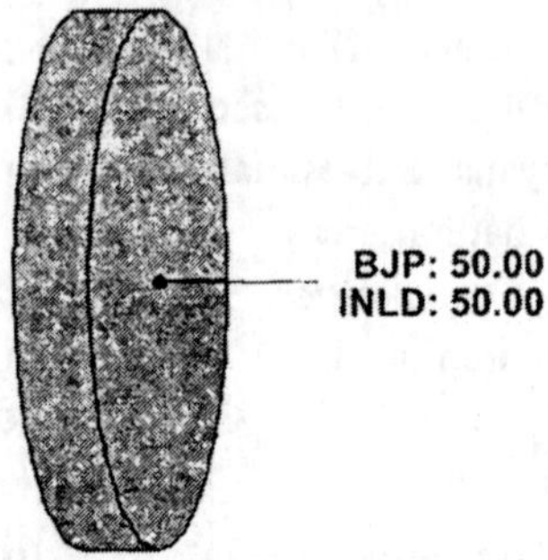

Swing %

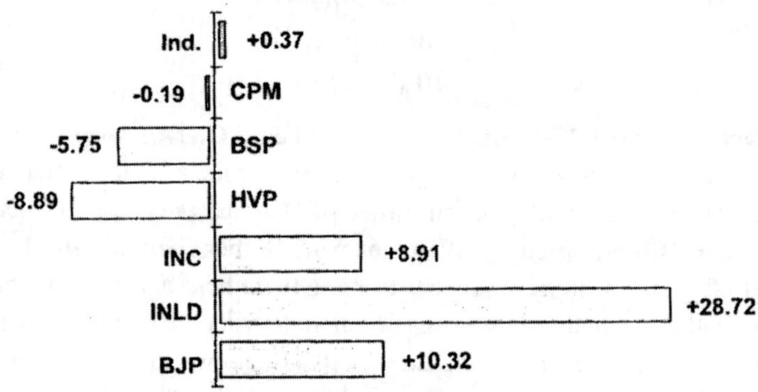

Gains & Losses

Party	Current Win	Prev. Win	Re-tained	Gained	Gained from	Lost	Lost to	Net
BJP	5	1	1	4	BSP-1, INC-2 HLDR-1	0	-	+4
INLD	5	0	0	5	INC-1, HVP-1 HLDR-3	0	-	+5
HLDR	0	4	0	0	-	4	INLD-3, BJP-1	-4
INC	0	3	0	0	-	3	BJP-2, INLD-1	-3
BSP	0	1	0	0	-	1	BJP-1	-1
HVP	0	1	0	0	-	1	INLD-1	-1
Total	10	10	1	9		9		0

party then going under the name of Haryana Lok Dal (Rashtriya). Ally INLD too won five seats for 28.72 per cent, one more than what his earlier party won for 25.90 per cent in 1998. It wrested a seat each from the Congress and HVP, while retaining three HLDR seats. Two SC seats were shared by BJP and INLD, with the first snatching Ambala from BSP, and the second taking the Sirsa seat it had won last time as HLDR.

Former Congress chief minister Bhajan Lal, who went out of power in the simultaneous assembly poll in 1996, lost Karnal by 147,854 votes to BJP's I.D. Swami, whom he had defeated by 52,061 votes in 1998. Haryana Congress chief Bhupinder Singh Hooda, who had thrice in a row defeated Chautala's father, 'Tau' Devi Lal, 85, a former deputy Prime Minister on his home turf of Rohtak since 1991, lost to little known Inder Singh of INLD by 1,44,693 votes.

Bansi Lal's son Surender Singh who had defeated his own brother and Chautala's son Ajay Chautala last time finished a distant third in Bhiwani with the junior Chautala trouncing Dharamvir of Congress by over two lakh votes.

BJP's Sudha Yadav, widow of a Kargil martyr, unseated Inderjit Singh of Congress in Mahendergarh and Kailasho Devi retained Kurukshetra for INLD instead of Chautala's old party. A third woman candidate contesting on the SP ticket lost her deposit in Rohtak.

In the 1967 poll, the first after the formation of the state, the Congress won seven of the nine seats with 44.1% votes. Two other seats were shared by the Bharatiya Jan Sangh and an independent. The Sangh and the independents polled a fifth of the votes each.

After the 1969 split in Congress, Indira Gandhi's Congress (I) won seven seats in 1971 as its votes went zooning up to 52.6%. The Congress (O) faction polled 11.3%, but a seat eluded it.

The Jan Sangh, which would re-emerge as the BJP in 1984, kept its seat though its vote share dropped to 11.2%, while a new Vishal Haryana Party won the remaining seat with 9.1% votes.

Congress (I) was completely swept away by the 1977 Janata wave failing to win even a single seat though it polled 18% votes. The Janata claimed all seats, now raised to ten, with a massive 70.4% mandate. The Vishal Haryana Party cornered 4.6% votes.

Congress (I) won back half the seats in 1980 with 32.6%. The Janata Party itself could win only one seat for 28.1% votes, while breakaway Janata Party Secular bagged four seats for 33.5% votes. The Congress made a clean sweep in 1984 as its vote share soared to its highest ever of 55%. Jan Sangh now in its BJP incarnation polled 7.5%, while Lok Dal polled 19.1%. The Congress decline began in 1989 when its tally dropped to four for 46.2% votes as the newly formed Janata Dal bagged six for 38.9%. BJP failed to win a seat though it polled 8.3% votes. Congress staged a comeback in 1991 wining all but Bhiwani, which went to Bansi Lal's HVP.

Key Contests

Bhiwani. Bansi Lal, chief minister during 1968-75 and 1986-87, won thrice from Bhiwani since 1980 as a Congress nominee. In 1996 his son Surender Singh defeated Jangbir Singh, who won on HVP ticket in 1991 but switched over to the Congress before the poll.

Rohtak. Former deputy prime Minister Devi Lal was elected from both Rohtak and Sikar in Rajasthan in 1989, but kept Sikar. In 1991 and again in 1996 he was defeated by Bhupendra Singh of the Congress.

Kurukshetra. Gulzari Lal Nanda, twice interim Prime Minister, won from here in 1967 and 1971, when it was called Kaithal.

Faridabad. The constituency with most Muslims in Haryana (25%) was represented by Maulana Abul Kalam Azad in 1957 when it formed part of the Gurgaon seat.

HIMACHAL PRADESH

History. Formed as a centrally administered territory on April 15, 1948 with the merger of 30 former hill states of Punjab, it became a Part C state in 1951. Some more hilly areas of Punjab were added to it in November 1966. It became the 18th state of India on January 25, 1971.

Communities. Muslims and Sikhs under 2%, Scheduled Castes 25%, Scheduled Tribes 5%. Communities include Rajputs and Ghiraths. Chamars and Koris are the major Scheduled Castes while the Gaddis are predominant among Scheduled Tribes.

Population (1991)	:	5,170,877
Area	:	55,673 sq km
Languages	:	Hindi, Pahari
Capital	:	Shimla
Lok Sabha Seats	:	4 (SC 1)

Election 1999 : BJP Consolidates its Hold

BJP consolidated its hold on the hill state a year after coming to power as it made a clean sweep of all the four seats in alliance with scam tainted former communications minister Sukh Ram's Himachal Vikas Congress (HVC). Despite an adverse swing of 5.16 per cent that reduced its share from 51.43 to 46.27 per cent, BJP retained its three seats. While former BJP chief minister Shanta Kumar held on to the Kangra seat he had regained from the Congress in 1998, party colleagues Suresh Chandel and Maheshwar Singh kept the Hamirpur and Mandi seats.

Ally HVC wrested the fourth Shimla seat from the Congress with Lt Col Dhani Ram Shandil of HVC defeating his Congress rival by 46,930 votes as the latter's overall vote share went down by 2.38 points to 39.52 per cent. Congress had won all the four seats in 1996, but was left with only one in 1998 when it was also dislodged from power in the simultaneous assembly poll, held nine months before term.

Maheshwar Singh won the Mandi seat for BJP with the highest margin of 131,025 votes. He had taken the seat for the party with a similar margin in June 1998 after Sukh Ram, who played the kingmaker in the state with his four MLAs after the February poll, retired from the contest. Ram had won the seat for the Congress thrice since 1984.

HVC finished third in the popularity stakes polling 12.37 per cent, up 8.80 points, of the vote pie. The remaining 1.84 per cent was shared

Electorate	:	37,76,547
Turnout	:	21,49,712
Turnout %	:	56.92%
Valid Votes	:	21,33,704
Invalid & Missing	:	16,008
Candidates	:	22

HIMACHAL PRADESH

Seats: 4 (General: 3; SC: 1)

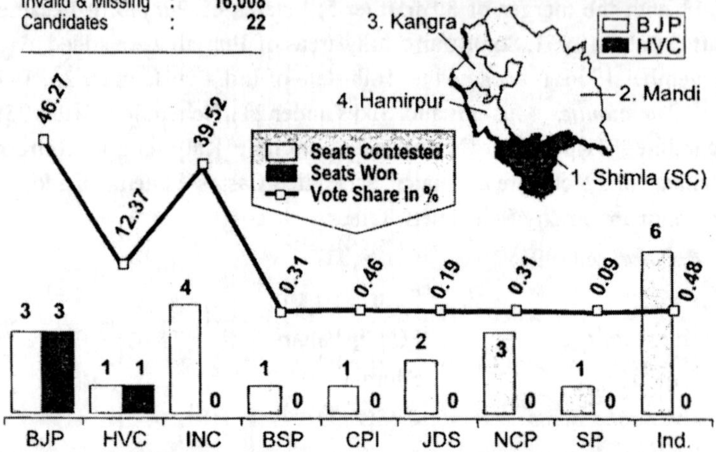

Vote & Seat Share

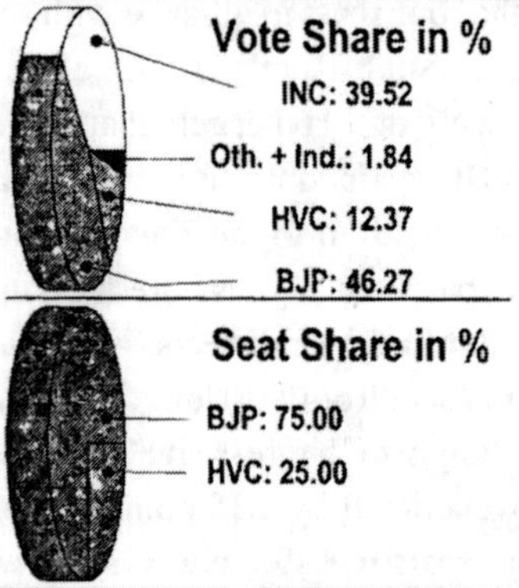

Swing %

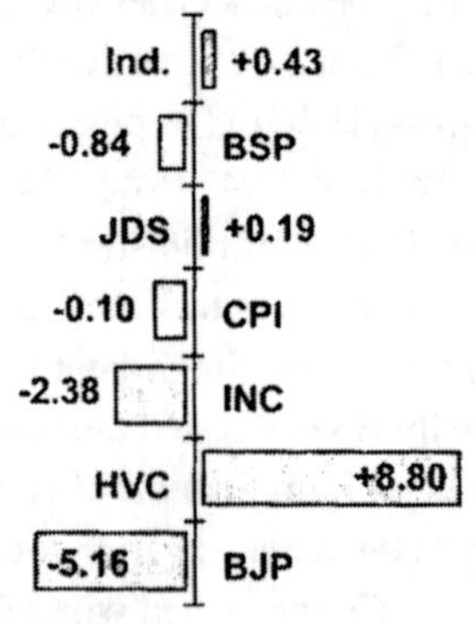

Gains & Losses

Party	Current Win	Prev. Win	Re-tained	Gained	Gained from	Lost	Lost to	Net
BJP	3	3	3	0	-	0	-	0
HVC	1	0	0	1	INC-1	0	-	+1
INC	0	1	0	0	-	1	HVC-1	-1
Total	4	4	3	1		1		0

by CPI (0.46 per cent), BSP and NCP (0.31 per cent each), JDS (0.19 per cent) and SP (0.09 per cent) besides five independents (0.48 per cent).

BJP, which had polled 42.58 per cent in the lone SC seat last time left it to ally HVC to do the battle in Shimla. In a six-cornered contest, HVC polling 52.77 per cent as against a mere 4.05 per cent in 1998 wrested it from the Congress even as it raised its share by 1.31 points to 43.89 per cent. Rest of the 3.84 per cent SC vote was shared by CPI (1.96 per cent), JDS (0.60 per cent), NCP (0.43 per cent) and an independent woman candidate (0.81). Excepting eight candidates of the Congress, BJP and HVC all other 14 lost their deposits. These included the lone woman candidate Asha Chauhan contesting as an independent in Shimla.

Unni 1977 Congress had been making a clean sweep in Himachal with its vote share ranging between 47.3% in 1957 and 75.8% in 1971, two years after the Congress split. But the Congress (I) lost all the seats in the Janata tide of 1977 even though 38.6% still voted for it. The Janata then cornered 57.2%. Congress recovered all the four seats in 1980 raising its vote share to 52.1% and repeated the performance in 1984 with its vote share soaring to 67.6%. However, it lost three seats to BJP in 1989 in the face of an over 15% swing that saw its vote share reduced to 42%. Bharatiya Jan Sangh made its presence felt for the first time in 1952 when it won 10.7% votes. Its share was more than halved in 1971, but the party bounced back in its BJP incarnation to gradually increase its vote share from 10.6% in 1980 to an all time high of 45.3% in 1989 when it won three seats as well. The Janata Dal in its first outing in 1989 won 7.19% votes and saw it reduced to 6.97% in 1991 and less than half a per cent five years later.

Key Contests

Kangra. BJP leader Shanta Kumar won from here in 1989, but resigned next year to become chief minister. He contested again in 1996, but lost to Sat Mahajan of the Congress.

Mandi. Former chief minister Virbhadra Singh won it for the Congress in 1971 and 1980. Former union minister, Sukh Ram took it for the party in 1984, only to lose it in 1989. He wrested it in 1991 and retained it in 1996.

JAMMU & KASHMIR

Seats: 6 (General: 6)

Electorate	:	50,24,427
Turnout	:	16,26,908
Turnout %	:	32.38%
Valid Votes	:	15,70,771
Invalid & Missing	:	56,137
Candidates	:	83

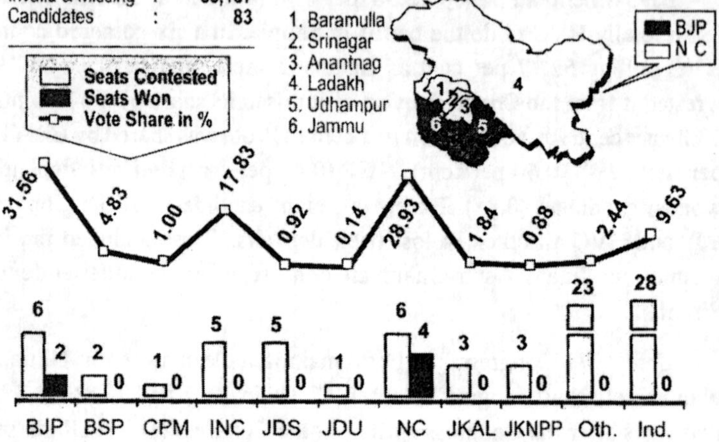

Vote & Seat Share

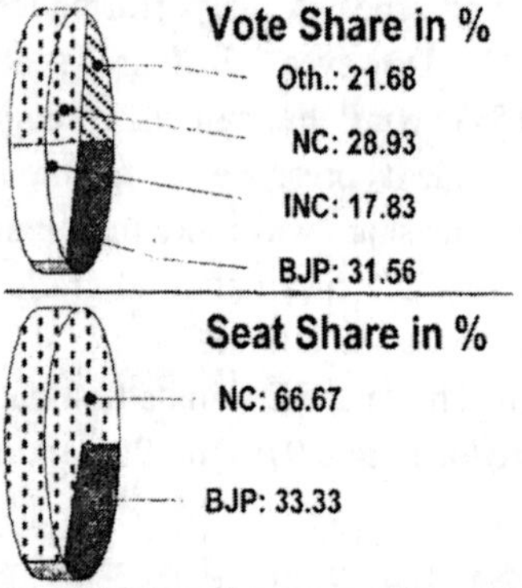

Swing %

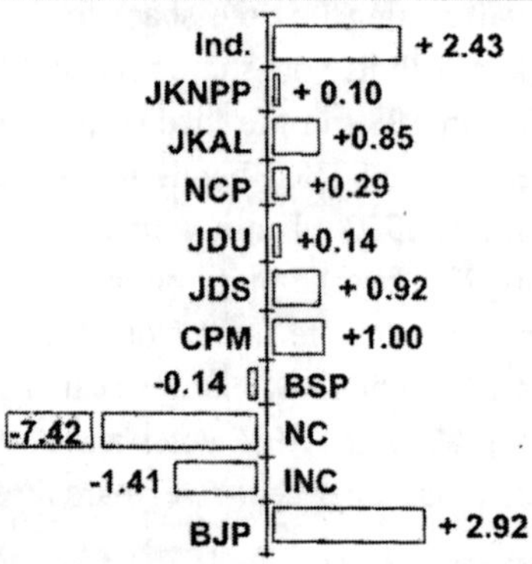

Gains & Losses

Party	Current Win	Prev. Win	Re-tained	Gained	Gained from	Lost	Lost to	Net
BJP	2	2	2	0	-	0	-	0
INC	0	1	0	0	-	1	NC-1	-1
NC	4	3	3	1	INC-1	0	-	+1
Total	6	6	5	1	-	1	-	0

JAMMU AND KASHMIR

History. Known as the paradise on earth for its scenic beauty Kashmir was a part of the Mughal empire under Akbar. After a period of Afghan rule, it was annexed by Ranjit Singh, the Sikh ruler of Punjab in 1819. Next year he handed over Jammu to Gulab Singh. Kashmir too was made over to him in 1846 after the battle of Sabraon. The State acceded to India on October 26, 1947 after an armed attack from Pakistan. A part of it is still under Pakistani occupation.

Communities. Hindus 33%, Muslims 65%, Scheduled Castes 9%. Pandits form the principal Hindu community. Meghs, whose main occupation are weaving and leather work, are the predominant SCs.

Population (1991 projected)	:	7,718,700
Area	:	222,236 sq km
Languages	:	Kashmiri, Urdu, Dogri, Ladakhi
Capital	:	Srinagar (summer), Jammu (winter)
Lok Sabha Seats	:	6—Jammu 2, Kashmir 3, Ladakh 1

Election 1999 : Abdullah Does One Better

The National Conference of Chief Minister Farooq Abdullah, which had won half of the six seats in 1998 on return to the poll fray after its 1996 boycott, did one better dislodging Congress from Anantnag to oust it from the valley. And in the foothills, BJP retained its Udhampur and Jammu seats, to make the Congress eclipse complete in the picturesque state, which went to the polls in the shadow of the gun. The poll in Anantnag was postponed by a couple of weeks after BJP candidate Ghulam Haider Noorani was killed in a mine blast. National Conference again topped the popularity stakes picking up all the four seats in the valley, one gained from Congress, despite an adverse over seven per cent swing that pushed its vote share down to 28.93 per cent. Helped by a near three per cent swing, BJP saw its share rising to 31.56 per cent, but its tally of two remained unchanged as its four losing candidates could not even save their deposits. A 1.41 point anti-Congress swing reduced its vote share to 17.83 per cent as former Janata Dal union home minister, Mufti Mohamad Sayeed, deserted it again. Sayeed, who had won Anantnag for it after coming back to the party in 1998, formed his own People's Democratic Party. Sayeed lost his seat to Ali Mohammad Naik of NC by 13,492 votes, while another former union minister Maqbool Dar, who had won the seat for JD in 1996 finished fifth as a JDU candidate.

BSP put up two instead of four candidates and still managed to poll almost as many votes—4.83 per cent as against 4.97 per cent last time, but both lost their deposits. Two local outfits, J&K Awami League and J&K National Panthers Party took away 2.72 per cent. The remaining 14.13 per cent vote was shared by CPM (one per cent), JDS (0.92 per cent), JDU (0.14 per cent), and 23 others (2.44 per cent) besides 28 independents (9.63 per cent). Vishno Datt Sharma of BJP trounced his NC rival Rajinder Singh Chib by 142,019 votes in Jammu, the highest in state. But chief minister Abdullah's son Omer Abdullah defeated Mufti Sayeed's daughter Mehbooba contesting as an independent after father and daughter broke away from Congress, by 36,859 votes in Srinagar.

Prof Saif-ud-din Soz, who parted company with NC on the issue of backing the BJP led coalition, finished fourth as an independent in the Baramulla seat he had won four times in a row in the past, despite the backing of Congress and CPM. Former party colleague Abdul Rashid Shaheen kept it for NC. Of the 83 candidates in fray, 68, including 25 independents and 14 nominees of six national parties, lost their deposits. All the six women candidates too could not save theirs.

Kashmir used to nominate its representatives to the Lok Sabha until 1967 when the first elections were held. The Congress won five of the six seats then with 50.5% and repeated the feat in 1971 polling 54.1%—its best as yet. But the Congress conceded two seats to the NC in 1977 as its vote share dropped to its lowest ever of 16.4%. It gave up two more seats in 1980 even as it polled 18.7% to recover a bit of its votes. Winning back two seats in 1984, the Congress raised its vote share to 30.2% in 1984 and 38.9% in 1989 even as it lost a seat.

Rival National Conference had won three seats in each of the three previous elections with its highest ever vote in 1984 when it polled 46.2%. Its lowest came five years later when it polled 6.8% votes, but still won three seats with Srinagar seat coming its way uncontested and a poor turnout in Anantnag and Baramulla.

Among other vote getters, the Janata Party polled 8.2% in1977 and 8.6% in 1980, but a seat eluded it. The Urs faction of the Congress won a seat in 1980, with 14.5% votes.

Key Contests

Baramulla. NC leader Saifuddin Soz won it in 1984 and 1989. In 1996 PCC president Ghulam Rasool Kar defeated an independent backed by a surrendered militant group.

Srinagar. Bakshi Ghulam Mohammed, Prime Minister of the state from 1953 to 1963, won it as an NC nominee in 1967. Sheikh Abdullah's widow won it in 1977 and his son Farooq Abdullah got it uncontested in 1980. In 1996 Mir Magami of the Congress scraped through beating Farooq Ahmad Indrabi of the Janata Dal by just 1,599 votes.

PUNJAB

Seats: 13 (General: 10; SC: 3)

Electorate	:	1,56,91,898
Turnout	:	88,21,396
Turnout %	:	56.22%
Valid Votes	:	87,54,530
Invalid & Missing	:	66,866
Candidates	:	120

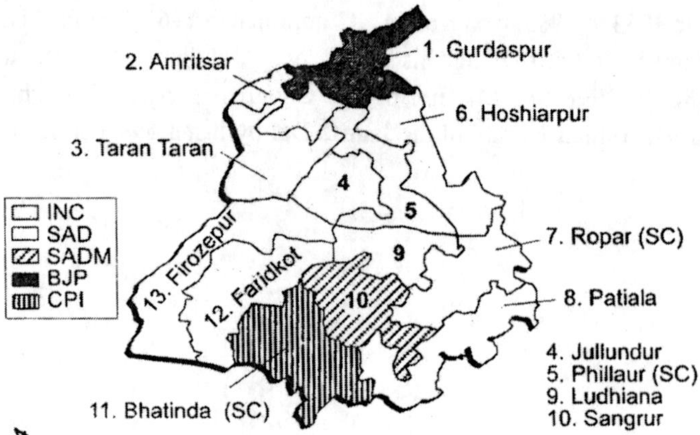

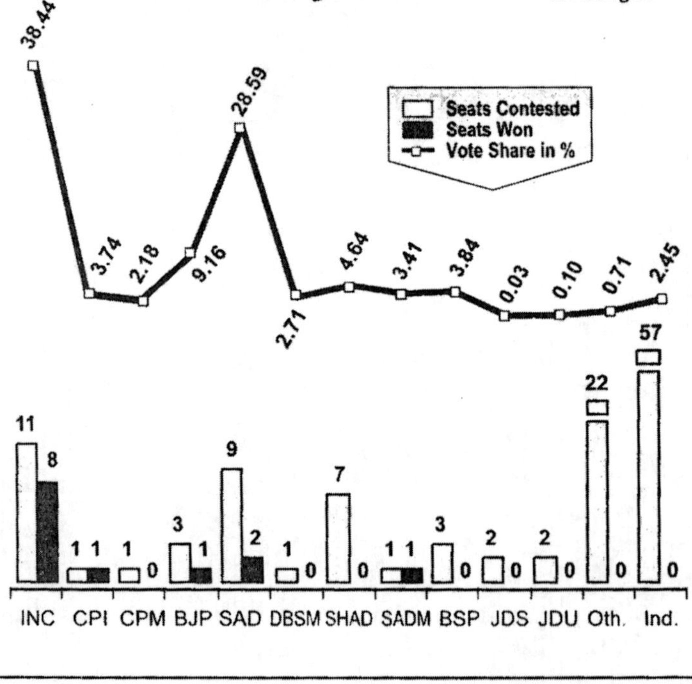

PUNJAB

History. Punjab, the land of seven rivers, was annexed by the British in 1849 and made a separate province in 1937. At the time of partition, Punjab was divided between India and Pakistan. Patiala and East Punjab States Union (PEPSU) was integrated with it on Nov. 1, 1956. Ten years later it was divided into two states Punjab and Haryana, sharing a common capital, Chandigarh.

Communities. Hindus 37%, Sikhs 61%, Scheduled Castes 27%, Communities include Aroras, Khatris and Jats. Adi Dharmis, Balmikis, Dumnas/Mahashas and Majhabis are the principal Scheduled Castes.

Population (1991)	:	20,281,969
Area	:	50,362 sq km
Languages	:	Punjabi, Hindi
Capital	:	Chandigarh
Lok Sabha Seats	:	13 (SC 3)

Election 1999: Congress on Comeback Trail

A row between chief minister Parkash Singh Badal and long time Shiromani Gurdwara Parbandhak Committee president Gurcharan Singh Tohra, an anti-incumbency wave and an over 14 per cent swing, helped Congress and its Left allies capture nine of the 13 seats in the land of five rivers. Polling 44.36 per cent in the border state, where it had been completely wiped out only last year, the Congress-led front left only three seats to the SAD-BJP-DBSM combine with 40.46 per cent votes, and one to a United Front floated by Tohra, including his Sarbhind Shiromani Akali Dal and three other Akali factions besides BSP with 11.89 per cent votes.

The Congress, which had drawn a blank once earlier in the face of 'Janata' wave in 1977, won the lion's share of eight seats with 38.44 per cent, 12.59 points more than last time, while CPI wrested the Bhatinda (SC) seat from Badal's Akali Dal with 3.74 per cent, up 0.34 points, but CPM could not win the Sangrur seat although it added 2.18 per cent, up 1.12 points, votes to the alliance kitty. Four of Congress gains came from Badal's party, two from BJP and one from an independent in Phillaur (SC), while it wrested Jalandhar won for JD last time by former Prime Minister Inder Kumar Gujral with the backing of SAD and its ally BJP.

Punjab

Vote Share (in %)

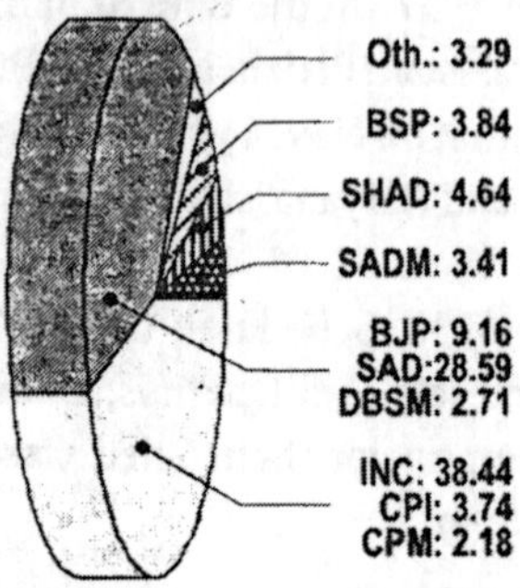

Seat Share (in %)

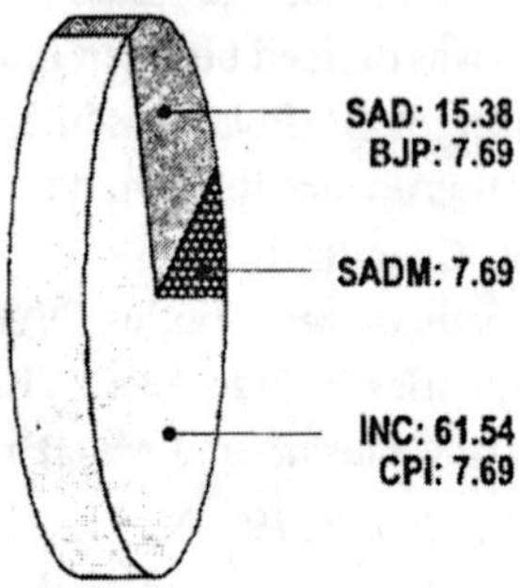

Swing %

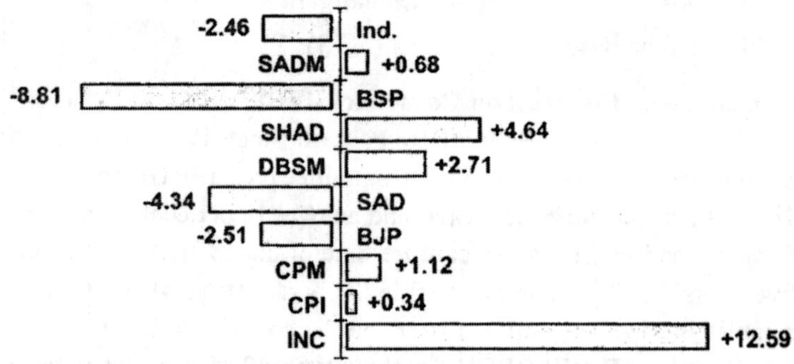

Gains & Losses

Party	Current Win	Prev. Win	Re-tained	Gained	Gained from	Lost	Lost to	Net
SADM	1	0	0	1	SAD-1	0	-	+1
BJP	1	3	1	0	-	2	INC-2	-2
INC	8	0	0	8	BJP-2, JD-1 SAD-4, IND-1	0	-	+8
JD	0	1	0	0	-	1	INC-1	-1
CPI	1	0	0	1	SAD-1	0	-	+1
SAD	2	8	2	0	-	6	INC-4, CPI-1 SADM-1	-6
IND	0	1	0	0	-	1	INC-1	-1
Total	13	13	3	10		10		0

With SAD no longer willing to support him, Gujral did not contest this time.

In the rival alliance, SAD polling 28.59 per cent, 4.34 points less, managed to hold on to only two of the eight seats it had, yielding six to Congress and one to CPI besides losing Sangrur to Simranjit Singh Mann, leading another Akali faction. Mann avenged his 1998 defeat at the hands of union minister Surjit Singh Barnala by trouncing him by 86,317 votes. Ally BJP with 9.16 per cent votes, 2.51 points less, lost two of its three seats, both to Congress, with only film star Vinod Khanna, who had won with over one lakh votes last time, managing to hold on to Gurdaspur with just 1,399 votes. He again squeaked past five times Congress MP, Sukhbans Kaur Bhinder. Another ally, Democratic Bahujan Samaj Morcha lost Phillaur (SC) seat won by its nominee Satnam Singh Kainth as an independent last time, but it added 2.71 per cent to the alliance share.

In the third 'United Front', Tohra's party collected 4.64 per cent votes in seven seats, but could not win any. BSP gathered 3.84 per cent, less than a third of its 1998 share of 12.65 per cent, again without success. In winning, Mann alone gave the UF 3.41 per cent votes, 0.68 points more than his four candidates got last time.

The remaining 3.29 per cent of the vote pie was shared by 83 others. All the 57 independents as also all the seven candidates of Tohra party and two of BSP were among the 92 deposit losers. In the three SC constituencies, Congress taking two, topped with 29.95 per cent with CPI bringing in 16.61 per cent to win the third. SAD share dropped ten points from 36.16 per cent as it lost two seats. Ally DBSM lost the third seat even as it collected 12 per cent SC vote. In the third front, Tohra's party took 8.15 per cent, while BSP's share dropped from 28 to 4.79 per cent. Besides Barnala, Badal's son Sukhbir Singh, who too had found a berth in the last Vajpayee government, lost in Faridkot. So did Prabhjot Kaur, widow of former Rajasthan governor Darbara Singh in Jalandhar. Punjab BJP chief Daya Singh Sodhi lost to former Congress union minister R L Bhatia in Amritsar.

'Maharani' Parneet Kaur, wife of Punjab Congress chief and scion of Patiala house, won Patiala leaving a Tohra loyalist Prem Singh Chandumajra trailing in the third place. Kaur and Santosh Chowdhary of the Congress, who won the Phillaur (SC) seat, were the only two of the 14 women candidates to get elected.

Before the division of Punjab, Congress did its best in 1957 winning 21 of the 22 seats with 51.3% and its worst five years later when it lost seven seats in the face of a ten per cent swing against it. In 1967 after the separation of Haryana, the Congress won 9 of the 13 seats with 37.3% raising it to 10 with 46% in 1971. But the Congress lost it all to the Akali Dal-Janata combine in 1977 though it still polled 34.9% votes. Making a recovery in 1980, the Congress put in its best performance winning 12 seats with 52.5%. The 1985 poll, 15 months after Operation Blue Star, saw its seats slashed by half as it votes slumped to 37.6%. But the worst was to come in 1989 when it could win only two seats for an all-time low of 26.5% votes.

Congress faced its first serious challenge from the Akalis in 1971 when they polled 30.9% votes, though winning only one seat. Raising it to 42.3% in 1977 they won nine seats in their second best performance so far. By 1980 their vote share plunged by about 20 points to 23.4% and they were left with only one seat. Bouncing back in 1985 they won seven seats for 37.2%. But in 1989 it was the Mann faction of the Dal which won six seats for 29.2%. Before this Sant Fateh Singh faction of the Akali Dal won three seats for 22.6% in 1967.

The BJP won its first seat in 1998 with its forerunner Jan Sangh getting one for 12.5% in 1967. The Sangh had won three in 1962 in the composite state with 15.2%. The highest it polled was in 1957 when it got 16% votes without a seat.

The JD won a seat in 1989 with 5.46% votes. The CPI got one in 1957 with 16.8% and two in 1971 with 6.2%, while the CPI(M) won its only seat in 1977 with 4.9%.

Key Contests

Hoshiarpur. In 1996, BSP leader Kanshi Ram defeated Kamal Choudhary of the Congress by 10,946 votes. Choudhary had defeated Mayawati who became UP chief minister in 1995, in 1991.

Zail Singh, who became President in 1982, was elected from Hoshiarpur in 1980.

Ludhiana. Jaswant Kaur, widow of slain chief minister Beant Singh, of the Congress lost to Amrik Singh Aliwal of the Akali Dal in 1996.

Her defeat sparked off a row in Punjab Congress with detractors of chief minister Harcharan Singh Brar accusing him of sabotaging Jaswant Kaur's election. Prominent Akali leader Jagdev Singh Talwandi was elected from here in 1977.

Electorate	:	3,10,76,825
Turnout	:	1,67,45,717
Turnout %	:	53.88%
Valid Votes	:	1,65,70,177
Invalid & Missing	:	1,75,540
Candidates	:	165

RAJASTHAN

Seats: 25 (General: 18; SC: 4; ST: 3)

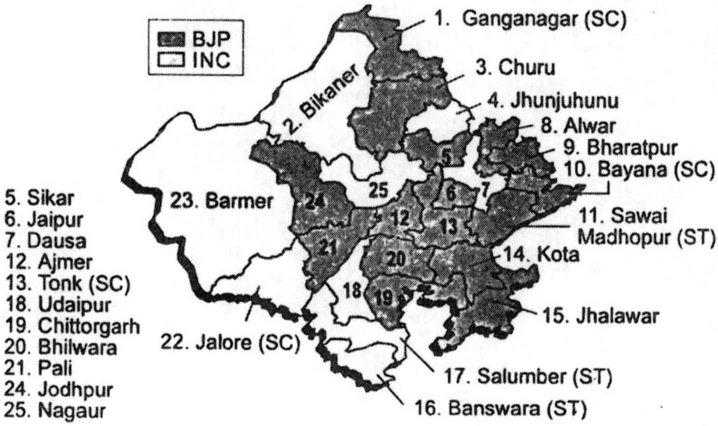

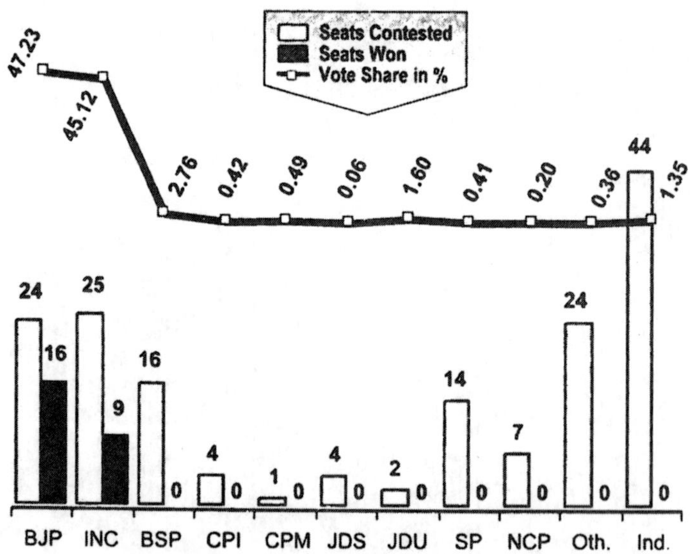

RAJASTHAN

History. Formed with the amalgamation of 19 former princely states, Rajasthan in its present form came into being on Novermber 1, 1956. The process of integration began on March 17, 1948 with four princely states forming the Matsya Union and ended with Ajmer joining the desert state.

Communities. Muslims 8%, Jains 2%, Scheduled Castes 22%, Scheduled Tribes 17%. Communities include Jats, Vaishyas, and Rajputs. Chamars, Meghwals and Balais are major Scheduled Castes. Minas and Bhils are dominant Scheduled Tribes.

Population (1991)	:	44,005,990
Area	:	342,239 sq km
Languages	:	Rajasthani, Hindi
Capital	:	Jaipur
Lok Sabha Seats	:	25 (SC 4, ST 3)

Election 1999: Desert State Deserts Congress

An anti-incumbency wave coupled with Jat disenchantment, did the Congress in, only year and a half after it won 18 of the 25 seats in a spectacular repeat of its 1980 performance in the state. A minor 0.67 per cent swing in its favour notwithstanding, the party's share of seats was slashed to just half as many. But Vajpayee, Kargil and Pokhran, generated a much stronger 5.58 per cent swing for rival BJP to help it raise its seat share from five to sixteen less than a year after it was ousted from power in the November 1998 Assembly elections.

Polling 45.12 per cent as against 44.45 in the February 1998 Lok Sabha poll, Congress lost a dozen seats to BJP but recovered one from it while former union ministers Buta Singh and Sis Ram Ola, now back in Congress retained their Jalore (SC) and Jhunjhunu seats. Denied a ticket by the Congress, Buta Singh contested as an independent in 1998, while Ola made a one-man Congress (S) outfit after the return of the breakaway Tiwari faction to the party fold.

Former Lok Sabha speaker Balram Jakhar shifting from Bikaner to Sikar lost by 28,173 votes to sitting BJP member Subhash Mehariya. Former chief minister Jagannath Pahadia suffered defeat in Bayana, while former Congress minister Natwar Singh's son Jagat Singh lost his father's Bharatpur seat by 97,018 votes. Congress also lost Jodhpur, earlier represented by chief minister Ashok Gehlot five times since 1980 by

Rajasthan

Vote Share (in %)

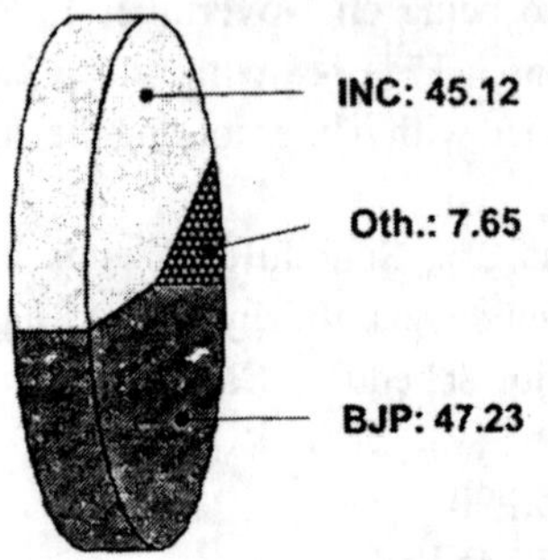

Seat Share (in %)

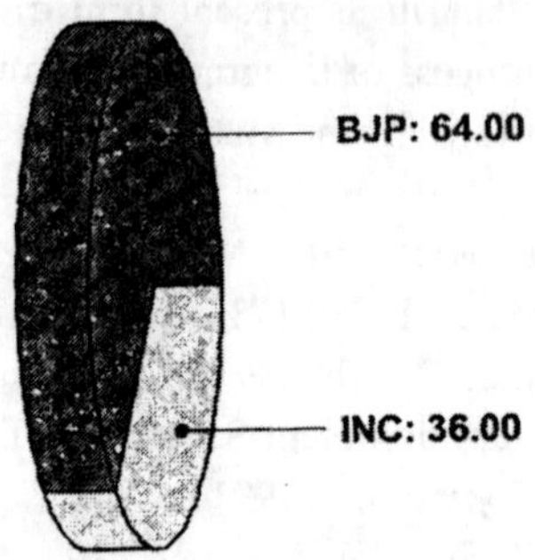

Swing %

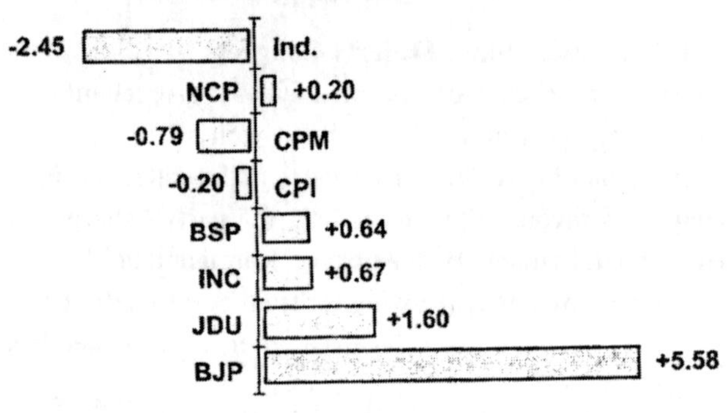

Gains & Losses

Party	Current Win	Prev. Win	Re-tained	Gained	Gained from	Lost	Lost to	Net
AIICS	0	1	0	0	-	1	INC-1	-1
BJP	16	5	4	12	INC-12	1	INC-1	+11
INC	9	18	6	3	AIICS-1, BJP-1 IND-1	12	BJP-12	-9
IND	0	1	0	0	-	1	INC-1	-1
Total	25	25	10	15		15		0

113,287 votes. Only senior Congress leader Rajesh Pilot retained Dausa, while state Congress chief Girija Vyas won back Udaipur.

The only major loss for BJP was the defeat of national vice president Bangaru Laxman at the hands of Buta Singh in Jalore though he managed to reduce the margin of Singh's victory from 1.66 lakh to 35,924. Minister of State for external Affairs, Vasundhara Raje and Girdhari Lal Bhargava won Jhalawar and Jaipur for the fifth time in a row since 1989. Raje's margin of victory at 152,415 was the highest in the state followed by that of Bhargava with 141,790.

External Affairs Minister Jaswant Singh, who had lost in 1998 in Chittorgarh, from where he had won twice in the past, did not contest this time having come to Rajya Sabha in the meantime. But his son Manavendra Singh, a journalist who has worked in the Territorial Army, lost his maiden contest in Barmer to Col. Sona Rama Chowdhury of Congress by 32,140 votes.

The remaining 7.65 per cent of the vote pie was shared by BSP (2.76), JDU (1.60), CPM (0.49), CPI (0.42), SP (0.41) and NCP (0.20). Four JDS candidates polled a minuscule 0.06 per cent besides 24 others and 44 independents taking 1.71 per cent. Except BJP and Congress, candidates of all other parties lost deposits. Among the 114 who could not save their deposits were 44 independents, 15 nominees of BSP, 14 of SP, seven of NCP, four of CPI and a CPM candidate.

In the four SC seats, BJP polled 50.14 per cent as against 38.26 per cent last time to win three seats. The Congress polled nearly seven per cent more votes to raise its SC share from 37.15 to 44.13 per cent, but could win only Jalore, losing the two other seats it had won last time. The remaining 5.73 per cent SC vote was shared by BSP (2.62), NCP (0.42), SP (0.35) and independents (0.85).

Congress won two of the three ST constituencies, polling 51.73 per cent as against a little over 50 per cent last time, but lost Sawai Madhopur to BJP. The latter polled 30.02 per cent, 6.22 points down from 1998, while ally JDU brought in 15.34 per cent to raise the alliance total to 45.36 per cent. The rest of 2.71 per cent ST vote was shared by CP (1.35), BSP (0.97), SP (0.39). Only three of the 15 women candidates succeeded including Vasundhra Raje of BJP from Jhalawar and Girija Vyas of Congress from Udaipur.

The Congress did its best in 1984 when it swept clean all the 25 seats with 52.7% votes. Its worst came only five years later as it lost all the seats facing a near 16 per cent negative swing slashing its vote share down to 37%. In terms of votes, 1977 was even worse. Polling just 30.6%, it could save only one seat as the Janata tide in the north swept away the other 24 with a record 65.2% voter support. The Congress polled its highest in 1957 when it won 19 seats with 53.6% votes.

BJP's forerunner Jan Sangh joining battle in 1952 with one seat for three per cent had gradually raised its tally to four for 12.4% by 1971. As BJP, it failed to win a seat in 1984 though it polled 23.7%. Coming into its own in 1989, BJP wrested 13 from the Congress thanks to a six-point swing in its favour. Two years later contesting all the 25 seats on its own, BJP lost a seat but raised its vote share to 40.88%. It overtook the Congress in 1996 polling its highest of 42.36%, but could not increase its tally of 12.

After its 1977 victory, the Janata Party saw its tally reduced to four for 31.7% in 1980 before fading into oblivion. The Janata Dal too after its initial success in 1989, when it won 11 seats for 25.68% votes, has not had any luck. Its vote share too has come down from 6.16% in 1991 to just 2.63%.

Success has eluded the CPI so far though it polled 4.8% in 1957. The CPI(M) won its only seat—Bikaner—in 1989 with 2.1% vote.

Earlier the Swatantra Party had a bit of success in 1967 when it won eight seats for 27%. Independents did pretty well in the first poll in 1952 when they won six seats for 29.2%. Karni Singh won a record five times in a row as an independent from 1952 to 1971 from Bikaner.

Key Contests

Chittorgarh. Jaswant Singh, who served as finance minister in BJP's short-lived government at the centre won for the second time from here in 1996, but lost in 1998.

Dausa. Former union minister Rajesh Pilot won for the fifth time from Dausa in 1999. He represented Bharatpur in 1980 and shifted to Dansa in 1989.

Nagaur. Nathu Ram Mirdha of the Congress won from here for the sixth time in 1996. He was the only Congress candidate to win from Rajasthan in 1977. The one time he lost was in 1984 when he contested on the Lok Dal ticket.

UTTAR PRADESH

Seats: 85 (General: 67; SC: 18)

Electorate	:	10,30,11,967
Turnout	:	5,50,78,345
Turnout %	:	53.47%
Valid Votes	:	5,40,83,249
Invalid & Missing	:	9,95,096
Candidates	:	1,208

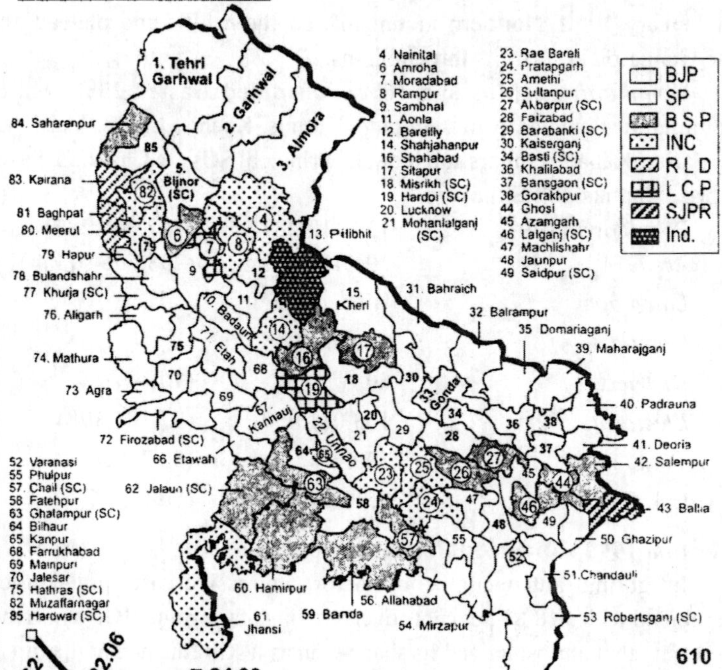

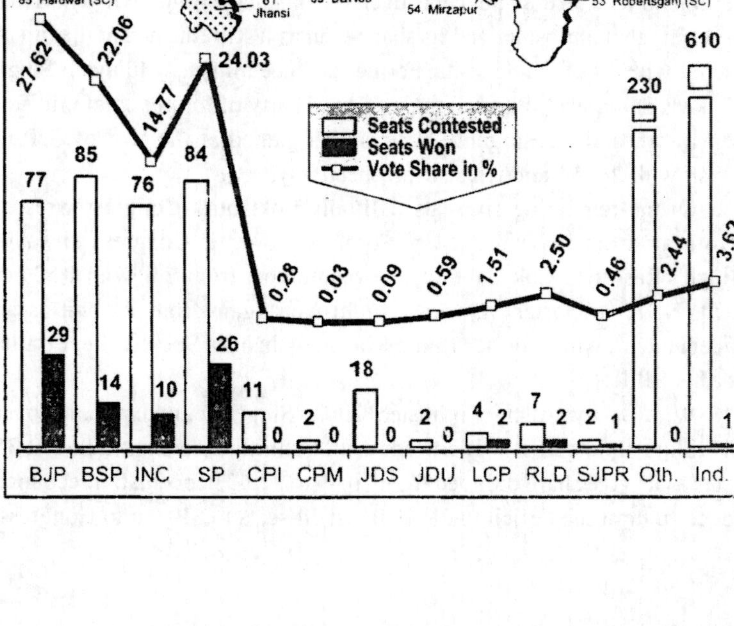

UTTAR PRADESH

History. India's most populous state, but ranking fourth in area, was formed by the British combining Agra and Oudh in 1877. Its name was shortened to United Provinces in 1935. It was renamed as Uttar Pradesh in January 1950. Northern mountains, southern hills and plateau and the Ganga plain form its three regions.

Communities. Muslims 16%, Scheduled Castes 23%. Major communities include Ahirs, Rajputs, Kurmis, Kachis, Lodhs, Vaishyas, Gadarias, Kahars, Gujjars and Kewats. Principal SCs are Chamars, Pasis, Koris, Khatiks and Shilpkars.

Population (1991)	:	139,112,287	(132,067,287)
Area	:	294,411 sq km	(238,566 sq km)
Languages	:	Hindi, Urdu	
Capital	:	Lucknow	
Districts	:	80	(70)
Electorate (99)	:	103,011,967	(97,184,398)
Turnout	:	53.47%	(53.75%)
Lok Sabha Seats	:	85-SC 18	(80-SC 17)

Election 1999 : Divided BJP Helps Opposition

Infighting, anti-incumbency factor, aggressive caste polarisation combined with an 8.87 per cent adverse swing, gave ruling BJP a massive drubbing that almost halved its share even as it still finished at the top of the lot with 29 of the 85 seats. Former defence minister Mulayam Singh Yadav's Samajwadi Party, Bahujan Samaj Party of former chief minister Mayawati, and a resurgent Congress, all gained at the cost of BJP to finish with 26, 14 and ten seats, respectively.

Of the remaining six seats, BJP ally Loktantrik Congress wrested two seats from SP with 1.51 per cent votes, while Congress ally Ajit Singh's Rashtriya Lok Dal took an even number from BJP with 2.50 per cent. NDA supporter Maneka Gandhi won again from Pilibhit as an independent, while former Prime Minister Chandra Shekhar kept Ballia for his SJPR.

With Backward chief minister Kalyan Singh facing dissidence over his ruling style and at loggerheads with Central leadership, BJP lost 35 seats as its vote share dropped from 36.49 to 27.62 per cent, but recouped seven to limit the deficit to 28. BJP lost 14 seats to SP, ten to Congress,

Uttar Pradesh

Vote Share (in %)

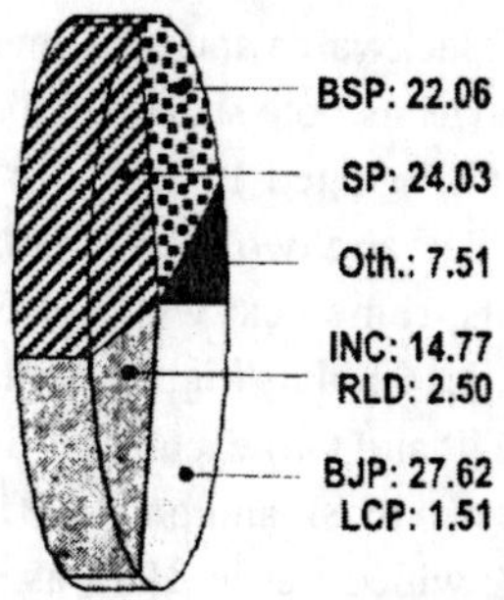

Seat Share (in %)

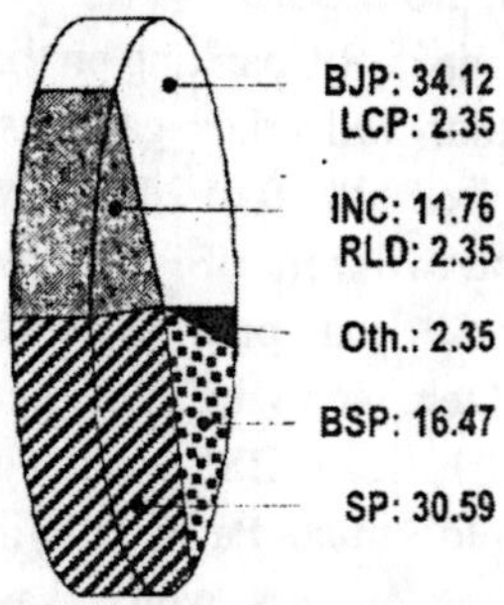

Swing %

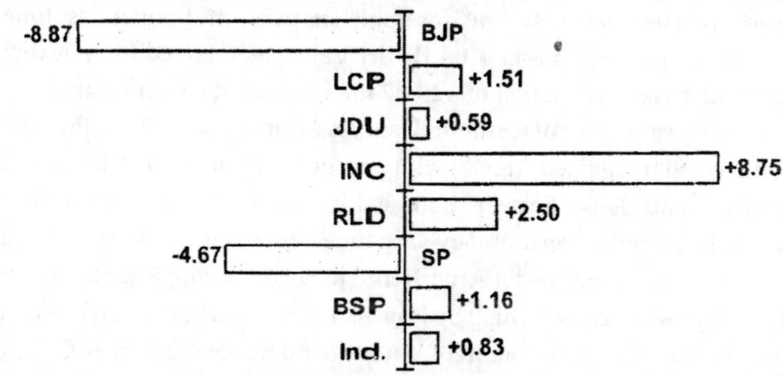

Gains & Losses

Party	Current Win	Prev. Win	Re-tained	Gained	Gained from	Lost	Lost to	Net
BJP	29	57	22	7	BSP-1, SP-6	35	INC-10, BSP-9 SP-14, RLD-2	-28
LCP	2	0	0	2	SP-2	0	-	+2
INC	10	0	0	10	BJP-10	0	-	+10
RLD	2	0	0	2	BJP-2	0	-	+2
BSP	14	4	1	13	BJP-9, SAP-2, SP-2	3	BJP-1, SP-2	+10
SP	26	20	10	16	BJP-14 BSP-2	10	BJP-6, BSP-2 LCP-2	+6
SJPR	1	1	1	0	-	0	-	0
SAP	0	2	0	0	-	2	BSP-2	-2
Ind	1	1	1	0	-	0	-	0
Total	85	85	35	50		50		0

nine to BSP and two to RLD with six of its seven gains coming from SP and one from BSP.

Yadav's SP, banking on the support of Backwards and Muslims with its secular credentials, gained six seats even as its vote share fell by 4.67 points from 28.70 to 24.03 per cent. In all SP gained 16 seats, 14 from BJP and two from BSP, but lost ten, six to BJP and two each to BSP and LCP. BSP, championing the cause of Dalits, came next with 14 seats, a gain of ten, won with 22.06 per cent votes, 1.16 points higher. Gaining a total of 13 seats, BSP wrested nine from BJP and two each from SP and erstwhile Samata Party, but yielded three, two to SP and one to BJP.

The Congress, which was completely wiped out in 1998 as it had been once before in the Janata wave of 1977, came back into reckoning. In snatching all its ten seats from BJP, it polled 14.77 per cent votes, nearly two and half times the miserable six per cent it polled last time.

While Prime Minister Atal Bihari Vajpayee retained his Lucknow seat with a reduced margin of 123,624 in the face of a spirited challenge from the former ruler of Kashmir, Congress' Karan Singh, Party President Sonia Gandhi regained Amethi with a record margin of 300,012. Gandhi family friend Satish Sharma, humbled by BJP's Sanjay Singh in Rajiv Gandhi's Amethi constituency last time, defeated the former Prime minister's estranged cousin Arun Nehru in neighbouring Rae Bareli after some aggressive campaigning by Priyanka. Congress heavyweight Narain Dutt Tewari won back Nainital from former defence minister K C Pant's wife Ila Pant of BJP. SP leader Mulayam Singh Yadav won from both Sambhal and Kannauj, former BSP chief minister Mayawati got in from Akbarpur, while Jat leader Ajit Singh regained his Baghpat citadel.

BJP leader Murli Manohar Joshi retained his Allahabad seat, but Mukhtar Abbas Naqvi, who defeated Noor Bano of Congress in Rampur in 1998 to get a berth in the Vajpayee government as a first-timer Muslim MP in saffron colours, lost to the very Begum by over one lakh votes. State Congress chief Salman Khurshid's journalist wife Louis Khurshid too tumbled in her maiden electoral venture.

Only ten candidates, among them cinestar Raj Babbar, won with margins of over one lakh, while five won with margins of less than five thousand with BSP candidate Pyare Lal edging past his SP rival Arun Kumari with only 105 votes in Ghatampur. Besides 3.62 per cent polled by 610 independents, 263 candidates of other parties including JDU

(0.59), CPI (0.28), JDS (0.09) and CPM (0.03) shared the remaining 3.43 per cent vote.

Of the 18 SC constituencies, BJP won seven with 26.52 per cent as against 11 with 37.1 per cent last time. Ally LCP took another with 3.21 per cent, while SP and BSP equally shared the remaining ten with 26.57 and 25.98 per cent votes respectively. As SP share went down 3.72 points from 30.29 per cent, BSP marginally increased its support by 0.66 points. Congress polled 11.13 per cent instead of about four per cent in 1998, but again without success. Left polled 0.54 per cent SC vote, while independents took about two per cent and others twice as much.

Sonia and Maneka Gandhi, the two *'bahus'* (daughters-in-law) of former prime minister Indira Gandhi were among nine of the 55 women candidates who won. Except LCP and JDU, candidates from every major party lost deposits with Congress topping the list with 47 followed by 24 of SP, 21 of BSP, 18 of JDU, 11 of CPI, two of CPM and one of BJP in a total of 964, including 608 independents.

Politics in Uttar Pradesh, which has given India eight of its 12 Prime Ministers, was dominated by the Congress until 1967, when the first non-Congress government headed by Charan Singh, assumed office in the state. In the first post-Nehru poll that year, Congress could win only 47 of the 85 Lok Sabha seats with 33.4% votes as against 81 for 53%—its highest ever—in 1952.

Calling a mid-term poll, a year ahead of schedule, in 1971, Indira Gandhi raised the Congress tally to 73 for 48.6% only to lose it all in 1977. Polling 25% votes, her party could not win even a single seat. She herself lost in Rae Bareli and son Sanjay in Amethi in the poll held after 21 months of her Emergency rule. The newly formed Janata Party made a clean sweep of all the 85 seats with 68.1% in an as yet unmatched performance.

Indira Gandhi however returned to power in 1980 as the Congress won 51 seats in UP for 35.9%. Its tally rose to an all time high of 83 for 51.03% in 1984. But within five years, Congress found itself going downhill. It could win only 15 seats for 31.8% in 1989, while the newly formed Janata Dal took 54 for 35.9%. But by 1991 it too was down to 22 for 21.62% before sliding further to just two for 4.27% in 1996.

UP rejected both JD and the Congress in 1991 as BJP emerged as a new force. Polling 32.83%, it won 51 seats—a long way up from 1984 when it drew a blank polling 6.4% votes, and 8 for 7.6% in 1989. Earlier, BJP's forerunner Jan Sangh had gradually raised its votes from 7.3% in 1952, when it failed to win a seat, to 22.2% in 1967 to bag 12 seats.

Only other notable performance was that of Janata Party Secular which won 29 seats with 29% votes in 1989. Lok Dal too polled 21.6% in 1984 but could win only two seats.

On the left front, CPI's best performance was in 1967 when it won five seats for 3.3% votes and 1971 when it got four for 3.7%. CPI(M) has won a seat only in 1967 and 1989. It has never polled more than the 1.2 % it did in 1967.

Key Contests

Allahabad. It has been the choice of the likes of Lal Bahadur Shastri (1952, 57), V.P. Singh (1980), H.N. Bahuguna (1971), and Amitabh Bachchan (1984). V.P. Singh later won from Fatehpur in 1989 and 1991 as a JD candidate.

BJP leader Murli Manohar Joshi wrested it from Saroj Dubey of JD by 99,585 votes in 1996.

Amethi. The constituency of Rajiv Gandhi was retained by family friend Satish Sharma in 1996, but lost it in 1998. The only seat to be retained by Congress in 1996, Amethi had always voted for the Congress except 1977, when Sanjay lost. He won from here in 1980. Rajiv Gandhi took it in 1984 defeating sister-in-law Maneka Gandhi by 3.15 lakh votes. He defeated Raj Mohan Gandhi of JD in 1989, but died without knowing that he had won in 1991 too. Satish Sharma got it in a by-election. Sonia Gandhi won it in 1999.

Ballia. Chandra Shekhar, Prime Minister in 1990-91, won in 1999 for the Seventh time since 1977, all but twice on a different ticket. In 1996 he was a nominee of the Samata Party. He was defeated once as a Janata Party candidate in 1984.

Ghosi. One of the five seats won by Congress from UP in 1991 was lost in 1996. Winner was again Kalpanath Rai who bagged it for the Congress in 1989 and 1991, but contested as an independent in 1996 on being denied the Congress ticket because of alleged involvement in the Hawala case.

Lucknow. Once represented by Vijaya Lakshmi Pandit, Lucknow returned BJP leader Atal Bihari Vajpayee for the fourth time since 1991. He defeated film star Raj Babbar of the Samajwadi Party by 118,671 votes in 1996. He has won five times earlier from Balrampur (1957, 67), Gwalior (1971) and New Delhi (1977, 80). He has lost twice—once in Balrampur in 1962 and then in 1984 when Madhav Rao Scindia of the Congress defeated him in Gwalior.

Nainital. It has been the constituency of Narain Dutt Tiwari and K.C. Pant. Pant won it thrice between 1962 and 1971. Tiwari won it in 1980, but lost in 1991. In 1996 he wrested the seat from BJP's Balraj Pasi.

Phoolpur. Jawaharlal Nehru won it in 1957 and 1962, his sister Vijaya Lakshmi Pandit in 1967 and V.P. Singh in 1971. Congress has won it only twice since then. BSP leader Kanshi Ram lost in 1996 to JPS Patel of SP by 17,071 votes.

Uttaranchal

Seats: 5 (General: 4; SC: 1)

Electorate	:	58,27,569
Turnout	:	28,45,743
Turnout %	:	48.83%
Valid Votes	:	28,13,784
Invalid Votes	:	31,959
Candidates	:	51

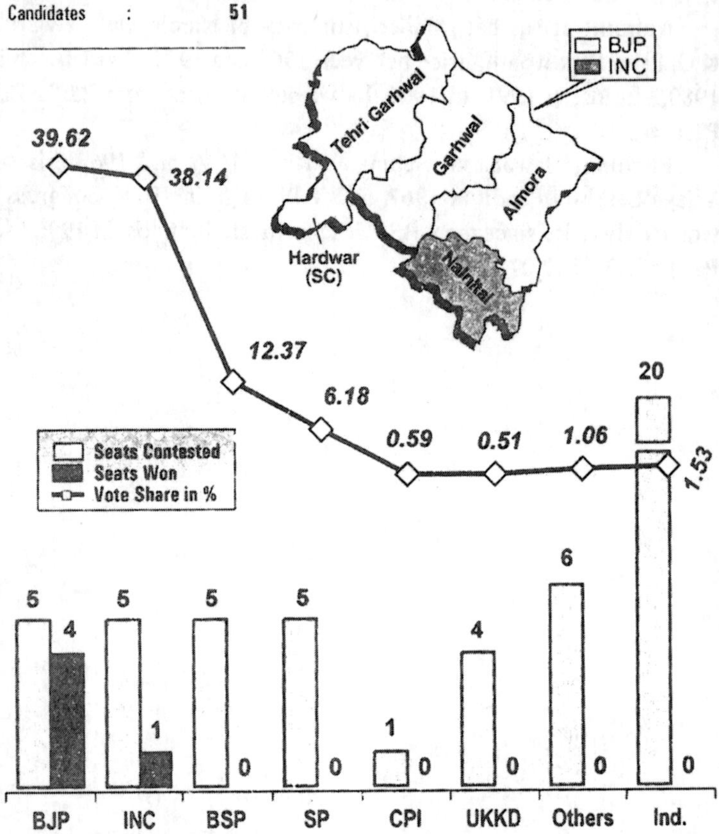

GAINS & LOSSES

Party	Current Win	Previous Win	Re-tained	Gained	Gained from	Lost	Lost to	Net
BJP	4	5	4	0	-	1	INC-1	-1
INC	1	0	0	1	BJP-1	0	-	+1
Total	5	5	4	1		1		0

UTTARANCHAL

History. Uttaranchal became the 27th Indian state on November 9, 2000. Nityanand Swami of BJP was sworn in as the first chief minister as the party holds 17 seats in the 31 member provisional house. The state assembly will eventually have a strength of 60.

Comprising the hill areas of India's most populous state of Uttar Pradesh, the region first heard a demand for political autonomy way back in 1923. A group of Kumaonese met the Lt. Governor of the composite state then known as the United Provinces to claim that Kumaon had always remained an independent political unit. The movement picked up momentum in the early 1970s with the *Chipko Andolan* (to save the trees), an anti-liquor agitation and stirs against large dams giving it the socio-political impetus. Uttarkhand Sangharsh Vahini and Uttarakhand Kranti Dal were formed shortly after the declaration of internal emergency in 1975.

Population (1991)	:	7,045,000
Area	:	55,845 sq km
Languages	:	Hindi
Capital	:	Dehradun
Districts	:	13—Almora, Bageshwar, Chamoli, Champawat, Dehradun, Hardwar, Nainital, Pauri Garhwal, Pithoragarh, Rudraprayag, Tehri Garhwal, Udham Singh Nagar, Uttarkashi
Electorate (99)	:	5,827,569
Turnout	:	48.83%
Lok Sabha Seats	:	5 (SC 1)
Party Position	:	BJP 4 (–1), Congress 1 (+1)

Election 1999 : Lion's Share for BJP

In the 1999 poll held before the formation of Uttraranchal, the region that now makes the state, returned all but one of BJP's five candidates.

But the victory of former chief minister, Narrayan Datt Tiwari, now back in the Congress, over Balraj Pasi of BJP by 112,407 votes denied the saffron party a clean sweep like the one it had made in 1998.

Thus gaining one seat, Congress finished second in the popularity stakes with 38.14%, just one and a half points behind BJP's 39.62% that brought it four seats.

Mayawati's Bahujan Samaj Party came next with 12.37% votes with Samajwadi Party ending up a distant fourth with 6.18%. Among other national parties, CPI collected about 0.6%, while JDS failed to get even a sixth of that. Independents and other smaller parties equally shared the remaining three per cent votes.

In the Hardwar SC seat, Harpal Singh Sathi polling 35.52% for the BJP pipped Ramesh Kumar Burman of BSP (30.59%) by 32,847 votes, leaving the Congress a distant third with 20.95%.

DELHI

History. Founded in the 11th century by the Tomars, Delhi passed into the hands of Muslim rulers in 1192. The British annexed it in 1857 after deposing Mughal Emperor Bahadur Shah and made it their capital in 1912. It became a Union Territory on November 1, 1956 and got a Metropolitan Council ten years later. In December, 1991 it was named the National Capital Territory with a legislative assembly—a sort of half-way house to full statehood.

Communities. Muslims 8%, Sikhs 7%, Christians 1%, Scheduled Castes 19%. It has a large number of migrants from various states, particularly labour from Uttar Pradesh, Bihar and Rajasthan.

Population (1991)	:	9,420,614
Area	:	1,483 sq km
Languages	:	Hindi, Punjabi, Urdu
Capital	:	Delhi
Lok Sabha Seats	:	7(SC 1)

Election 1999 : Capital Gains for BJP

Less than a year after an 'onion wave' drove BJP out of power in the national capital in the November 1998 Assembly poll, the saffron party made a clean sweep of the seven Lok Sabha seats as the pendulum swung again as it has between the erstwhile Jan Sangh and the Congress since 1962.

Polling 51.76 per cent—up 1.03 points from 50.73 it polled in February 1998—BJP not only dislodged Meira Kumar, daughter of former deputy Prime Minister Jagjivan Ram from the Karol Bagh SC constituency, but also humbled the architect of 1991 economic reforms, former finance minister Manmohan Singh making his first electoral foray in South Delhi.

BJP widened the popularity gap with Congress from eight to 9.81 points as the rival party drew a blank for the second time since 1977 with its share coming down by 0.69 points from 42.64 to 41.95 per cent in a two-horse race. BSP finished way behind with its three candidates, polling 2.24 per cent, all losing deposit. A JDS candidate accounted for 1.39 per cent, while 79 others, including 52 independents collected 2.66 per cent.

Former BJP chief executive councillor, Vijay Kumar Malhotra came

Electorate	:	87,39,313
Turnout	:	38,02,815
Turnout %	:	43.51%
Valid Votes	:	38,02,732
Invalid & Missing	:	83
Candidates	:	97

DELHI

Seats: 7 (General: 6; SC: 1)

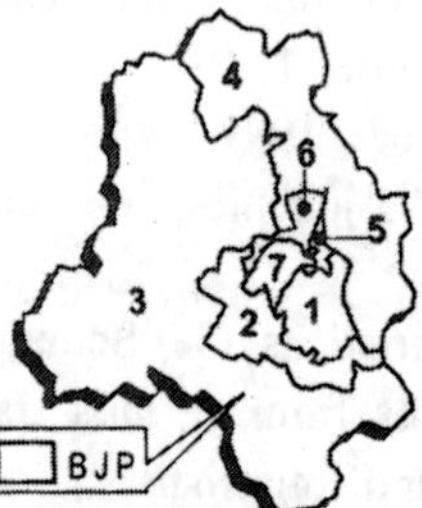

1. New Delhi
2. South Delhi
3. Outer Delhi
4. East Delhi
5. Chandni Chowk
6. Delhi Sadar
7. Karol Bagh (SC)

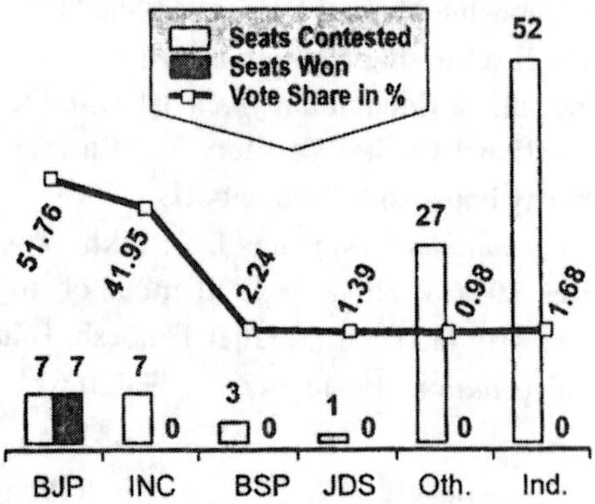

Vote & Seat Share

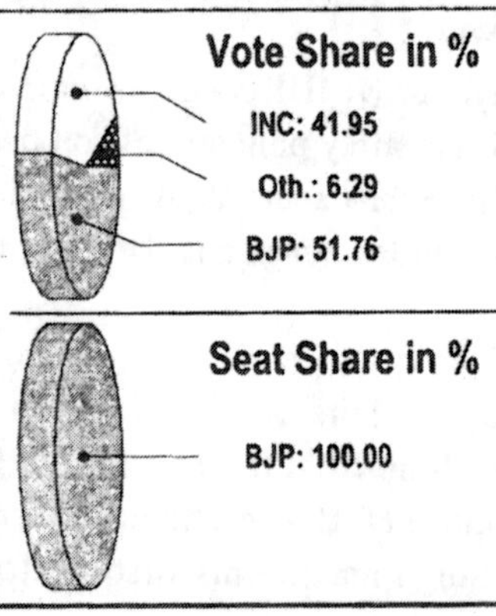

Swing %

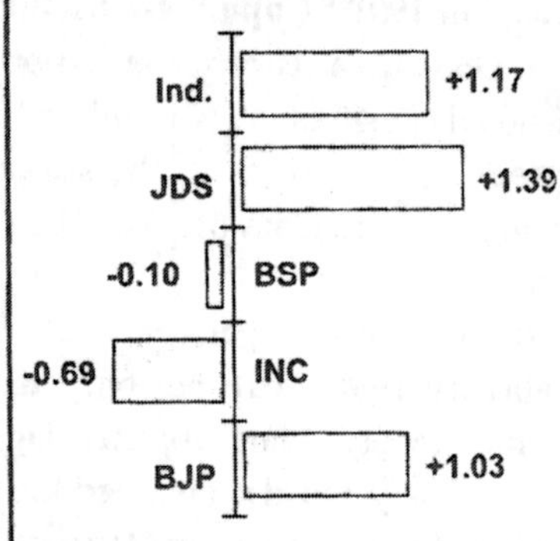

Gains & Losses

Party	Current Win	Prev. Win	Re-tained	Gained	Gained from	Lost	Lost to	Net
BJP	7	6	6	1	INC-1	0	-	+1
INC	0	1	0	0	-	1	BJP-1	-1
Total	7	7	6	1		1		0

back to South Delhi after 22 years to take on Manmohan Singh in place of former chief minister Sushma Swaraj, who went to distant Bellary to join a high profile battle with Congress President Sonia Gandhi. While Malhotra defeated Singh by 29,999 votes, party colleague Vijay Goel hung on to Chandni Chowk with just 1,995 votes with Shoaib Iqbal of JDS playing spoilsport for Congress in the Muslim-dominated constituency with a *fatwa* in his favour from the Imam of Jama Masjid.

Urban Development Minister, Jagmohan again won from prestigious New Delhi defeating R K Dhawan of the Congress, while former chief minister Madan Lal Khurana and Lal Bihari Tiwari retained Delhi Sadar and East Delhi. Another former chief minister Sahib Singh Verma won Outer Delhi for BJP with the highest margin of 202,472. With votes ranging between 157 and 41, 9 11 (BSP- Outer Delhi), all but 15 of the 97 candidates, including 52 independents forfeited their deposits.

Delhi Mayor Anita Arya of BJP was only one of the seven women candidates to emerge successful. In wresting the Karol Bagh seat for BJP, she brought the party 49.93 per cent SC votes. Loser Meira Kumar gave Congress 45.07 per cent, while the rest of five per cent was shared by BSP (2.21 per cent), NCP (0.59 per cent) and eight others.

In the first Lok Sabha elections in 1952, Congress won three of the four seats with 49.4% votes, leaving one to the Kisan Mazdoor Praja Party, which won 7.3% votes. Bharatiya Jan Sangh polled 25.9% votes but could not win a seat. Congress won all the five seats in the next two elections as the Jan Sangh gradually narrowed the popularity gap to poll 32.7% votes in 1962. It turned the tables on the Congress in 1967 winning six of the seven seats for 46.7% votes as the Congress vote share dropped to 38.8%. After the 1969 Congress split, Indira Gandhi's Congress (I) bounced back to reclaim all the seven seats with 64.4% votes. The Sangh still secured 29.6% votes but no seats. Congress (I) lost all the seven seats in the Janata tide in 1977 though it did poll 30.2% votes against Janata's 68.2%. Congress recovered six seats in 1980 with 50.4% votes as Janata held on to one with 37.9%.

Congress again made a clean sweep in 1984 following the assassination of Indira Gandhi polling its highest ever vote of 68.7%. The Sangh, now in its BJP incarnation failed to win a seat though it polled 18.8% votes. In 1989, thanks to seat adjustments with Janata Dal it won four seats for 26.19%, while JD took one for 16.29%. The Congress had to rest content with only two though it polled 43.41% votes. In the tenth round in 1991, Congress took two while five went to BJP although both polled almost equal votes—39.57% for the Congress and 40.21 for the BJP.

Key Contests

New Delhi. BJP leader Atal Behari Vajpayee won it in 1977 and 1980 as the Janata Party candidate. Former defence minister K.C. Pant took it in 1984. L.K. Advani regained it for BJP in 1989. He won again in 1991 but resigned to let defeated Congress candidate Rajesh Khanna get in in a bye-election. Khanna lost the seat to BJP's Jagmohan in 1996.

CHANDIGARH

History: Designed by French architect Le Corbusier as the capital of Punjab, it became a union territory on November 1, 1966 after the creation of Haryana. It still serves as the joint capital of the two states.

Communities: Sikhs 22%, Scheduled Castes 13%, Balmikis and Chamars are the most numerous SCs.

Population (1991)	:	642,015
Area	:	114 sq km
Languages	:	Hindi, Punjabi
Capital	:	Chandigarh
Lok Sabha Seats	:	1

Election 1999 : Congress Upsets BJP

Pawan Kumar Bansal of Congress not only finally succeeded in winning back the Union Territory from BJP in his third attempt in three years, but also humbled the saffron party's national vice president, Krishan Lal Sharma. Bansal had defeated BJP's Satya Pal Jain to first win the seat in 1991, but lost it to Jain in 1996 and his determined bid to unseat his old rival came a cropper in 1998 even as he increased the party share by 8.91 points to 38.70 per cent.

This time he added another 8.3 points to claim 47 per cent of the vote pie to wrest the seat from BJP, which too raised its vote share by 2.71 points from 42.36 to 45.07 per cent with Sharma as its nominee instead of Jain in the 16-cornered contest.

All the 14 other candidates sharing the rest of 7.93 per cent vote lost their deposits with BSP claiming 2.75 per cent, SP 1.72 per cent, a BSP faction 0.15 per cent and a small party 0.17 per cent besides ten independents, who took away 3.15 per cent. Losers included all the three women candidates.

In the first election in 1967, after Chandigarh became a Union Territory on November 1, 1966 following the creation of Haryana, BJP's forerunner Jan Sangh won the seat with 48.7 per cent only to lose it in 1971 with 23.3 per cent. As BJP it gradually raised its share from 5.6 per cent in 1984 to 39.05 per cent in 1996 to score its first win. It retained the seat in 1998 with 42.36 per cent.

Congress has won the seat five times in nine elections since 1971, losing it to Janata Party (66.1 per cent) in 1977, Janata Dal (42.1 per cent) in 1989, and BJP in 1996 (39.05 per cent) and 1998

Electorate	:	5,85,656
Turnout	:	2,82,879
Turnout %	:	48.38%
Valid Votes	:	2,82,816
Invalid & Missing	:	63
Candidates	:	16

CHANDIGARH

Seats: 1 (General: 1)

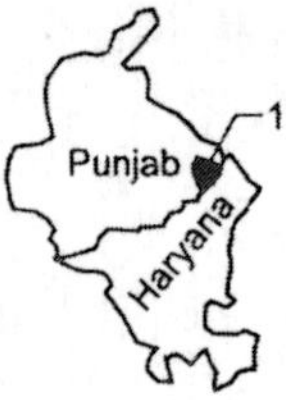

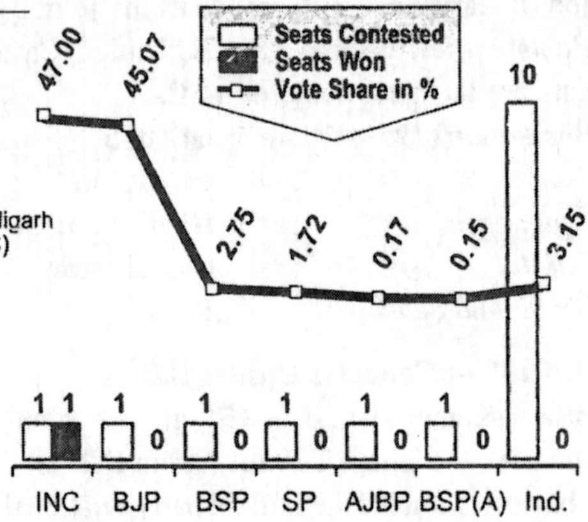

Vote & Seat Share

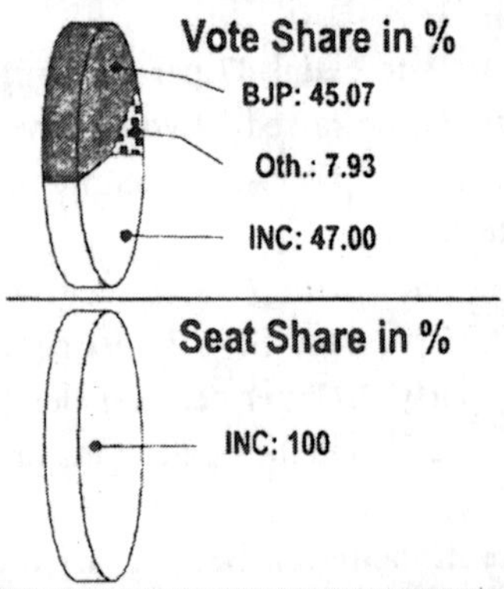

Swing %

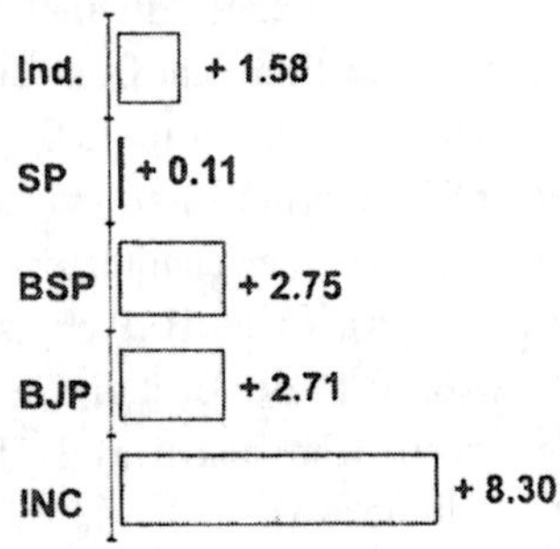

Gains & Losses

Party	Current Win	Prev. Win	Re-tained	Gained	Gained from	Lost	Lost to	Net
BJP	0	1	0	0	-	1	INC-1	-1
INC	1	0	0	1	BJP-1	0	-	+1
Total	1	1	0	1		1		0

(42.36 per cent). Congress did its best in 1971 when it polled 66.9 per cent and its worst in 1967 with 23 per cent.

The Janata Party won the seat in 1977 with 66.1% and the JD in 1989 with 42.1%. The Swatantra Party had polled 20.9% in 1967 in any other notable performance.

SOUTH

Seats: 132	Candidates: 937

Electorate	:	15,43,98,280
Turnout	:	10,09,49,226
Turnout %	:	65.38%
Valid Votes	:	9,82,82,354
Invalid & Missing	:	26,66,872

Party	Seats Contested	Seats Won	Lost Deposit	1999 Vote%	1998 Vote%	Vote Swing %
BJP + Allies	**132**	**73**	**19**	**40.28**	**35.95**	**+4.33**
BJP	48	19	14	12.29	15.44	-3.15
JD(U)	16	3	5	3.24	-	+3.24
DMK	19	12	0	6.41	5.64	+0.77
MDMK	5	4	0	1.65	1.70	-0.05
MADMK	1	1	0	0.40	0.30	+0.10
PMK	8	5	0	2.42	1.65	+0.77
TDP	34	29	0	13.53	10.84	+2.69
TRC	1	0	0	0.34	0.38	-0.04
INC + Allies	**133**	**48**	**5**	**42.40**	**37.12**	**+5.28**
INC	101	35	0	34.05	28.79	+5.26
ADMK	29	10	5	7.17	7.16	+0.01
KEC(M)	1	1	0	0.36	0.38	-0.02
MUL	2	2	0	0.82	0.79	+0.03
BSP	11	0	11	0.16	0.28	-0.12
CPI	12	0	4	2.34	2.86	-0.52
CPM	22	9	7	5.51	4.49	+1.02
JD(S)	36	0	31	2.87	-	+2.87
NCP	8	0	8	0.03	-	+0.03
FBL	8	0	8	0.06	-	+0.06
KEC	1	1	0	0.37	0.35	+0.02
NTRTDP (LP)	13	0	13	0.06	0.41	-0.35
TMC	28	0	21	2.09	5.50	-3.41
AIMIM	1	1	0	0.46	0.52	-0.06
ATDP	20	0	20	0.25	-	+0.25
PT	10	0	8	0.58	0.47	+0.11
Others	94	0	94	0.52	9.94	-9.42
Ind.	408	0	406	2.01	2.11	-0.10
Total	**937**	**132**	**655**	**100.00**	**100.00**	**0.00**

CHAPTER 8

THE SOUTH: CONSOLIDATION OF NDA

Despite major reverses in Karnataka, BJP-led National Democratic Alliance consolidated its gains across the Vindhyas with new strategic alliances pushing it to the top slot in the southern region that sends 132 members to the Lok Sabha. In all BJP and allies won 73 seats with 40.28 per cent votes, a gain of 23 over 50 seats picked up with 29.65 per cent votes last time. However, the gains were less due to an apparent near eleven per cent swing than to switching of allies in Andhra and Tamil Nadu.

The Congress alliance, finishing 25 behind, too managed to add four seats, not counting ten seats picked up by CPM and allies, who were on the opposite side of the political divide in Kerala. With a 12.44 point swing, the Congress alliance picked up 48 seats for 42.40 per cent as against 44 for 29.96 per cent in 1998. Left picked up 8.22 per cent of the popular vote, though CPI drew a blank for its 2.34 per cent votes. More than half the voters (50.62 per cent) opted for the Congress and Left allies, but thanks to new equations NDA won five seats for every four of the 58 claimed by them together.

With constituents of the erstwhile United Front going their different ways, it became a two horse race with only one seat going to a third party, Salahuddin Owaisi of AIMIM, who 'hit a six' in Hyderabad. Parties outside the alliances polled 7.09 per cent votes with 408 independents sharing 2.01 per cent.

Among the NDA supporters, TDP whose 12 winners could not save the BJP alliance in the crucial confidence vote in April, raised its strength to 29, gaining 14 seats from Congress, two from CPI and one from BJP with a regional swing of 2.69 points pushing its vote share to 13.53 per cent. BJP itself picked up 19 seats for 12.29 per cent votes, one less than the 20 it had won for 15.44 per cent, indicating an adverse swing of 3.15 points.

Gaining six seats from the Congress, three in Andhra, two in Karnataka and one in Andaman and Nicobar Islands, and one each from Janata Dal (Andhra) and TMC (Tamil Nadu), BJP lost eight to Congress in Karnataka and conceded one to TDP in Andhra. Switching sides, DMK gained seven seats in Tamil Nadu, six from rival AIADMK and one from CPI, but lost Pondicherry to Congress to double its tally of six for 5.64 per cent votes to 12 for 6.41 per cent with a tiny swing of 0.77 points.

Similarly, PMK (5), MDMK (4) and MGRADMK (1) snatched a seat each from former ally Jayalalitha. Only Tamizhaga Rajiv Congress leader, V Ramamurthy lost his Salem seat.

In Karnataka, however, new found ally JDU formed by chief minister J H Patel's faction of Janata Dal and commerce minister Ramakrishna Hegde's Lok Shakti, could win only three seats for 3.24 per cent votes.

It indicated an over five point drop in their popularity considering that Lok Shakti and erstwhile Janata Dal, then in opposition to each other, had won three seats each with an 8.37 per cent regional vote share. In the opposition, Congress on its own won 35 seats, a net loss of six, despite a favourable swing of 5.26 points that pushed up its vote share to 34.05 per cent from 28.79 per cent last time.

In all it lost 24 seats, 15 to TDP, six to BJP (three in Andhra, two in Karnataka besides Andamans) and one each to JDU (Karnataka), CPM (Kerala) and Kerala Congress. But it recouped 18, eight from BJP, two each from JD, LS (all in Karnataka), CPI (Kerala) and TMC (Tamil Nadu), and one apiece from TDP (Andhra) and DMK (Pondicherry).

AIADMK, back in the company of Congress, lost the clout that had made it play kingmaker in 1998. It lost ten seats in all to finish with a tally of ten for 7.17 per cent votes, instead of 18 for just about the same share last time. DMK accounted for six of its losses, while MDMK took two and PMK and MGRADMK, one each. Its two gains were at the cost of MDMK and TRC. Muslim League and Kerala Congress (M) retained their two and one seats in Kerala with just about the same share of 0.82 and 0.36 per cent respectively.

In the Left, CPM won nine, three more than last time, with a one per cent swing that pushed its regional share to 5.51 per cent. Its gains were at the cost of Janata Party (Tamil Nadu), Congress and RSP (both Kerala). But CPI lost all its five seats in the region as its vote share dropped from 2.86 to 2.34 per cent. The Congress (Kerala) and TDP (Andhra) gained two each, while one was snatched by DMK (Tamil Nadu). LDF partner Kerala Congress won a seat with 0.37 per cent votes.

Among others, TMC lost three seats even as it collected 2.09 per cent votes, a 3.41 point drop, to draw a blank. So did JDS failing to pick up even one of the four seats held by Janata Dal. Janata Party too lost its lone seat. As a national party, BSP put up eleven candidates, but failed to impress the southern voter.

ANDHRA PRADESH

Seats: 42 (General: 34; SC: 6; ST: 2)

Electorate	:	4,93,43,692
Turnout	:	3,40,92,966
Turnout %	:	69.09%
Valid Votes	:	3,27,00,670
Invalid & Missing	:	13,92,296
Candidates	:	285

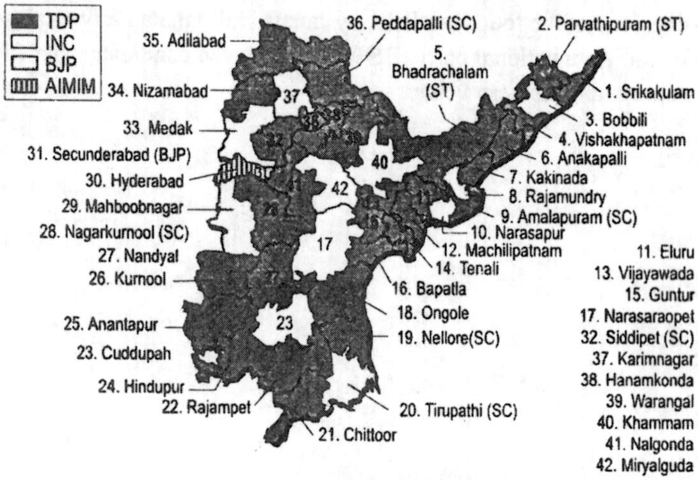

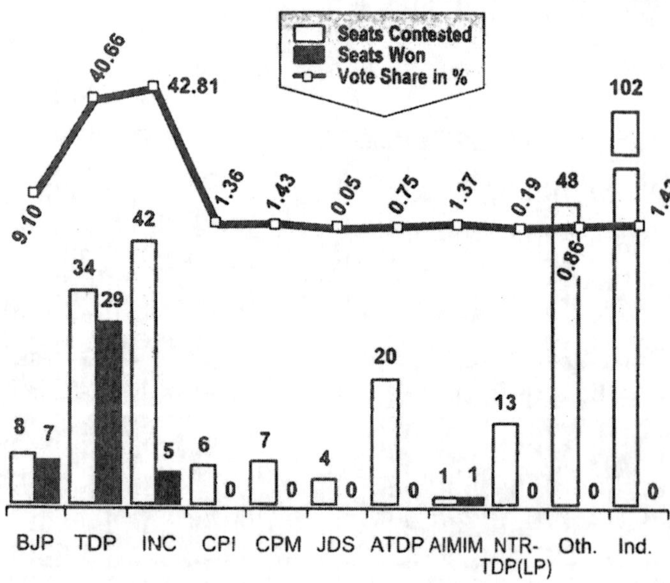

ANDHRA PRADESH

History. The fifth largest state in India, both in area and population, it was carved out of the Telugu-speaking areas of Madras on Oct. 1, 1953. Nine districts from the Nizam's Hyderabad state were added to it on November 1, 1956. It has three distinct regions called Andhra, made up of nine coastal districts, Rayalseema, consisting of four interior districts and Telengana, made up of capital Hyderabad and nine adjoining districts.

Communities. Muslims 9%, Christians 3%, Scheduled Castes 5%, Scheduled Tribes 6%. Others include Reddys/Kapus, Kammas, Turpu Kapus, Balijas and Telagas.

Population (1991)	:	66,508,008
Area	:	275,068 sq km
Languages	:	Telugu and Urdu
Capital	:	Hyderabad
Lok Sabha Seats	:	42 (SC 6, ST 2) Coastal 19, Rayalseema 28, Telengana 15

Election 1999: Naidu Again Plays Kingmaker

Thanks to a strategic alliance with the BJP, Chief Minister Chandrababu Naidu overcame the anti-incumbency factor to again emerge as the king-maker at the Centre with his TDP making the fourth largest haul of Lok Sabha seats at 29. With BJP taking seven more seats, the allies cornered 85.71 per cent of the seats together polling nearly half the total votes (49.76 per cent). Apart from the alliance with BJP, computer-savvy Naidu's record of good governance, his populist Deepam scheme to provide cooking gas to rural women and infighting in Congress, all helped TDP record its second best performance since 1984 when it won 30 seats with 44.8 per cent votes. Its worst was in 1989 when it could win only two seats with 34.5 per cent votes.

Leaving BJP to contest eight seats, TDP increased its tally about two-and-a half times with a mighty 8.69 point swing gaining it 18 seats. Of these, 15 came from the Congress, two from CPI and one from ally BJP. But it lost the Bobbilli seat to Congress' B Satyanarayana to finish with a net gain of 17 with 40.66 per cent votes as against 31.97 per cent last time for a dozen seats.

BJP, which had chosen to ally with the rival TDP (LP) led by N T Rama Rao's widow Lakshmi Parvathi last time, agreed to play second

Andhra Pradesh

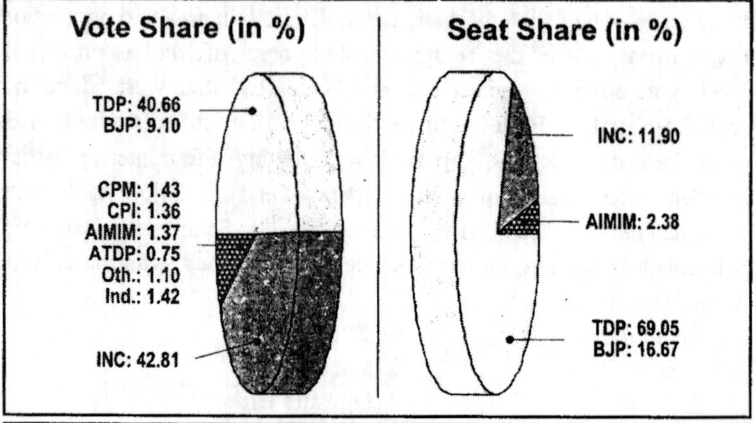

Swing %

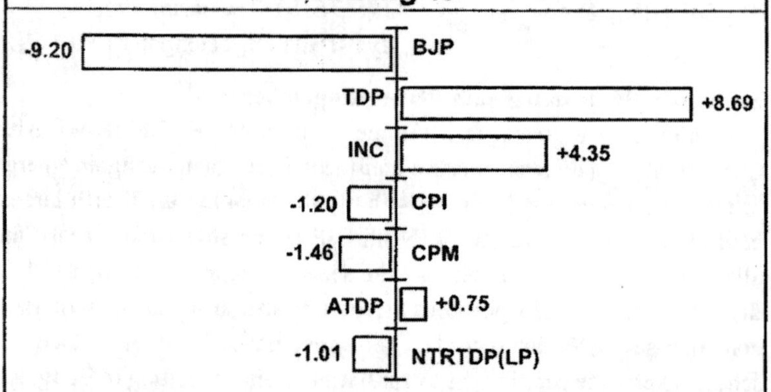

Gains & Losses

Party	Current Win	Prev. Win	Re-tained	Gained	Gained from	Lost	Lost to	Net
AIMIM	1	1	1	0	-	0	-	0
BJP	7	4	3	4	INC-3, JD-1	1	TDP-1	+3
INC	5	22	4	1	TDP-1	18	BJP-3, TDP-15	-17
JD	0	1	0	0	-	1	BJP-1	-1
CPI	0	2	0	0	-	2	TDP-2	-2
TDP	29	12	11	18	BJP-1, INC-15 CPI-2	1	INC-1	+17
Total	42	42	19	23		23		0

fiddle to Naidu this time by contesting only eight seats instead of 38. It won all but one of them to return the second highest success ratio of 87.5 per cent.

In the process, it gained four seats, three from the Congress and one from JD even as its vote share dropped by 9.2 points from a record 18.3 per cent last time. Conceding a seat to ally TDP, BJP made a net gain of three in its tally of seven for 9.1 per cent votes. A 4.35 per cent swing pushed Congress to the top of popularity stakes with a 42.81 per cent vote, but failure to make adjustments with the Left sent its tally crashing to five, one less than the previous lowest of six in 1984.

At that time TDP under popular matinee idol NTR, had swept the polls in Andhra even as the rest of India gave the Congress under Rajiv Gandhi a massive mandate. In all, the Congress lost 18 seats, 15 to TDP and three to BJP, but wresting Bobbili from TDP ended up with a net loss of 17.

All India Majlis-e-Ittehadul Muslimeen (AIMIM) was the only other successful party retaining its lone seat even as its vote share dropped marginally from 1.52 to 1.37 per cent. Its leader Salahuddin Owaisi won the city of Charminar, Hyderabad for the sixth time in a row. He again defeated Baddam Reddy of the BJP, whom he had bettered in both 1991 and 1998.

In the Left, CPI which had won two of the three seats it contested last time with a vote share of 2.56 per cent, chose to put up a fight in six seats, but lost them all as its vote share dropped to 1.36 per cent. CPM too contested seven instead of three, but could not win any again as its vote share too halved from 2.89 to 1.43 per cent.

NTR's widow Lakshmi Parvathi's party not only again came a cropper, but also saw its vote share slashed to a minuscule 0.19 per cent, about a sixth of its vote in 1998, but way down from the 10.66 per cent it won on debut in 1996. Anna TDP, floated by a son of NTR, too could not win any of the 20 seats it contested, but collected 0.75 per cent votes. Of the six SC seats, TDP won five with 43.98 per cent wresting two from the Congress with an over 11 per cent swing in its favour. Ally BJP took the sixth seat from the Congress with a 7.83 per cent vote share. Congress lost all the three SC seats though at 43.51 per cent it polled six per cent more votes. Polling 44.58 per cent votes, almost double of the 23.67 per cent it got last time, TDP grabbed both the ST seats wresting one from

CPI, which saw its vote share drop to 9.11 per cent, over eleven points down from 20.65 per cent in 1998.

In the two ST seats too Congress polled about three per cent more votes, but its 40.88 per cent votes could not win it any seat. Four independents and a TDLP candidate took away the remaining 5.43 per cent ST votes. Only four of the 18 women contestants won. Among the losers were two former Congress chief ministers, K Vijay Bhaskar Reddy and N Bhaskar Rao, and former union ministers P Shiv Shankar and P Upendra.

Prominent Congress winners included former chief minister, N Janardhana Reddy from Narasaraopet, Renuka Chowdhury, who had switched from TDP, from Khammam and former Janata Dal spokesman S Jaipal Reddy from Miryalguda. BJP's junior union minister Bandaru Dattatraya made it from Secunderabad.

In the simultaneous assembly poll, Naidu returned to power with his TDP winning 180 of 294 seats as against 219 in 1994, while ally BJP at 12 increased its tally four fold. Congress too pushed its score nearly three-and-a-half times from 26 to 90. While CPI lost all its 19 seats, CPM could hold on to only two of its 15. At nine, independents and others too dropped a seat.

Launched by Nandamuri Taraka Rama Rao on May 28, 1982, Telugu Desam won 30 seats with 44.82% votes on its first run for the Lok Sabha in 1984 after the assassination of Mrs Indira Gandhi. Five years later, Andhra switched back to Congress electing 39 of its candidates with 50.9%. TDP share dropped to 34.45 per cent, but it won the party only two seats. In 1991, the TDP votes dropped by another two per cent, but it won 13 seats, wresting as may as 12 from the Congress. Nine of these additional seats came in the first phase of elections before the assassination of Rajiv Gandhi and three after. Before 1984, Andhra poll scene was dominated by the Congress which had never polled less than 40 per cent votes in the state until 1996.

Key Contests

Nandyal. P.V. Narasimha Rao, Prime Minister during 1991-96, defeated Bhuma Venkata Nagi Reddy of the TDP by 98,408 votes in 1996. In November 1991, Rao had won by a record 5.80 lakh votes after G P Reddy vacated the seat on his becoming the Prime Minister. Also elected from Berhampur in Orissa, Rao chose to resign the Nandyal seat in 1996. Rao who served as Chief Minister of Andhra Pradesh during 1971-73 won from Hanamkonda in 1977 and 1980. In 1984 and 1989 he was elected from Ramtek in Maharashtra.

Electorate	:	3,43,04,429
Turnout	:	2,31,08,498
Turnout %	:	67.36%
Valid Votes	:	2,23,53,851
Invalid & Missing	:	7,54,647
Candidates	:	130

KARNATAKA

Seats: 28 (General: 24; SC: 4)

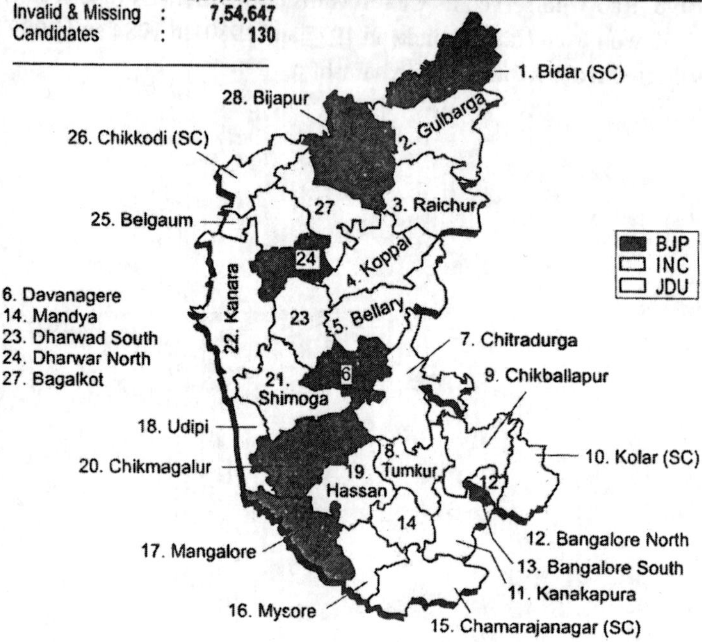

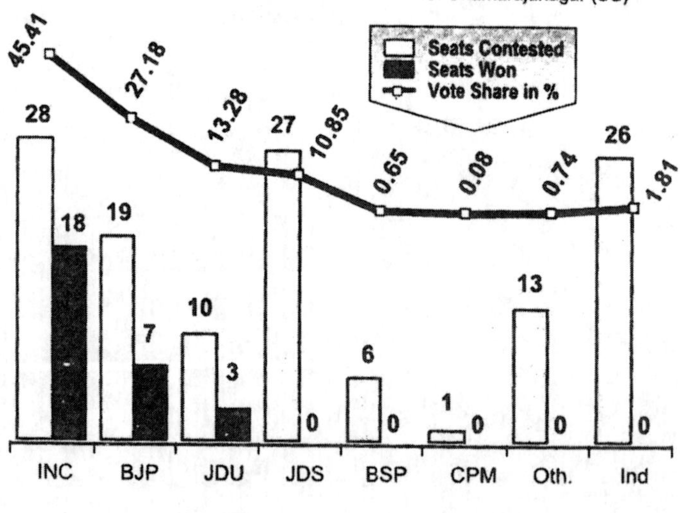

KARNATAKA

History. Founded in 1399 by the Wodeyars, the princely state of Mysore became a Kannada-speaking state on Nov. 1, 1956 with the inclusion of such areas of Hyderabad, Bombay and Madras. It was renamed Karnataka on Nov. 1, 1973.

Communities. Muslims 12%, Christians 2%, Scheduled Castes 15%, Scheduled Tribes 5%. Major communities include Lingayats, Vokkaligas, Edigas and Marathas. Adi Karnatakas, Bhovis and Banjaras are the main Scheduled Castes while Naikdas are the principal Scheduled Tribe.

Population (1991)	:	44,977,201
Area	:	191,791 sq km
Languages	:	Kannada, Urdu, Tamil
Capital	:	Bangalore
Lok Sabha Seats	:	28 (SC 4)—North 10, Coastal 2, Mysore 16

Election 1999 : Congress Stages a Comeback

An uneasy alliance between the BJP and Janata Dal (United)—bringing together Ramakrishna Hegde's Lok Shakti and chief minister, J H Patel's Janata Dal—helped Congress spurred by Party President Sonia Gandhi stage a remarkable comeback with all the incumbency sins of Patel visited against the alliance.

Helped by a 9.19 per cent swing in its favour, Congress doubled its Lok Sabha tally to 18 with 45.41 per cent votes as against nine for 36.22 per cent last time. As many as eight of Congress' dozen gains came from BJP with two each yielded by the erstwhile Lok Shakti and Janata Dal. But it also lost two to BJP and one to JDU to finish with a net gain of nine. BJP, opposing the Patel government tooth and nail till the other day, suddenly found itself on the same side and paid a heavy penalty for it. Although at 27.18 per cent, it polled a wee bit more (0.23 per cent) than the 26.95 per cent last time, the new equations nearly halved the BJP tally from 13 to seven.

Patel's Janata Dal and Hegde's Lok Shakti, which had won three seats each with 21.69 and 11.5 per cent votes last time, lost half of them with their new incarnation JDU polling 13.28 per cent, just 40 per cent of their combined share in 1998. Both lost two seats each to Congress and conceded one apiece to the new JDU, which wrested Chitradurga from the Congress. Two of JDU's tally of three came from the four SC

Karnataka

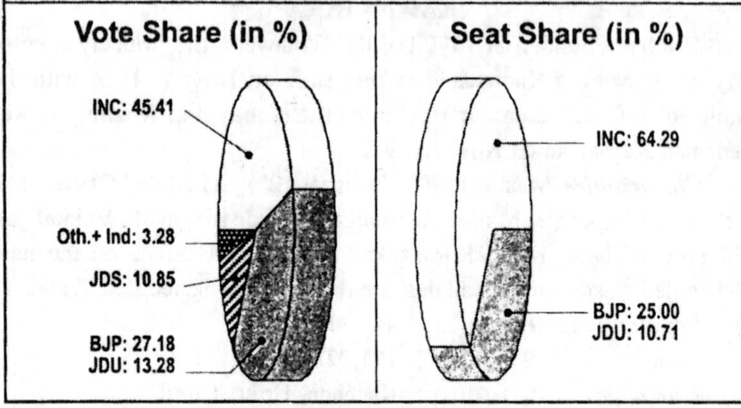

Swing %

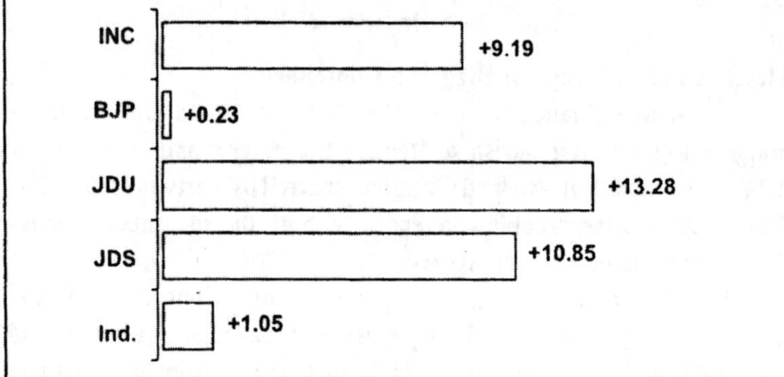

Gains & Losses

Party	Current Win	Prev. Win	Re-tained	Gained	Gained from	Lost	Lost to	Net
BJP	7	13	5	2	INC-2	8	INC-8	-6
INC	18	9	6	12	BJP-8, JD-2 LS-2	3	BJP-2, JDU-1	+9
JD	0	3	0	0	-	3	INC-2, JDU-1	-3
JDU	3	0	0	3	INC-1, JD-1 LS-1	0	-	+3
LS	0	3	0	0	-	3	INC-2, JDU-1	-3
Total	28	28	11	17		17		0

seats with nearly half the SC vote. BJP and Congress shared the other two with an identical quarter of the SC vote pie. No other party put up a candidate in the reserved seats, which were shared equally last time by the BJP, Lok Shakti, Congress and JD with 19.54, 15.66, 32.54, and 27.98 per cent votes respectively.

Former Prime Minister, H D Deve Gowda's JD (Secular), which had contested all but one of the 28 seats, was completely routed though it managed to garner 10.85 per cent votes. Gowda, who had vowed to "rise from the ashes" after the Congress pulled the rug from under him, lost to G Puttaswamy Gowda of the Congress in his native Hassan by 1,41,757 votes.

Bellary witnesssed a high profile battle between a *desi* (native) daughter and a *videshi* (foreign) daughter-in-law. The constituency, which has always returned a Congress candidate since the first poll, though with reducing margins, again chose Italian born Sonia Gandhi over BJP's Sushma Swaraj. Gandhi won with over 56,000 votes only to give it up later in favour of Amethi in Uttar Pradesh, from where too she had won with a record margin of 300,012 votes.

The biggest win in the state was recorded by R L Jalappa of the Congress, who defeated his JDU rival in Chikballapur by 211,198 votes. Former Congress union ministers Margaret Alva and C K Jaffer Sharief won from Kanara and Bangalore North. Former chief minister, S Bangarappa, now back in Congress, made it from Shimoga. But another former chief minister M Veerappa Moily lost a close race to BJP's Dhananjaya Kumar in Mangalore. Civil Aviation Minister Ananth Kumar won Bangalore South for the BJP. Gandhi and Alva were the only two of eleven women contestants to emerge winners.

In the parallel assembly poll, Congress recorded a facile victory grabbing 132 of the 224 seats at stake, a massive gain of 96 over the 36 it had in 1994. BJP too added four seats to its kitty to finish with 44. The split Janata Dal was the biggest loser with its 'United' and 'Secular' factions finishing with 19 and nine seats, 87 less than its 1994 total of 115. BSP and CPM lost a seat each, while ADMK gained one and 19 independents made it this time as against 16 last time. Karnataka Congress president S M Krishna became the new chief minister in place of Janata Dal's J H Patel, who himself finished a poor third in his home constituency of Channagiri.

Politics in Karnataka had been dominated by the Congress until the 1980s. In the first election in 1952, Congress won ten of the eleven seats in Mysore as it was then called, leaving only one seat to Kisan Mazdoor Praja Party backed by 23% voters. The trend continued even after enlargement of Mysore with Congress winning 23 of the 26 seats in 1957 with 55.5% votes. Its popularity dipped a bit in the first post-Nehru elections in 1967 when Congress could win only 18 of the 27 seats with 49% votes. After the 1969 Congress split, Indira Gandhi's party won all the 27 seats with the backing of 70.9% voters—its highest ever. And even as the Janata wave swept north India in 1977, 56.8% Karnataka voters gave her party 26 of the 28 seats. The Janata could win only two though it polled 39.9% votes indicating a sharp polarisation. Congress wrested another seat from the Janata in 1980, polling 56.3%, dropped three in 1984 in the face of a five per cent negative swing only to regain them in 1989 even as its vote share fell to its then lowest of 48.9%. Two years later Congress dropped four seats as its popularity slumped further to 42.13%. It took a nosedive in 1996 to hit rock bottom—five for 30.31% votes.

Before it joined the Janata Party, BJP's predecessor Bharatiya Jan Sangh saw its vote share progressively drop from 4.2% in 1952 to 1.9% in 1971. Picking up again as BJP in 1984, its popularity zoomed from 4.68% to 28.78% in 1991, when it opened its account for the first time with four seats.

The Janata Party won two seats for 39.9% in 1977, lost one in 1980 as its vote share dropped to 22.9%. It won four seats with 35.1% votes in 1984, but could not get any with 10.6% five years later. Lending its name to Samajwadi Janata Party of then Prime Minister Chandrashekhar, it got a seat for 3.82% votes in 1991, Gowda being the lone winner.

Other than that the only notable performance in the past was by Swatantra Party which won five seats in 1967 for 14.3% votes. Congress (O) and Urs factions too polled 16.4% and 16.7% votes in 1971 and 1980 respectively, but a seat eluded either.

Key Contests

Chikmagalur. Chosen by Indira Gandhi to enter Lok Sabha through a by-election after her defeat at Rae Bareli in 1977, Chikmagalur had always returned Congress until 1996 when B.L. Shankar of JD defeated two term Congress MP D.K. Tharadevi.

Hassan. Former Prime Minister H.D. Deve Gowda entered Lok Sabha for the first time from here in 1991 as a Samajwadi Janata Party candidate. He resigned his seat in December 1994 to become chief minister after the JD victory in Karnataka. After losing the office of Prime Minister, Gowda won again in 1998, but lost in 1999.

Chikkodi (SC). Former Congress minister, B. Shankranand had won seven times in a row from here since 1967. He could not equal Jagjivan Ram's record of eight straight wins as he went down to Ratnamala Dhareshwar of JD in 1996.

Electorate	:	2,20,55,375
Turnout	:	1,54,46,826
Turnout %	:	70.04%
Valid Votes	:	1,53,77,980
Invalid & Missing	:	68,846
Candidates	:	142

KERALA

Seats: 20 (General: 18; SC: 2)

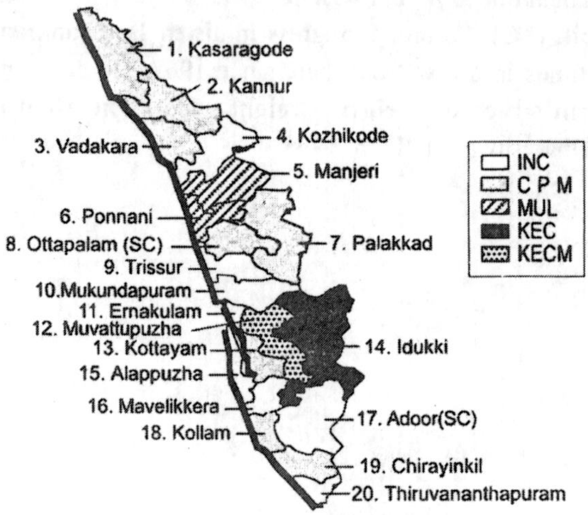

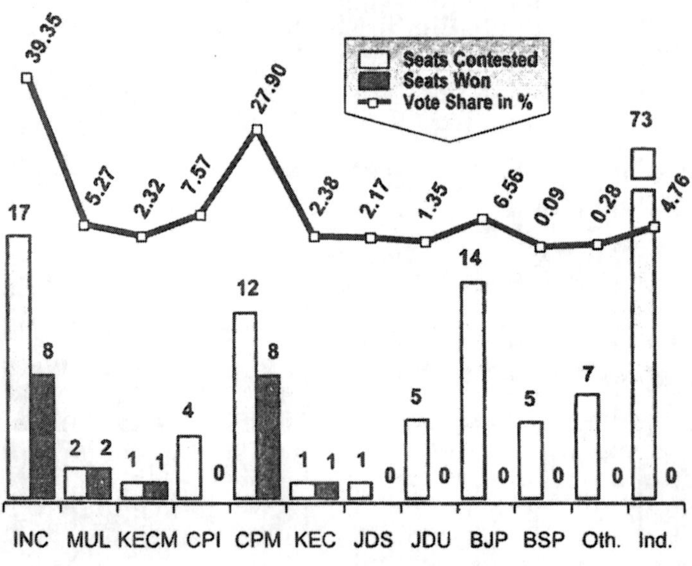

KERALA

History. Kerala came into being on November 1, 1956 by the merger of Travancore-Cochin state and Malabar district of Madras. It has three geographic regions—highlands, midlands and low lands.

Communities. Muslims 22%, Christians 21%, Scheduled Castes 10%. Major communities include Ezhavas and Nairs. Pulayans and Cherumans are the principal Scheduled Castes.

Population (1991)	:	29,698,518
Area	:	38,863 sq km
Languages	:	Malayalam
Capital	:	Thiruvananthapuram
Lok Sabha Seats	:	20 (SC 2)—Malabar 9, Central 3, Travancore-Cochin 8

Election 1999 : A Vote for Status Quo

The Congress-led United Democratic Front (UDF) and the ruling Left Democratic Front (LDF) headed by the CPM finished with honours even, as Kerala voted for status quo giving them the same 11-9 tally as in 1998. Congress again won eight seats for the UDF, which had lost power in the simultaneous assembly polls in 1996, with 39.35 per cent votes.

Allies Muslim League and Kerala Congress (Mani) brought the other three retaining their two and one seats with 5.27 per cent and 2.32 per cent votes respectively to give the combine 46.94 per cent votes with only 0.86 extra points. Itself polling just 0.68 points more than the 38.67 per cent it got last time, Congress retained six seats, wrested two seats from CPI, but lost one apiece to the CPM and the rival Kerala Congress to finish with its old tally of eight.

The rival LDF polling 43.54 per cent, 3.68 points more, kept its share of nine. CPM retained its six and gained a seat each from Congress and RSP, which did not put up a candidate in Kollam following a split in the party with a faction led by Baby John breaking away.

Ally Kerala Congress wrested another seat from Congress, but CPI lost both its seats to Sonia Gandhi's party to give LDF the same old score. CPM itself won eight instead of six seats for the front with 27.90 per cent—6.90 points more. CPI added another 7.57 per cent—0.75 points less, KEC 2.38 per cent—0.18 points more, and JDS 2.17 per cent to its

Kerala

Vote Share (in %)

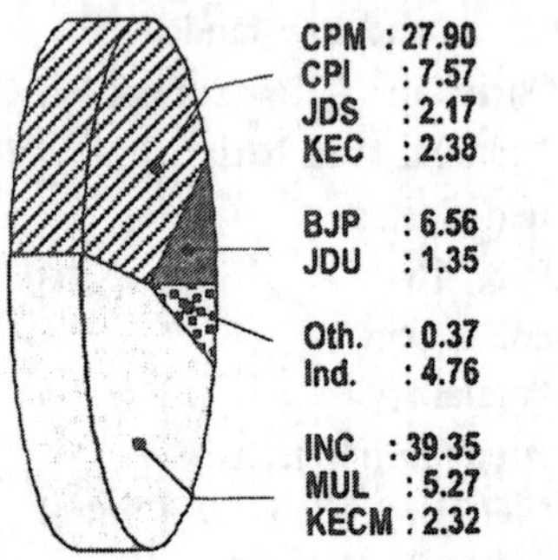

Seat Share (in %)

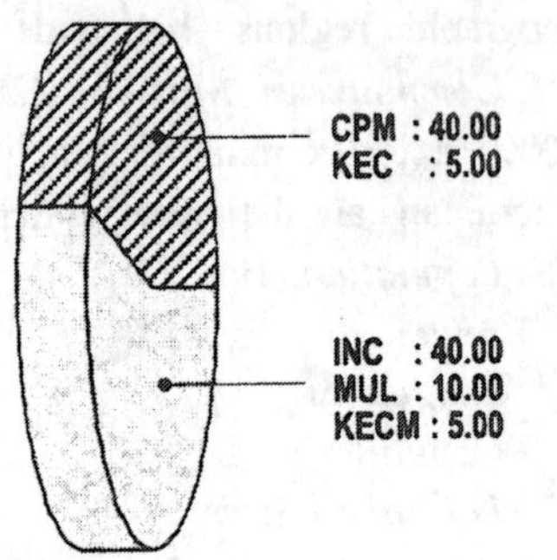

Swing %

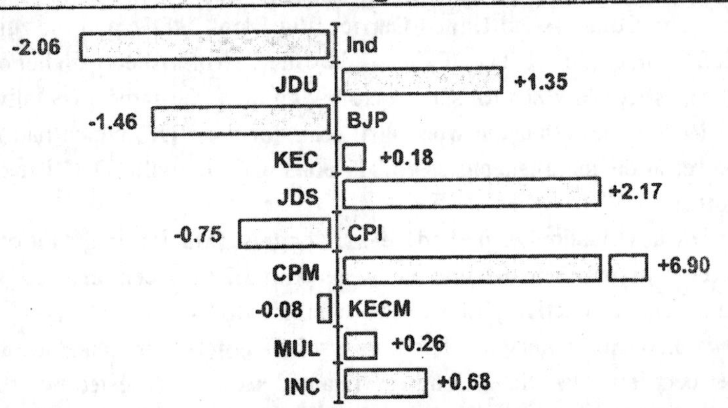

Gains & Losses

Party	Current Win	Prev. Win	Re-tained	Gained	Gained from	Lost	Lost to	Net
CPI	0	2	0	0	-	2	INC-2	-2
CPM	8	6	6	2	INC-1, RSP-1	0	-	+2
INC	8	8	6	2	CPI-2	2	CPM-1, KEC-1	0
KEC	1	0	0	1	INC-1	0	-	+1
KECM	1	1	1	0	-	0	-	0
MUL	2	2	2	0	-	0	-	0
RSP	0	1	0	0	-	1	CPM-1	-1
Total	20	20	15	5	-	5	-	0

vote bank. BJP, which too floated a new front, not only failed again to open its account, but its vote share slid 1.46 points to 6.56 per cent from 8.02 per cent in 1998 as it fielded only 14 candidates instead of 20. All but one of them lost their deposits.

The Congress and CPM shared the two SC seats with 46.30 per cent—up 1.28 points, and 24.40 per cent—up 0.46 points, respectively. CPI lost a SC seat to Congress as its vote share dropped 2.38 points to 21.38 per cent. BJP, which again contested both the SC seats, won 7.82 per cent votes, about 0.80 points more. Of the 13 women candidates in fray, only A K Premajam of CPM retained her Badagara seat.

Former Congress chief minister, K Karunakaran, shifted from Thiruvananthapuram to defeat E.M. Sreedharan, son of veteran CPM leader E M S Namboothiripad in Mukundapuram. His son K Muraleedharan too defeated C. M Ibrahim of JDS in Kozhikode. But in Kannur, A P Abdullakkutty, 30-year-old president of the Students Federation of India, fielded by CPM upset the applecart of Congress' M Ramachandran, who had been winning the seat since 1984. But top Malayalam actor Murali, who has played the revolutionary in hits like *Lal Salaam* and *Rakthasakshikal Zindabad,* lost to Congress' V M Sudheeran in Alappuzha, which was once represented by Communist veterans like PT Punnoose, P K Vasudevan Nair and Susheela Gopalan.

Kerala, the first state to vote a Communist government to power in 1957, returned nine CPI candidates to the Lok Sabha that year with 37.5% votes. Congress won six for 34.8%, leaving the remaining three to independents and the Praja Socialist Party. In 1962, the Congress and the CPI shared six seats each leaving an equal number to others. The first post-Nehru elections in 1967 saw the Congress strength reduced to just one though at 36.2% it had polled higher than even before. It was the CPI(M) which took the dominant share winning nine seats for 24.6% votes. CPI and the Samyukta Socialist Party won three apiece with about 8% vote each. Entering the coalition era in 1971, Congress saw six of its seven candidates win with 19.8% votes. Its best performance came in 1989 in winning 14 seats for 41.70% votes.

CPI(M)'s best came in 1967 with nine wins for 24.6% though in 1971 it polled nearly two per cent more at 26.2%. Its worst was in 1977 when 20.3% votes could not win it a seat. CPI did its best in 1957 when it won nine for 37.5% votes, while its poorest performance came in 1989 when it could not win a single seat though it polled 6.2%. The Muslim League has been winning two seats right from 1962 with its vote share ranging between 4.5% in 1962 and 6.6% in 1957.

Key Contests

Badagara. Former union minister K.P. Unnikrishnan recorded six straight wins from here between 1971 and 1996, first as Congress and then thrice as a candidate of his Indian Congress (Socialist). But he suffered a defeat in 1996 after merging his IC(S) with the Congress.

Ottapalam (SC). K.R. Narayanan won it thrice between 1984 and 1991 as a Congress nominee. He quit in 1992 to become Vice President. CPI(M) wrested the seat from the Congress in 1996.

Electorate	:	4,77,07,688
Turnout	:	2,76,79,492
Turnout %	:	58.02%
Valid Votes	:	2,72,30,040
Invalid & Missing	:	4,49,452
Candidates	:	362

TAMIL NADU

Seats: 39 (General: 32; SC: 7)

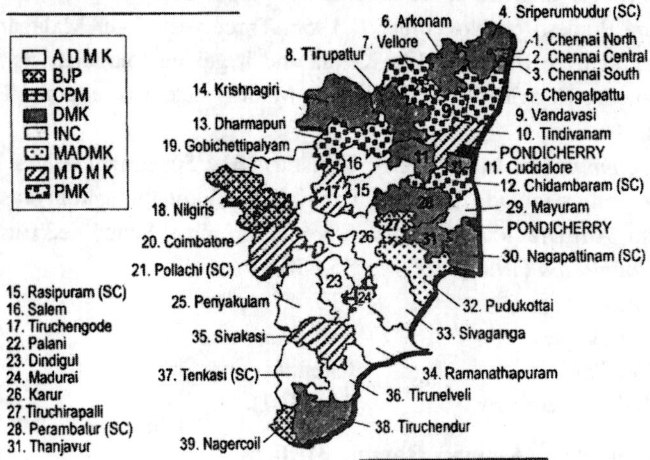

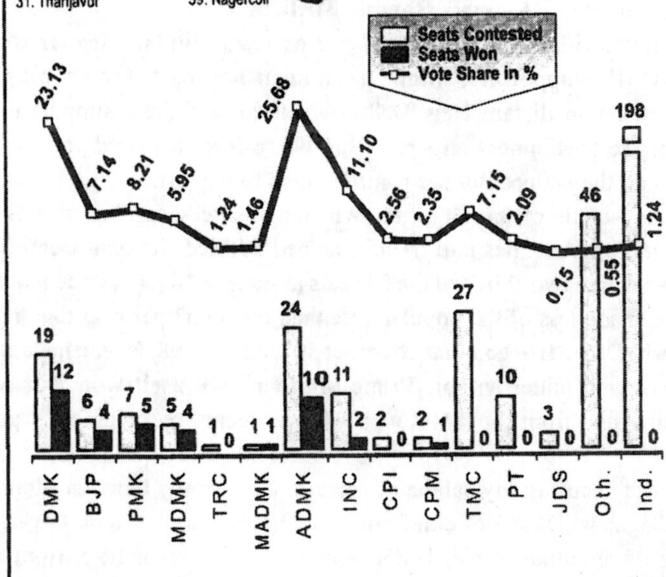

TAMIL NADU

History. The home of Dravida culture, Tamil Nadu came under British sway with the formation of the East India Company at Madras in 1639. Eleven districts of old Madras were made over to the new state of Andhra Pradesh on November 1, 1956. Three years later Malabar and Kasargod were transferred to Kerala and it gained four districts from Travancore-Cochin. On Jan. 14, 1969, Madras state was renamed Tamil Nadu.

Communities. Muslims 5%, Christians 6%, Scheduled Castes 18%. Communities include Vellalas, Vanniars, Mukkulathors, Idaiyans and Nadars, Adi Dravidas and Pallans are the principal Scheduled Castes.

Population (1991)	:	55,858,946
Area	:	130,058 sq km
Languages	:	Tamil
Capital	:	Chennai
Lok Sabha Seats	:	39 (SC 7)

Election 1999 : Amma's Gamble Misfires

Jayalalitha, *Puratchi Thalaivi* or revolutionary leader to her AIADMK supporters, might have been hoping to again play the kingmaker in distant New Delhi, when she withdrew support to the Vajpayee government on April 14, 1999 to force the third poll in three years on the nation. But her gamble failed to pay off.

In a battle of three Fronts, switched alliances, turning friends into enemies and enemies into friends, helped BJP led National Democratic Alliance win two-thirds of the 39 seats at stake. At 47.13 per cent, it won just a shade less of the popular vote than the 47.53 per cent that helped the AIADMK-BJP combine to corner 30 seats in 1998. Promising a stable government under an able Prime Minister, BJP itself won four seats, gaining one from the TMC with 7.14 per cent votes, just 0.28 points more.

But accusing Jayalalitha of corruption, new ally Dravida Munnetra Kazhagham (DMK) of chief minister M Karunanidhi, took the largest slice of the alliance pie. DMK won 12 seats, wresting six from rival AIADMK and one from CPI, with 23.13 per cent votes, indicating a three-point swing in its favour. Two other former Jayalalitha allies Pattali Makkal Katchi (PMK) and Marumalarchi Dravida Munnetra Kazhagam

Tamil Nadu

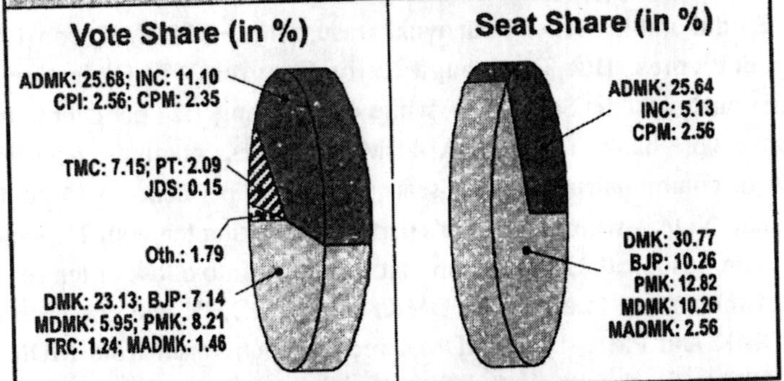

Swing %

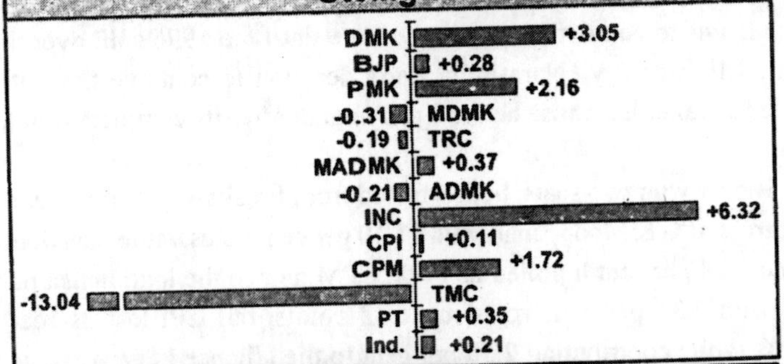

Gains & Losses

Party	Current Win	Prev. Win	Re-tained	Gained	Gained from	Lost	Lost to	Net
ADMK	10	18	8	2	TRC-1, MDMK-1	10	DMK-6, MDMK-2 MADMK-1, PMK-1	-8
BJP	4	3	3	1	TMC-1	0	-	+1
CPI	0	1	0	0	-	1	DMK-1	-1
CPM	1	0	0	1	JP-1	0	-	+1
DMK	12	5	5	7	CPI-1, ADMK-6	0	-	+7
INC	2	0	0	2	TMC-2	0	-	+2
JP	0	1	0	0	-	1	CPM-1	-1
MADMK	1	0	0	1	ADMK-1	0	-	+1
MDMK	4	3	2	2	ADMK-2	1	ADMK-1	+1
PMK	5	4	4	1	ADMK-1	0	-	+1
TMC	0	3	0	0	-	3	BJP-1, INC-2	-3
TRC	0	1	0	0	-	1	ADMK-1	-1
Total	39	39	22	17		17		0

(MDMK) brought in five and four seats with 8.21 and 5.95 per cent votes, both gaining a seat each from AIADMK.

So did another rebel Tirunavukkarasu, whose MADMK won 1.46 per cent votes. But Tamizhaga Rajiv Congress (TRC) leader V Ramamurthi lost his Salem seat, while contributing 1.24 per cent to the alliance vote bank. The rival AIADMK-Congress combine, accusing NDA of communalism, won 13 seats with 41.69 per cent—5.44 points less than NDA—with Jayalalitha's party contributing ten with 25.68 per cent, a minuscule 0.21 point drop that translated into a loss of ten seats. Six of these went to arch rival DMK, two to MDMK and one each to MADMK and PMK, but AIADMK recouped one each from MDMK and TRC to finish with a net deficit of eight.

The Congress, which had helped one or the other of the rival Kazhagams to come to power in the state until the 1996 split over then Prime Minister P V Narasimha Rao's decision to continue ties with a tainted Jayalalitha, chose her company again after its complete rout last time.

It now won two seats, both wrested from breakaway Tamil Maanila Congress of G K Mooppanar, with 11.10 per cent votes, more than double of the 4.78 per cent it polled in 1998. CPM gained the lone Janata party seat with 2.35 per cent votes, up 1.72 points, but CPI lost its seat to DMK, while contributing 2.56 per cent to the alliance kitty.

The TMC-led third front, saying it opposed both corruption and communalism, came a cropper although it won 9.4 per cent votes for its labours with TMC alone contributing 7.15 per cent, about a third of the 20.19 per cent it polled last time in alliance with DMK. TMC lost two seats to the Congress and one to BJP, while allies Puthiya Tamizhagam (PT) and JDS also failed to open their accounts, but brought in 2.09 and 0.15 per cent votes. All three JDS candidates lost their deposits.

Five of the seven SC seats were won by NDA with 46.74 per cent of the popular vote. DMK took three with 22.45 per cent, while PMK and MDMK shared one each with 12.98 and 6.23 per cent votes. BJP did not win a SC seat, but brought in 5.08 per cent votes. Rival AIADMK won the other two seats with 29.72 per cent as against five for 40.92 per cent last time. With CPI contributing 6.75 and the Congress 3.17 per cent, the alliance share in the reserved seats was 39.64 per cent. The Third

Front took away 12.81 per cent of the SC vote with TMC getting 8.19 against 20.14 per cent last time and PT notching 4.62 per cent.

A total of 276 candidates, including all the 198 independents, lost their deposits. TMC was the biggest loser with 21 followed by All India Forward Bloc and PT eight each. Only one of the 16 women candidates, Dr V Saroja of the AIADMK won in Rasipuram. Jayalalitha's foe-turned-friend-turned-foe, maverick Janata Party leader Subramanian Swamy, lost his deposit in Madurai to CPM's P Mohan. Former TMC union finance minister P Chidambaram was defeated in Sivaganga. Two former DMK ministers Murasoli Maran and T R Baalu retained their Madras Central and South seats with the latter winning by a margin of 240,184, the highest in the state. Power Minister Rangarajan Kumaramangalam won Tiruchirapalli for BJP, while Mani Shankar Aiyar, now back in Congress, made it from Mayiladuturai.

T T V Dhinakaran, a nephew of Jayalalitha's friend Sasikala Natarajan, accused in a FERA violation case, got in from Periyakulam, but another Jaya nominee, controversial former Supreme Court judge, V Ramaswamy, lost to MDMK leader Vaiko in Sivakasi.

Congress dominated politics in the old Madras state until 1967 when the Dravida Munnetra Kazhagam (DMK) led by C.N. Annadurai upset its applecart. From its best ever score of 31 seats for 46.5% in 1957, the Congress was reduced to just three for 41.7%. Politics in Tamil Nadu was never the same again after that. DMK won 25 seats for 35.8% that year and practically repeated the feat in 1971 winning 23 for 35.3%. Congress (I) found itself playing a bit part winning nine seats for 12.5%. while rival Congress(O) polled 30.4% but could win only one seat. Politics in the state took another turn in 1977 with a split in the DMK. Cinestar M.G. Ramachandran leading the rival AIADMK won it 18 seats for 30.5%, while DMK was left with only one seat for 18%. Alliance politics now came to the fore with Congress trading assembly seats for those in Parliament. The strategy not only helped the Congress gradually raise its share in the Lok Sabha to 28 in 1991 with 42.75% votes. but also hold the key to power in the state. With whichever of the two regional parties it sided, that won. It was thus that the AIADMK was reduced to just two for 25.4% votes in 1980 before striking it rich again between 1984 and 1991 in alliance with the Congress. Similarly DMK won 16 seats for 23% siding with the Congress in 1980. A break in the alliance in 1984 saw its tally crashing down to two, though at 25.9% it polled nearly three per cent more. But the worst was yet to come. DMK drew a blank in both 1989 and 1991, when its vote share too slid down to 22.69% in the poll after Rajiv Gandhi's May 21 assassination at Sriperumbudur. An anti-establishment vote and a revolt in the Congress helped it turn the tables on AIADMK and Congress together in 1996.

Among other parties, the CPI(M) won four seats in 1967 for 6.9%. The Swatantra won six seats in 1967 for 9.2% while eight independents won in 1957 with 81 of them polling 39.8%.

Key Contests

Madras South. This has been the constituency of former President R. Venkataraman, C.N. Annadurai, T.T. Krishnamachari and Vyjayanthimala. Venkataraman won it in 1977 and 1980. He had won earlier from Thanjavur in 1952 and 1957. DMK leader Murasoli Maran won it in 1971. From 1996 to 1999 he was returned from Madras Central.

Nagercoil. K. Kamaraj, Congress president from 1964 to 1968, won it in 1971. N. Dennis, who had won it four times in a row since 1984, retained it on the TMC ticket in 1996.

Sivaganga. Former Finance Minister P. Chidambaram, won it thrice for congress from 1984 to 1991. Switching over to TMC in 1996 the rebel minister defeated a former party colleagues M. Gowrishankaran by over 2.47 lakh votes. He lost the seat in 1999.

Tenkasi (SC). TMC leader M. Arunachalam won it for the sixth time in a row in 1996. The rebel leader who had been winning it for the Congress since 1977 defeated V. Selvaraj of the Congress by about 96,000 votes.

ANDAMAN AND NICOBAR ISLANDS

History. A group of more than 3,000 islands in the Bay of Bengal, were occupied by the British after driving out the Dutch in the 18th century. The first settlement was established in North Andamans in 1789. The British used it as a penal settlement between 1857 and 1942 when the Japanese occupied it. They came back into British hands on October 9, 1945. After becoming a part of free India in 1947, they were made a union territory in 1956.

Communities. Tribals 18%, Christians 26%, Muslims 9%. Tribal communities include the Great Andamanese, Jarawas and Onges.

Population (1991)	:	280,661
Area	:	8,249 sq km
Languages	:	Hindi, Tamil, Bengali, English
Capital	:	Port Blair
Lok Sabha Seats	:	1

Election 1999 : BJP Ends Long Congress Reign

BJP finally ended the 22-year-old Congress reign in the 3,000 picturesque islands since the first Lok Sabha poll there in 1967 with Bishnu Pada Ray polling 52.74 per cent votes—a massive 17.21 point swing—to defeat his Congress rival by a wide margin of 13,947 votes.

BJP had in 1998 come quite close—a margin of just 544 votes—to dislodging Congress' Manoranjan Bhakta, who had won the lone seat for the sixth time in a row to record the party's ninth straight win. Congress' best came in 1971, when K R Ganesh polled 61.5 per cent votes. The Congress, in fact, this time polled 7.26 per cent more votes to shore up its vote share to 43.17 per cent from its lowest ever of 35.91 per cent in 1998 as against BJP's 35.53 per cent. But it could not match the rise of saffron party which had polled 4.85 per cent in its first foray in 1991 raised it to 24.25 in 1996 and added another 11.28 per cent last time.

A candidate of Sharad Pawar's Nationalist Congress Party polled just 1,015 votes and lost his deposit. So did two independents, including a woman, together polling 3.39 per cent—up 0.86 points—votes. Indian Congress Socialist, that has now merged with NCP, had finished third with 20.36 per cent votes last time.

CPM, which had slipped to the fourth position in 1998 with only

Electorate	:	2,47,300
Turnout	:	1,47,098
Turnout %	:	59.48%
Valid Votes	:	1,45,791
Invalid & Missing	:	1,307
Candidates	:	5

A & N Islands

Seats: 1 (General: 1)

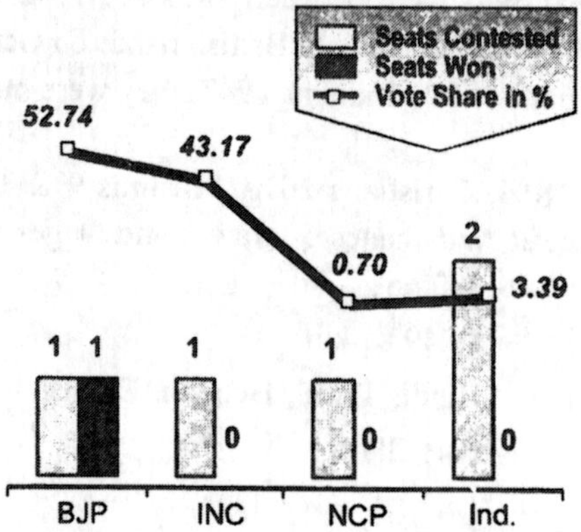

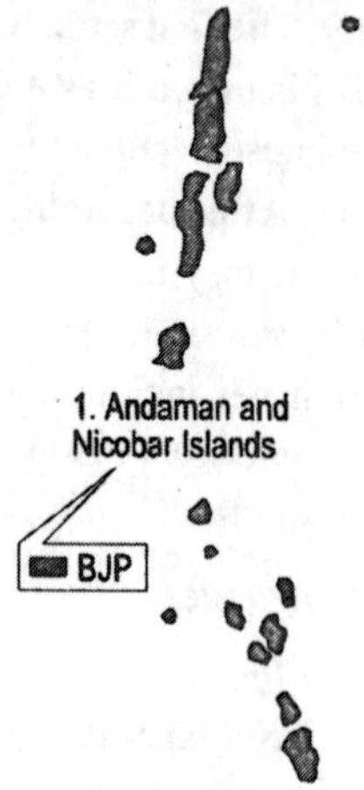

Vote & Seat Share

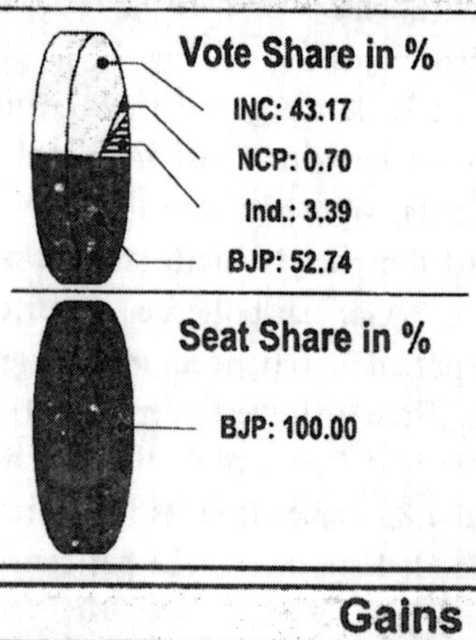

Swing %

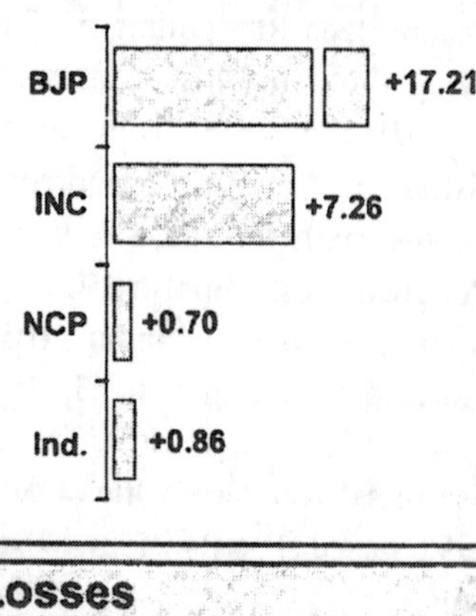

Gains & Losses

Party	Current Win	Prev. Win	Re-tained	Gained	Gained from	Lost	Lost to	Net
BJP	1	0	0	1	INC-1	0	-	+1
INC	0	1	0	0	-	1	BJP-1	-1
Total	1	1	0	1		1		0

5.67 per cent, did not put up a candidate this time. Starting with 20.3% in 1980, CPM polled its highest ever of 44.14% in 1991, lost a massive 30 per cent in 1996 and suffered a further erosion of 8.65 points in 1998.

Congress did its best in 1971 when K.R. Ganesh polled 61.5% votes. He had won it in 1967 too with 52.6% votes. Lok Dal polled 31.34% in 1984 and the Janata Dal 16.96% in 1989.

LAKSHADWEEP

Seats: 1 (ST: 1)

Electorate	:	37,620
Turnout	:	30,172
Turnout %	:	80.20%
Valid Votes	:	29,860
Invalid & Missing	:	312
Candidates	:	4

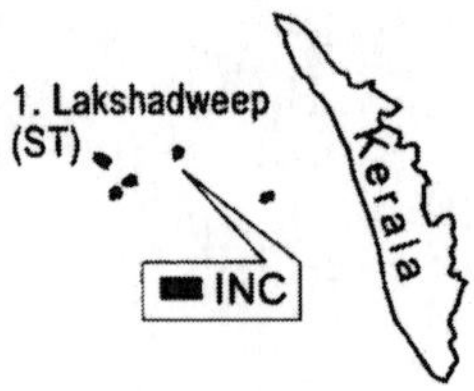

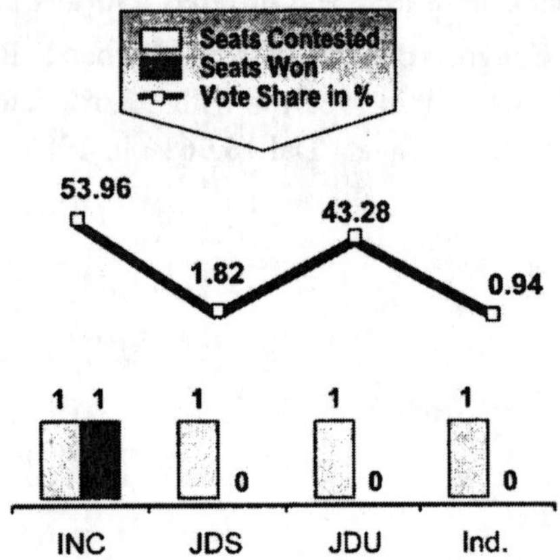

Vote & Seat Share

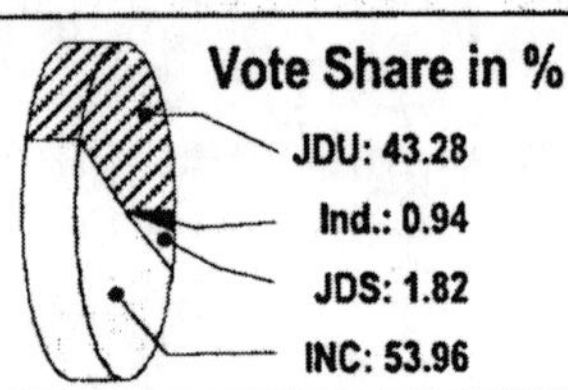

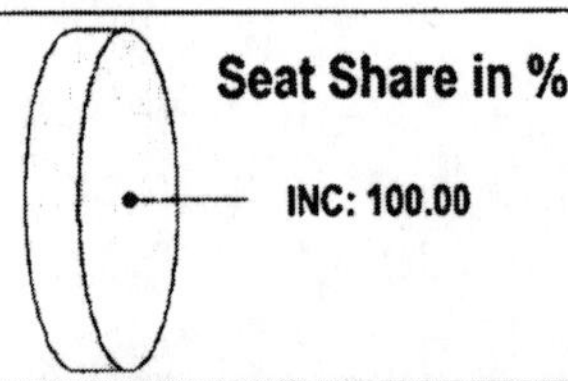

Swing %

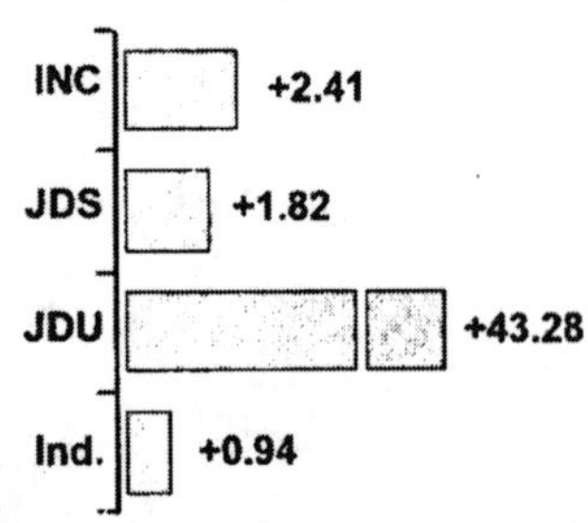

Gains & Losses

Party	Current Win	Prev. Win	Re-tained	Gained	Gained from	Lost	Lost to	Net
INC	1	1	1	0	-	0	-	0
Total	1	1	1	0	-	0	-	0

LAKSHADWEEP

History. The smallest Lok Sabha constituency is an archipelago of 36 islands, only ten of which are inhabited. The English took over all the islands in 1854. Made a Union Territory in 1956 as Laccadive, Minicopy and Amindivi Islands, it was renamed Lakshadweep in 1973.

Communities. Muslims 95%, Hindus 5%. Mostly Muslim, leading tribes include Koyas, Malimis, Melacheris, Raveris and Thakrus.

Population (1991)	:	51,407
Area	:	32 sq km
Languages	:	Malayalam
Capital	:	Kavaratti
Lok Sabha Seats	:	1 (ST)

Election 1999 : Sayeed Keeps Going

PM Sayeed, Deputy Speaker in the 12th Lok Sabha, did it yet again. For the tenth time in a row, he won the smallest Lok Sabha constituency, all but twice for the Congress. He contested the first poll as an independent in 1967, was returned unopposed as a Congress nominee in the second and stood for the rival Urs Congress in 1980.

Except in 1967, when he beat another independent, A T Arnakad, and in 1971 when he was elected unopposed, Sayeed had since 1977 always faced Mohammed Koya as his opponent, thrice as an independent, as a nominee of Janata Party in 1980 and that of Janata Dal after 1991. But this time, Koya, a doctor by profession, chose not to contest.

In the event, Sayeed, a lawyer by profession, who served as a minister in both the Charan Singh and Narasimha Rao governments, defeated his JDU rival, Dr K P Muthukoya by a record 3,189 votes, more than thrice his 964 margin last time. He had won the first election by 367 votes and just scraped through with 281 votes in 1991.

In percentage terms, Congress votes went up 2.41 points to 53.96 per cent. Sayeed did his best for the Congress in 1967 when he polled 58.6 per cent and his worst in 1991 when he polled 50.6 per cent. In 1980, when he won the seat for Urs Congress with 56.4 per cent votes, Congress (I) polled just 3.9 per cent.

Rival Muthukoya polled 43.28 per cent votes for JDU as against 48.45 per cent by Janata Dal last time. A JDS candidate polled 542 votes (1.82 per cent) and lost his deposit. So did an independent with even less-281 votes (0.94 per cent). As always, Lakshadweep, recorded a high 80.20 per cent turnout, but it was about five per cent less than in 1998.

Once a part of the Calicut constituency in Kerala, Lakshadweep Islands were consolidated into a Union Territory in 1956 and given representation in Lok Sabha the next year with the nomination of K Nalla Koya Thangal by the President of India. He was re-nominated in 1962 and the first poll conducted in 1967.

PONDICHERRY

History. Founded by the French in 1674, it was taken by the Dutch in 1693, but returned to the French in 1699. Mahe on the Malabar Coast was occupied around 1721, Yanam in 1731 and Karaikal in 1738. Once the British established their paramountcy over India, they let the French continue in Pondicherry. The French transferred it to India in 1954 and it became a Union Territory in 1962.

Communities. Muslims 6%, Christians 9%, Scheduled Castes 16%. Vanniars and Vellalas are the principal communities. Adi Dravidas and Parayans are dominant among SCs.

Population (1991)	:	807,785
Area	:	492 sq km
Languages	:	Tamil, Malayalam, French
Capital	:	Pondicherry
Lok Sabha Seats	:	1

Election 1999 : Return of the Congress

Former chief minister, M O H Farook won the erstwhile French enclave back for the Congress, which took it for the eighth time since 1967. It had conceded the seat to AIADMK in 1977 and DMK snatched it in 1998.

Farook polled 37.17 per cent votes—a swing of 5.05 points—to defeat his PMK rival by 24,188 votes. PMK polled 31.73 per cent—9.38 points less than the 41.11 per cent polled by DMK last time when it finally dislodged the Congress after finishing runner—up four times since 1980.

The TMC, which is still part of the ruling coalition in Pondicherry even after parting ways with DMK, finished third with Home Minister Kannan polling only 25.16 per cent votes. Six independents collecting 5.94 per cent lost their deposits. The Congress did its best in 1980 when it polled 66.5 per cent with its worst coming in 1998 after parting company with AIADMK, which won the seat in 1977 with 53.3 per cent.

BJP, which had doubled its vote share from 1.97 per cent in 1991 to 4.42 per cent in 1996, had left it to its then ally AIADMK to do the battle in Pondicherry in 1998. New-found partner PMK took up the NDA challenge this time.

PONDICHERRY

Seats: 1 (General: 1)

Electorate	:	7,02,176
Turnout	:	4,44,174
Turnout %	:	63.26%
Valid Votes	:	4,44,162
Invalid & Missing	:	12
Candidates	:	9

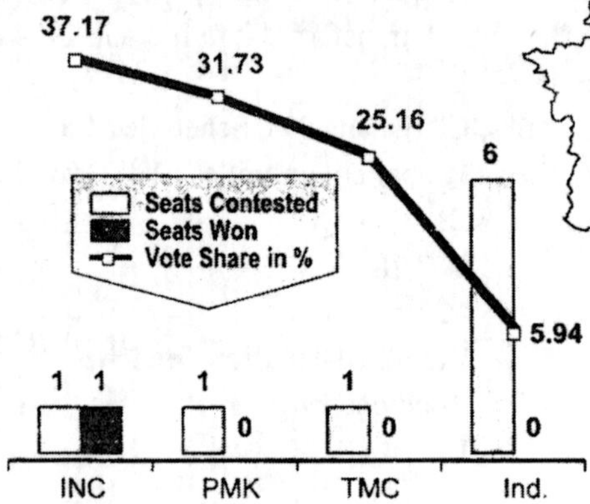

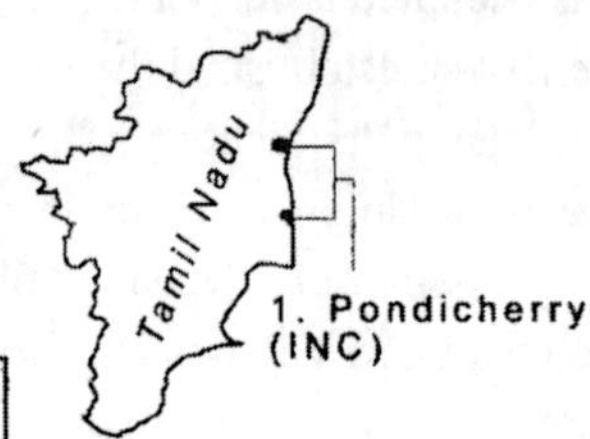

Vote & Seat Share

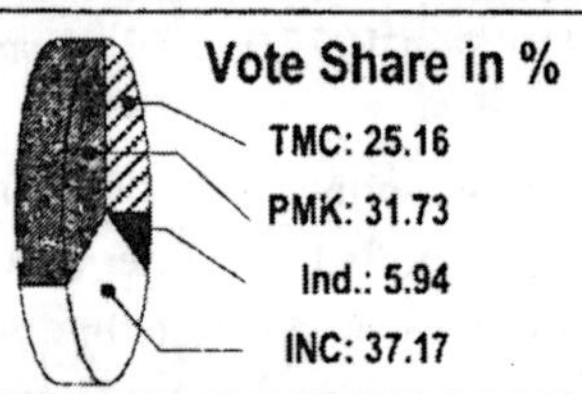

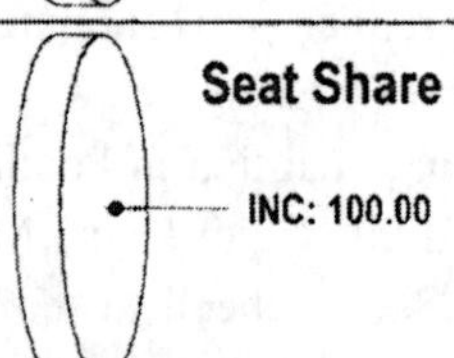

Swing %

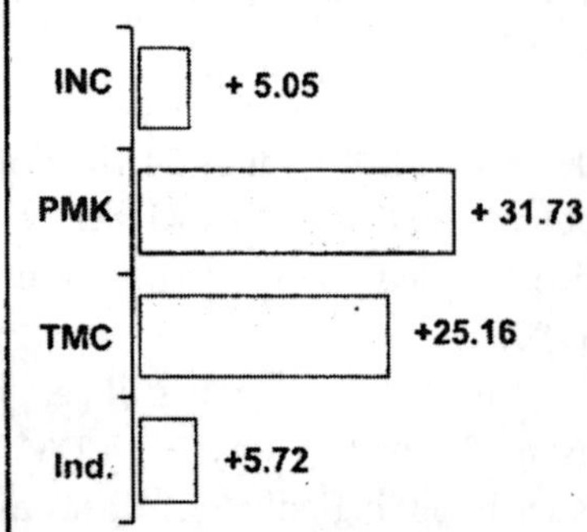

Gains & Losses

Party	Current Win	Prev. Win	Re-tained	Gained	Gained from	Lost	Lost to	Net
DMK	0	1	0	0	-	1	INC-1	-1
INC	1	0	0	1	DMK-1	0	-	+1
Total	**1**	**1**	**0**	**1**	**-**	**1**	**-**	**0**

Only other notable performances have been those of the Janata Party, which was the runner-up in 1977 and 1980 with 44.4 and 26.7 per cent votes, and the People's Front which finished third in 1967 with 26.9 per cent.

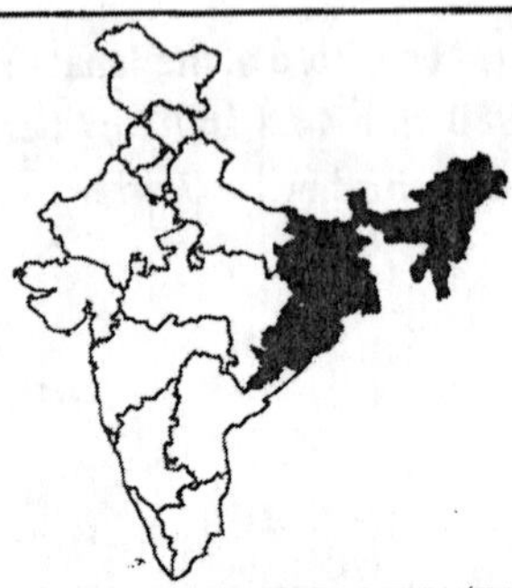

EAST

Seats: 142	Candidates: 1,097

Electorate	:	15,04,35,679
Turnout	:	9,97,15,542
Turnout %	:	66.28%
Valid Votes	:	9,85,16,153
Invalid & Missing	:	11,99,389

Party	Seats Contested	Seats Won	Lost Deposit	1999 Vote%	1998 Vote%	Vote Swing %
BJP + Allies	**140**	**74**	**12**	**40.87**	**31.08**	**+9.79**
BJP	69	36	5	18.97	17.99	+0.98
JD(U)	26	18	4	7.55	-	+7.55
BJD	12	10	0	4.44	3.69	+0.75
TC	29	8	2	9.50	8.94	+0.56
MSCP	2	1	1	0.23	0.19	+0.04
SDF	1	1	0	0.11	0.10	+0.01
ANC	1	0	0	0.07	0.17	-0.10
INC + Allies	**144**	**30**	**44**	**28.45**	**28.85**	**-0.40**
INC	101	23	36	18.19	18.75	-0.56
RJD	43	7	8	10.26	10.10	+0.16
BSP	53	0	52	0.61	0.33	+0.28
CPI	19	3	13	2.47	2.98	-0.51
CPM	40	24	4	13.99	14.11	-0.12
JD(S)	18	0	18	0.06	-	+0.06
NCP	44	2	41	0.82	-	+0.82
AGP	8	0	3	1.20	1.07	+0.13
FBL	6	2	3	1.24	1.22	+0.02
JMM	23	0	20	0.99	1.33	-0.34
MPP	1	0	0	0.15	0.12	+0.03
RSP	5	3	1	1.52	1.64	-0.12
UDP	1	0	0	0.11	0.21	-0.10
BPSP	2	0	0	0.62	-	+0.62
CPML	35	1	32	1.17	0.86	+0.31
MCO	1	0	0	0.36	0.26	+0.10
PDF	1	0	0	0.18	-	+0.18
URMCA	1	0	0	0.25	0.15	+0.10
Others	162	0	161	1.15	13.70	-12.55
Ind.	393	3	385	3.79	2.09	+1.70
Total	**1097**	**142**	**789**	**100.00**	**100.00**	**0.00**

CHAPTER 9

THE EAST: TURNING SAFFRON

Thanks to strategic tie-ups, BJP-led National Democratic Alliance at last gained an upper hand in the eastern region as it stormed Bihar and Orissa and made impressive inroads in Assam and West Bengal even as Congress and the Left held on to their respective strongholds. And though NDA did not make much of an impact in the northeast in terms of seats, its candidates succeeded in making their presence felt with substantial votes. The alliance with 74 seats cornered 52.11 per cent of the 142 seats at stake in the region. With 36 seats, BJP's own share of the regional seat pie was 25.35 per cent.

The rival Congress-RJD alliance could muster only 30 seats, a little over one fifth of the total, as it lost a dozen with another good show by Sonia Gandhi's party in Assam unable to offset the rout in Orissa despite a bit of improvement in West Bengal. While ally Laloo's luck ran out in Bihar, Leftists did somewhat better in harvesting 33 seats, or 23.24 per cent of the total, with three independents and Pawar's Nationalist Congress Party taking the remaining five.

Picking up 40.87 per cent, BJP alliance turned out to be the biggest vote catcher in the eastern region with a combined swing of 4.24 per cent. The 1998 alliance had got 36.63 per cent of the regional votes. Leading the pack of allies was BJP with its 36 seats for 18.97 per cent, up one point. New found ally Janata Dal (United) brought in 18 seats with 7.55 per cent votes instead of 5.91 per cent by George Fernandes' Samata last time, while Trinamool Congress contributed more votes—9.50 instead of 8.94 per cent—for its eight seats. Biju Janata Dal, bringing up the rear with 4.44 per cent, up 0.75 points, won ten seats for NDA. Swings for BJP ranged from an adverse 11.59 points in Manipur, 1.02 per cent in Bihar to a positive 3.44 per cent in Orissa and 5.35 per cent in Assam.

The alliance made its greatest haul in Bihar where it won 41 seats to gain 11 thanks to the consolidation of anti-Laloo vote with the merger of ally Samata with last time's adversary Janata Dal. Orissa brought in three fresh gains with an 8.94 per cent swing as an extra two came in from West Bengal with 2.54 per cent more votes. And in the northeast too, BJP gained a seat in Assam as it made its first pickings in Brahmaputra valley.

BJP itself gained 14 seats, eight from the Congress alone—four in Bihar and two each in Orissa and Assam-five from RJD in Bihar and one from CPM in West Bengal. But it also lost three seats to the Congress—two in Bihar and one in Assam—two to RJD and one apiece to CPM and an independent to finish with a net gain of seven. New ally JDU gained ten seats from RJD, while retaining seven of the ten Samata and the lone JD seat in Bihar. Old ally Biju Janata Dal wrested two from the Congress as it conceded another to it in Orissa, while Trinamool Congress did the same with CPM in West Bengal.

A tiny half a per cent adverse swing with a greater polarisation of votes across the region, cost the rival Congress-RJD alliance 11 seats as its combined vote slipped from 28.85 to 28.45 per cent. Congress itself lost only one, but the RJD conceded ten. As a further 0.56 point erosion brought its tally down to 23 for 18.19 per cent, Congress yielded eleven seats in all. Eight of these went to BJP, four in Bihar and two each in Assam and Orissa, where it lost two more to BJD and the Tura seat in Meghalaya to NCP with former Lok Sabha speaker P A Sangma switching sides.

In turn, it recovered ten seats, three from BJP—two in Bihar and one in Assam—two from Arunachal Congress and one each from Samata in Bihar, BJD in Orissa, UMF in Assam and CPM and RSP in West Bengal. Swings for Congress ranged from an adverse 4.1 per cent in Orissa and 1.91 per cent in West Bengal to a favourable 1.54 per cent in Bihar. Ally RJD polling 10.26 per cent could win only seven of the 43 seats it contested even as it raised its regional vote share up a notch from 10.10 per cent that brought it 17 seats last time. In all it lost 15 seats, ten to JDU and five to BJP, but recouped two each from BJP and Samata and one from the defunct Rashtriya Janata Party in Bihar as none of its seven candidates contesting outside Bihar could succeed.

With the United Front of yore in disarray, the Left won 33 seats with CPM alone taking 24 for 13.99 per cent instead of 26 for almost as much (14.11 per cent). Retaining its two seats in Tripura, CPM lost two to Trinamool Congress and one each to BJP and Congress in West Bengal, but also recouped one from Trinamool Congress there. It also won a seat from BJP in Bihar.

Dropping half a per cent vote, CPI retained its three seats in West Bengal, but lost one in Manipur to NCP to finish with a tally of three for 2.47 per cent. RSP lost one of its four seats to Congress in West Bengal as it polled 1.52 per cent, down 0.12 points, but Forward Bloc retained its two for 1.24 per cent. Another Left party, CPML gained a seat in Assam from ASDC with its 35 candidates in the region gathering 1.17 per cent. Not only did the NDA do well in general seats, but also won 19 of the 37 reserved seats with BJP itself raking in a dozen. Of the 20 SC seats, eleven went to NDA with a combined vote share of 45.63 per cent. BJP won four for 20.81 per cent, allies JDU and BJD brought in three each with 7.61 and 7.54 per cent votes, while Trinamool took one for 9.67 per cent.

The Left won seven for 23.48 per cent with CPM taking four for 14.61, RSP two for 5.27 and Forward Bloc one for three per cent. Congress-RJD combine polled more votes—27.29 per cent-but could win only one seat each with Laloo Yadav's party contributing 15.08 and Congress 12.21 per cent. The remaining 3.6 per cent of the SC vote was shared among others by BSP (1.27 per cent) and NCP (0.33 per cent). BJP again topped with eight wins in 17 ST seats with 32.26 per cent with allies Trinamool Congress (3.10 per cent), BJD (2.79 per cent) and JDU (0.31 per cent) bringing in 6.2 per cent votes to raise the NDA ST vote share to 38.46 per cent.

Four ST seats were shared by the Left with 14.48 per cent, as CPM took two for 7.55 and RSP and CPML one each for 4.14 and 2.38 per cent respectively. Congress took two for 26.06 per cent, while rival NCP got one for 1.35 per cent. Two independents also won sharing the rest of the twenty per cent vote, with two factions of JMM taking about two per cent.

In the seven smaller Northeastern states, the Congress won four of the eleven for 31.26 per cent, gaining two from Arunachal Congress, retaining the Nagaland seat and losing one in Meghalaya to NCP. For the NDA, Sikkim Democratic Front (2.45 per cent) and Manipur State

Congress Party (5.05 per cent) retained their seats to give the alliance two for 21.26 per cent as Arunachal Congress (1.61 per cent) lost its two seats to Congress.

Six BJP candidates polled 7.54 per cent, but none succeeded. Nor did one each of Trinamool Congress (3.96 per cent) and JDU (0.64 per cent). Left finished third in popularity stakes with 19.59 per cent, about one and a half point behind NDA supporters. CPM polling 15.39 per cent retained both the seats in Tripura, but CPI (0.90 per cent) lost a seat to NCP in Manipur and ally Manipur People's Party could not win though it brought 3.30 per cent votes.

Among others, new entrant NCP topped with a win each in Meghalaya and Manipur with 7.69 per cent, while one independent replaced another in Mizoram as the rest shared about a fifth of the North-eastern vote.

The three tribal seats were shared by CPM (Tripura), NCP (Manipur) and an independent (Mizoram). With the Left cornering 26.20 per cent of the ST vote, and the independents taking in as much, Congress polled 13.52 and BJP 12.58 per cent ahead of NCP with 9.28 per cent. Trinamool Congress too garnered 5.31 per cent but without success.

Electorate	:	5,88,25,863
Turnout	:	3,58,62,673
Turnout %	:	60.96
Valid Votes	:	3,56,51,151
Invalid & Missing	:	2,11,522
Candidates	:	497

BIHAR

Seats: 54 (General: 41; SC: 8; ST: 5)

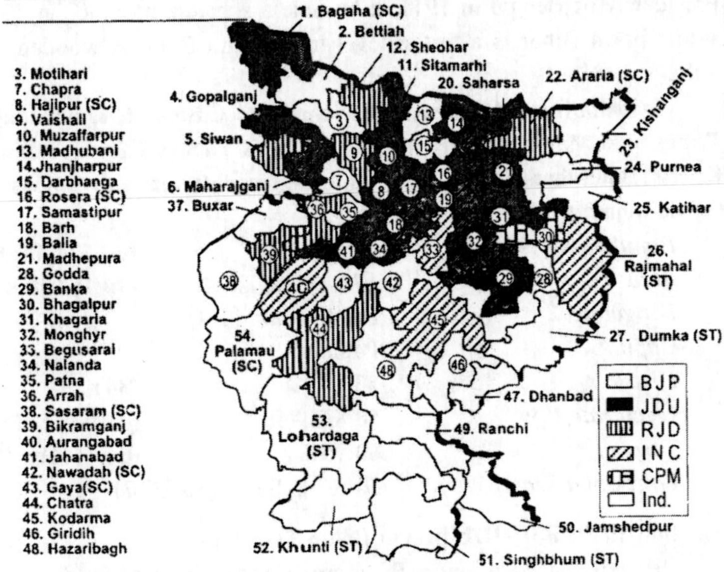

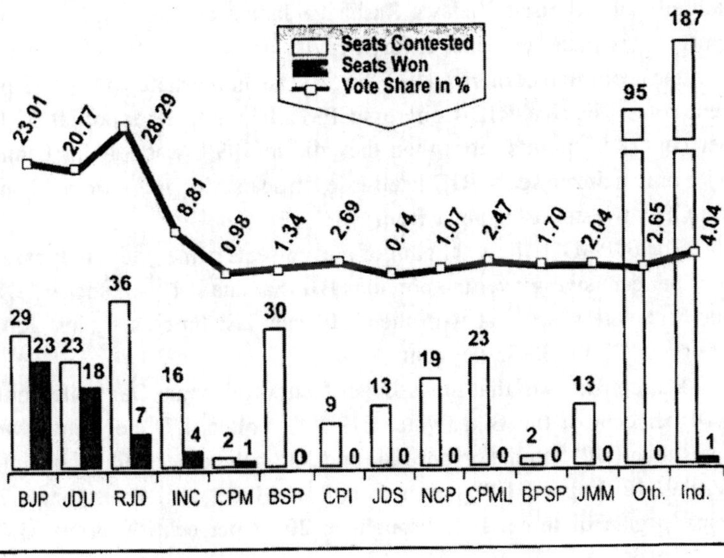

BIHAR

History. Tracing its history to the Mauryan empire, the British wrested it from the Nawabs of Bengal in 1764. Broken away from the Presidency of Bengal in 1911, it became a separate province in 1936. While north Bihar is a fertile level tract, south Bihar is wooded and hilly.

Communities. Muslims 15%, Scheduled Castes 16%, Scheduled Tribes 11%. Major communities include Ahirs/Yadavs, Kurmis, Rajputs, Koeris, Bhumihars and Kahars. Santhals, Hos, Mundas and Oraons are the dominant tribes.

Population (1991)	:	86,374,465	(64,574,465)
Area	:	173,877 sq km	(94,163 sq km)
Languages	:	Hindi, Maithili, Urdu	
Capital	:	Patna	
Districts	:	52	(34)
Electorate (99)	:	58,825,863	(43,907,882)
Turnout	:	60.96%	(64.15%)
Lok Sabha Seats	:	54-SC 8, ST 5 (40-SC 7)	

Election 1999: BJP-JDU Storm Laloo Territory

New political equations in Bihar proved the undoing of fodder scam-tainted Laloo Prasad Yadav's Rashtriya Janata Dal as despite polling more votes than last time, it lost heavily as the rival BJP-Janata Dal (United) combine cornered 41 of the 54 seats in the state with 43.78 per cent votes. The rival RJD-Congress-CPM alliance together polling 38.08 per cent, 3.83 points more than they did in 1998, was left far behind with only a dozen seats. RJD itself lose ten seats, Congress dropped one, but CPM wrested Bhagalpur from BJP.

For BJP-JDU, the vital gain of eleven seats came with an apparent four per cent swing over the previous BJP-Samata Party alliance's 39.77 per cent vote share that won them 30 seats last time as against RJD-Congress' 22 for 33.85 per cent.

But considering that the 'secular' faction of Janata Dal polled only 0.14 per cent of the Bihar vote, BJP-JDU polled 4.71 per cent fewer votes than BJP, Samata on one side and JD on the other polled last time. While BJP dropped 1.02 points to poll 23.01 per cent votes for its 23 seats, a gain of three, JDU brought in 20.77 per cent. This was 3.69

Bihar

Vote Share (in %)

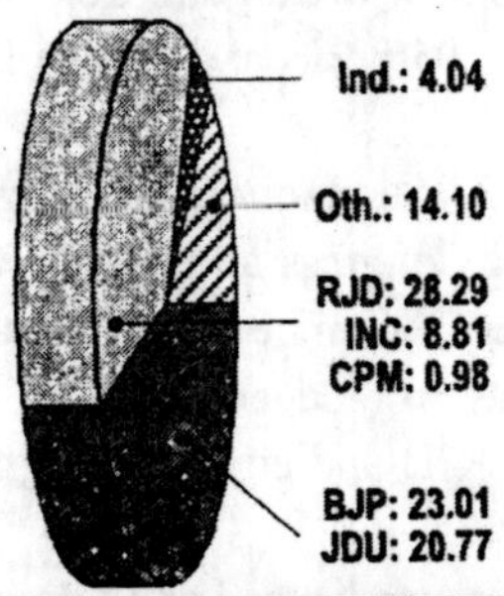

Seat Share (in %)

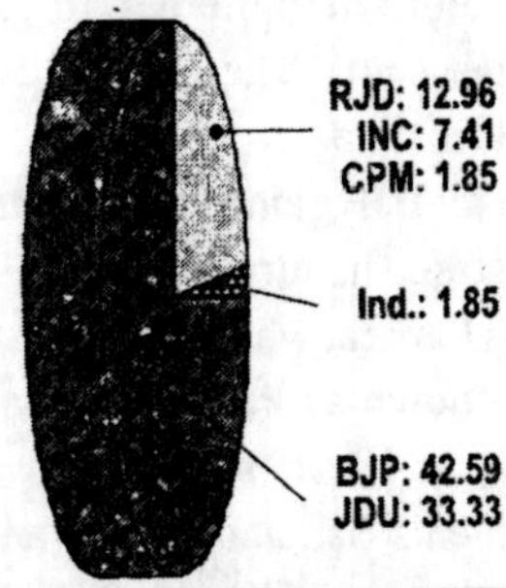

Swing %

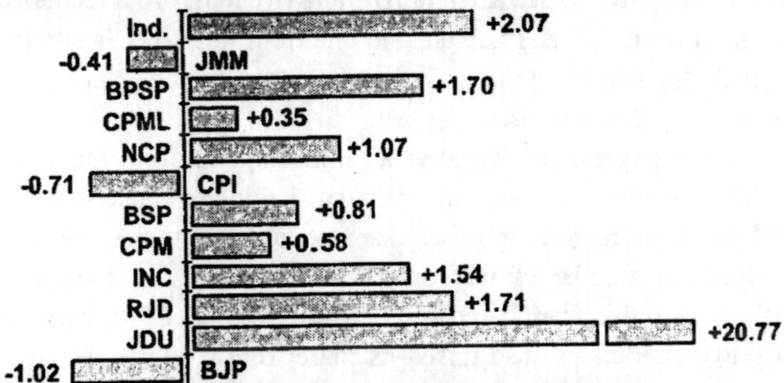

Gains & Losses

Party	Current Win	Prev. Win	Re-tained	Gained	Gained from	Lost	Lost to	Net
BJP	23	20	14	9	RJD-5, INC-4	6	RJD-2, INC-2 CPM-1, IND-1	+3
INC	4	5	1	3	SAP-1, BJP-2	4	BJP-4	-1
CPM	1	0	0	1	BJP-1	0	-	+1
JD	0	1	0	0	-	1	JDU-1	-1
JDU	18	0	0	18	RJD-10, SAP-7, JD-1	0	-	+18
RJD	7	17	2	5	BJP-2, SAP-2 RJP-1	15	JDU-10, BJP-5	-10
SAP	0	10	0	0	-	10	JDU-7, RJD-2 INC-1	-10
RJP	0	1	0	0	-	1	RJD-1	-1
Ind	1	0	0	1	BJP-1	0	-	+1
Total	54	54	17	37		37		0

points less than the 24.46 per cent secured by George Fernandes' Samata (15.74 per cent) and Sharad Yadav-led JD (8.72 per cent) separately in 1998 before they merged to form JDU along with Hegde's Lok Shakti (0.11 per cent). The two LS candidates at 0.05 per cent got even fewer votes this time.

In all BJP gained nine seats, five from RJD and four from Congress, but lost six in turn, two each to RJD and Congress and one to CPM besides Purnea, which was wrested by former SP nominee, Rajesh Ranjan, better known as Pappu Yadav contesting as an independent. Ally JDU brought in 18 seats with ten wrested from RJD and eight coming from constituents Samata (seven) and JD (one).

In the rival alliance, RJD finished with seven instead of 17 despite a little 1.71 point swing that raised its vote share from 26.58 to 28.29 per cent. It really lost 15 seats, ten to JDU and five to BJP, but recouped five, two each from BJP and Samata and one from Rashtriya Janata Party of alleged don Anand Mohan Singh, who formed another party and lost narrowly by 2,535 votes.

Ally Congress, which after an initial uproar from the state unit, agreed to contest only 16 seats RJD was willing to concede, too polled 1.54 points more votes to raise its share from 7.27 to 8.81 per cent, but dropped a seat, to be left with only four. It actually lost as many to BJP, but recouped two from it and another from Samata. CPM, which put up only two candidates, also raised its share from 0.40 per cent to nearly one per cent as it wrested a seat from BJP.

But CPI refusing RJD's offer of three seats, fielded nine candidates, none of whom could win as its vote share slid by 0.71 points from 3.40 to 2.69 per cent. The rest of 15 per cent vote was shared by CPML (2.47 per cent), two factions of JMM (2.47 per cent), Pawar's NCP (1.07 per cent), BSP (1.34 per cent) and 291 independents and others in a contest of 497. All but two of the 187 independents lost their deposits with 196 others, including 29 of BSP, 18 of Pawar's NCP and 13 of JDS. Only four of the 20 women candidates won with former union minister Kanti Singh regaining the Bikramganj seat for RJD.

Dogged by the fodder scam, RJD chief Laloo Yadav was humbled in Madhepura seat by Sharad Yadav, who had replaced him as JD president after the 1997 party split, but not before a bit of drama with Laloo going to court demanding a repoll because of alleged rigging. When he won despite denial of a repoll, Sharad Yadav claimed that his margin of victory would have been much higher than the 30,319 he got. Former union minister Taslimuddin of RJD, with a controversial past also lost Kishanganj to BJP, but alleged don M Sahabuddin retained his Siwan seat for RJD.

Defence Minister George Fernandes retained his Nalanda seat for JDU instead of Samata, as did Ram Vilas Paswan, who had given JD its lone seat in Bihar in 1998, winning his Hajipur (SC) seat with 105,504 votes. Other notable winners were Finance Minister Yashwant Sinha in Hazaribagh, former railway minister Nitish Kumar in Barh and BJP Union minister Babulal Marandi in Dumka. Cricketer Kirti Azad, who was clean bowled by would-be Congress chief minister Sheila Dikshit in November 1998 assembly elections in Delhi, wrested Darbhanga from RJD for BJP.

Polling more than half the votes (50.88 per cent), BJP-JDU combine won all but one of the eight SC seats with half of them again going to BJP for 30.03 per cent instead of 28.99, while three were taken by ally JDU with 20.85 per cent. RJD could retain only one with 41.32 per cent. Rest of the 7.80 per cent SC vote was shared by BSP (2.57 per cent), CPML (1.52 per cent), NCP (0.92 per cent) and 33 others and independents (2.79 per cent). BJP also won four of the five tribal seats with 41.48 per cent instead of three for 40.03, while Congress lost one of its two ST seats even as it raised its vote share by 7.29 points from 29.21 to 36.50 per cent. Four JMM candidates polled 17.50 per cent, but in vain while the rest of 4.52 per cent was shared by 23 others and independents.

Politics in Bihar was dominated by the Congress until 1967 when it lost power in the state, but managed to win 34 Lok Sabha seats with the backing of 34.8% voters—down 11% from the first general election in 1952 when it won 45 seats with 45.8% votes. Congress retrieved its position a bit in 1971 when it won 39 seats with 40.1% votes. But the 1977 Janata wave completely swept it away. It could not with even a single seat though it polled 22.9% votes. The newly formed Janata Party, on the other hand, won a massive mandate wresting 52 seats with the backing of 65% voters. The Congress bounced back in 1980 to win 30 seats for 36.4% votes and four years later saw its tally zooming to 48 with the sympathy wave in the wake of Prime Minister Indira Gandhi's assassination. Its popularity touched the highest ever figure of 51.8%.

But the renewed honeymoon lasted only five years. In 1989 its tally plunged to four with 28.1% votes. Two years later it lost three more seats to finish with only one seat procured with 24.16%. The Janata Dal era began in Bihar in 1989 when the party won 31 seats for 36.40% votes. It added one more seat in 1991 despite an over two per cent drop in its vote share. But the BJP has been progressively enlarging its vote bank—from 6.93% in 1984—when it failed to win a seat—to over 24% in 1998, with 20 seats.

Key Contests

Barh. Samata Party leader Nitish Kumar won the seat for Janata Dal in 1989 and 1991. In 1996, he defeated former JD colleague Vijay Krishna by a margin of over ten per cent.

Chapra. JD president, Laloo Prasad Yadav won as a Janata Party candidate in 1977 and as a JD nominee in 1989, but resigned in April 1990. BJP's Rajiv Pratap Rudi wrested the seat in 1996.

Kishanganj. The constituency with more Muslims than all but four other constituencies, returned journalist M.J. Akbar in 1989, but preferred Syed Shahabuddin, a former IFS member, in 1991. In 1996, it opted for Taslimuddin of JD, whose later appointment as minister of state for home in the Gowda government caused a great deal of controversy because of his alleged criminal record.

Hajipur. Ram Vilas Paswan has been elected to the Lok Sabha seven times, six times from Hajipur and once from Rosera in 1991. He won with a record margin of 5.05 lakhs in 1989.

Sasaram. Scheduled Caste leader Jagjivan Ram won eight times in a row—from 1962 to 1984 —the first five times as a Congress candidate. But his daughter Meira Kumar failed to win it back for the Congress in 1989 and 1991. BJP candidate Muni Lal wrested it from the JD in 1996.

JHARKHAND

History. Jharkhand became the 28th state of India on November 15, 2000, the birth anniversary of legendary Birsa Munda, leader of an insurrectionary tribal peasant movement way back in 1895. Babulal Marandi of BJP took over as the first chief minister with the National Democratic Alliance led by BJP enjoying an upper hand in the 81-member house.

Carved out of Bihar, the region has witnessed movements for separation since the late thirties though the struggle for self-rule can be traced more than two centuries back with Tika Manji waging a major protest in 1772. An Adivasi Mahasabha (Tribal Council) was launched in 1938 followed by the formation of Jharkhand Party by Moreng Gonke in 1950 to back the demand for an Adivasi homeland. Emerging as a major opposition with 21 seats in the Bihar assembly in 1952, it repeated its performance five years later, before waning away in the sixties. The movement received fresh impetus when Santhal leader Shibu Soren formed Jahrkhand Mukti Morcha in 1972. A tripartite agreements among the centre, Bihar and Jharkhand leaders led to the formation of the Jharkhand Area Autonomous Council in 1995. Jharkhand has rich reserves of iron ore and coal and several industries including those run by the house of Tata.

Population (1991)	:	218,00,000
Area	:	79,714 sq km
Languages	:	Hindi
Capital	:	Ranchi
Districts	:	18 : Bokaro, Chhatra, Deogarh, Dhanbad, Dumka, Garwa, Giridih, Hazaribagh, Koderma, Lohardaga, Pakur, Palamau, Ranchi, Sahibganj, Singhbhum (East), Singhbhum West),
Lok Sabha Seats	:	14 (SC 1, ST 5)
Party Pasition	:	BJP 11(-1), Congress 2, RJD 1 (+1)

Election 1999 : BJP Takes Centre Stage

Polling 45.53% votes in the election before the formation of Jharkhand, BJP won all but three of the 14 seats in the region even as it

Electorate	:	1,49,17,981
Turnout	:	76,97,554
Turnout %	:	51.60%
Valid Votes	:	75,90,428
Invalid Votes	:	1,07,126
Candidates	:	125

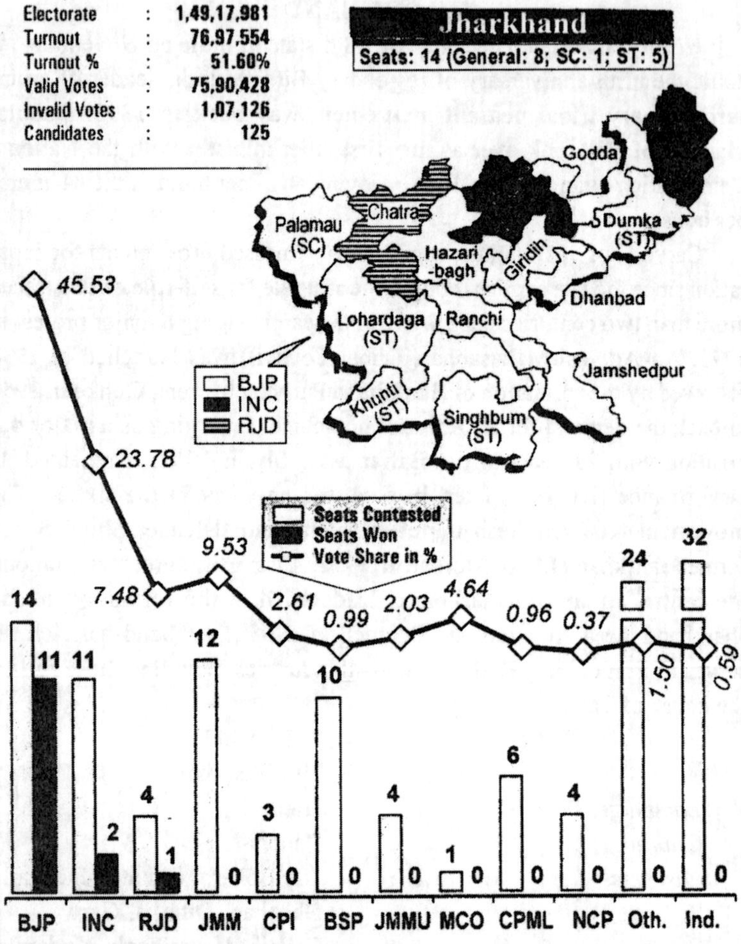

GAINS & LOSSES

Party	Current Win	Previous Win	Re-tained	Gained	Gained from	Lost	Lost to	Net
BJP	11	12	9	2	INC-2	3	INC-2, RJD-1	-1
INC	2	2	0	2	BJP-2	2	BJP-2	0
RJD	1	0	0	1	BJP-1	0	-	+1
Total	14	14	9	5		5		0

conceded Chhatra seat to RJD. BJP lost two more seats—Rajmahal (ST) and Kodarma to Congress, but wrested two other ST seats—Singhbhum and Lohardaga—from it to limit its losses to one.

The Congress finished second in the popularity stakes with 23.78% votes with two seats again, while RJD gained its lone seat with 7.48%. Jharkhand Mukti Morcha (JMM) polled more—9.53%—to take third place, but a seat eluded it with JMM(U) taking away about two per cent votes.

CPI polled 2.61%, while BSP and CPI(ML) garnered about one per cent each. Independents and others shared the remaining ten per cent.

Winning four of the five ST seats with 46% votes, BJP finished over nine points ahead of the Congress, while wresting Lohardaga and Singhbhum and retaining Dumka and Khunti.

Polling 53.37% votes, it also kept the Palamau SC seat with RJD taking a 36.65% votes share.

Electorate	:	2,41,87,460
Turnout	:	1,34,50,484
Turnout %	:	55.61%
Valid Votes	:	1,32,67,000
Invalid & Missing	:	1,83,484
Candidates	:	105

ORISSA

Seats: 21 (General: 13; SC: 3; ST: 5)

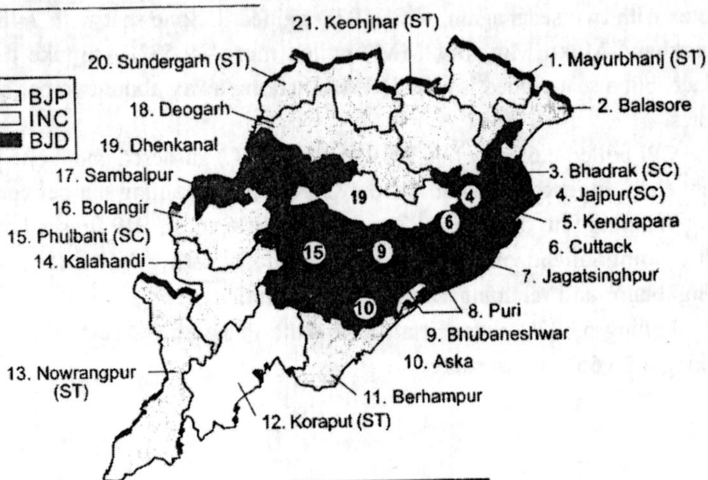

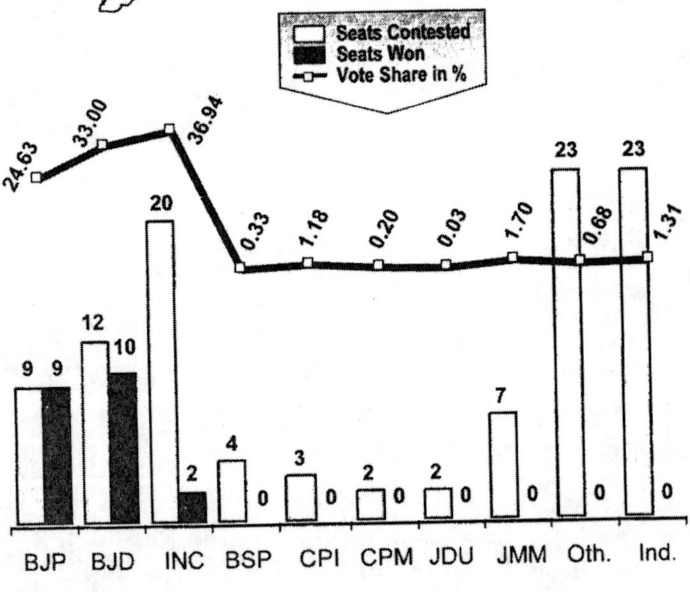

ORISSA

History. Known as Kalinga in the olden days, Orissa was taken over by the British in 1803 and made a part of the Bengal Presidency. It was made a separate province in 1936. After independence, 25 princely states of Orissa were merged with it on August 19, 1949. Orissa ranks tenth in area and eleventh in population.

Communities. Scheduled Castes 16%, Scheduled Tribes 25%. Major communities include Gauras/Goalas, Khandayats, Telis, Kewats and Tantis/Tatwas. Panos, Doms, Gandas and Dhobas are the principal Scheduled Castes. Dominant Scheduled Tribes are Khonds, Gonds, and Santhals.

Population (1991)	:	31,659,736
Area	:	155,707 sq km
Language	:	Oriya
Capital	:	Bhubaneswar
Lok Sabha Seats	:	21 (SC 3, ST 5)—Coastal 10, Western 5, Tribal 6

Orissa: BJP—BJD Tide Sweeps Congress Away

A near nine per cent swing coupled with a strong anti-incumbency vote against the ruling Congress, helped BJP and its ally Biju Janata Dal, floated by popular Orissa leader Biju Patnaik's son Naveen, all but sweep away the Congress leaving it with just two of the 21 seats. Together cornering more than half of the popular vote—57.63 per cent instead of 48.69 per cent last time—the BJP-BJD combine snatched three seats from the Congress as an adverse 4.1 per cent swing reduced the Congress vote share to 36.94 per cent in a virtual two-horse race.

Claiming the legacy of Biju, Naveen Patnaik's BJD raised its popular share by 5.5 points to 33 per cent to win ten seats, gaining two from and losing one to Congress to finish with a net gain of one. Ally BJP, also adding 3.44 points to its share polled nearly a quarter of the state vote (24.63 per cent), to win nine, snatching two from Congress while holding on to the seven it had won in 1998.

In its worst performance after 1989, when it could win only three seats with 38.4 per cent and 1977, when it got four for 38.2 per cent, Congress lost four of its five seats. Two each went to BJP and BJD, but

Orissa

Vote Share (in %)

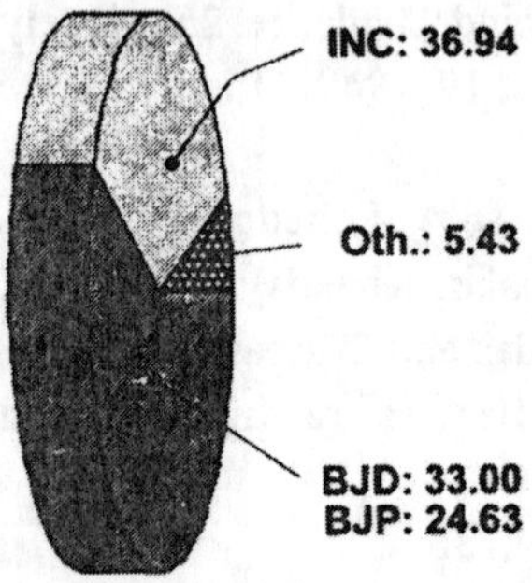

Seat Share (in %)

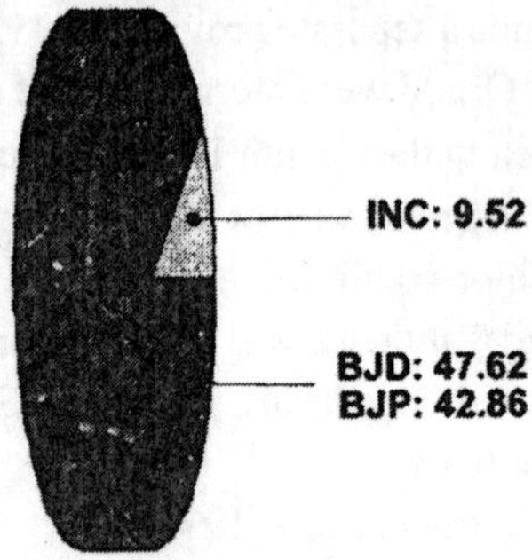

Swing %

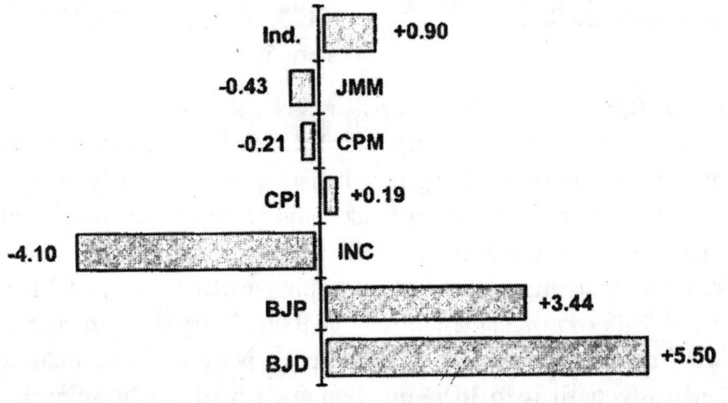

Gains & Losses

Party	Current Win	Prev. Win	Re-tained	Gained	Gained from	Lost	Lost to	Net
BJD	10	9	8	2	INC-2	1	INC-1	+1
BJP	9	7	7	2	INC-2	0	-	+2
INC	2	5	1	1	BJD-1	4	BJD-2, BJP-2	-3
Total	21	21	16	5		5		0

Congress recouped one from BJD to finish with it lowest tally of two for 36.94 per cent. The rest of 5.4 per cent vote pie was divided among Jharkhand Mukti Morcha (1.70 per cent), the Left (1.47 per cent), BSP (0.33 per cent) and 23 independents (1.31 per cent) besides half a dozen sundry parties.

Candidates of all parties, except BJD, BJP and Congress and all the 23 independents were among the 63 deposit losers in a contest of 105. The only seat Congress could retain was Koraput won last time by chief minister Giridhar Gamang, whose controversial vote in Lok Sabha during the confidence vote in April 1999 had brought the Vajpayee government down. His wife Hemabati won it by a slender margin of 12,216 votes now.

Former union minister Kamakhya Prasad Singh Deo won the only other seat for the party, Dhenkanal with the lowest margin of 3,752 votes as state Congress chief Hemananda Biswal made a vain bid to dislodge Debendra Pradhan of BJP in Deogarh and lost by 86,644 votes. BJD leader Naveen Patnaik won his father's Aska seat again by 256,675 votes, the highest margin in the state, while a former prince, Bikram Kesari Deo retained Kalahandi seat for BJP by over one lakh votes. He was among a dozen BJP-BJD candidates to do so. Only two of eight women contestants made it with Hemabati Gamang winning Koraput for Congress and a *bahu* of the erstwhile Bolangir royal family, Sangeeta Singh Deo retaining her seat by a wider margin of 180,869 votes.

While BJD won all the three SC seats with 58.05 per cent, 12.62 points more than the 45.43 per cent that gave it two in 1998, Congress lost its only seat as its SC vote share dropped by 3.42 points from 43.70 to 40.28 per cent. BSP took about one per cent SC vote while five others polled 0.62 per cent. BJP won four of the five ST seats 45.74 per cent, up 7.84 points, to wrest one from Congress. BJD doing battle for the combine in the fifth ST seat polled 8.82 per cent to give it 54.56 per cent of the ST vote pie, but could not dislodge Congress from Koraput. While Congress ST vote dropped 2.70 points from 39.75 to 37.05 per cent, JMM failed to win a seat even as it polled 6.66 per cent. Eight other candidates, including one of Pawar's NCP, shared 1.29 per cent.

The Congress had put in its best performance in 1984 after Indira Gandhi's assassination when it won 20 seats with 57.5% as it did in

1980 with 56.1%. And its worst was in 1989 when it could win only three seats for 38.4%—one less than the four it won with 38.2% votes against the Janata tide in 1977.

That year the Janata won 15 seats for 51.8%, but lost it all in 1980 though it polled 14.1%. By 1984 it regained a seat polling 32% votes. The Janata Dal won 16 seats in its first outing in 1989 for 49.5%, but lost all but six in 1991 as its vote share plunged nearly 15 points to touch 34.62%. It lost two more this time with its vote share going down to a little over 30%.

BJP has progressively increased its vote share from 1.2% in 1984 to 24.63% with nine seats in 1999.

Most other parties, including the CPI and CPI(M) have never won more than a seat or two. Only Swatantra Party won eight seats in 1967 for 30.9% and three in 1971 for 15.9%, while the Gantantra Parishad won seven seats in 1957 with 29.1%, and Biju Patnaik's Utkal Congress polled 23.6% in 1971 but could win only one seat.

Key Contests

Berhampur. In 1996 P.V. Narasimha Rao chose this constituency with about 35% Telugu-speaking people, as his second seat after Nandyal in Andhra, from where he had entered the Lok Sabha in 1991. He won both and kept Berhampur, which has always voted Congress, except in 1952 when it opted for CPI.

Aska. JD leader Biju Patnaik wrested it from the Congress in 1996 defeating R.C. Rath, who had won it thrice for the Congress.

Patnaik also won from Cuttack where colleague Srikant Jena had beaten Jayanti Patnaik, wife of Chief Minister J.B. Patnaik in the previous last two elections.

In the past, Biju Patnaik had thrice won from Kendrapara between 1977 and 1984 as a Janata Party candidate.

WEST BENGAL

Seats: 42 (General: 32; SC: 8; ST: 2)

Electorate	:	4,65,27,770
Turnout	:	3,57,44,108
Turnout %	:	76.82%
Valid Votes	:	3,52,90,663
Invalid & Missing	:	4,53,445
Candidates	:	309

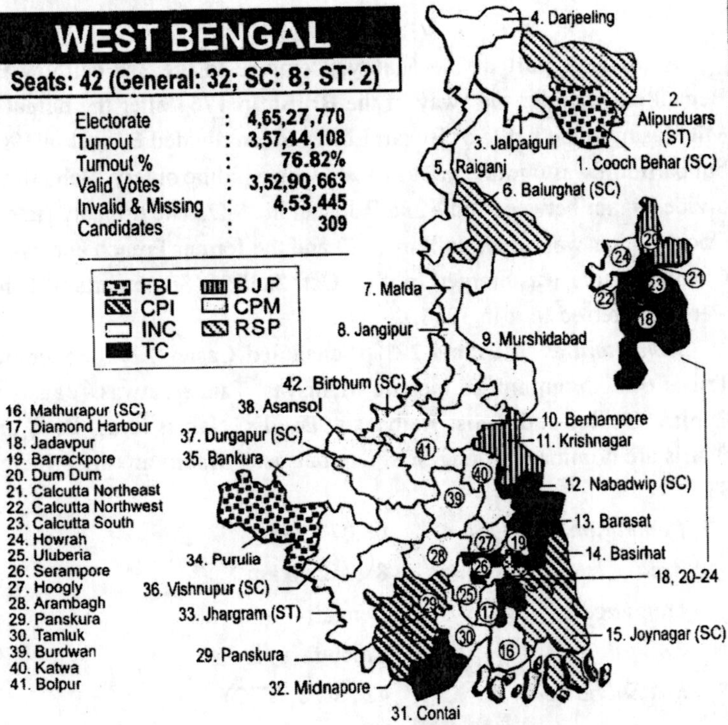

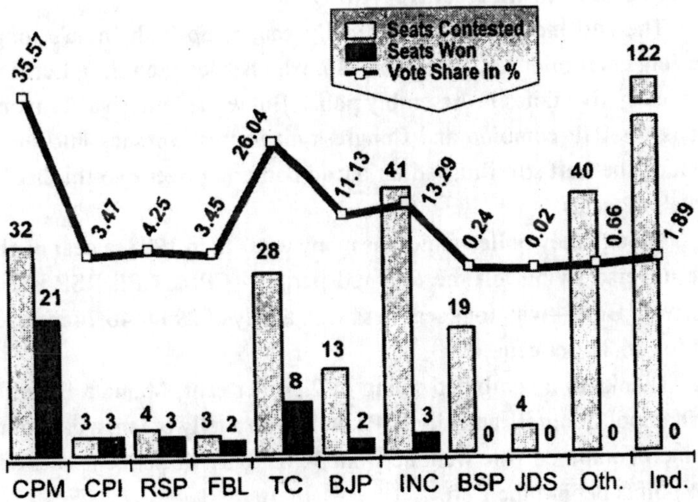

WEST BENGAL

History. A part of the Mauryan empire in the 3rd century BC Bengal came under the sway of the British in 1764 after the defeat of Mir Kasim in the battle of Buxar. Lord Curzon divided Bengal in 1905, but partition was undone in 1911 following a public outcry. Bengal was divided again between India and Pakistan in 1947. The princely state of Cooch Behar was added to it in 1950 and the former French enclave of Chandranagore was merged in it on Oct. 2, 1954. Some parts of Bihar were transferred to it in 1956.

Communities. Muslims 22%, Scheduled Castes 22%, Scheduled Tribes 6%. Communities include Mahisyas, Tantis/Tatwas, Vaishyas, Banias, Goalas and Telis. Rajbansis, Bagdis, Namasudras, Pods and Bauris are dominant among SCs. Santhals and Oraons are the principal STs.

Population (1991)	:	68,077,965
Area	:	88,752 sq km
Language	:	Bengali
Capital	:	Calcutta
Lok Sabha Seats	:	42 (SC 8, ST 2)

Election 1999 : Still Red, But Not Quite

The anti-incumbency rule finally caught up with India's longest serving chief minister, Jyoti Basu, 86, who has led the ruling Left Front to victory five times in Assembly polls. But while both rival Trinamool Congress-BJP combine and Congress made fresh inroads into the red citadel, the Left still finished far ahead cornering over two-thirds of the state's 42 seats.

Though they polled almost as many votes as in 1998, a near negligible adverse swing left the four red parties—CPM, CPI, RSP and the Forward Bloc—with four seats less with a tally of 29 for 46.74 instead of 33 for 46.83 per cent.

Thanks to a combined swing of 2.54 per cent, Mamata Banerjee's Trinamool Congress and ally BJP notched up a tally of ten, a gain of two as their combined vote went up from 34.63 to 37.17 per cent—less than ten points behind the Left.

West Bengal

Vote Share (in %)

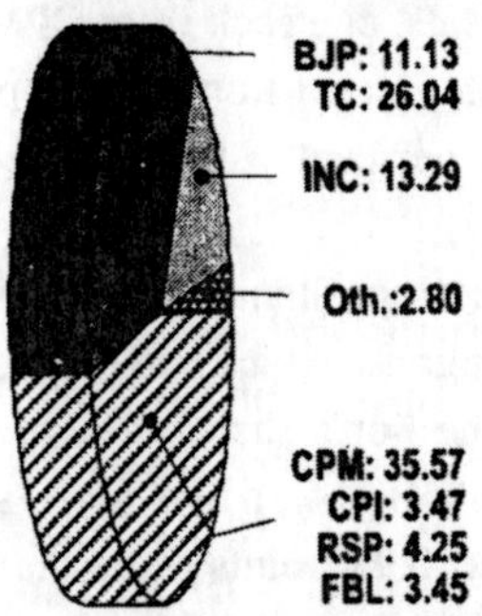

Seat Share (in %)

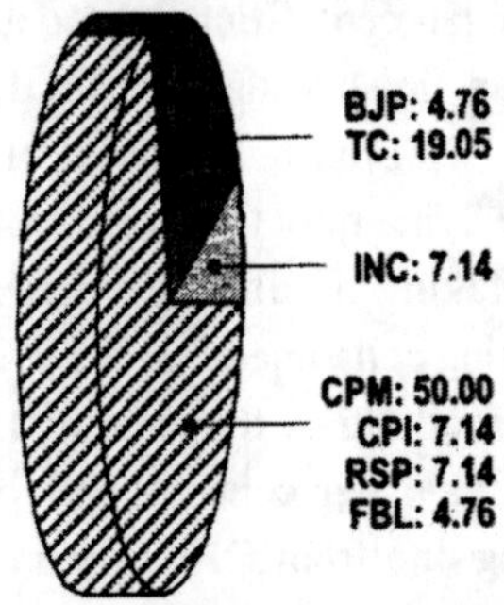

Swing %

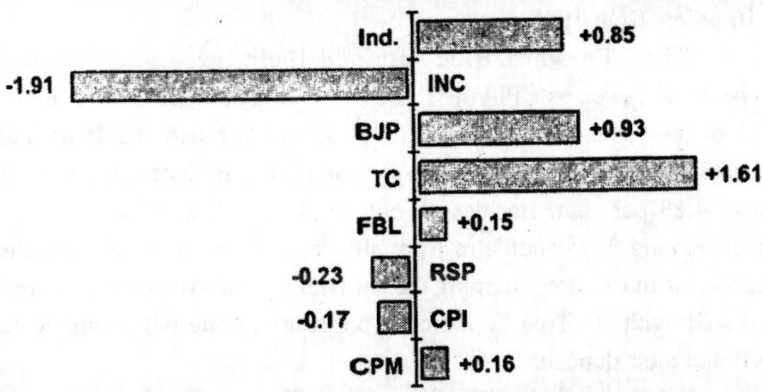

Gains & Losses

Party	Current Win	Prev. Win	Re-tained	Gained	Gained from	Lost	Lost to	Net
BJP	2	1	1	1	CPM-1	0	-	+1
TC	8	7	6	2	CPM-2	1	CPM-1	+1
INC	3	1	1	2	CPM-1, RSP-1	0	-	+2
CPI	3	3	3	0	-	0	-	0
CPM	21	24	20	1	TC-1	4	BJP-1, INC-1, TC-2	-3
RSP	3	4	3	0	-	1	INC-1	-1
FBL	2	2	2	0	-	0	-	0
Total	42	42	36	6		6		0

But what worried the Left was the fact that the TC-BJP combine finished in second position in 25 seats with votes ranging between 31 and 46 per cent. Congress too gained two seats, one each from CPM and RSP, to finish with three for 13.29 per cent, an erosion of 1.91 points since 1998, but only a third of its near 40 per cent vote share in 1996 before Trinamool Congress broke away.

Making an almost clean sweep of metropolitan Calcutta and its adjoining constituencies, the Trinamool Congress, which had helped BJP get a foothold in the state in 1998, took the lion's share of eight seats with 26.04 per cent-up 1.61 points. BJP brought in two more seats, gaining one from CPM, for 11.13 per cent, 0.93 points more than last time. For the Left Front, CPM picked up 21 seats, snatching one from Trinamool Congress, but returning two to it and losing one each to Congress and BJP to finish with a net loss of three, with 35.57 per cent, up 0.16 points from 1998.

CPI and Forward Bloc retained their three and two seats respectively, even as CPI vote share came down a fraction of a point to 3.47 per cent and that of FB went up by almost as much to 3.45 per cent. But RSP lost one of its four seats to Congress as its vote fell just a little bit to 4.25 per cent. Besides all but one of the 122 independents, 97 others among 309 candidates from all parties except the Left, lost their deposits with Congress topping the list with 31 followed by BSP with 19 and NCP with 10. Two Trinamool Congress and one BJP nominee also forfeited their deposits.

Cornering nearly half the SC vote (49.27 per cent), the Left won all but one of the eight SC seats, with CPM taking four for 31.27 instead of five for 30.92 per cent. RSP took two for 11.39 per cent, down 0.40 points and the Forward Bloc one for 6.56 per cent, up 0.98 points. Trinamool Congress wrested a SC seat from CPM with 21.02 per cent votes, while ally BJP brought in 17.07 per cent without any success to give the combine 38.09 per cent share of the SC pie. Congress contested all the eight SC seats, but in vain polling 10.22 per cent. Others, including BSP (0.47 per cent) and 14 independents (1.72 per cent) shared the remaining 2.42 per cent of the votes polled.

The two ST seats were again shared by CPM and RSP with 25.91 per cent—down 2.5 points, and 25 per cent—down 0.91 points, to give the Left a combined ST share of 50.91 per cent. Though success again eluded it, Trinamool-BJP combine polled ten per cent more votes to raise its share from 24.09 to 34.09 per cent with Trinamool Congress bringing in 18.86 per cent, 8.41 points more, and BJP 15.23 per cent, up 1.59 points. At 10.22 per cent, Congress did no better than earlier. All others shared 7.27 per cent ST vote with Norain faction of Jharkhand Party cornering 5.45 per cent, Jharkhand Mukti Morcha 0.68 per cent, and BSP and NCP 0.23 per cent each.

India's first Communist home minister Indrajit Gupta won his eleventh Lok Sabha election, for the fifth time from Midnapore, while CPM leader Somnath Chatterjee scored his fifth straight win from Bolpur. Former Congress minister Ajit Kumar Panja retained his Calcutta North East seat for Trinamool Congress, while his elder brother Ranjit Panja kept the Barasat seat he had snatched in 1998 after the death of Forward Bloc leader Chitta Basu, who had held it for over 20 years. BJP state leader Tapan Sikdar, who gave the saffron party its first victory in the red bastion in 1998 by unseating CPM leader Nirmal Kanti Chatterjee, retained his Dum Dum seat defeating the new CPM nominee Anil Bhattacharya by 134,561 votes.

State Congress President A B A Ghani Khan won for the seventh time from Malda, but with a much smaller margin of 24,553, while CPM's Basudeb Acharia performed a similar feat in Bankura. Congress leader Priya Ranjan Dasmunshi unseated three-time winner Subrata Mukherjee of CPM in Raiganj. Amar Roy Pradhan, 65, of Forward Bloc achieved the unique distinction of winning the same seat eight times in a row with his victory in Coochbehar SC seat. CPI leader Gita Mukherjee's seventh straight win in Panskura made her the only woman in West Bengal to do so. Besides Mukherjee and Mamata Banerjee, only three others of the 26 women candidates made it.

The Congress kept its hold on West Bengal for 20 years after independence doing its best in 1952 when it won the most seats, 24, and 1957 when it polled the highest, 48.2%. Its Lok Sabha tally was reduced to 14 for 39.7% in 1967 as it lost power in the state. The Congress did its worst ever in 1977 when it could win only three seats for 29.4%. Except in 1984 when the Congress won 16 seats for 48.2%, the Congress has failed to bag more than four-five seats since the rise of the red star in 1977.

The CPI(M) has been going from strength to strength since its debut in 1967 when it won five seats for 15.7%. Raising its tally to 20 for 34.3% in 1971, CPI(M) forged an alliance with RSP and the Forward Bloc while making seat adjustments with the newly formed Janata Party in 1977.

The three left parties won 23 seats, with CPI(M) taking 17 for 26.2%, while Janata took 15 for 21.5% leaving only three to the Congress. The Left hasn't looked back since, its best coming in 1980 when it won 38 seats, including three of the CPI, and cornered 54% votes. A dip came in 1984 when the left scored 26 for 48.4%.

Going it alone. CPI's best was in 1962 when it won nine seats for 29.4%. Independents did well in 1967 when seven of them won polling 15.3% votes. BJP forerunner Jan Sangh won two seats for 5.9% way back in 1952.

Key Contests

Barasat. In 1996 Forward Bloc leader Chitta Basu won for the fifth time since 1977. The only time he lost was in 1984 when T.K. Ghosh of the Congress defeated him by 13,000 votes.

Berhampur. RSP leader Tridib Chaudhari won it seven times between 1952 and 1980. He lost for the first time in 1980 to AC Sinha of the Congress by just 4,000 votes. RSP wrested the seat in 1989 and won it again in 1991. In 1996 Promothes Mukherjee of RSP defeated Siddhartha Shankar Ray, who had given up the Indian Ambassador's post in Washington to contest. Ray had won from Raiganj in 1971.

Bolpur. CPI(M) leader Somnath Chatterjee scored his third straight win from Bolpur in 1996. He had earlier won from Burdwan and Jadavpur. Mamata Banerjee of the Congress defeated him in Jadavpur in 1984.

Calcutta South. Mamata Banerjee, who had scored the biggest margin of victory among Congress candidates in 1991, won again in 1996 defeating Shakti Mukherjee of CPI(M) by 9,424 votes.

Midnapore. CPI leader Indrajit Gupta, who became India's first communist home minister, won his ninth Lok Sabha election in 1996.

He has been elected thrice from Midnapore and two times each from Basirhat, Calcutta South West (now Jadavpur) and Alipore. He defeated Durgapada Roy of the Congress by 210,649 votes here in 1996.

Electorate	:	1,42,78,058
Turnout	:	1,02,00,743
Turnout %	:	71.44%
Valid Votes	:	99,07,200
Invalid & Missing	:	2,93,543
Candidates	:	115

ASSAM

Seats: 14 (General: 11; SC: 1; ST: 2)

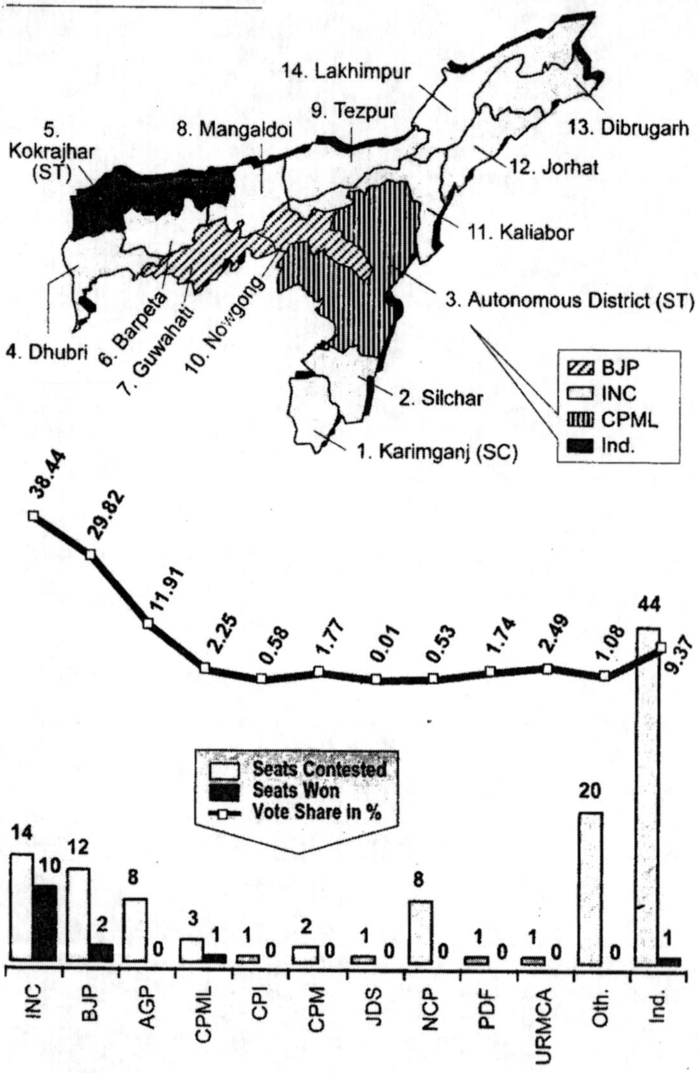

The North East

ASSAM

History. Conquered by the Ahoms in the 13th century. Assam became a British protectorate in 1826. Cachar was annexed to it in 1832 and Jaintia Hills three years later. It became a separate province in 1874 and came under a governor in 1921. On partition, the predominantly Muslim district of Sylhet went to East Pakistan (now Bangladesh). The North Eastern Frontier Agency was separated from it in 1948. Nagaland was carved out of Assam in 1963 and Meghalaya and Mizoram in 1972. Barak and Brahmaputra valley are its two major regions.

Communities. Scheduled Castes 7%, Scheduled Tribes 11%. They include Patnis, Boro Kacharis, Lalungs, Mikirs/Karbis and Miris. Precise estimate of Muslims not available.

Population (1991)	:	22,414,322
Area	:	78,438 sq km
Languages	:	Assamese, Bengali (Barak valley)
Capital	:	Dispur
Lok Sabha Seats	:	14 (SC 1, ST 2) Barak valley 2, Hill Districts 1, Brahmaputra Valley 11

Election 1999: Congress Holds As Lotus Blooms in Brahmaputra

Helped by a 5.35 per cent swing and an anti-establishment vote, BJP gained a foothold in the Brahmaputra valley, even as Congress held on to a lion's share of ten in 14 despite a little erosion in its vote bank, while the ruling Asom Gana Parishad (AGP) could not recover even a bit of the ground it lost in 1998. Ousted from power in the simultaneous Assembly poll in 1996, when it could win only five Lok Sabha seats, Congress maintained its doubled tally of ten in 1998, even as its vote share went down 0.53 points from 38.97 to 38.44 per cent. But its success appeared to be more due to a split of rival vote between BJP and AGP.

Though BJP could win only two seats instead of one, its maiden success in Brahmaputra valley, posed a direct challenge to Chief Minister Prafulla Kumar Mahanta's AGP's hopes of a revival in the state. Winning the prestigious seats of Guwahati and Nowgong, Mahanta's

Assam

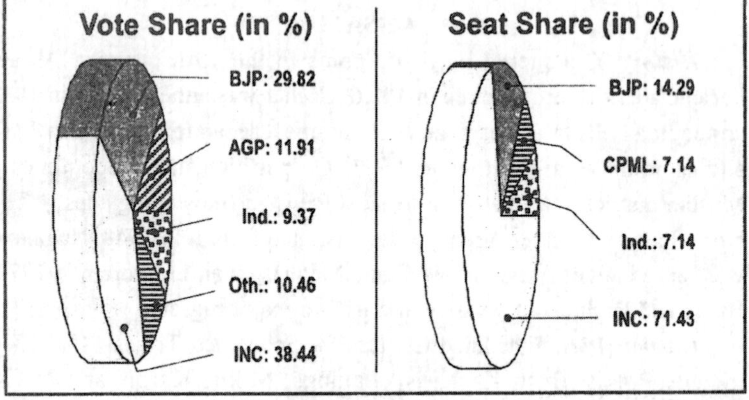

Swing %

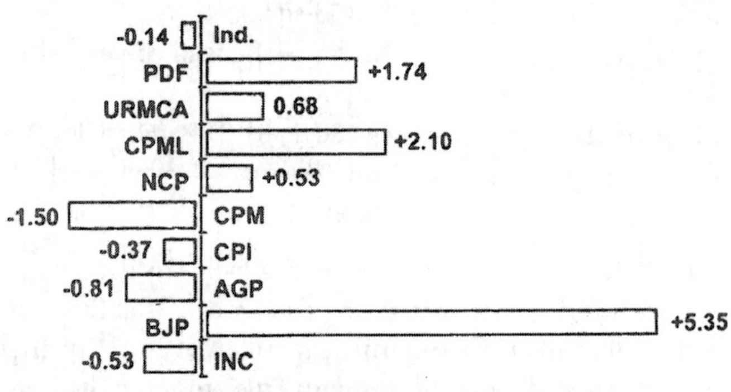

Gains & Losses

Party	Current Win	Prev. Win	Re-tained	Gained	Gained from	Lost	Lost to	Net
ASDC	0	1	0	0	-	1	CPML-1	-1
BJP	2	1	0	2	INC-2	1	INC-1	+1
CPML	1	0	0	1	ASDC-1	0	-	+1
INC	10	10	8	2	BJP-1, UMF-1	2	BJP-2	0
UMF	0	1	0	0	-	1	INC-1	-1
Ind.	1	1	1	0	-	0	-	0
Total	**14**	**14**	**9**	**5**		**5**		**0**

home district, BJP raised its vote share from 24.47 to 29.82 per cent. Formed in 1985 by then leaders of the All Assam Students' Union riding high on a popularity wave following the anti-foreigners stir, Mahanta's AGP was hit hard by the anti-incumbency factor.

Losing all its five seats in 1998 with a massive 14.45 point fall in its vote share two years after coming to power, AGP again drew a blank as its popularity suffered a little more erosion of 0.81 points to push down its share to 11.91 per cent. CPML, whose two candidates had lost their deposits last time, won the Autonomous District ST seat with 2.25 per cent state vote with three-time winner Jayanta Rongpi switching over from Autonomous State Demand Committee (ASDC). The second ST seat of Kokrajhar was retained by an independent, Sansuma Khungur Bwismuthiary sharing 9.37 per cent vote with 43 others without party affiliation.

Both the other Communist parties again remained seat-less as they lost a little vote with CPM polling 1.77 per cent—down 1.50 points—and CPI getting 0.58 per cent instead of 0.95 per cent. Pawar's NCP, which had fielded eight candidates, drew a miserable half per cent, while the United Reservation Movement Council of Assam (2.49 per cent), People's Democratic Front (1.74 per cent) and sundry other parties shared the remaining six per cent in a contest of 115.

Congress heavyweight Santosh Mohan Dev defeated BJP union minister Kabindra Purakayastha in Silchar by 107,752 votes to avenge his 1998 loss. State Congress president Tarun Gogoi won again in Kaliabor as did controversial lottery king Mani Kumar Subba in Tezpur.

Congress' Abdul Hamid also retained Dhubri where polling was postponed to October 28 following the abduction and subsequent killing of BJP candidate Pannalal Oswal. But Congress suffered a setback in Guwahati and Nowgong with its candidates, Bhubaneswar Kalita and Nripen Goswami losing their seats to BJP.

However, it wrested Silchar from BJP and gained Barpeta with last time winner A F Golam Osmani merging his faction of United Minorities Front with the Congress. Karimganj, the lone SC seat, was won again by Congress with nearly half the vote (49.56 per cent), close to ten points more than the 39.88 per cent it got last time.

BJP too added 5.18 points to raise its SC vote share from 38.24 to 43.42 per cent with AGP, which had polled 19.7 per cent last time, leaving it to ally CPM to join the battle. CPM polled 4.97 per cent, while the remaining 2.05 per cent was shared by independents and others including NCP, which got less than half a per cent vote. The two ST seats were shared by the CPML and an independent candidate, with 16.07 and 32.82 per cent votes. Two regional parties, URMCA (18.97 per cent) and PDF (14.92 percent) together polled 33.89 per cent with Congress getting 16.45 per cent. Less than one per cent was left for four others, while BJP, which had taken 14.17 per cent last time did not field an ST candidate. Only two of the ten women candidates emerged successful with state Youth Congress president Ranee Narah of Congress, the lone winner of 1998, retaining Lakhimpur.

Before 1985, when the Assam accord was signed, Congress dominated the polities in Assam polling between 45.1% in 1962 and 57% in 1971. Its vote share fell to its lowest ever of 23.6% in 1985 when the state went to the polls almost a year after the eighth general elections in 1984. Elections were not held in Assam in 1989.

Key Contests

Barpeta. Former President, Fakhruddin Ali Ahmed was elected from Barpeta in 1967 and 1971 as a Congress candidate. Udhab Barman of the CPI (M) won the seat in 1991 and retained it in 1996.

ARUNACHAL PRADESH

History: The land of the dawn-lit mountains, Arunachal, acquired a separate identity in 1914 with the British separating some tribal parts of Assam to form the North Eastern Frontier Tract. New Delhi took over its administration in 1948 after renaming it the North Eastern Frontier Agency (NEFA). It became a union territory on Jan. 20, 1972 as Arunachal Pradesh and the 24th State of India on Feb. 20, 1987. Thinly populated, it is the 13th largest state of India. Bigger than Assam or Punjab.

Communities: Hindus 30%, Christians 5%, Buddhists 14%, Scheduled Tribes 70%. Major hill tribes include Adi Gallongs, Adi Minyongs, Adi Padams, Bangnis, Hill Miris, Nishis, Noctes, Tagins and Wanchos.

Population (1991)	:	864,558
Area	:	83,743 sq km
Languages	:	Monpa, Aka, Miji, Sherdukpen, and other tribal languages.
Capital	:	Itanagar
Lok Sabha Seats	:	2

Election 1999: Congress Comes Back

Congress bagged both the Lok Sabha seats in Arunachal Pradesh as Chief Minister Mukut Mithi led the party to a spectacular victory in the parallel assembly poll. The return of Congress came just eight months after toppling rebel Congress leader Gegong Apang, who had ruled the state for 19 years in January 1999.

Thanks to a massive 33 per cent swing, Congress snatched back from Apang's Arunachal Congress, the two seats it had held for 16 years since 1980. It also raised its vote share from 23.90 to 56.92 per cent—24 per cent higher than the rival BJP-ANC alliance's 32.92 per cent.

Apang's party, which had conceded one seat to ally BJP, lost the other too as its support plunged sharply by about 36 points from 52.47 to 16.62 per cent. Ally BJP, which had finished third in 1998 with 21.75 per cent, in opposition to both the Congresses, retained its place in its fourth electoral foray, but with a 5.45 point lower share of 16.30 per cent.

The remaining ten per cent of the vote was shared by Pawar's NCP (7.77 per cent) and an unrecognised Ajeya Bharat Party (2.39 per cent).

ARUNACHAL PRADESH

Seats: 2 (General: 2)

Electorate	:	6,11,099
Turnout	:	4,41,229
Turnout %	:	72.20%
Valid Votes	:	4,25,663
Invalid & Missing	:	15,566
Candidates	:	6

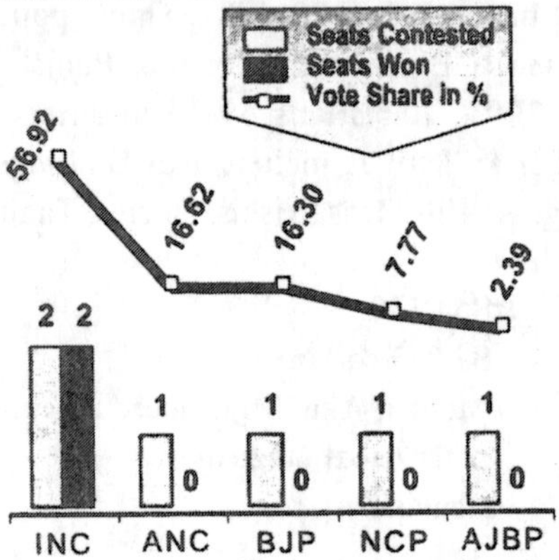

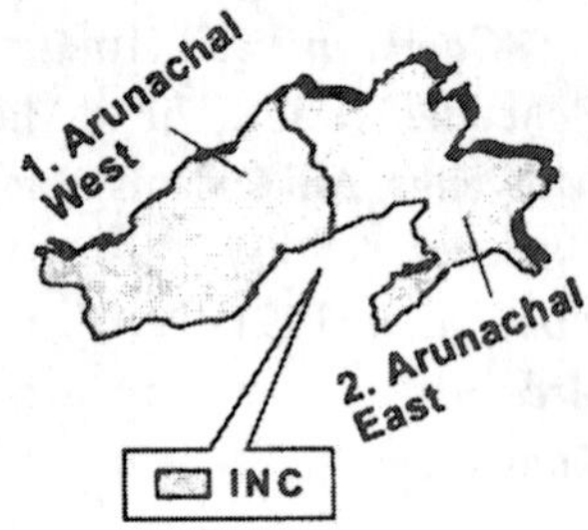

Vote & Seat Share

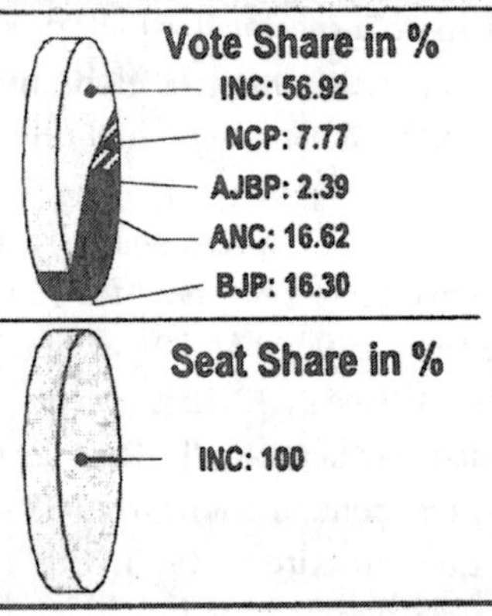

Swing %

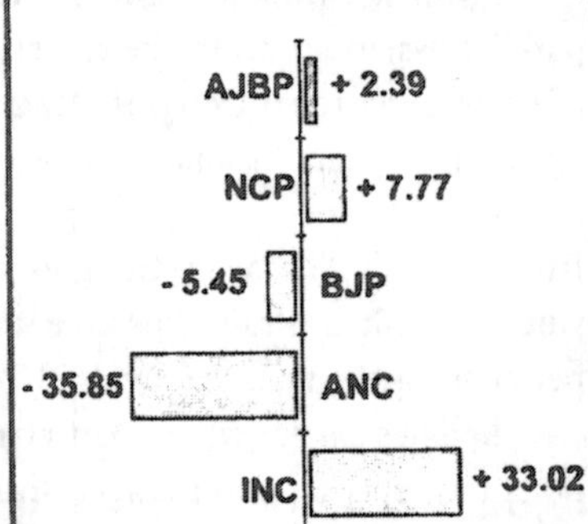

Gains & Losses

Party	Current Win	Prev. Win	Re-tained	Gained	Gained from	Lost	Lost to	Net
ANC	0	2	0	0	-	2	INC-2	-2
INC	2	0	0	2	ANC-2	0	-	+2
Total	2	2	0	2		2		0

in a five-party contest. There were no women candidates among the six in fray. Apang's son Omak Apang, who had found a berth in the last Vajpayee government in return for ANC support, lost his Arunachal West seat by 60,723 votes to Jarbom Gamlin of Congress.

The Arunachal East seat was again won by Wangcha Rajkumar, but for Congress this time. Rajkumar, who beat BJP's Tapir Gao by 41,403 votes, won it as an independent in 1996 and as an ANC nominee last time.

Until 1989, the main opposition to Congress had been coming from the People's Party of Arunachal (PPA), which opted out after three unsuccessful runs in 1980, 1984 and 1989 when it polled 40.2, 34.6 and 35.2 per cent, respectively. JD was the main rival in 1991 with 24.7 per cent, while two independents, allegedly backed by Apang, won both the seats in 1996 with 53.8 per cent.

In the parallel assembly poll, chief minister Mithi pulled off a spectacular victory wresting all but seven of the 60 assembly seats, a clear gain of ten. Mithi's predecessor Apang, who had ruled the state for 19 years, most of it for the Congress, was the lone member of his Arunachal Congress to get elected. Ally BJP again came a cropper as all its 23 candidates lost, while Pawar's NCP won four seats and independents the remaining two.

MANIPUR

Seats: 2 (General: 1; ST: 1)

Electorate	:	13,71,969
Turnout	:	9,00,181
Turnout %	:	65.61%
Valid Votes	:	8,93,588
Invalid & Missing	:	6,593
Candidates	:	18

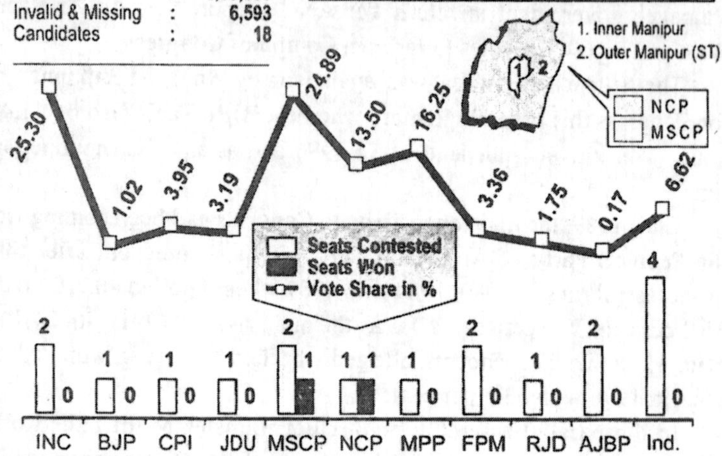

Vote & Seat Share

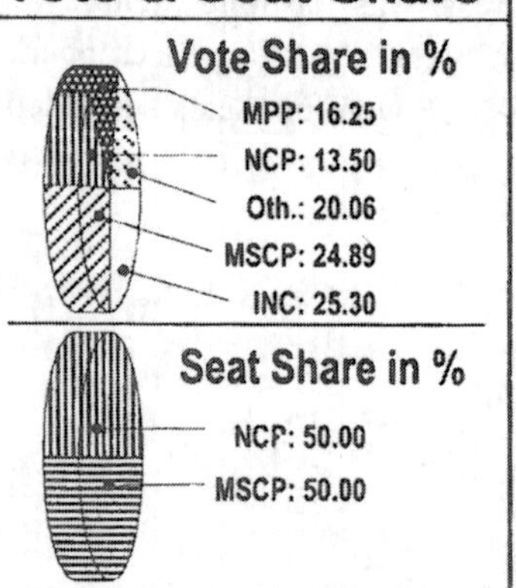

Swing %

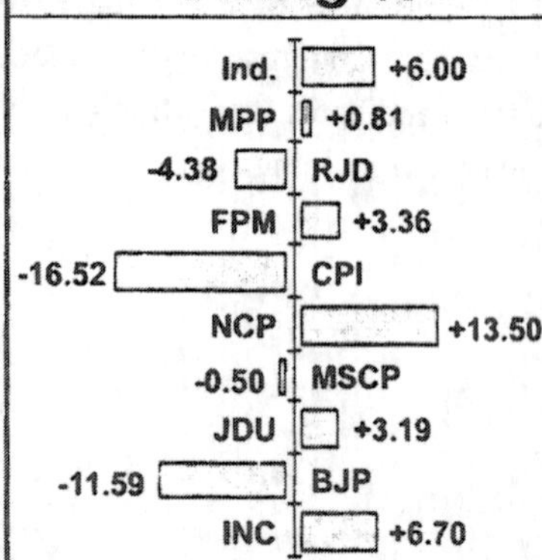

Gains & Losses

Party	Current Win	Prev. Win	Re-tained	Gained	Gained from	Lost	Lost to	Net
MSCP	1	1	1	0	-	0	-	0
NCP	1	0	0	1	CPI-1	0	-	+1
CPI	0	1	0	0	-	1	NCP-1	-1
Total	2	2	1	1		1		0

MANIPUR

History. The princely state of Manipur came under the British in 1891. After independence, it was integrated with India in October 1949. Made a union territory in 1956, it became a full state on January 21, 1972.

Communities. Hindus 61%, Muslims 6%, Christians 30%, Scheduled Tribes 28%. Major tribes are Aimols, Anals, Kukis, Paites, Tangkhuls and Thados. Meiteis, the largest community in the valley and foothills of Manipur, are settled agriculturalists.

Population (1991)	:	1,837,119
Area	:	22,327 sq km
Languages	:	Manipuri
Capital	:	Imphal
Lok Sabha Seats	:	2 (ST 1)

Election 1999: Shared Spoils

Despite a 6.7 per cent swing that put it at the top of the popularity stakes with 25.30 per cent, Congress could not regain either of the two seats it had lost in 1998 thanks to a split in the party. The breakaway Manipur State Congress Party (MSCP), now allied with the NDA, retained one while new entrant NCP took the other from CPI.

Thounoujam Chaoba Singh, who had first won the Inner Manipur seat in 1996 for the Congress, kept it again under the banner of MSCP. Holkhomang Haokip, who had as a BJP candidate lost to CPI's Kim Gangte in the Outer Manipur ST seat in 1998, won it for Pawar's NCP this time as Gangte switched over to JDU. Singh defeated a human rights activist, Khaidem Mani contesting on the Manipur People's Party (MPP) ticket as a joint candidate of the Secular Democratic Front, including CPI, CPM and JDS by 8,195 votes. Congress candidate Nimaichand Luwang trailed in the third place. MSCP with one win, came second in popularity chart with 24.89 per cent, a half point drop, followed by MPP with 16.25 per cent, up 0.81 points, but without a win. BJP contesting the outer Manipur seat in opposition to ally MSCP and JDU both, polled about one per cent, 2.17 points behind JDU's 3.19 per cent. NCP wrested the Outer ST seat from CPI to finish fourth with 13.50 per cent, leaving the left party way down with only 3.95 per cent instead of 20.47 per cent. Nine others, including four independents, shared about 11.9 per cent of the vote pie in a contest of 18. Two women, including last time's sole female winner Gangte lost.

In the 13 rounds since 1952, the Congress drew a blank thrice, kept one five times and won both on as many occasions. Starting with one for 23.8% in 1952, the Congress did its best in 1977 polling 45.3%. Its worst was in 1998 when it lost both seats with its vote share falling to 18.60%.

The Manipur People's Party entered the fray in 1971, but won a seat only in 1991 polling its highest of 23.5% in 1977 and its lowest of 6.70% in 1996. The CPI won a seat in 1967 and 1980 with its best of 28.9% in 1967 and its worst in 1996 with 4%. Independents have won a seat twice in 1957 and 1967. The Janata wave of 1977 hardly touched Manipur with only 8.6% voters opting for it. But it did go upto 17.6% in 1980 before fading away. Earlier the Socialist Party won a seat each in 1952 and 1962 with 19.3% and 26.3% votes.

Electorate	:	11,78,250
Turnout	:	6,61,999
Turnout %	:	56.18%
Valid Votes	:	6,54,330
Invalid & Missing	:	7,669
Candidates	:	14

MEGHALAYA

Seats: 2 (General: 2)

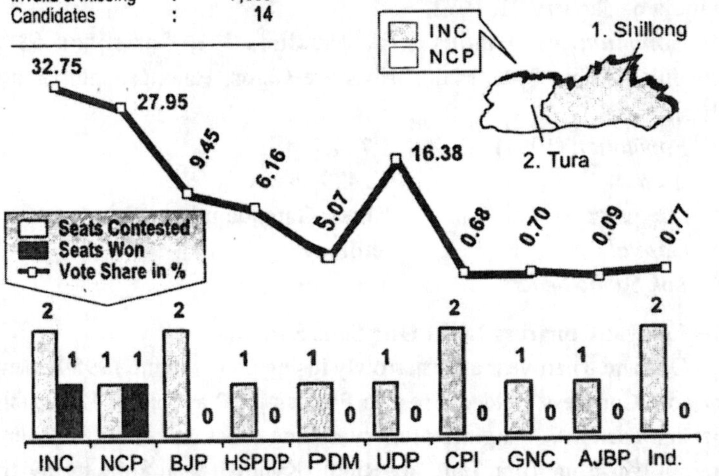

Vote & Seat Share

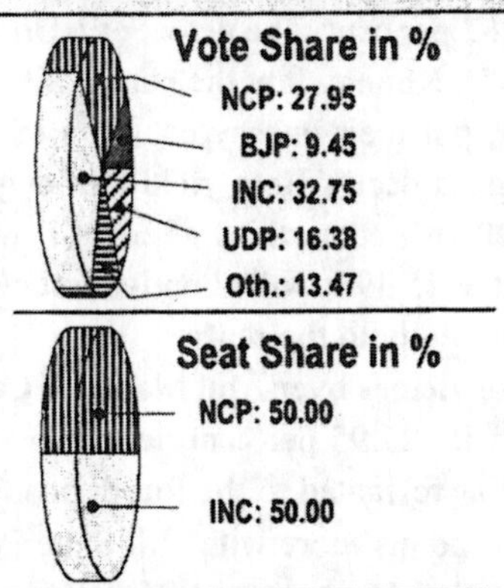

Swing %

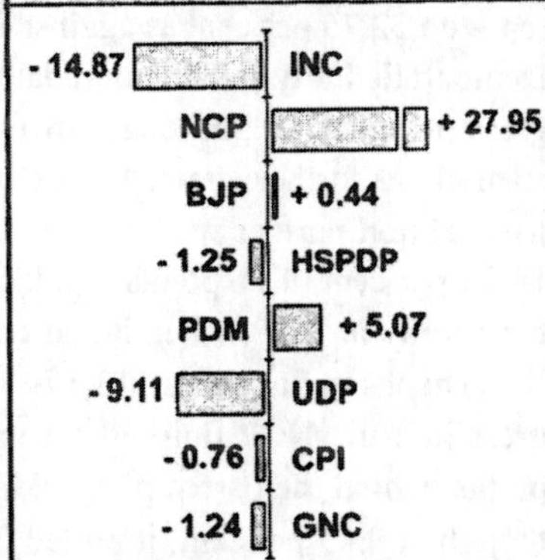

Gains & Losses

Party	Current Win	Prev. Win	Re-tained	Gained	Gained from	Lost	Lost to	Net
INC	1	2	1	O	-	1	NCP-1	-1
NCP	1	0	0	1	INC-1	0	-	+1
Total	2	2	1	1		1		0

MEGHALAYA

History. Meghalaya, the abode of the clouds, was carved out of Assam as an autonomous region on April 2, 1970. It became a full state of India on January 21, 1972.

Communities. Hindus 19%, Muslims 3%, Christians 53%, Scheduled Tribes 81%. Major tribes are Garos, Hajongs, Jaintias and Khasis.

Population (1991)	:	1,774,778
Area	:	22,429 sq km
Languages	:	Khasi, Garo, Jaintia
Capital	:	Shillong
Lok Sabha Seats	:	2

Meghalaya: Congress Loses One Sans Sangma

One and a half year after narrowly losing power in the 1998 Assembly poll, Congress yielded a seat to Pawar's NCP as former Lok Sabha speaker Purno A. Sangma, after switching sides recorded his fourth straight win from Tura. But Paty Ripple Kyndiah won Shillong for the second time for Sonia Gandhi's party.

Despite a downswing of 14.87 points, Congress still finished at the top with 32.75 per cent as against 47.62 per cent. The defeat of a United Democratic Party (UDP) candidate S.D. Khongwir at the hands of Congress' Kyndiah in Shillong, however, put their uneasy coalition in the state under further strain. With Congress declining to yield Shillong to its coalition partner in the state, UDP still came third after NCP with 16.38 per cent, 9.11 points less than the 25.49 it polled on its first electoral foray in 1998, when it had contested both the seats.

Thanks to Sangma's 113,579-vote victory over Atul Marak of Congress in Tura, NCP finished second with 27.95 per cent, less than five points behind the parent party. BJP was relegated to the fourth position though at 9.45 per cent, it polled 0.44 points more with Hill State People's Democratic Party coming next with 6.16 per cent, 1.25 points less. CPI, which like Congress and BJP, contested both the seats polled only 0.68 per cent, less than half of its 1.44 per cent share in 1998, to finish behind two local parties, People's Democratic Movement with 5.07 per cent and Garo National Council with 0.70 per cent. Two independents and an unregistered party together shared 0.86 per cent.

Except two Congress and one candidate each of NCP and UDP, all the ten others in fray lost their deposits. There were no women candidates this time unlike in 1998 when BJP had put up two.

Except for the victory of an independent H.S. Lyngdoh way back in 1977, the congress dominated the scene until 1996. It did its best in 1980 winning the Tura seat with 74.3% votes with no elections held in Shillong that year. It won both seats in 1984 with 62.4% and recorded its lowest vote in 1977 when it won one seat for 35.9%.

The only major challenge until 1996 came from independents who polled 64.1% in 1977. Starting with 6.3% in 1980, CPI touched its lowest of 1.39% in 1996. The All Party Hill Leaders Conference contested only once in 1980 to poll 11.8%.

Electorate	:	4,48,649
Turnout	:	2,93,455
Turnout %	:	65.41%
Valid Votes	:	2,91,786
Invalid & Missing	:	1,669
Candidates	:	7

MIZORAM

Seat: 1 (ST: 1)

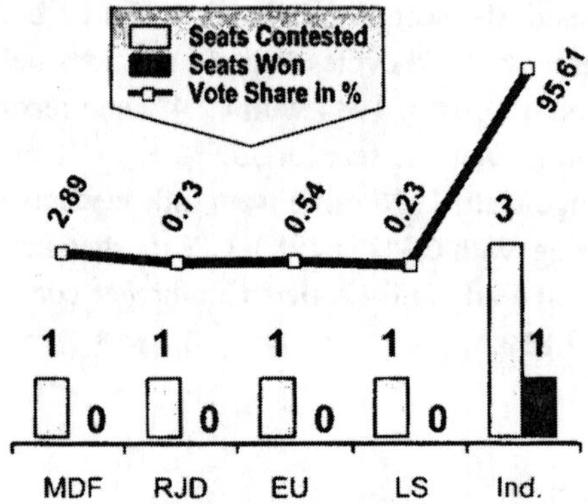

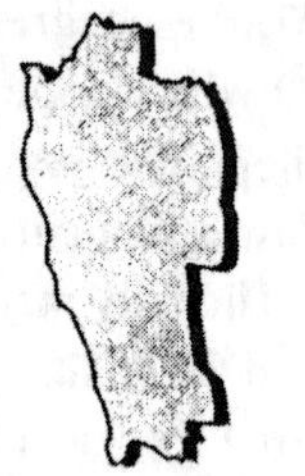

1. Mizoram (ST)
(Ind)

Vote & Seat Share

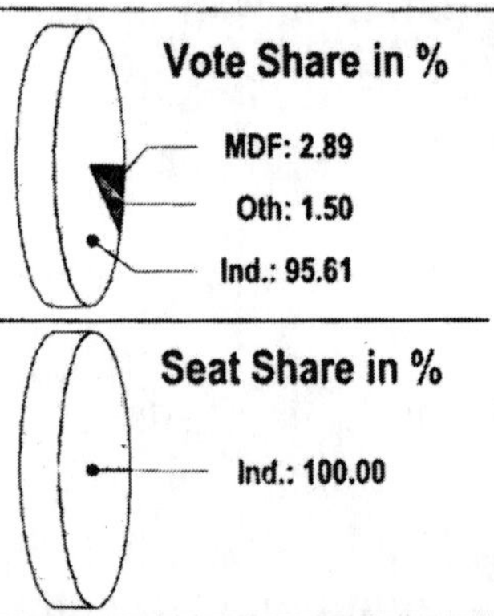

Swing %

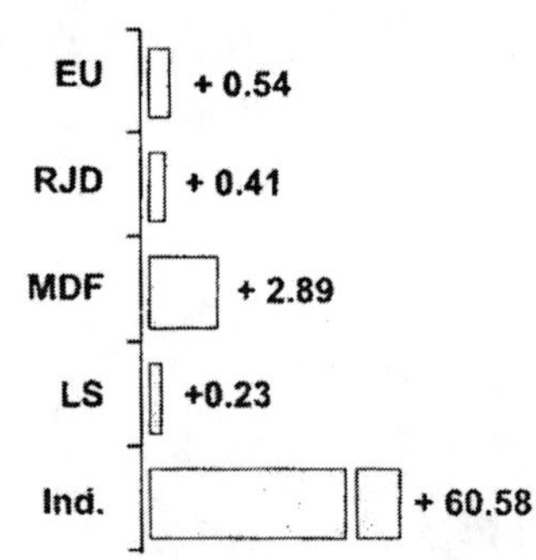

Gains & Losses

Party	Current Win	Prev. Win	Re-tained	Gained	Gained from	Lost	Lost to	Net
Ind.	1	1	1	0	-	0	-	0
Total	1	1	1	0	-	0	-	0

MIZORAM

History. Mizoram, the land of the Mizos, was annexed by the British in 1891 and made a part of Assam in 1898 as Lushai Hill District. Made a union territory in 1972, it became the 23rd state of India following a peace accord with the Mizo National Front. Signed on June 30, 1986, the peace accord ended two decades of insurgency.

Communities. Hindus 8%, Christians 84%, Buddhists 8%, Scheduled Tribes 94%. Major tribes are Lushais and Chakmas.

Population (1991)	:	689,756
Area	:	21,081 sq km
Languages	:	Mizo, English
Capital	:	Aizawl
Lok Sabha Seats	:	1 (ST 1)

Election 1999: Congress Opts Out

An independent candidate, Vanlalzawma, jointly sponsored by the ruling Mizo National Front (MN F) and Mizo People's Conference (MPC), defeated another independent backed by a Congress-led opposition alliance by a record margin of 68,659 votes, to shatter its hopes of regaining a foothold in the state.

The Congress, which had been pipped at the post by 535 votes in a close contest last time, chose to sponsor Rokamlova with MNF (Nationalist) and JDS after its popularity slipped down to 34.86 per cent in 1998 from a peak 48.5 per cent in 1989. BJP, which had polled 2.94 per cent last time, also did not put up a candidate this time, but it apparently made no difference to the outcome. With the winner (58.80 per cent) and the loser (35.27 per cent) together polling over 94 per cent votes, the rest of the six per cent was shared by five others, including a third independent, who all lost deposits.

Among others, Maraland Democratic Front polled 2.89 per cent followed by RJD (0.73 per cent), Ephraim Union (0.54 per cent) and Lok Shakti (0.23 per cent). There were no women among the seven candidates. Before it lost the seat in 1998, Congress had won it four times in a row from 1984 when a former police officer, Lalduhoma took it without contest.

C Silvera retained it for the Congress in the next three elections between 1989 and 1996. The seat was won by Mizo Union candidate

Sangliana in the first parliamentary election in 1972 and by an independent, R Rothuama in 1977 and 1980.

The Congress did its worst in the first poll in 1977 when it polled 37.10% and recorded its highest vote of 48.45% in 1989. The JD contested only in 1991 when it polled 23.48%.

The Mizo National Front, which took part in the elections for the first time in 1989, gradually increased its vote share from 31.28% in 1989 to 37.63% in 1996, but it is yet to score a victory.

The Mizoram seat was won by an independent R. Rothuama in 1977 and 1980 polling 58% and 53% votes. People's Conference finished second in 1980 polling 42% votes with Congress staying out. A local outfit, the Democratic Party won 19.31% votes in 1989.

NAGALAND

History. The former Naga Hills district of Assam and the former Tuensang Frontier division of the North East Frontier Agency (NEFA) were made a centrally administered area in 1957. Conferred the status of a state in January 1961, Nagaland was officially inaugurated on Dec. 1, 1963

Communities. Hindus 15%, Christians 81%. Scheduled Tribes 89%. Major tribes are Aos, Semas, Konyaks, Chakhesangs, Angamis and Lothas.

Population (1991)	:	1,209,546
Area	:	16,579 sq km
Languages	:	Ao, Konyak, Angami, Seema, Lotha and English
Capital	:	Kohima
Lok Sabha Seats	:	1

Election 1999: Congress Shaken but not Stirred

Despite an adverse 15.52 per cent swing, Congress kept its hold over the lone Nagaland Lok Sabha seat it had won back in 1996. But two regional parties made considerable inroads into some of its traditional strongholds as an independent won a by-election to the state Assembly in a parallel poll. The victory margin of the Congress candidate K Asungba Sangtam, who had polled a record 86.70 per cent in the poll boycotted by a few militant groups in 1998, was reduced from 73.40 to 48.77 per cent though in real terms he won with a higher margin of 353,598 votes.

This third straight victory for the Congress was its fifth in six elections since 1984. Losing the seat to the Nagaland People's Council in 1991, Congress recovered it in 1996 after NPC's winner Imchelemba defected to it. A rival independent candidate, Shurhozelie, backed by Nagaland People's Council and Nationalist Democratic Movement, gave a neck-to-neck fight in several Assembly segments, overtaking him in five of them, but finished a poor second with 22.42 per cent.

New player BJP came third with 5.12 per cent votes relegating Lok Shakti, which had gathered 13.30 per cent votes in a straight contest against Congress last time, to the fourth slot with 0.79 per cent. A second independent polled less than half a per cent vote, but all three

NAGALAND

Seat: 1 (General: 1)

Electorate	:	9,55,914
Turnout	:	7,28,313
Turnout %	:	76.19%
Valid Votes	:	7,25,045
Invalid Votes	:	3,268
Candidates	:	5

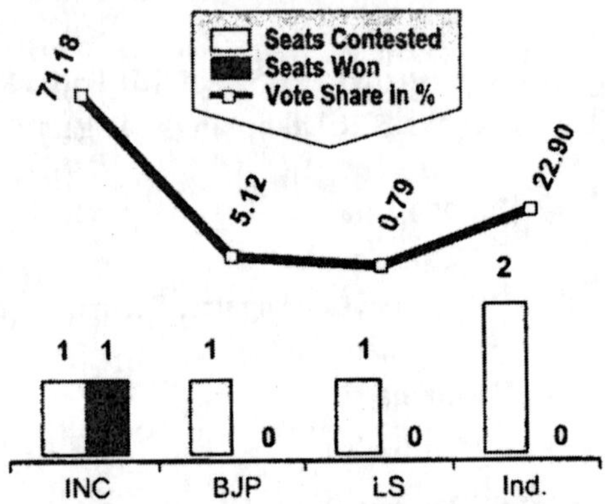

1. Nagaland (INC)

Vote & Seat Share

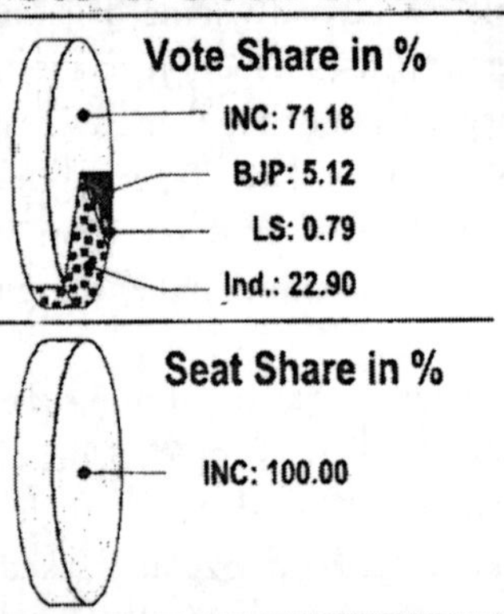

Swing %

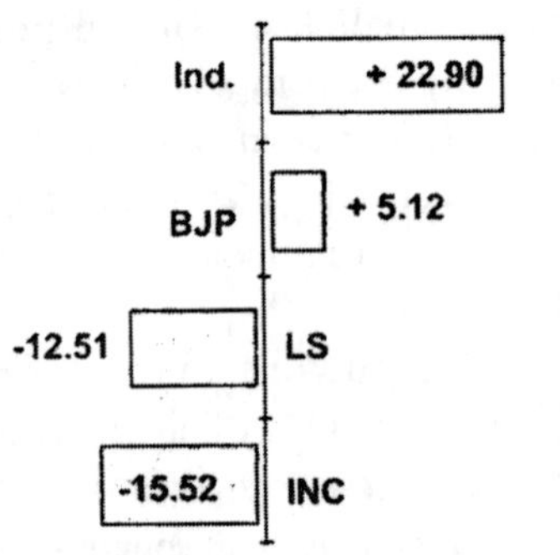

Gains & Losses

Party	Current Win	Prev. Win	Re-tained	Gained	Gained from	Lost	Lost to	Net
INC	1	1	1	0	-	0	-	0
Total	1	1	1	0	-	0	-	0

lost their deposits in an all-male five-cornered contest.

Nagaland's ninth Lok Sabha poll since 1971 recorded a 76.19 per cent turn out, more than one and a half times the 45.41 per cent it saw in 1998 in the face of a boycott call by the underground Naga Ho Ho (Parliament).

After the formation of Nagaland on December 1, 1963, the Naga National Organisation won the seat without contest in 1967 with present Congress Chief Minister S C Jamir as its nominee.

The United Front of Nagaland polling 63.9% votes wrested the seat from NNO (36.1%) in a straight contest in 1971. The United Democratic Front polling 51.7% took the seat in 1977 defeating the Congress (48.3%) in another straight contest. UDF lost in 1980 to an independent Chingwang polling 51%. Switching over to Congress, Chingwang won to raise the party's vote share to its highest ever—64.6% in 1984. His Naga National Democratic Party opponent polled 29.4% while an independent got six per cent. The Congress retained the seat in 1989 polling 60.3% as against 39.7% by an NPC nominee, only to lose it in 1991 to NPC which polled 52.6% that year with BJP getting 3% in its sole venture in Nagaland.

The state has witnessed six straight contests since 1971 with triangular fights in 1984, 1991 and 1996.

SIKKIM

Seat: 1 (General: 1)

Electorate	:	2,55,253
Turnout	:	2,08,670
Turnout %	:	81.75%
Valid Votes	:	2,05,133
Invalid & Missing	:	3,537
Candidates	:	4

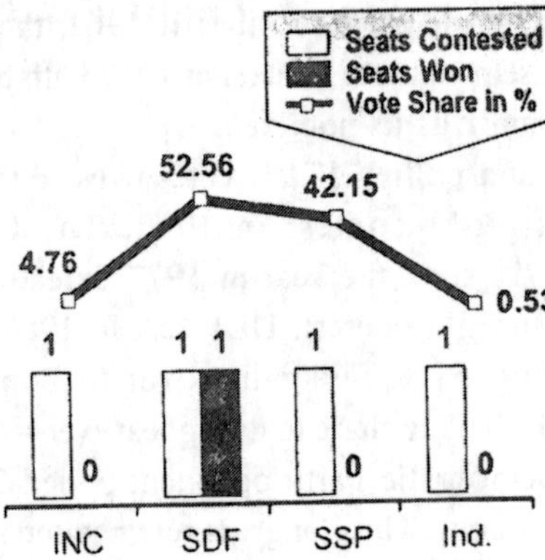

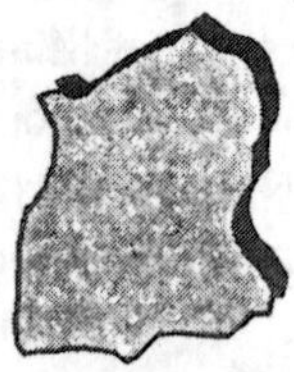

1. Sikkim
(SDF)

Vote & Seat Share

Vote Share in %

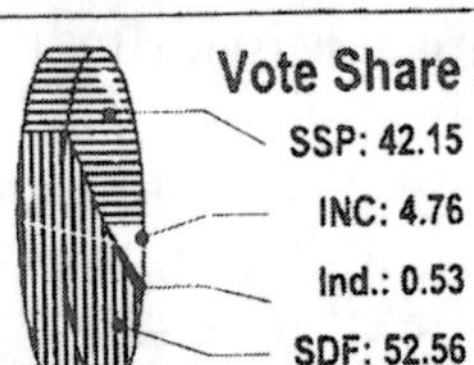

Seat Share in %

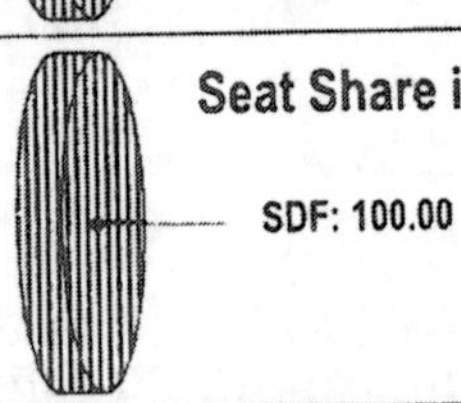

Swing %

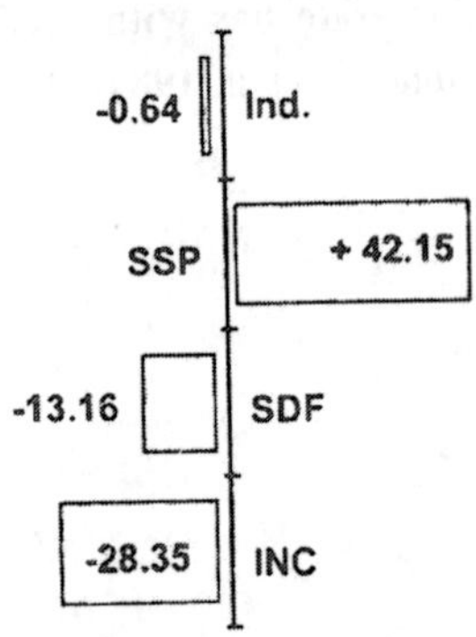

Gains & Losses

Party	Current Win	Prev. Win	Re-tained	Gained	Gained from	Lost	Lost to	Net
SDF	1	1	1	0	-	0	-	0
Total	1	1	1	0	-	0	-	0

SIKKIM

History. Ruled by the Chogyals during the British period, Sikkim became an associate state of India in 1974. It finally joined India as its 22nd state on April 26, 1975 after the state assembly resolved on April 10 to abolish the institution of the Chogyal. The Parliament later amended the Constitution (38th amendment) to give effect to the merger.

Communities. Buddhists 29%, Christians 3%, Scheduled Castes 7%, Scheduled Tribes 24%. Gorkhalis/Nepalis are the majority community. Kamis are the principal SCs, while Bhutias and Lepchas are dominant STs.

Population (1991)	:	406,457
Area	:	7,096 sq km
Languages	:	Lepcha, Bhutia, Hindi, Nepali, Limbu
Capital	:	Gangtok
Lok Sabha Seats	:	1

Election 1999: SDF Stays Put

The ruling Sikkim Democratic Front (SDF) of Chief Minister Pawan Kumar Chamling not only hung on to the state's lone seat despite a massive 13.16 per cent swing against it, but also returned to power sweeping the parallel Assembly poll.

"Giant killer" Bhim Prasad Dahal, a former bureaucrat, who had defeated long-time chief minister Nar Bahadur Bhandari, by over 82,000 votes to score his party's first Lok Sabha victory in 1996, completed a hat-trick. But his margin of victory dipped to a little modest 50,949 votes in 1998 and a worrying 21,362 this time. Polling 52.56 per cent, as against 72.15 in 1996 and 65.72 per cent in 1998, Dahal got the better of Satish Chandra Rai of Bhandari's Sikkim Sangram Parishad (SSP), back in fray after opting out of the 1998 poll, with 42.15 per cent in a four-cornered contest all-male contest.

Congress, whose Sanchaman Subba had collected 33.11 per cent as combined opposition candidate last time, saw its vote share plunge down 28.35 points to 4.76 per cent, making up about a seventh of its 1998 total. Somnath Poudiyal of Congress with 9,762 votes as also an independent polling only 1,077 votes, or 0.53 per cent, lost their deposits.

Congress won the first election in 1977 without contest. Sikkim

Janata Parishad took the seat in 1980 with 61.6 per cent vote. Bhandari won it as an independent in 1984 with 72.4 per cent. His SSP won it in 1989 and retained it in 1991 polling a record 90.1 per cent. SDF wrested the seat in 1996 with 72.7 per cent and has kept it since.

Bhandari's wife won it in a by-election after he became chief minister for the second time in March 1985 heading a Sikkim Janata Parishad government. Dil Kumari Bhandari lost the seat as a Congress candidate in 1989 to SSP's N. Thapa, who polled 68.5%.

Only other notable performance have been those of the Sikkim Prajatantra Congress polling 10% votes in 1980 and the Rising Sun Party winning 9.6% in 1989.

In the parallel Assembly poll, SDF won a three-fourths majority with 24 seats in the 32-member house. Rival SSP finished with seven, while the Sangha non-territorial seat, representing monasteries in the state went to an independent backed by the ruling party. Re-elected from his native Damthang constituency for the fifth time in a row, Chief Minister, Pawan Kumar Chamling, who dislodged Bhandari in 1994, again headed the new government. Bhandari, who ruled the state for about 15 years, won from Rhenock, but narrowly lost his traditional seat of Soreng by a mere 66 votes to an SDF candidate.

TRIPURA

History. The pincely state of Tripura acceded to India on October 15, 1949. It became a union territory on Sep. 1, 1956 and a full state on Jan. 21, 1972.

Communities: Muslims 7%, Buddhists 3%, Scheduled Castes 16%, Scheduled Tribes 29%. Namasudras and Jaliya Kaibartas are the principal SCs, while Tripuris and Riangs are prominent STs.

Population (1991)	:	2,757,205
Area	:	10,486 sq km
Languages	:	Bengali, Kakbarak Manipuri
Capital	:	Agartala
Lok Sabha Seats	:	2 (ST 1)

Election 1999: Marxists Romp Home Again

Three years after wresting the two state seats from the Congress, the ruling Left Front consolidated its hold over them thanks to a 7.44 per cent swing that put it far ahead of rival BJP-Trinamool Congress alliance and relegating Congress to a poor third.

Polling 56.24 per cent instead of 48.80 per cent last time, CPM retained both for the Front. While former state home minister, Samar Chowdhury, defeated a Trinamool Congress nominee in Tripura West by 198,399 votes, a tribal leader, Bajuban Reang, overcame the BJP candidate in Tripura East ST seat by 150,500 votes.

Former Congress chief minister, Sudhir Ranjan Majumder, contesting under the banner of breakaway Trinamool Congress, in Tripura West gathered 14.46 per cent. In the East, BJP's Jishnu Debbarma polled 12.82 per cent, up 4.63 points, to give the alliance a combined share of 27.28 per cent, less than half of the Left Front pie.

With its longstanding electoral ally, Tripura Upajati Juba Samiti (TUJS) too backing the BJP-Trinamool combine, the Congress finished third with its 42.12 per cent share slashed by two-thirds to only 13.88 per cent, its lowest since 1980, when it had polled 22.6 per cent. It was a far cry from the peak of 82.83 per cent polled in 1991. Eleven others, including five independents, shared the remaining 2.6 per cent with Pawar's NCP polling a miserable 1895, or 0.16 per cent.

Both candidates of the Congress, which had held the two seats for 12 years between 1984 and 1996, lost their deposits. So did eleven others

TRIPURA

Seats: 2 (General: 1; ST: 1)

Electorate	:	17,95,394
Turnout	:	12,23,687
Turnout %	:	68.16%
Valid Votes	:	12,04,594
Invalid & Missing	:	19,093
Candidates	:	17

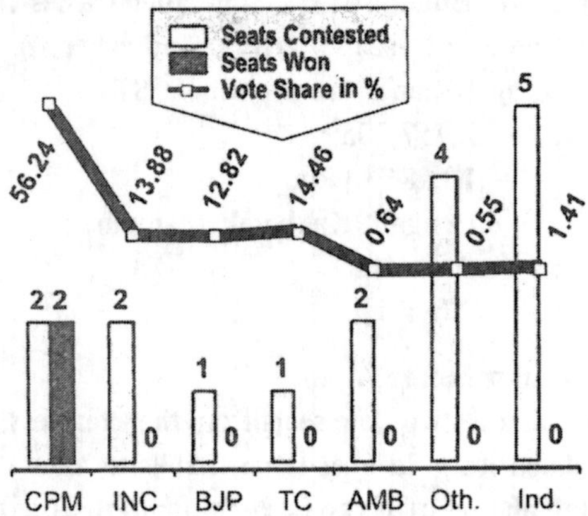

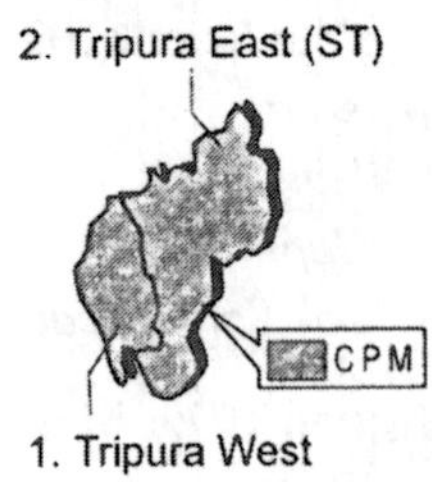

Vote & Seat Share

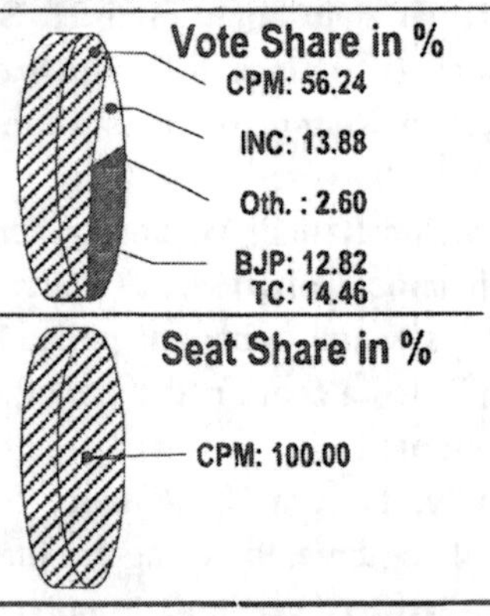

Swing %

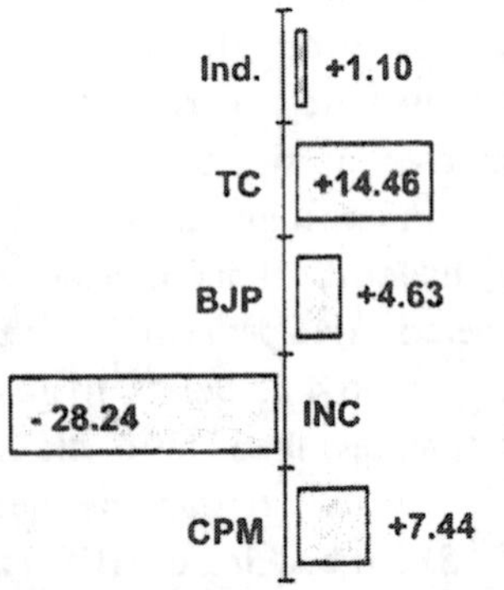

Gains & Losses

Party	Current Win	Prev. Win	Re-tained	Gained	Gained from	Lost	Lost to	Net
CPM	2	2	2	0	-	0	-	0
Total	2	2	2	0	-	0	-	0

of all parties except CPM, BJP and Trinamool among the 17 candidates, all males. In the lone ST Tripura East seat, winner CPM again took the lion's share with 54.81 per cent with BJP trailing it with about half as much at 27.76 per cent.

The Congress finished third with 15.07 per cent with the rest of the 2.36 per cent ST vote shared by a candidate of Amra Bangalee Party (1.04 per cent) and an independent (1.32 per cent).

CPI won both the Tripura seats in the first election in 1952. Conceding one to Congress in 1957, it again won both in 1962. Congress wrested them in 1967 when CPM.entered the poll fray. CPM has won both the seats six times since 1971, while Congress did it thrice since 1967 sharing a seat with CPI in 1957 and Janata party in 1977.

Tripura Upjati Juba Samiti polled 6.2% in 1977 and 13.5% in 1980, but did not get a seat.

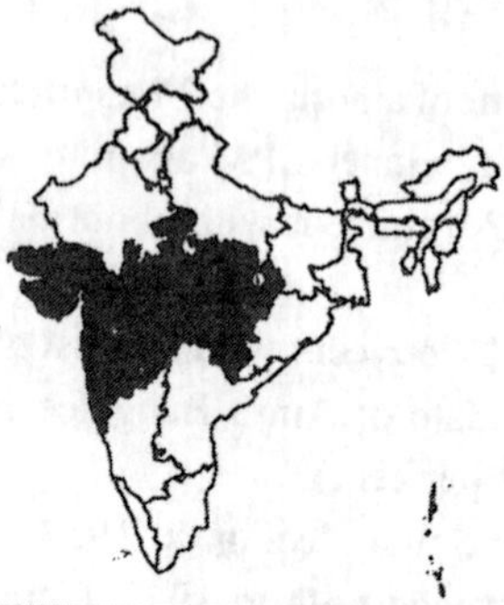

WEST

Seats: 118	Candidates: 789

Electorate	:	13,43,28,276
Turnout	:	7,47,94,555
Turnout %	:	55.68%
Valid Votes	:	7,25,35,217
Invalid & Missing	:	22,59,338

Party	Seats Contested	Seats Won	Lost Deposit	1999 Vote%	1998 Vote%	Vote Swing %
BJP + Allies	**141**	**79**	**24**	**43.92**	**44.76**	**-0.84**
BJP	96	64	1	36.12	36.46	-0.34
SHS	34	15	12	7.72	8.30	-0.58
JDU	11	0	11	0.08	-	+0.08
INC + Allies	**119**	**28**	**9**	**38.35**	**42.21**	**-3.86**
INC	112	28	4	37.68	40.43	-2.75
RPI	7	0	5	0.67	1.78	-1.11
BSP	47	0	42	1.99	3.42	-1.43
BBM	4	1	0	0.95	-	+0.95
CPI	6	0	6	0.13	0.29	-0.16
CPM	4	0	4	0.25	0.29	-0.04
GGP	20	0	20	0.25	0.25	0.00
JDS	9	1	7	0.45	-	+0.45
NCP	57	6	26	10.01	-	+10.01
PWP	2	1	1	0.39	0.36	+0.03
SJPR	2	0	2	0.02	0.01	+0.01
SP	29	0	28	0.66	1.44	-0.78
Others	86	0	86	0.58	5.20	-4.62
Ind.	263	2	261	2.05	1.77	+0.28
Total	**789**	**118**	**516**	**100.00**	**100.00**	**0.00**

CHAPTER 10

THE WEST: MAJOR GAINS FOR BJP

Western India with 118 seats in the Lok Sabha, brought good cheer to BJP as it swept Goa for the first time, maintained its dominant position in Gujarat and Madhya Pradesh and thanks to a split in Congress made major gains in Maharashtra. On the debit side was only the loss of two seats of Dadra and Nagar Haveli and Daman and Diu even as Maharashtra slipped out of the BJP-Shiv Sena combine's hands in the parallel Assembly poll.

Although the Congress and the Nationalist Congress Party of Sharad Pawar came together in an uneasy alliance in Maharashtra after the polls to dislodge the BJP-Sena government the split cost them dearly in the Lok Sabha poll.

In an essentially two-horse race, BJP-Sena captured 79 seats making up two-thirds of the total leaving only 28 to Congress. Sonia Gandhi's party turned out to be the biggest loser conceding 24 seats with BJP-Sena combine gaining 18 seats and the newly formed NCP taking six. RPI lost all the four seats it had won last time in alliance with Congress and SP, which again drew a blank with all its 29 candidates biting dust. With four major parties taking 113 or 95.76 per cent of the total, only five seats were left to be shared by JDS, the Peasants and Workers Party (PWP), Bharipa Bahujan Mahasangha (BBM), an RPI faction in Maharashtra and an independent.

Together polling 43.84 per cent, down 0.92 points from 44.76 per cent last time, BJP and Shiv Sena contributed 64 and 15 seats to the alliance kitty with either party gaining nine seats. Across the board, BJP polling 36.12 per cent, down 0.34 points, gained 21 seats, 19 of them from Congress alone. It wrested seven seats from Congress in Maharashtra, five each in Gujarat and Madhya Pradesh and two in Goa. It also took a seat each from RPI and ally Shiv Sena.

In turn it lost a dozen seats, all but one to Congress, which took six in Madhya Pradesh and four in Gujarat, besides Daman and Diu. Another seat was wrested by the BJP winner last time turning independent in Dadra and Nagar Haveli. Shiv Sena, putting up 34 candidates, a dozen of them in opposition to BJP outside Maharashtra, polled 7.72 per cent votes to gain eleven seats, nine from Congress and two from RPI. All its gains were in Maharashtra as was the loss of a seat each to Congress and ally BJP. Another NDA partner, JDU contested eleven seats in Gujarat and Madhya Pradesh, again in opposition to BJP to poll a minuscule 0.08 per cent. The Congress practically going it alone, polled 37.68 per cent as against 40.43 per cent last time to yield 36 seats across the region. Ally RPI bringing in another 0.67 per cent votes, lost all the four seats it won for the alliance last time.

The heaviest loss (24) was, of course, in Maharashtra, where Shiv Sena sliced away nine, BJP seven, NCP six and JDS and an RPI faction one each. BJP accounted for another 12, taking five each in Gujarat and Madhya Pradesh and two in Goa. But Congress recouped a dozen losses, eleven from BJP in Madhya Pradesh (6), Gujarat (4) and Daman and Diu (1). It wrested another seat from Shiv Sena in Maharashtra to limit its regional deficit to 24.

New entrant, Pawar's NCP contesting 57 seats sliced away ten per cent votes but could win only six seats, in Maharashtra alone, all at the expense of Congress. Six CPI and four CPM candidates, together polled 0.38 per cent for the Left. The estranged Congress and NCP between them polled 47.69 per cent—3.85 points more than the BJP and Shiv Sena, indicating how different Maharashtra poll story might have been without the Congress split. Three other parties, BBM (0.95 per cent), JDS (0.45 per cent) and PWP (0.39 per cent), won a seat each. BSP's 47 candidates gathered nearly two per cent votes, but without any success. Voters again rejected independents with only two of the 257 contestants getting in with 2.05 per cent vote.

BJP-Sena combine won all but two of the eleven SC seats in the region, with a combined vote share of 44.22 per cent with BJP taking the lion's share of seven for 36.11 per cent. Both Sena candidates won to bring in 8.11 per cent. At 36.65 per cent, Congress polled a little more than BJP, but only one of its candidates won. The only other success was that of RPI leader, Ramdas Athawale, who contested as an independent after failing to win recognition for his faction.

Athawale and 17 other independents together shared 8.43 per cent of the SC vote. Four NCP candidates too lost, polling 4.87 per cent. So did seven of the BSP and five of SP picking up 4.65 and 0.54 per cent votes, respectively.

BJP won two thirds of the 18 ST seats too with 42.70 per cent votes. Allies Shiv Sena and JDU added 0.67 points to the vote share to take the alliance total to 43.37 per cent but failed to win a seat. At 43.51 per cent, Congress alone polled more votes, but could win only four seats as its support was spread unevenly. NCP polled 5.53 per cent, but all its nine candidates lost as did four of CPM with 1.84 per cent of the regional ST vote. JDS won a seat in Maharashtra with about two per cent votes, while all seven BSP candidates lost, gathering 1.48 per cent. A BJP winner turned independent, succeeded in Dadra and Nagar Haveli polling 0.96 per cent of the regional ST vote with 16 other non-party candidates.

Electorate	:	9,08,777
Turnout	:	4,09,944
Turnout %	:	45.11%
Valid Votes	:	4,09,794
Invalid & Missing	:	150
Candidates	:	16

GOA

Seats: 2 (General: 2)

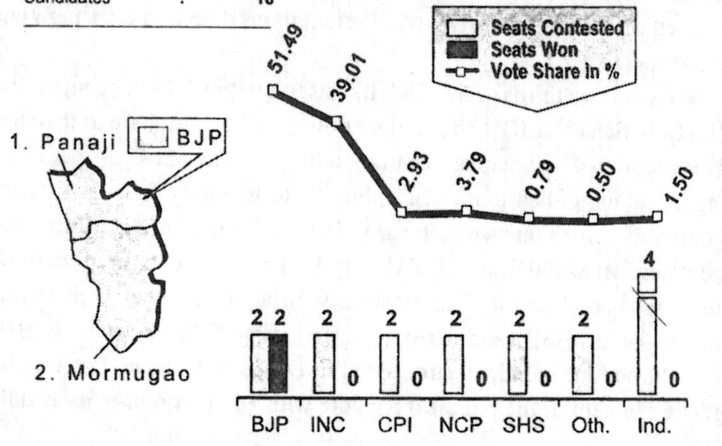

Vote & Seat Share

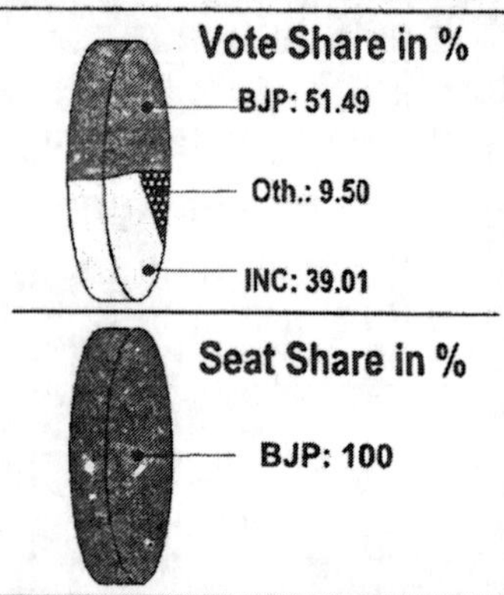

Swing %

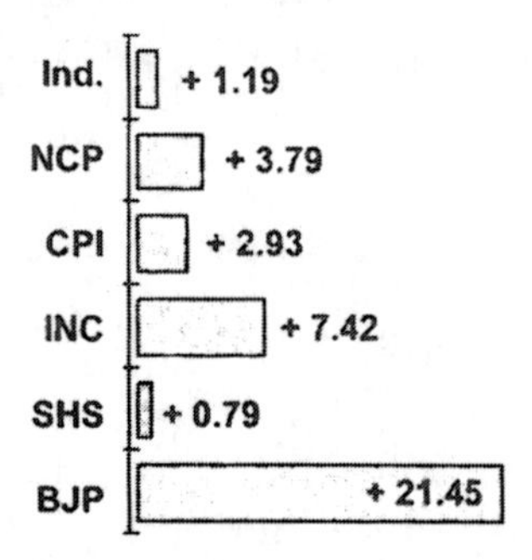

Gains & Losses

Party	Current Win	Prev. Win	Re-tained	Gained	Gained from	Lost	Lost to	Net
BJP	2	0	0	2	INC-2	0	-	+2
INC	0	2	0	0	-	2	BJP-2	-2
Total	2	2	0	2		2		0

GOA

History. Tracing its history back to the Mauryas, Goa was captured by the Portuguese in 1510. Diu and Daman, both on the Gujarat coast, were annexed in 1534 and 1559 respectively. After 451 years of colonial rule, Goa, Daman and Diu were liberated on Dec. 19, 1961 and made a union territory. Goa became a full state of India on May 30, 1987, while Daman and Diu were retained as a separate union territory. Goa is India's smallest state.

Communities. Christians 30%, Muslim 4%, Scheduled Castes 2%, Scheduled Tribes 1%. Communities include Brahmins, Vaishyas, Marathas, Bhandaris and Gomantaks.

Population (1991)	:	1,169,793
Area	:	3,702 sq km
Languages	:	Konkani, Marathi
Capital	:	Panaji
Lok Sabha Seats	:	2

Election 1999: BJP Storms Sun'n Sand State

Just four months after coming to power in the former Portuguese enclave after June Assembly elections, the Congress lost both the state seats to Bharatiya Janata Party, which first made its presence felt in the tourist paradise in 1991, when it finished third in the popularity stakes.

Polling 51.49 per cent, second only to Congress' record 57.7 per cent in 1991, BJP defeated Congress candidates with wide margins thanks to a massive swing of 21.45 per cent even as the rival party share too went up by 7.42 points to 39.01 per cent. BJP's Shripad Yasso Naik defeated former union minister Ramakant Khalap in Panaji by a margin of 36,721 votes, while Angle Ramakant Soiru got the better of Alemao Joaquim Braz by 14,457 votes in Mormugao.

A dozen candidates, among them two each of Sharad Pawar's Nationalist Congress Party (NCP), CPI and BJP ally Shiv Sena lost their deposits in either seat even as they polled a paltry 3.79, 2.93 and 0.79 per cent votes. So did six others, including four independents together collecting 1.50 per cent. Congress chief minister Luizinho Faleiro attributed the party defeat to factors, ranging from less time for campaigning to heavy showers on the polling day, but the absence of local Maharashtrawadi Gomantak Party (MGP) for the first time in Goa's electoral history, did help BJP.

The rise of BJP began in 1991, when for the first time it polled a sizeable 15.6 per cent, to finish third. Five years later, its own vote share dropped to 13.75 per cent, but its presence helped MGP and another local party, United Goans Democratic Party (UGDP), snatch both the seats from the Congress.

Congress regained the seats in 1998 despite more erosion in its vote bank thanks ironically to BJP coming within striking distance. A massive 16.29 point swing in its favour then raised its vote share to 30.04 per cent—just about one and a half per cent less than the Congress share of 31.59 per cent votes, 2.78 points down from 1996. Congress wrested the Panaji seat from MGP and took back the Mormugao seat from UGDP in 1998 essentially due to BJP slicing away more of the MGP-UGDP vote rather than that of the Congress.

MGP, which could muster only 13.17 per cent votes in 1998—as against its highest of 40.5 per cent in 1977—did not field a candidate this time, leaving the two national parties to fight it out.

In the first election after liberation in 1967, one seat was picked up by an independent candidate polling 40.6% while the other went to United Goans Sequeira Group polling 36% in both the seats it contested. Congress managed to get 5.5% in its first electoral outing, but raised its share to 24.4% in 1971, when it also won a seat. The other went to UGSG polling 24.7%. In 1977, the two seats were shared by the Congress and the MGP, both polling about 40% votes each. The newly formed Janata Party failed to win a seat but picked up 14.7% votes. Three years later with Eduardo Faleiro siding with the Urs group in Congress, Indira Gandhi's party could muster only 12.2% votes. Four years later with Faleiro back in its fold Congress put both the seats in its kitty with 46.2% votes. But in 1989, MGP polling 27.8% snatched one away. Faleiro kept his seat even as the Congress marginally increased its vote share to 47.4%. The newly formed Janata Dal too polled 18.1% votes, but in vain. In 1991, Congress polling its highest ever vote of 57.66% recaptured the two seats, only to lose them both five years later.

In the June 1999 Assembly elections, the Congress won an absolute majority claiming 21 of the 40 seats, three more than in 1994. BJP raised its share from four to ten, while MGP saw its strength reduced from

12 to four. Two other local parties, UGDP and GRCP won two each, with one going to an independent.

In the 1989 Assembly poll, MGP had given a close fight to Congress, winning 18 seats as against the latter's 20 with the remaining two seats going to independents.

Key Contests

Mormugao. Lisbon born Eduardo Faleiro won the seat five times in a row from 1977 to 1991 for the Congress except in 1980 when he stood for the Urs group of the party. A former minister of state for external affairs, Faleiro tasted his first defeat in 1996 at the hands of Churchil Braz Alemao of the UGDP.

Electorate	:	2,94,93,840
Turnout	:	1,38,75,575
Turnout %	:	47.05%
Valid Votes	:	1,36,14,729
Invalid & Missing	:	2,60,846
Candidates	:	159

GUJARAT

Seats: 26 (General: 20; SC: 2; ST: 4)

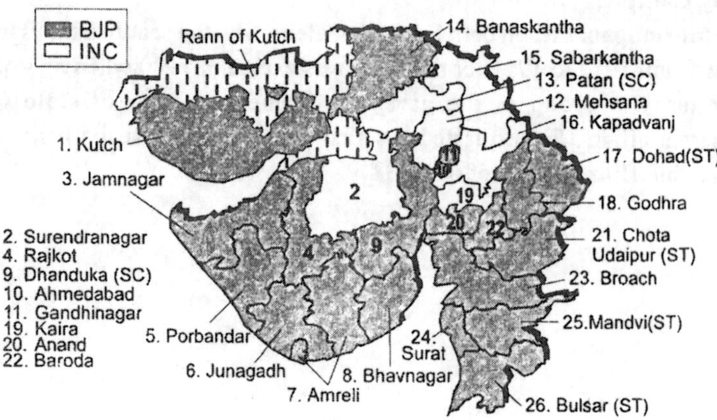

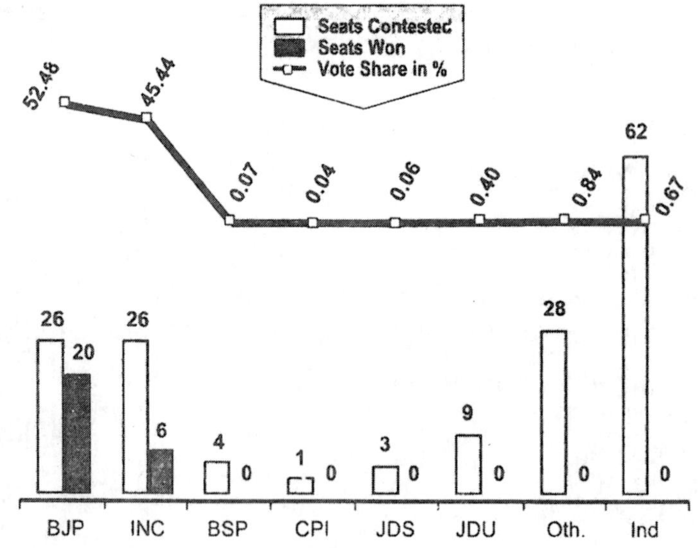

GUJARAT

History. Formed on May 1, 1960 out of the main Gujarati speaking areas of Bombay and the former states of Saurashtra and Kutch, it's the tenth most populous state of India. The Saurashtra peninsula is hilly. Kutch on the northeast is barren and rocky. The rest, known as Gujarat, is generally plain.

Communities. Muslims 9%, Scheduled Castes 8%, Scheduled Tribes 15%. Major communities include Patels, Kolis and Bharwads. Vankars/ Dheds, Bhambis, Bhils, Dhodias and Dublas are major SC and STs.

Population (1991)	:	41,309,582
Area	:	196,024 sq km
Languages	:	Gujarati, Marathi
Capital	:	Gandhinagar
Lok Sabha Seats	:	26 (SC 2, ST 4) Kutch 1, Saurashtra 7, Gujarat 18

Election 1999: BJP Stays in Saddle

Less than two years after storming back into power in the parallel Assembly poll, in 1998, BJP consolidated its hold on the state in the Lok Sabha too. Winning 20 of the 26 seats with 52.48 per cent votes, an over four point swing over 48.28 per cent it polled last time, it added a seat to its tally. The Congress tally was reduced from seven to six even as its vote share went up by nearly nine points from 36.49 to 45.44 per cent.

The results indicated that the Congress did not get all the 10.21 per cent votes polled by BJP rebel leader Shankersinh Vaghela's Rashtriya Janata Party, now merged with it. RJP was completely wiped out last time with 13 of its 20 candidates losing deposit. The anti-incumbency factor and the grave water crisis in Saurashtra apparently did not hurt BJP though it did lose Surendranagar, the district most affected by water shortage, and three other seats to Congress. But it wrested five other seats from Congress to finish with an extra seat. It won all but five of the 20 general seats with the support of 41 per cent voters, 8.66 points less than the 49.66 per cent that gave it one more seat last time.

It also lost one of the two SC seats even as it polled 48.76 per cent, more than three points up over 45.44 it got in 1998. But it won all the four ST seats, instead of one with 51.11 per cent votes, an over ten per

Gujarat

Vote Share (in %)

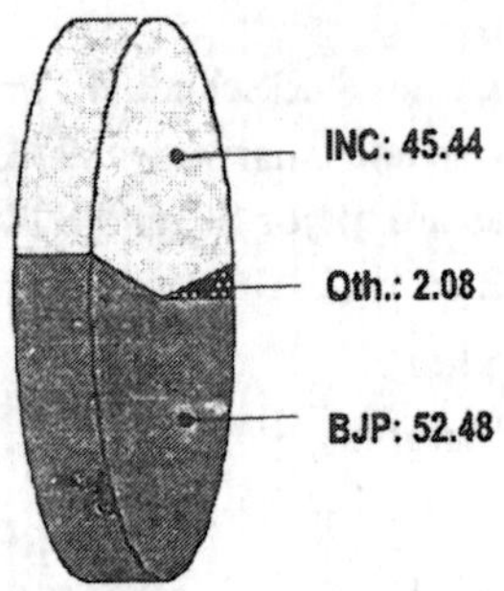

Seat Share (in %)

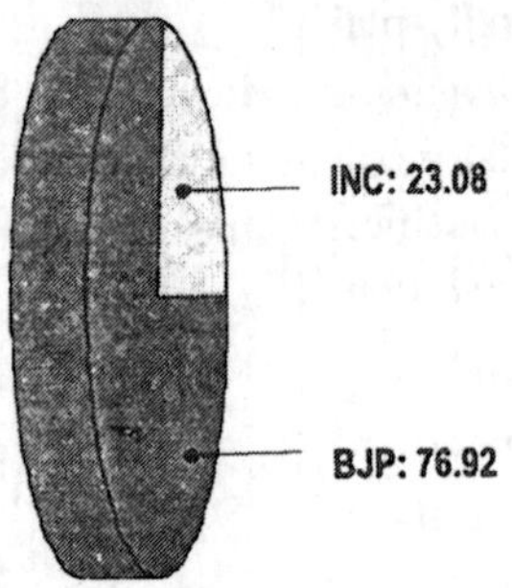

Swing %

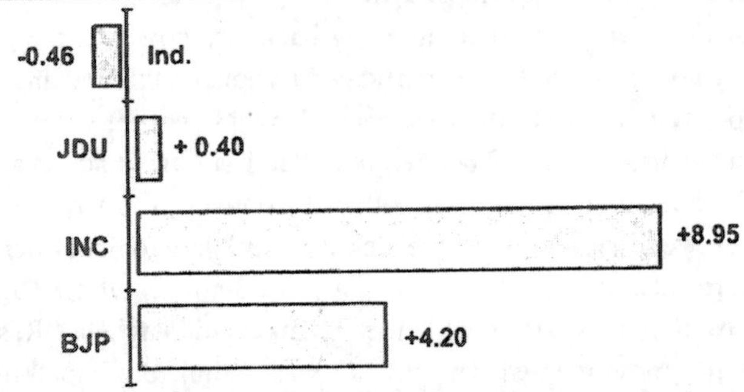

Gains & Losses

Party	Current Win	Prev. Win	Re-tained	Gained	Gained from	Lost	Lost to	Net
BJP	20	19	15	5	INC-5	4	INC-4	+1
INC	6	7	2	4	BJP-4	5	BJP-5	-1
Total	26	26	17	9		9		0

cent swing over 40.72 it polled in the tribal areas last time. The Congress polled 34.59 per cent votes to win five general seats, one extra, and claimed an SC seat with 50.07 per cent votes, up 16.83 points. But it lost all its three ST seats while polling 46.56 per cent-down 1.74 points-in tribal areas.

Other parties, including CPI (0.58 per cent) and JDU (0.14 per cent), polled 1.17 per cent SC votes and 2.33 per cent ST votes with Pawar's NCP alone taking 1.26 per cent of the latter. Home Minister Lal Krishna Advani, won back the Gandhinagar seat for BJP taking on former chief election commissioner, T N Seshan.

Undertaking a barefoot campaign in the state capital, Seshan wooed voters with some Bollywood Hindi: *"Hum to dil de chuke sanam* (I've given my heart)," and *"Hum dulhaniya lene aye hain* (I've come to take the bride)." Seshan lost by 188,927 votes, but had the satisfaction of polling 3,000 more votes in the Gandhinagar Assembly segment.

Former RJP chief minister, Vaghela, now with Congress, won Kapadvanj with 165,381 votes, but it was union Textile Minister Kashiram Rana who won Surat for BJP with the state's highest margin of 249, 197 votes. Party colleague Vallabh Kathiriya, a cancer surgeon who made news with a 3.54 lakh vote victory in Rajkot last time, won again, but with a greatly reduced margin of 86,747 votes.

Losing three seats to BJP, Congress could win only four general seats with 34.49 per cent votes, but it won three of the four ST seats with 48.30 per cent. Its lone SC seat was won with 33.24 per cent votes. In all 107 candidates lost their deposits, including all the 62 independents. So did nine nominees of JDU, seven each of NCP and SP, six of Shiv Sena, four of BSP and three each of RPI and JDS. Only three of the seven women candidates, two from BJP and one from Congress, emerged successful, all retaining their seats, but former Ahmedabad mayor Bhavnaben Dave of BJP lost her seat in Surendranagar.

In the 1962 poll, the first after the formation of Gujarat, the undivided Congress won 16 seats with 52.6% votes but conceded four to the newly formed Swatantra, which cornered 25% votes. In the next election, Swatantra overtook the Congress to win 12 seats with 39.9% votes. While Congress bagged one seat less, it polled seven per cent more votes at 46.9%. But in 1971, two years after a major split, Congress (I) led by Indira Gandhi and the rival Congress (O) both won

11 seats each. But Congress (I) with 44.9% votes polled 5.2% more votes. In 1977, in the face of the Janata wave, Congress (I) won 10 seats with 46.9%, while the Janata took the rest with 49.5%. Congress(I) bounced back in 1980 winning all but one of the 26 seats with its highest ever vote share of 54.8%. The Janata could pick up only one seat though it polled 36.9% votes. In the next round Congress dropped a seat and 1.6% votes even as Janata Party saw its vote share plummet down to 16.6%. BJP picked up one seat, but garnered 18.6% votes to begin its rise to power even as Janata Dal briefly shared the spoils in 1989. While JD won 11 seats with 27.8% votes then, BJP won 12 with 30.47%. Within two years it had eclipsed all others.

Key Contests

Gandhi Nagar. BJP president L.K. Advani won it in 1991 along with New Delhi and decided to keep it. After he resigned the seat a few months before the poll in the wake of the Jain Hawala case, the party's prime ministerial candidate Atal Behari Vajpayee decided to contest from here too besides Lucknow to keep it warm for Advani. He too won both in 1996, but chose to keep Lucknow.

Sabarkantha. Gulzarilal Nanda, twice interim Prime Minister, after the deaths of Jawaharlal Nehru and Lal Bahadur Shastri, represented it from 1952 to 1967, when he shifted to Kaithal in Haryana. Nisha Amarsingh Chaudhary (Congress) wrested it in 1996 from BJP's Arvind Trivedi, who acted as Ravana in the *Ramayana* TV serial.

Surat. Morarji Desai, Prime Minister during 1977-79, won five times from Surat, thrice as Congress candidate. He won as Congress(O) candidate in 1971 and as the Janata Party nominee in 1977. BJP leader Kashiram Rana won the seat for the third time in a row in 1996 by a margin of over 175,000, the highest in the state.

Electorate	:	4,70,22,915
Turnout	:	2,57,43,398
Turnout %	:	54.75%
Valid Votes	:	2,53,56,387
Invalid & Missing	:	3,87,011
Candidates	:	344

MADHYA PRADESH

Seats: 40 (General: 25; SC: 6; ST: 9)

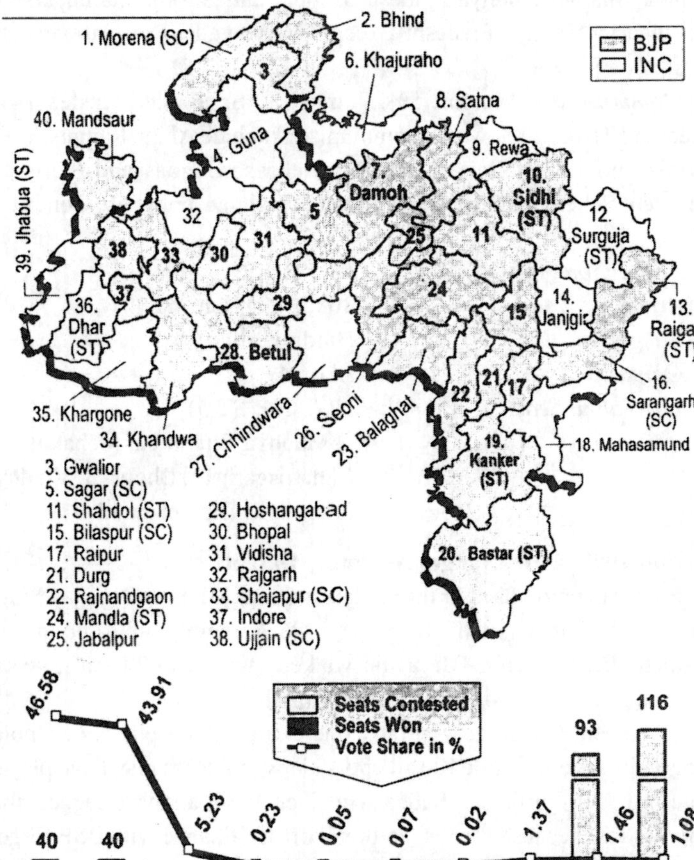

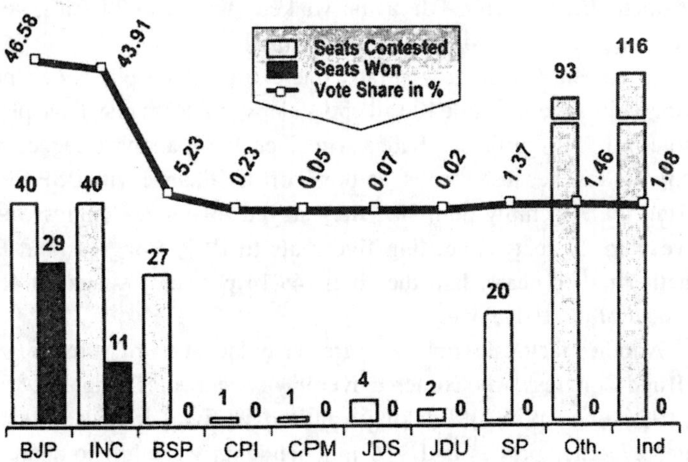

MADHYA PRADESH

History. India's largest state was formed on November 1, 1956 with the merger of 17 Hindi-speaking districts of then Madhya Pradesh, Madhya Bharat, Vindhya Pradesh, Bhopal and Sironj, and enclave of Rajasthan in Madhya Pradesh. Except for the valleys of Narmada and Tapti, it's a plateau.

Communities. Muslim 5%, Jains 1%, Scheduled Castes 14%, Scheduled Tribes 22%. Major communities include Ahirs, Rajputs, Telis, Kurmis and Lodhs. Jatavs, Balais, Mehras, Gandas and Kolis are prominent Scheduled Castes. Dominant Scheduled Tribes are Gonds and Bhils.

Population (1991)	:	48,581,170
Area	:	308,252 sq km
Languages	:	Hindi, Urdu
Capital	:	Bhopal
Lok Sabha Seats	:	29 (SC 4, ST 5) —Madhya Bharat 12, Mahakosal 7, Chhattisgarh 11, Bhopal 3, Vindhya Pradesh 4, Bundelkhand 3

Election 1999: BJP Avenges Assembly Defeat

Barely ten months after the Congress Chief Minister Digvijay Singh pulled off a victory in the November 1998 Assembly polls defying the anti-incumbency factor, BJP again walked away with 29 seats, nearly three fourths of the spoils in a virtual straight contest.

At eleven, Congress won only one extra seat despite a 4.51 point swing in its favour. While Kargil and Vajapyee factors may have played a role in BJP's fourth Lok Sabha win since 1989, analysts suggest that Congress lost because it chose to break off its alliance with BSP forged during the Assembly poll. Had they stayed together, Congress might have won 20 seats conceding five seats to BSP. Congress and BSP together polled nearly half the votes (49.14 per cent) as against 46.58 per cent of the BJP alone.

Another factor possibly was greater polarisation of votes between BJP and Congress, who cornered over 90 per cent votes as against 85 per cent last time. With BSP taking a little over five per cent, instead of nine, 27 other parties and 116 independents were left to share the

Madhya Pradesh

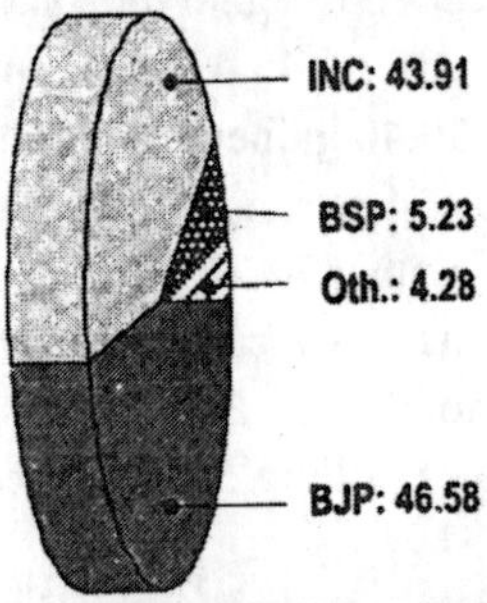

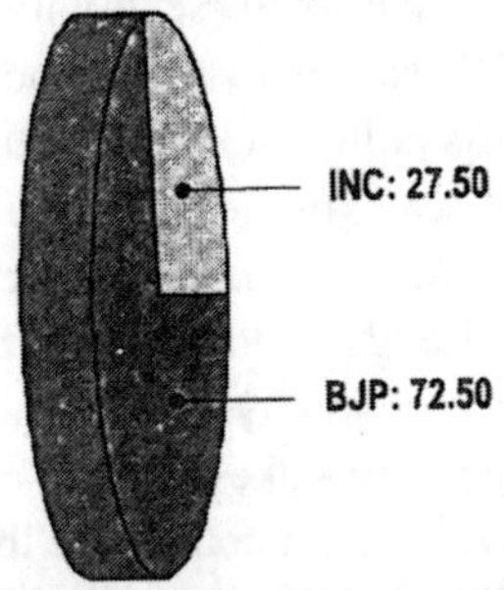

Swing %

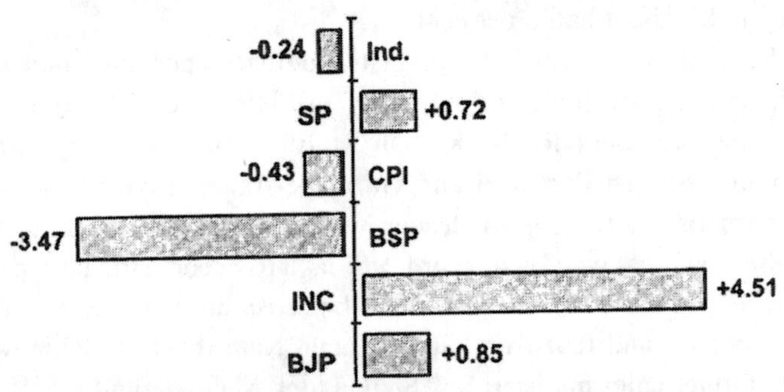

Gains & Losses

Party	Current Win	Prev. Win	Re-tained	Gained	Gained from	Lost	Lost to	Net
BJP	29	30	24	5	INC-5	6	INC-6	-1
INC	11	10	5	6	BJP-6	5	BJP-5	+1
Total	40	40	29	11		11		0

remaining four per cent. Despite a little 0.85 point swing over the 45.73 per cent it polled in 1998, BJP lost a seat.

Though it wrested five seats from the Congress, the saffron party lost six to the former. It won 17 of the 25 general seats with 46.28 per cent instead of 19 with 45.76 per cent votes, but polled 1.77 points more to win all the six SC seats with 49.51 per cent. BJP again took six of the nine ST seats with a 1.19 point higher share of 45.47 per cent. The Congress polling 43.91 per cent as against 39.40 gained a seat. Its eight general seats, two extra, were won with 43.74 per cent votes, up 4.67 points, while its three ST victories came with 47.43 per cent with a simlar rise. But it lost its only SC seat even as its six candidates brought the party polling 39.86 per cent, 3.7 point more votes. BSP came third in the popularity stakes with 27 of its candidates polling 5.23 per cent, yet only five of them could save their deposits.

All but 10.65 per cent of the SC vote was cornered by the Congress and BJP with BSP polling 5.31 per cent and SP about one per cent. Others shared 7.1 per cent of ST vote with BSP taking 2.77 per cent, CPI 1.16 and SP about half a per cent.

Several Congress bigwigs tasted defeat. They included party spokesman, Ajit Jogi, former chief minister Motilal Vora, state Congress president Radha Kishan Malviya and two Rajya Sabha members, Suresh Pachouri and Gufran-e-Azam. Five former state ministers also lost. Congress leader Madhavrao Scindia, shifting from Gwalior to Guna, won by a record 2.14 lakh to become the only person in Madhya Pradesh to win nine Lok Sabha elections in a row, five times from Gwalior and four from Guna. Kamal Nath retained Chhindwara, while former chief minister, S C Shukla took Mahasamund.

A former BJP chief minister, Sunder Lal Patwa who had lost to Kamal Nath last time came in from Hoshangabad. BJP union ministers, Uma Bharti, Ramesh Bais and Satya Narain Jatiya also won, but Nitish Bhardwaj, Krishna of the small screen, lost to Digvijay Singh's younger brother, Laxman Singh in Rajgarh.

Excepting BJP, Congress and five candidates of BSP, all others totalling 259 lost their deposits. They included 116 independents together polling 1.08 per cent. Of the 23 women candidates, only three won, all of them of BJP, while all the four Congress nominees lost. The winning BJP women included Uma Bharti, who shifted from the temple town of Khajuraho to Bhopal to record her fifth victory in a row.

Politics in Madhya Pradesh was dominated by the Congress until 1967 when it lost power in the state for the first time. In the Lok Sabha poll that year, the Congress won 24 of the 37 seats for 40.8% as against 35 for 52.1% in 1957 after the formation of the enlarged state. In 1971, the Congress share came down to 21 though its votes went up to 45.6%. The Janata wave of 1977 all but swept away the Congress leaving it with just one seat for 32.5% votes—its worst performance to date. The Janata then took 37 seats for 57.9%—the highest polled by any party so far. The Congress bounced back in 1980 to win 35 seats for 47.2% and then made a clean sweep of all the 40 seats with its best ever 57.1% votes. But 1989 saw a reversal of fortunes with the luck finally turning for the BJP. The Congress could win only eight seats for 37.7% while the BJP won 27 for 39.7%.

Two years later, the wheel of fortune again turned for the Congress as it polled 45.30% to win 27 seats. The BJP share was reduced to 12 with 41.88%. Earlier, BJP's forerunner Jan Sangh posed a challenge to Congress as it gradually increased its vote share from 4.9% in 1952 to 33.36% in 1971 when it won seats. A seat had eluded Jan Sangh Until 1962 when it won three for 17.9%—3.9% up from 1957 when it drew a blank. Then with a close to twelve point swing the Sangh raised its tally to ten in 1967 with 29.6% votes. In its first outing as BJP after the Janata interlude in 1984, it secured the backing of 30% voters but no seat. Five years later, though BJP came into its own to win 27 seats for 39.7%. Raising its vote share to 41.88% by 1991 it found the seats going down to 12. Apart from Janata Party, the only other party to put up a creditable performance was the Praja Socialist Party which polled 16.1% in 1957 and 12.3% in 1962 to win three seats. The Socialist Party too polled 12.2% in 1952 but it could not win a seat.

Key Contests

Bhopal. Dr Shanker Dayal Sharma, elected President in 1992, won from here in 1971 and 1980 on the Congress ticket. Sushil Chandra Verma kept it for the BJP between 1989 and 1996. Uma Bharati shifted from Khajuraho to win it in 1999.

Chhindwara. The only constituency in the Hindi belt which has always voted Congress even in the face of the 1977 Janata tide. Former union minister Kamal Nath won it six times between 1980 and 1999. His wife Alka Nath won it for the Congress in 1996.

Guna. Vijaya Raje Scindia won from Guna four times and once each from Gwalior and Bhind. The only time she lost was in Bhind in 1984. She shifted to Jhalswer in Rajasthan in 1998.

Gwalior. Former union minister Madhav Rao Scindia has won five time from Gwalior after representing Guna thrice between 1971 and 1980. Denied a Congress ticket in 1996, he floated his own MPVC party and won. In 1984 he defeated Atal Behari Vajpayee, who had won from here in 1971. Scindia returned to Guna in 1999 to record his ninth straight win to the Lok Sahba.

Electorate	:	1,22,57,507
Turnout	:	67,64,464
Turnout %	:	55.19%
Valid Votes	:	66,33,339
Invalid Votes	:	1,31,125
Candidates	:	91

Chattisgarh

Seats: 11 (General: 5; SC: 2; ST: 4)

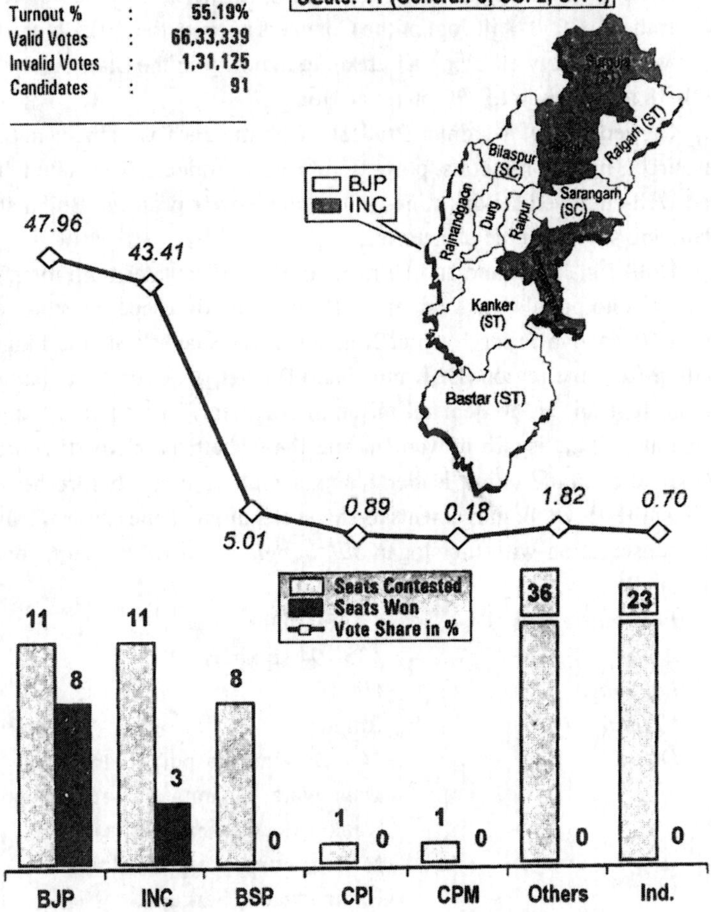

GAINS & LOSSES

Party	Current Win	Previous Win	Re-tained	Gained	Gained from	Lost	Lost to	Net
BJP	8	7	5	3	INC-3	2	INC-2	+1
INC	3	4	1	2	BJP-2	3	BJP-3	-1
Total	11	11	6	5		5		0

CHHATTISGARH

History. Chhattisgarh came into being as the 26th Indian state on November 1, 2000. Ajit Jogi of the Congress became the first Chief Minister with his party enjoying an absolute majority in the State Assembly with 48 members in the 90-member House.

Carved out of Madhya Pradesh, Chhattisgarh is rich in natural resources, mainly minerals, power, and forest products. The state inherited well-endowed Baldia mines, numerous power projects, Bhilai steel plant and several cement factories.

Unlike in Jharkhand and Uttranchal, two other states born together, there was no popular movement for the creation of a separate state with the first Madhya Pradesh Chief Minister Ravi Shankar Shukla himself hailing from the region. Dr Khubichand Baghel, a Congress parliamentarian, first raised the demand in the mid-sixties. Then came a Prathak (separate) Chhattisgarh movement and the Chhattisgarh Mukti Morcha launched by trade union leader Shankar Guha Niyogi, before he was killed in 1991. Other movements too have championed the cause of tribals and conservation with the slogan *Jal, Jungle aur Jamin* (water, forest, and land).

Population (1991)	:	17,600,000
Area	:	135,194 sq km
Language	:	Hindi
Capital	:	Raipur
District	:	16—Bastar, Bilaspur, Champa, Dantewara, Dhamtari, Durg, Jashpur, Kanker, Kawardha, Korba, Koriya, Mahasamund, Raigarh, Raipur, Rajnandgaon, Sarguja,
Electorate (99)	:	12,257,507
Lok Sabha Seats	:	11 (SC 2, ST 4)
Party Position	:	BJP 8 (+1), Congress 3 (- 1)

Election (1999) : BJP Gain but Congress Gets the State

Although the Congress formed the first government in the new state because of its unassailable position in the Assembly, it was the BJP that won all but three of the 11 Lok Sabha seats in the region that was to become Chhatisgarh.

Polling nearly half the votes (47.96%), the BJP retained five seats, wrested three from the Congress, while conceding two to it to finish with an additional seat.

The Congress, 4.55 points behind with 43.41% votes, held on to Janjgir and, wrested Mahasamund and Surguja ST seats from the BJP, but lost three others to it to end up with a net loss of one.

BSP came third in the popularity stakes with about five per cent votes with the two Left parties, CPI and CPI(M) together collecting a little over one per cent. Independents and other smaller parties shared the remaining 2.55% of the vote pie.

While a former Congress Chief Minister of Madhya Pradesh, Shyama Charan Shukla won the Mahasumund seat from the BJP beating Chandra Sekhan Sahu "Champu" by 15,435 votes, another, Moti Lal Vora bit the dust in Rajnandgaon. He lost to little known Dr Raman of BJP by 26,715 votes.

Polling 47.38% votes, the BJP also won three of the four ST seats, including Raigarh wrested from the Congress. In turn the Congress picked Surguja from the BJP to make its lone gain, while polling 44.82%.

Gaining Sarangarh from Congress, the BJP took both the SC seats with 46.26% votes, more than ten points ahead of its rival's 35.77%. BSP took 15.47% of the SC vote but even a single seat eluded it.

Electorate	:	5,67,32,152
Turnout	:	3,46,40,320
Turnout %	:	64.39%
Valid Votes	:	3,30,31,602
Invalid & Missing	:	16,08,718
Candidates	:	261

MAHARASHTRA

Seats: 48 (General: 41; SC: 3; ST: 4)

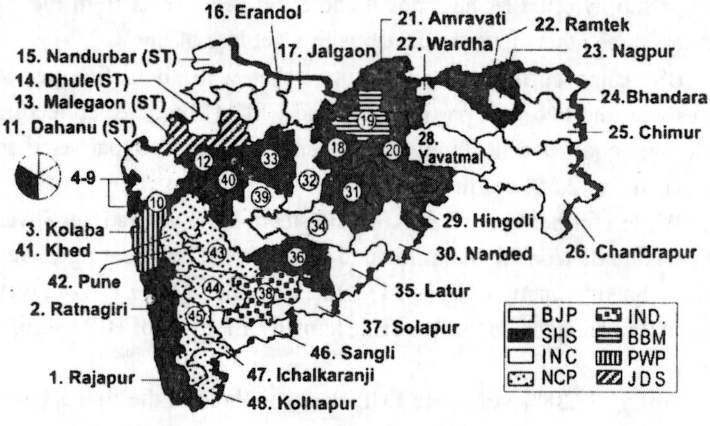

4. Mumbai South-BJP
5. Mumbai South Central-SHS
6. Mumbai North Central-SHS
7. Mumbai North East-BJP
8. Mumbai North West-INC
9. Mumbai North-BJP

10. Thane
12. Nashik
18. Buldhana(SC)
19. Akola
20. Washim
31. Parbhani

32. Jalna
33. Aurangabad
34. Beed
36. Osmanabad(SC)
38. Pandharpur (SC)

39. Ahmednagar
40. Kopargaon
43. Baramati
44. Satara
45. Karad

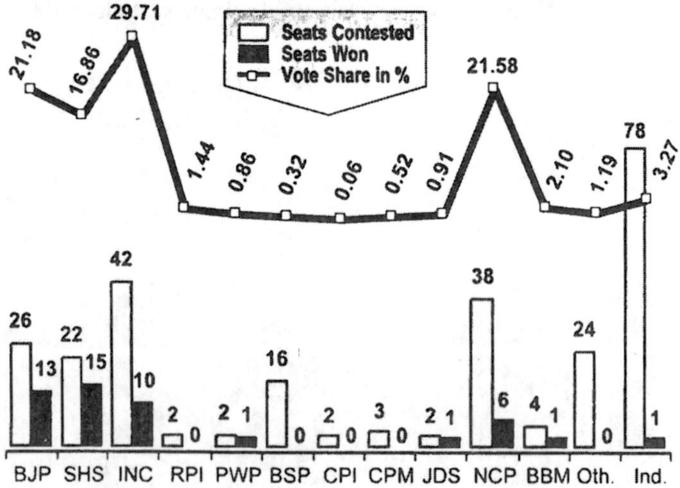

MAHARASHTRA

History. A part of the Mauryan empire, it was included in the Bombay Presidency by the British in 1818 after defeating the Marathas. It continued as a bilingual state of Bombay after independence and became Maharashtra on May 1, 1960 after the separation of Gujarat. India's third largest state, both in area and population, its three regions are Western Maharashtra, Vidarabha and Marathwada.

Communities. Muslims 10%, Buddhists 7%, Scheduled Castes 7%, Scheduled Tribes 6%. Major communities include Marathas/Kunbis and Lingayats. Mahars, Mangs and Bhambhis are among the principal Scheduled Castes. Dominant Scheduled Tribes are Gonds, Bhils and Koli Mahadevs.

Population (1991)	:	78,937,187
Area	:	307,690 sq km
Language	:	Marathi
Capital	:	Mumbai
Lok Sabha Seats	:	48 (SC 3, ST 4)—Konkan 5, Greater Bombay 6, Khandesh 6, Vidarbha 11, Marathwada 8, Western Maharashtra 12

Election 1999: Pawar Paves Way for BJP-Sena Combine

Maratha leader Sharad Pawar, architect of a magnificent win for the Congress in 1998 through an alliance with Republican Party of India and the Samajwadi Party, helped BJP-Shiv Sena alliance stage a comeback in the Lok Sabha poll even as it lost power in the parallel Assembly poll.

Though Pawar's newly formed Nationalist Congress Party itself could win only six seats, all at the cost of Congress, the split on the issue of party president, Sonia Gandhi's foreign origin, helped the BJP-Sena alliance win 28 of the 48 seats. Despite an adverse swing of 4.11 points that reduced their combined vote share from 42.15 to 38.04 per cent, the combine captured 18 extra seats with both partners gaining nine seats each, as BJP won 13 and Sena two more.

On the other hand, Congress and NCP going their separate ways, won the support of more than half the voters (51.29 per cent) but could win only ten and six seats, less than half of 33 secured by the united

Maharashtra

Vote Share (in %)

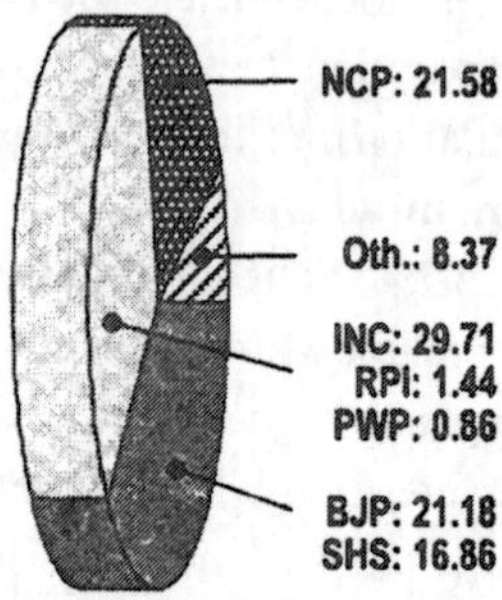

Seat Share (in %)

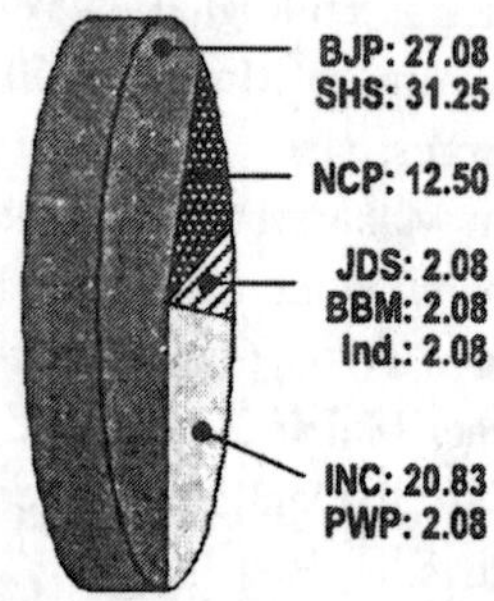

Swing %

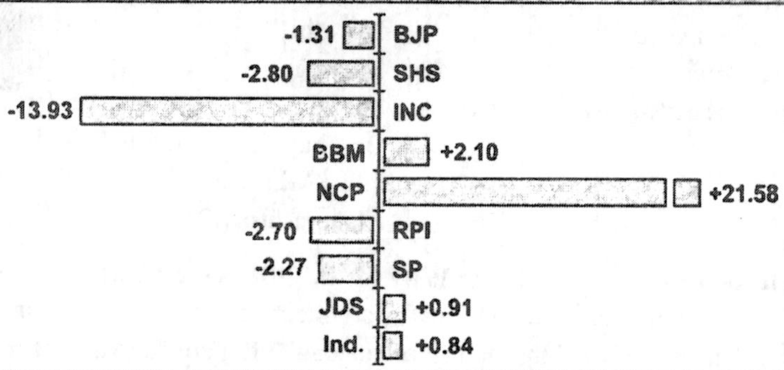

Gains & Losses

Party	Current Win	Prev. Win	Re-tained	Gained	Gained from	Lost	Lost to	Net
BJP	13	4	4	9	INC-7, RPI-1 SHS-1	0	-	+9
SHS	15	6	4	11	INC-9, RPI-2	2	INC-1, BJP-1	+9
INC	10	33	9	1	SHS-1	24	BJP-7, SHS-9 JDS-1, IND-1, NCP-6	-23
BBM	1	0	0	1	RPI-1	0	-	+1
PWP	1	1	1	0	-	0	-	0
RPI	0	4	0	0	-	4	SHS-2, BJP-1, BBM-1	-4
NCP	6	0	0	6	INC-6	0	-	+6
JDS	1	0	0	1	INC-1	0	-	+1
IND	1	0	0	1	INC-1	0	-	+1
Total	**48**	**48**	**18**	**30**		**30**		**0**

party in 1998. The Congress-NCP share was in fact 0.89 points higher than the 50.40 per cent won by the Congress-RPI-SP alliance that brought it 37 seats last time.

Polling 21.18 per cent votes, down 1.31 points, BJP itself wrested seven seats from the Congress, and one each from RPI and the Sena, while retaining all the four it had.

The Sena polling 16.86 per cent, 2.80 points less than the 19.66 per cent it got in 1998, also retained four seats, while gaining nine from the Congress and two from RPI. But it also lost one to INC and conceded another to ally BJP.

The split brought down the Congress vote share 13.93 points from 43.64 to 29.71 per cent leading to a loss of 23 seats. It yielded nine seats to Shiv Sena, seven to BJP, six to NCP and one each to JDS and Athawale faction of RPI. All the six NCP gains were at the cost of Congress as it sliced away 21.58 per cent vote. RPI, which had brought four seats to the Congress alliance last time, lost them all—two to Shiv Sena and one each to BJP and the local Bharipa Bahujan Mahasangha (BBM) as its vote share dropped by 2.70 points from 4.14 to 1.44 per cent.

Athawale faction of RPI gained a seat from Congress with 1.35 per cent, while Peasants and Workers Party (PWP) retained its Kolaba seat with 0.86 per cent votes, the same as earlier. JDS too gained a seat at the cost of Congress with 0.91 per cent votes. Of the three SC seats, two went to Shiv Sena with 25.86 per cent votes, while BJP could not win any but brought 7.32 per cent votes to raise the combine's total to 33.10 per cent. Ousted RPI leader, Ramdas Athawale, contesting as an independent, took the third seat with 19.50 per cent of the SC vote.

Congress and NCP polled 24.92 and 15.42 per cent SC vote, but a seat eluded either with about seven per cent of the vote shared by independents (6.67 per cent) and BSP (0.31per cent). BJP won two of the four ST seats with 30.84 per cent votes, while 34.06 per cent won Congress one with JDS wresting the fourth with 7.46 per cent vote. NCP and CPM polled 19.41 and 6.68 per cent in the tribal areas, but a seat eluded them. The remaining 1.55 per cent was shared by BSP (0.39) and others.

Prominent winners included union ministers Ram Naik (BJP) and Suresh Prabhu (Shiv Sena), and former Sena chief minister Manohar Joshi. For the Congress thespian Sunil Dutt checked the BJP-Sena sweep in Mumbai wresting the North-West constituency from BJP's Madhukar

Sarpotdar. Sitting MP Murli Deora lost Mumbai South to BJP's Jayawantiben Mehta, his 1998 rival. Former speaker Shivraj Patil won again from Latur, but former chief minister A R Antulay was defeated once more.

As an NCP candidate now, former chief minister Sharad Pawar won for the fifth time from Baramati with a record margin of 298,903 but close confidant and party treasurer Datta Meghe finished a poor third in Wardha. Four other NCP candidates lost the seats they won for the Congress last time.

Ousted RPI leader, Ramdas Athawale, shifting from Mumbai North Central to Pandharpur (ST), defeated BJP's Nagnath Kshirsagar by the second highest margin of 259,505 votes with Congress's Sandeepan Thorat, who had won this seat seven times in a row, relegated to the third position. More than half (134) of the 261 candidates, including 77 independents, lost their deposits. Others included 16 of BSP, seven of NCP, three of Congress and one each of BJP, Shiv Sena and Samajwadi Party.

Only four—Jayawantiben Mehta (BJP), Bhavana Gawli (Shiv Sena), Prabha Rao (Congress) and Nivedita Mane (NCP)—of the 17 women candidates emerged successful.

In the simultaneous assembly poll, BJP-Sena combine was ousted from power as its strength was reduced from 141 to 125 in a hung house of 288. The estranged Congress (75) and NCP (58) then joined hands to form a government with the backing of independents and others. Congress emerged as the single largest party with 75 seats, three less than 1995. Shiv Sena came next with 69, a loss of six. Newly-formed NCP was placed third with 58. Losing ten, BJP finished fourth with 56. PWP came next with five, while JDS, CPM and SP finished with two each. A dozen independents and seven others made up the rest.

The composite state of Bombay as also Maharashtra had generally favoured Congress with its score ranging between 37 for 48.5% in 1967 and 42 for 63.1% in 1971—its best ever. Even in the face of the Janata wave in 1977, Congress polled 47% votes to win 20 seats—its previous lowest tally. By 1984, the Congress raised its tally to a top point of 43 for 51.2%. But it lost 15 seats in 1989 with its votes falling to 45.4%. Bouncing back in 1991, the Congress won 38 seats for 48.40%.

Before this only in 1977, the Congress faced a major challenge from the Janata Party which then won 19 seats for 31.4%, while five other seats went to Peasants and Workers Party for 6.1%.

The Janata share fell to eight for 20.4% in 1980 and one for 7.6% in 1984. The Janata Dal won five for 10.95% in 1989 and drew a blank two years later for 9.88%.

Beginning with 2 seats for 3.4% in 1957, the Jan Sangh polled its highest 7.4% for nil in 1967. Raising it to 10.1% in its BJP incarnation in 1984, it won 10 seats for 23.7% in 1989 in alliance with the Shiv Sena. By 1991 its own share was down to five even as the Sena increased its tally from one to four with its votes rising from 1.2% to 9.45%.

Key Contests

Baramati. Former defence minister, Sharad Pawar has won it five times. He did it for the first time in 1984 as an Indian Congress Socialist nominee. He won it for the Congress thrice between 1991 and 1998 and for his own NCP in 1999.

Latur. Former speaker Shiv Raj Patil has won seven times from Latur since 1980.

Rajapur. JD leader Madhu Dandavate won it five times from 1971 to 1989. Sudhir Sawant of Congress ended his winning run in 1991.

Ramtek. Former Prime Minister P.V. Narasimha Rao was elected from here in 1984 and 1989.

DADRA & NAGAR HAVELI

Seats: 1 (ST: 1)

Electorate	:	98,376
Turnout	:	73,507
Turnout %	:	74.72%
Valid Votes	:	71,905
Invalid	:	1,602
Candidates	:	5

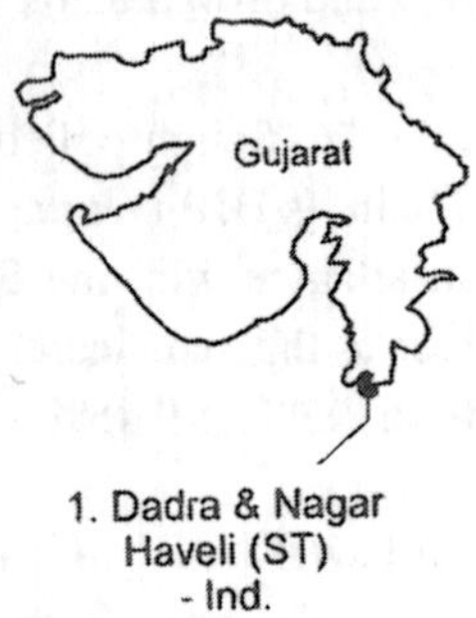

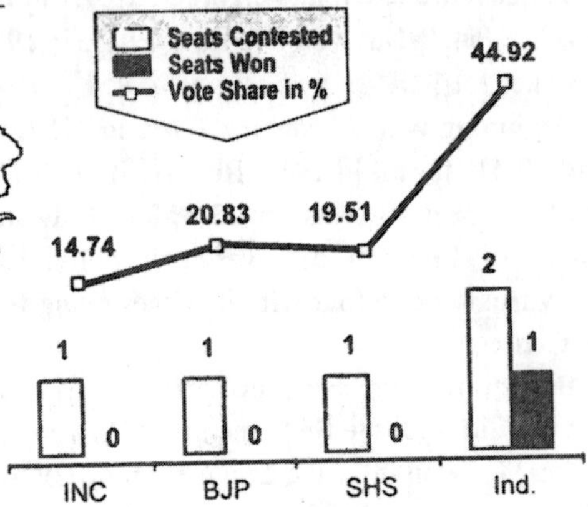

Vote & Seat Share

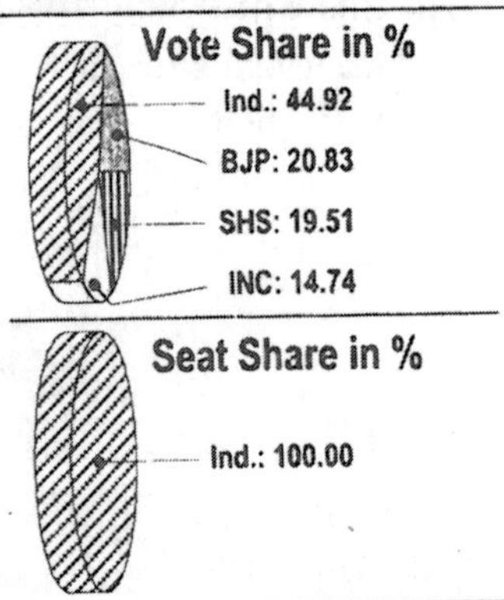

Swing %

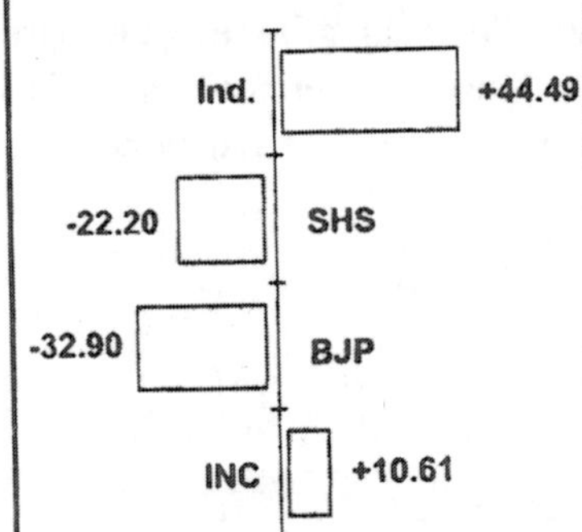

Gains & Losses

Party	Current Win	Prev. Win	Re-tained	Gained	Gained from	Lost	Lost to	Net
BJP	0	1	0	0	-	1	Ind.-1	-1
Ind.	1	0	0	1	BJP-1	0	-	+1
Total	1	1	0	1		1		0

DADRA AND NAGAR HAVELI

History. Assigned to the Portuguese by the Marathas in 1799, it was liberated in 1954 and was formally integrated into India on Aug. 11, 1961.

Communities. Scheduled Tribes 88%. Varlis are the most dominant.

Population (1991)	:	138,477
Area	:	491 sq km
Languages	:	Gujarati, Marathi
Capital	:	Silvassa
Lok Sabha Seats	:	1 (ST 1)

Election 1999: BJP Tastes Delkar Switch

Mohanbhai Delkar did it once again, but this time as an independent instead of as a BJP candidate in 1998 to end the victory run of Congress, which had been defeated only thrice earlier in nine elections. Delkar first won as an independent in 1989 defeating Congress' S J Gavali, who in turn, had given Congress its first defeat five years earlier as an independent.

Joining the Congress in 1991, Delkar again beat Gavali, then fighting as a BJP nominee. He repeated the feat in 1996, but switched over to BJP in 1998 to record his fourth straight victory from this tiny former Portuguese enclave.

As an independent now, Delkar polled 41.52 per cent, 12.21 points less than the 53.73 per cent he polled as the BJP nominee last time. It was quite a climb- down from 61.74 and 55.62 per cent he polled for the Congress in 1991 and 1996, respectively

His fifth victory this time reduced the BJP share by 32.9 points to 20.83 per cent. Shiv Sena came next with 19.51 per cent, less than half of 41.71 it polled last time. The Congress finished fourth even as it raised it share from its lowest of 4.13 in 1998 to 14.74 per cent, but its nominee again could not save his deposit. The Congress first lost to Delkar in 1989 polling 28.6 per cent. Its best came in 1980 when it won 61.9 per cent of the popular vote. Another independent winning 3.4 per cent votes also lost his deposit in the five-cornered contest. There were no women candidates again this time.

The Congress did its best in 1980 when it polled 61.9% and its worst in 1998 in gathering only 4.13%.

CPI(M)'s best came in 1971 when it polled 27.8% and the worst in 1989 with 10.8%. Only other notable performances in the past were by the Praja Socialist Party polling 16.6% in 1967, Congress (O) getting 33% in 1971 and the Janata Party taking 31.8% in 1977.

Electorate	:	72,216
Turnout	:	51,811
Turnout %	:	71.74%
Valid Votes	:	50,800
Invalid & Missing	:	1,011
Candidates	:	4

DAMAN & DIU

Seats: 1 (General: 1)

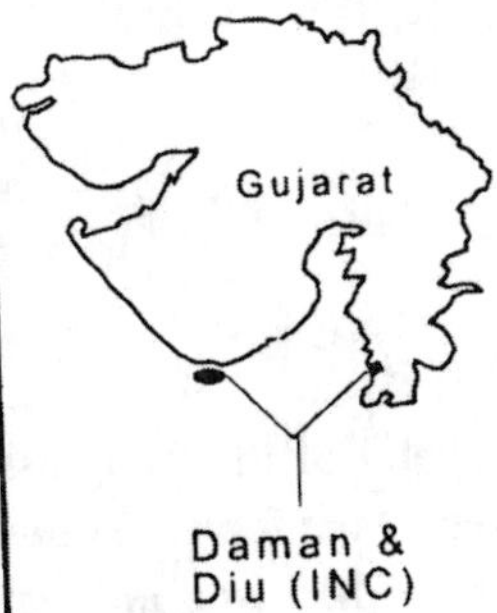

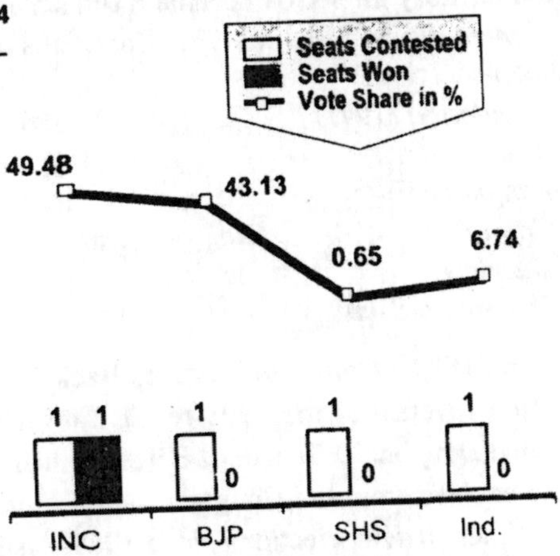

Vote & Seat Share

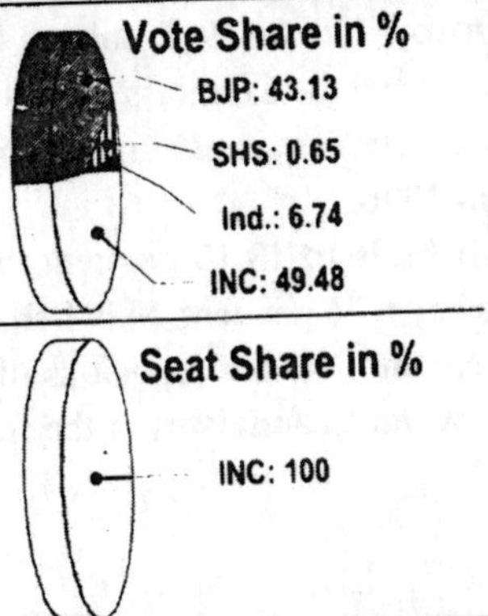

Swing %

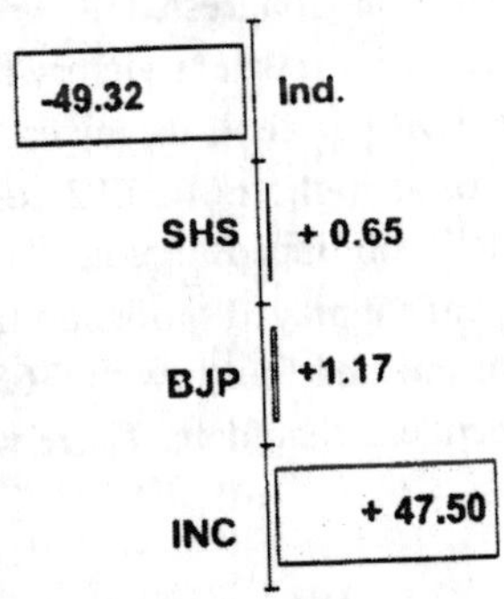

Gains & Losses

Party	Current Win	Prev. Win	Re-tained	Gained	Gained from	Lost	Lost to	Net
BJP	0	1	0	0	-	1	INC-1	-1
INC	1	0	0	1	BJP-1	0	-	+1
Total	1	1	0	1	-	1	-	0

DAMAN AND DIU

History. The Portuguese captured Diu in 1534 and annexed Daman in 1559. Liberated in 1961 along with Goa, they became a separate union territory after Goa became a full state in 1987.

Communities. Muslims 9%, Christians 3%. Siddis are the major Scheduled Tribe

Population (1991)	:	101,586
Area	:	121 sq km
Language	:	Gujarati
Capital	:	Daman
Districts	:	2
Lok Sabha Seats	:	1

Election 1999 : Congress Bounces Back

In a reversal of the 1998 result Dahyabhai Patel of the Congress defeated Devjibhai J Tandel of BJP, who had wrested the former Portuguese enclave from the Congress then. Loser Tandel had won the seat three times in four elections since 1989, losing to G K Tandel of the Congress in 1996. DJ first beat GK as an independent candidate in 1989.

Two years later he won the seat for BJP with GK turning independent. Back in Congress, GK wrested it from him in 1996 only to lose it two years later. Patel's victory this time raised the Congress share from a mere 1.98 per cent, its lowest, to 49.48 per cent, but still 1.14 points short of its highest of 50.62 per cent in 1996.

BJP too upped its vote share from 41.96 to 43.13 per cent, but an independent played spoilsport taking away 6.74 per cent. Shiv Sena candidate finished fourth with 0.65 per cent and lost his deposit as did the independent candidate. There were no women candidates in the fray.

CHAPTER 11

OF POLL PUNDITS AND PUNTERS

305? 287? 242?—That was the cryptic headline of an English daily on the morning after the last of five rounds of poll 1999 was completed on Sunday October 3, putting an (un)intended question mark on poll pundits.

How was the pollster with his computers and swing charts any better than the astrologers, palmists and sundry other fortune-tellers—some with computers too—to whom politicians of every hue had always turned?

If psephology or the art of predicting poll results, was indeed a science why didn't two and two always make four?

Pollsters, of course, had their margin of error, last minute swings and lying factor of voter not necessarily telling the truth, to fall back upon, but the Indian voter again foxed them all.

After the Supreme Court found "no merit" in the Election Commission plea for help to enforce its "guidelines", to keep the results of opinion and exit polls under wraps until the last elector had cast his vote, pollsters again had captive audiences glued to the tube.

Even as the Press Council insisted that its own ban on them stood, there was no stopping of punters. In fact, politicians took them more seriously as the *Satta Bazaar* was seen as a market without biases.

Afterwards, there were claims aplenty of "I told you so", but the fact remained that hardly anyone could get the full picture right this time with most pollsters and pundits either failing to gauge the mood swings or to translate them into seats.

Three major exit polls, said to be more accurate as they are conducted after the voter has actually cast his vote and cannot change his mind, gave the BJP-led National Democratic Alliance anything between 242 and 305 seats.

If an Insight poll on Star TV was on the dot with its 295-305 prediction for NDA, particularly after National Conference's backing actually raised its support base to 304, it was wide of the mark with its projected tally for either Congress and allies or others.

Together with the Left (43), Congress alliance won 179 seats whereas *Insight* had given it no more than 145-155. Similarly 'Others', excluding Left had 61 and with them 104—either too low or too high compared with 85-95, Star TV had foretold.

Similarly, a Doordarshan poll conducted by Development and Research Services (DRS) gave NDA 287, Congress and allies 174 and 'Others' 77—not exactly bull's eye.

Yet another survey conducted by CMCR-IMS for Maratni newspaper *Lokmat* gave BJP and allies only 242 with the rival Congress getting 227, leading to suggestions that the newspaper had let its prejudices get the better of it.

Similar blame was laid at the door of C-Voter-*Pioneer* when it suggested that the BJP front may bag 313-318 seats and Congress president Sonia Gandhi could find herself on a sticky wicket in Bellary with voters willing to give a *desi behan* a chance over a *videshi bahu.*

But then Lokmat appeared to be the only one to have judged the anti-BJP wave in UP correctly in projecting 38 seats for it when the alliance actually got 31, while DD had given it 46 and Star TV an even higher 48-52.

It again was on the dot with nine for Congress in Assam. And in West Bengal, if Star TV was right in projecting 29-33 seats for the Left (actual 29), DD was the only one to give Congress the three that it actually got.

But none could see the rout of RJD coming in Bihar with the three exit polls giving the Congress-RJD combine 20-22 seats, exactly double of the eleven they actually got.

They were equally off the mark in gauging the success of BJP-JDU alliance, which garnered 41 seats as against the projected 27-31.

Punters in Delhi offering even money on BJP getting 187 were almost right, but UP foxed them too. Though they did scale down their estimate of the BJP tally in UP from 48 to 38, it was still nine seats higher than what it actually got.

And although their estimate for the Congress was much lower than that of the pollsters, at 138 it was two dozen more.

Again while they offered only 30 paise on former finance minister Manmohan Singh making it from South Delhi, it was BJP's Vijay Kumar Malhotra who won despite 3:1 odds. Earlier, four major pollsters, *Centre for Media Studies* (CMS) for *Outlook, Development and Research Services* (DRS) for *The Times of India, Insight* for *India Today* and AC Nielsen for the *Hindustan Times*, too conducted opinion polls about a month before the elections.

Both the *Times/DRS* poll and *India Today/Insight* gave almost the same tally for the two major contenders, but Outlook/CMS projected a different picture.

While DRS gave BJP and allies 332 seats and *Insight* ranged it between 332 and 336, CMS projected the combine's tally at 279-289. Similarly, if DRS gave the Congress 138 and *Insight* 132-146, *CMS* gave it a much higher 152-162.

Insight made no predictions for the Third Front, but DRS gave it 73 with CMS suggesting 63-68. CMS alone gave 34-39 to others, which could go either way.

The *Outlook/CMS* poll based on a sample of 10,650 voters spread over 71 constituencies estimated the NDA share a bit low at 279-289 with 39.15 per cent with BJP itself getting 200 for 27.55 per cent. Its estimate for the Congress alliance was too high at 152-162 for 31.15 per cent with 135 seats for the Sonia party alone for 23.85 per cent.

The Nielsen survey, based on a sample of 76 constituencies in 15 states, was bang on target in predicting 300 seats for BJP and allies, excluding NC. But at 146, it gave ten seats more to the Congress combine and at 97 as many less to others. In terms of votes too it was fairly close in suggesting that NDA will get 41.6 per cent, just 0.92 points more than it actually did. It underestimated the Congress combine's vote by 3 33 points in giving it 30.4 per cent instead of 33.73 per cent. To others, it gave 28 per cent, 2.41 points more.

At the zonal level it gave BJP and allies 75 (+1) in the North, 71 (-2) in South, 78 (+4) in East and 76(-3) in West. Again while the Congress got 35 (+5), 46 (-2), 29 (-1) and 36 (+8) in the four zones, others' share was 41 (-6), 15 (+4), 35 (-3), and 6 (-5).

Pollsters suggested the fact that despite inaccuracies at the state level, if they did get their national tally right, it was not by accident but by design. The margin of error at the constituency level is much higher than at the state level. At the national level it is even lower.

For as the sample size increases, the errors tend to cancel each other out, psephologist G V L Narasimha Rao explained. Others fell on the late swing explanation—generally seen as the last refuge of the failed psephologist or the defeated candidate—with Kargil emerging as a key factor helping BJP and its allies.

Mapping the swings in public mood, Marketing and Development Research Associates (MDRA), an offshoot of CMS suggested that BJP could hope to get a peak figure of 210 if the polls were held in May 1999 after the Pawar split. Its tally would have been 200 if they were held just after Pokhran nuclear tests a year earlier. BJP was at its lowest ebb of 160 at the time of November '98 polls in four states. If Lok Sabha polls too had been held at the same time, the Congress might have touched the 230-seat peak. BJP's prospects improved by ten seats after Vajpayee's bus ride to Lahore in February with the Congress going down by the same number.

But surprisingly when two months later, he lost the vote of confidence, BJP gained 15 seats - possibly due to sympathy factor - even as Congress added five to its prospective tally. Later that month when the Congress failed to form an alternative government, BJP prospects improved by 20 seats, while Congress' prospects declined by 25.

The Pawar split in May chopped another 20 from the Congress share, while adding five to BJP kitty. Later that month as the Kargil crisis erupted, the odds were fairly evened with BJP poised to take 180 and the Congress 170. In June, as the Kargil campaign built up, BJP added five to its prospective tally, while Congress lost 20. In the post-Kargil scenario in July, BJP stood poised to take 190 and the Congress 145. In the event BJP took 182, but Congress with 114 fared much worse than what pollsters had expected.

Apart from last minute swings, undecided voters, turnout and lying factor can all upset a forecast even if it is based on a carefully planned survey, pollsters say.

Exit polls tend to be more accurate than opinion polls because there are no undecided voters and people tend to be less cagey after they have cast their votes.

Another pitfall in a multi-party situation is conversion of votes polled by a party into seats as splits and alliances and the spread of votes can make all the difference.

A device used by pollsters to convert a multi-party scenario into a two-party situation is the Index of Opposition Unity (IOU). Higher the IOU, lesser the split in opposition votes.

It did work at one time when one was looking at Congress and non-Congress situations. IOU is dead now that the Congress has lost power in all but a handful of states, say pollsters.

But some still swear by it saying it would work if computed for the dominant party in a state. For instance, it could be calculated for the CPM in West Bengal and BJP/Congress in Rajasthan or Madhya Pradesh.

IOU is determined by dividing the highest opposition party vote by the total opposition vote. An IOU of one would indicate total opposition unity as in a straight contest between two major parties, and an IOU of 0.5 would indicate a two way split of opposition votes.

But more than the IOU, the most important factor is how a typical constituency is picked up and how data is collected. Pollsters suggest that there are certain 'bell weather' constituencies reflecting the national or regional mood. Picked up on the basis of past voting patterns, these constituencies are used to gauge swings for or against a political party.

The swings, in turn, are superimposed on other seats to see who may win. Pollsters also resort to the "cube law" as a rough and ready reckoner of seats.

Evolved by western psephologists essentially for two party systems, it suggests that the seats won by a party are usually "in proportion to the cube of the percentage of votes polled by that party". Thus a two-percent swing should translate into eight per cent more seats.

Indian psephologists have modified the cube law too. Here the total votes of opposition parties are multiplied by the IOU and assigned to an 'ideal' second party to calculate the seats that might be won by all the 'opposition' parties together.

The 'swing' and 'split' factors are also taken into account. Sometimes the swings and splits cancel each other out and at other times they work in the same direction to give a new complexion to an electoral battle.

A study of all elections since 1952, however, suggests that the swings play a more decisive role. Fine tuning for the 'lying factor'—voters may not be telling the truth—and late mood swings can help pollsters make fairly accurate predictions.

Pollsters claim that a carefully planned exercise should not have more than two per cent margin of error for votes. But this could result in a ten per cent error in seats, enough to turn victory into defeat—and make or mar reputations.

If the last three general elections suggested that psephology has arrived in India, 1999 suggested that there are as yet many imponderables and methodologies need to be further improvised in tune with the emerging political situation.

Even before the results stretched the credibility of the opinion polls, they came in for criticism with the Press Council suggesting and the Election Commission imposing a ban on them.

Its January 20, 1998 guidelines prohibited the publication or broadcast of opinion and exit polls 48 hours before the first date of polling until the last date of polling.

Examples were cited of some western countries, which have put a ban on publication of opinion polls during the last week of an election or over the entire election period lest they may influence the outcome of the real thing.

The five-member constitutional bench of the Supreme Court did not lift the EC ban and merely expressed surprise at the Commission's hesitation in enforcing its own guidelines as it had claimed that they had the force of law under Article 324 of the Constitution.

"If you had assumed that you had powers to issue such guidelines then why are you doubting the very same powers by coming to the court seeking their enforcement," the bench asked the Commission. Faced with a no-win situation, the Commission quietly withdrew its directive.

Critics suggested that apart from the 'bandwagon'—backing the winning horse, or the 'counter-bandwagon'—rooting for the underdog, effect, opinion polls tended to focus on the eventual outcome and thus diverted attention from the issues.

Others doubted the extent to which opinion polls could affect the outcome of the election, but suggested they could nevertheless still play a positive role by focusing on issues instead of turning it into a betting game.

Responsibly conducted by professionals with clear indication of how, when, where and who did it to arrive at what conclusion, they were any day better than the informed guess work that the media tended to indulge in otherwise, they said.

"How does the EC plan to ban journalists and the Internet speculating or reporting on the trends," asked Dorab Sopariwalla, a leading market research professional and analyst.

As the elections were spread over a month, he wondered, wouldn't it give an unfair advantage to those who were on the winning side before the ban came, as the later trends would go unreported?

Informed readers do not take newspaper reports as seriously as the supposedly scientific opinion polls, countered Press Council Chairman, Justice P B Sawant.

In support of its contention, the Press Council in 1998 conducted an opinion poll of its own of 2,500 voters in Mumbai, Delhi and Chennai.

It was "alarmed" to find that half the voters had read and remembered a particular opinion poll and of them 70 per cent said they believed it.

Speaking in defence of the polls, a psephologist said opinion polls had become very important as a feedback channel with the decline in public confidence in politicians in the democratic world.

Conduct of reliable opinion polls in a vast, diverse and underdeveloped country like India was a difficult and complex exercise. And if for this reason some do not turn out to be accurate that should not be a reason for scrapping them, but only for having more of them, more frequently to make them better. As the polling industry grows, the good will drive out the bad, another said.

Lok Sabha Polls, 1952-1999 : Basic Data

Poll Year	Total Seats	Electorate in Million	Turnout in Million	Turnout in %	No. of Candidates	Forfeited Deposit	No. of Independents	Women Candidates	Women Winners	Expenditure in Million Rs
1952	489	173.21	105.94	61.16	1864	749	533	Not Available	22	104.6
1957	494	193.65	123.46	63.79	1591	465	481	45	27	59.0
1962	494	216.37	119.90	55.42	1985	854	480	70	34	78.1
1967	520	249.00	152.72	61.33	2447	1198	1134	67	31	109.5
1971	518	274.09	151.54	55.29	2784	1708	1224	86	22	144.3
1977	542	321.17	194.26	60.49	2439	1356	2821	70	19	298.1
1980	542	355.59	202.41	56.92	4620	3413	3792	142	28	370.7
1984	542	399.82	249.59	62.43	5313	4263	3712	164	44	782.8
1989	543	498.91	309.05	60.11	6160	5003	5687	198	27	1101.5
1991	543	514.13	317.61	56.66	8699	7518	5537	325	39	3025.2
1996	543	592.57	343.31	57.94	13952	12688	10635	599	40	5086.8
1998	543	605.88	375.45	61.97	4750	3486	1915	274	43	6547.6
1999	543	618.11	370.99	60.02	4648	3401	1945	277	48	6530.1

List of Parties

ABHM	Akhil Bharatiya Hindu Mahasabha
ADMK	All India Dravida Munnetra Kazhagam
ADSF	Akali Dal Sant Fateh Singh Group
AGP	Asom Gana Parishad
AIICS	All India Indira Congress (Secular)
AIICT	All India Indira Congress (Tiwari)
AIJP	All India Jharkhand Party
ANC	Arunachal Congress
APHLC	All Party Hill Leaders Conference
ASCF	All India Scheduled Castes Federation
ASDC	Autonomous State Demand Committee
BBM	Bhairpa Bahujan Mahasangha
BC	Bangla Congress
BJD	Biju Janata Dal
BJP	Bharatiya Janata Party
BJS	Bharatiya Jan Sangh
BKD	Bharatiya Kranti Dal
BSP	Bahujan Samaj Party
CSPJ	Chota Nagpur and Santhal Pargana Janata Party
CPI	Communist Party of India
CPM	Communist Party of India (Marxist)
CPML	Communist Party of India (Marxist-Leninist)
CWP	Commonweal Party
DBSM	Democratic Bahujan Samaj Morcha
DMK	Dravida Munnetra Kazhagam
DP	Democratic Party
FBL	All India Forward Bloc
GP	Ganatantra Parishad
GNLF	Gorkha National Liberation Front
HLDR	Haryana Lok Dal (R)
HLS	Haryana Lok Samiti
HSPDP	Hill State People's Democratic Party
HVC	Haryana Vikas Congress
HVP	Haryana Vikas Party
ICJ	Indian Congress (J)
ICS	Indian Congress (Socialist)
ICS-SCS	Indian Congress (Socialist-Sarat Chandra Sinha)
INC	Indian National Congress
INCI	Indian National Congress (I)
INCO	Indian National Congress (Organisation)
INCU	Indian National Congress (U)
INLD	Indian National Lok Dal
IPF	Indian People's Front
JD	Janata Dal
JD(G)	Janata Dal (Gujarat)
JDS	Janata Dal (Samajwadi) (1990-91)
JDS	Janata Dal (Secular)
JDU	Janata Dal (United)
JHP	Jharkhand Party
JMM	Jharkhand Mukti Morcha
JP	Janata Party
JPB	Janata party of Bihar
JPS	Janata Party (Secular)
JKD	Jharkhand Kranti Dal
KC	Kerala Congress
KCJ	Kerala Congress (J)
KCM	Kerala Congress (M)
KCP	Karnataka Congress Party
KLP	Krishakar Lok Party
KMPP	Krishak Mazdoor Praja Party
KNA	Kuki National Assembly
LCP	Loktantrik Congress Party
LKD	Lok Dal
LS	Lok Shakti
LSS	Lok Sevak Sangh
MCOR	Marxist (Coordination)
MADMK	MGR Anna Dravida Munnetra Kazhagam
MDMK	Marumalarchi Dravida Munnetra Kazhagam
MGP	Maharashtrawadi Gomantak Party
MIM	All India Majlis-e-Ittehad ul Muslimeen
MNF	Mizo National Front
MPP	Manipur People's Party
MPVC	Madhya Pradesh Vikas Congress
MSCP	Manipur State Congress Party
MUL	Muslim League
NC	Jammu & Kashmir National Conference
NCP	Nationalist Congress Party
NMGJ	Nutan Maha Gujarat Janata Parishad
NNDP	Naga National Democratic Party
NNO	Nagaland National Organisation
NPC	Nagaland People's Council
PDF	People's Democratic Front
PDP	People's Democratic Party
PF	People's Front
PMK	Pattali Makkal Katchi
PPA	People's Party of Arunachal
PPC	People's Conference
PSP	Praja Socialist Party
PT	Puthiya Tamizhagam
PTCA	Plains Tribals Council of Assam
PWP	Peasants and Workers' Party of India
RIS	Rising Sun Party
RJD	Rashtriya Janata Dal
RJP	All India Rashtriya Janata Party
RLD	Rashtirya Lok Dal
RPI	Republican Party of India
RPIK	Republican party of India (Khobragade)
RRP	Ram Rajya Parishad
RSP	Revolutionary Socialist Party
SAD	Shiromani Akali Dal
SADB	Shiromani Akali Dal (Badal)
SADM	Shiromani Akali Dal (Simranjit Singh Mann)
SAP	Samata Party
SDF	Sikkim Democratic Front
SHS	Shivsena
SHSAD	Sarb Hind Shiromani Akali Dal
SJPR	Samajwadi Janata Party (R)
SP	Socialist Party (1952-67)
SP	Samajawadi Party
SSP	Samyukta Socialist Party (1957-77)
SSP	Sikkim Sangram Parishad
Swatantra	Swatantra Party
TC	Trinamool Congress
TDP	Telugu Desam Party
TMC	Tamil Maanila Congress (Moopanar)
TNTP	Tamilnad Toilers Party
TPS	Telengana Praja Samiti
TRC	Tamzhaga Rajiv Congress
TTNC	Travancore Tamilnad Congress
TUJS	Tripura Upajati Juba Samiti
UC	Utkal Congress
UDF	United Democratic Front
UDP	United Democratic Party
UGDP	United Goans Democratic Party
UGSG	United Goans Sequeira Group
UFN	United Front of Nagaland
UMF	United Minorities Front
UMFA	United Minorities Front, Assam
VHP	Vishal Haryana Party

Lok Sabha By-Elections since 1999

Constituency	State	Winner	Votes Polled	Runner-up	Margin	Previous Winner
Bellary	Karnataka	INC (K. Basavana Gowd)	259,851	BJP	96,020	INC
Kannauj	Uttar Pradesh	SP (Akhilesh Yadav)	306,054	BSP	58,725	SP
Aska	Orissa	BJD (Kumudini Patnaik)	288,243	INC	179,474	BJD
Dausa	Rajasthan	INC (Rama Pilot)	349,439	BJP	65,264	INC
Tiruchirapalli	Tamil Nadu	ADMK (Dalit Ezhilmalai)	343,874	BJP	17,413	BJP
Shahjahanpur	Uttar Pradesh	SP (Rammurti Singh Verma)	151,890	INC	23,250	INC
Midnapore	West Bengal	CPI (Prabodh Panda)				CPI

Assembly Segment Composition of Lok Sabha Constituencies

State: Andhra Pradesh

1. SRIKAKULAM

Assembly No & Name

1. Ichapuram
2. Sompeta
3. Tekkali
4. Harishchandra
5. Narasannapeta
15. Amadalavalasa
16. Srikakulam

2. PARVATHIPURAM

Assembly No. & Name

6. Patapatnam
7. Kothuru
8. Naguru
9. Parvathipuram
10. Salur
13. Vunukuru
14. Palakonda

3. BOBBILI

Assembly No. & Name

11. Bobbili
12. Therlam
17. Etcherla
18. Cheepurupalli
19. Gajapathinagaram
20. Vizianagaram
21. Sathivada

4. VISHAKHAPATNAM

Assembly No. & Name

22. Bhogapuram
23. Bheemunipatnam
24. Vishakhapatnam I
25. Vishakhapatnam II
26. Pendurthi
27. Uttarapalli
28. Srungavarapukota

5. BHADRACHALAM

Assembly No. & Name

29. Paderu
37. Chintapalli
38. Yellavaram
71. Gopalapuram
73. Polavaram
274. Bhadrachalam
275. Burgampahad

6. ANAKAPALLI

Assembly No. & Name

30. Madugula
31. Chodavaram
32. Anakapalli
33. Paravada
34. Elamanchili
35. Payakaraopeta
36. Narsipatnam

7. KAKINADA

Assembly No. & Name

42. Jaggampeta
43. Peddapuram
44. Prathipadu
45. Tuni
46. Pithapuram
47. Sampara
48. Kakinada

8. RAJAHMUNDRY

Assembly No. & Name

39. Burugupudi
40. Rajahmundry
41. Kadiam
50. Anaparthy
51. Ramachandrapuram
52. Alamuru
72. Kovvur

9. AMALAPURAM

Assembly No. & Name

49. Tallarevu
53. Mummidivaram
54. Allavaram
55. Amalapuram
56. Kothapeta
57. Nagaram
58. Razole

10. NARASAPUR

Assembly No. & Name

59. Narasapur
60. Palacole
61. Achanta
62. Bhimavaram
63. Undi
64. Penugonda
66. Attili

11. ELURU

Assembly No. & Name

65. Tanuku
67. Tadepalligudam
68. Ungutur
69. Dendulur
70. Eluru
74. Chintalapudi
87. Kaikalur

12. MACHILIPATNAM

Assembly No. & Name

82. Nuzvid
83. Gannavaram
84. Vuyyur
85. Gudivada
86. Mudinepalli
88. Malleswaram
89. Bandar

13. VIJAYAWADA

Assembly No. & Name

75. Jaggayyapet
76. Nandigama
77. Vijayawada West
78. Vijayawada East
79. Kankipadu
80. Mylavaram
81. Tiruvuru

14. TENALI

Assembly No. & Name

90. Nidumolu
91. Avanigadda
93. Repalle
94. Vemur
95. Duggirala
96. Tenali
102. Mangalagiri

15. GUNTUR

Assembly No. & Name

99. Pratipad
100. Guntur I
101. Guntur II
103. Tadikonda
104. Sattenapalli
105. Peddakurapadu
110. Chilakularipet

16. BAPATLA

Assembly No. & Name

92. Kuchinapudi
97. Ponnur
98. Bapatla
111. Chirala
112. Parchur
113. Martur
114. Addanki

17. NARASARAOPET

Assembly No. & Name

106. Gurzala
107. Macherla
108. Vinukonda
109. Narasaraopet
120. Cumbum
121. Darsi
122. Markapur

18. ONGOLE

Assembly No. & Name

115. Ongole
116. Santhanuthalapadu
117. Kandukur
118. Kanigiri
119. Kondepi
124. Udayagiri
125. Kavali

19. NELLORE

Assembly No. & Name

126. Allur
127. Kovur
128. Atmakur
129. Rapur
130. Nellore
131. Sarvepalli
132. Gudur

20. TIRUPATHI

Assembly No. & Name

133. Sulurpet
134. Venkatagiri
135. Sri Kalahasti
136. Satyavedu
137. Nagari
138. Puttur
149. Tirupathi

21. CHITTOOR

Assembly No. & Name

139. Vepanjeri
140. Chittoor
141. Palmaner
142. Kuppam
143. Punganur
147. Pileru
148. Chandragiri

22. RAJAMPET

Assembly No. & Name

144. Madnapalle

145. Thamballapalle
146. Vayalapad
150. Kodur
151. Rajampet
152. Rayachoty
153. Lakkireddipalli

23. CUDDAPPAH

Assembly No. & Name
154. Cuddappah
155. Badvel
156. Mydukur
157. Proddatur
158. Jammalamadugu
159. Kamalapuram
160. Pulivendla

24. HINDUPUR

Assembly No. & Name
161. Kadiri
162. Nallamada
163. Gorantla
164. Hindupur
165. Madakasira
166. Penukonda
173. Dharmavaram

25. ANANTAPUR

Assembly No. & Name
167. Kalyandrug
168. Rayadrug
169. Uravakonda
170. Gooty
171. Singanamala
172. Anantapur
174. Tadpatri

26. KURNOOL

Assembly No. & Name
175. Alur
176. Adoni
177. Yemmiganur
178. Kodumur
179. Kurnool
180. Pattikonda
181. Dhone

27. NANDYAL

Assembly No. & Name
123. Giddalur
182. Koilkuntla
183. Allagadda
184. Panyam
185. Nandikotkur
186. Nandyal
187. Atmakur

28. NAGARKURNOOL

Assembly No. & Name
188. Achampet
189. Nagarkurnool
190. Kulwakurthi
191. Shadnagar
192. Jadcherla
195. Kollapur
203. Pargi

29. MAHBUBNAGAR

Assembly No. & Name
193. Mahbubnagar
194. Wanaparthy
196. Alampur
197. Gadwal
198. Amarchinta
199. Makthal
200. Kodangal

30. HYDERABAD

Assembly No. & Name
201. Tandur
202. Vicarabad
204. Chevella
215. Karwan
216. Yakutpura
217. Chandrayangutta
218. Charminar

31. SECUNDARABAD

Assembly No. & Name
206. Musheerabad
207. Himayatnagar
208. Sanathnagar
209. Secunderabad
210. Khairatabad
213. Asafnagar
214. Maharajgunj

32. SIDDIPET

Assembly No. & Name
211. Secunderabad Cantt
219. Medchal
220. Siddipet
221. Dommat
222. Gajwel
223. Narsapur
228. Ramayampet

33. MEDAK

Assembly No. & Name
224. Sangareddy
225. Zahirabad
226. Narayankhed
227. Medak

229. Andole
232. Kamareddy
233. Yellareddy

34. NIZAMABAD

Assembly No. & Name

230. Balkonda
231. Armoor
234. Jukkal
235. Banswada
236. Bodhan
237. Nizamabad
238. Dichpalli

35. ADILABAD

Assembly No. & Name

239. Mudhole
240. Nirmal
241. Boath
242. Adilabad
243. Khanapur
244. Asifabad
246. Sirpur

36. PEDDAPALLI

Assembly No. & Name

245. Luxettipet
247. Chinnur
248. Manthani
249. Peddapalli
250. Mydaram
251. Huzurabad
253. Indurthi

37. KARIMNAGAR

Assembly No. & Name

254. Karminagar
255. Choppandandi
256. Jagtial
257. Buggaram
258. Metpalli
259. Sircilla
260. Narella

38. HANAMKONDA

Assembly No. & Name

252. Kamalapur
261. Cheriyal
262. Janagaon
268. Ghanpur
270. Hanamkonda
271. Shyampet
272. Parkal

39. WARANGAL

Assembly No. & Name

263. Chennur
264. Dornakal
265. Mahbubabad
266. Narsampet
267. Wardhannapet
269. Warangal
273. Mulug

40. KHAMMAM

Assembly No. & Name

276. Kothagudem
277. Sathupalli
278. Madhira
279. Palair
280. Khammam
281. Shujatnagar
282. Yellandu

41. NALGONDA

Assembly No. & Name

205. Ibrahimpatnam
212. Malakpet
289. Nalgonda
291. Alair
292. Bhongir
293. Mungode
294. Deverkonda

42. MIRYALGUDA

Assembly No. & Name

283. Tungaturthi
284. Suryapet
285. Kodad
286. Miryalguda
287. Chalakurthi
288. Nakrekal
290. Ramannapet

State: **Arunachal Pradesh**

1. ARUNACHAL WEST

Assembly No. & Name

1. Lumla
2. Tawang
3. Mukto
4. Dirang
5. Kalaktang
6. Thrizino-Buragaon
7. Bomdila
8. Bameng
9. Chayangtajo
10. Seppa East
11. Seppa West
12. Pakke-Kasang
13. Itanagar
14. Doimukh

15. Sagalee
16. Yachuli
17. Ziro-Hapoli
18. Palin
19. Nyapin
20. Tali
21. Koloriang
22. Nacho
23. Taliha
24. Daporijo
25. Raga
26. Damporijo
27. Liromoba
28. Likabali
29. Basar
30. Along West
31. Along East
32. Rumgong
33. Mechuka

2. ARUNACHAL EAST

Assembly No. & Name

34. Tuting-Yinkgkiong
35. Pangin
36. Nari-Koyu
37. Pasighat West
38. Pasighat East
39. Mebo
40. Mariyang-Geku
41. Anini
42. Dambuk
43. Roing
44. Tezu
45. Hauyuliang
46. Chowkham
47. Namsai
48. Lekang
49. Bordumsa-Diyum
50. Miao
51. Nampong
52. Changlang South
53. Changlang North
54. Namsang
55. Khonsa East
56. Khonsa West
57. Borduria-Bagapani
58. Kanubari
59. Longding-Pumao
60. Pongchou-Wakka

State: **Assam**

1. KARIMGANJ

Assembly No. & Name

1. Ratabari
2. Patharkandi
3. Karimqanj North
4. Karimgang South
5. Badarpur
6. Hailakandi
7. Katlicherra
8. Algapur

2. SICHAR

Assembly No. & Name

9. Sichar
10. Sonai
11. Dholai
12. Udharbond
13. Lakhipur
14. Barkhola
15. Katigora

3. AUTONOMOUS DISTRICT

Assembly No. & Name

16. Haflong
17. Bokajan
18. Howraghat
19. Diphu
20. Baithalangso

4. DHUBRI

Assembly No. & Name

21. Mankachar
22. Salmara South
23. Dhubri
24. Gauripur
25. Golakganj
26. Bilasipara West
27. Bilasipara East
37. Goalpara East
38. Goalpara West
39. Jaleswar

5. KOKRAJHAR

Assembly No. & Name

28. Gossaigaon
29. Kokrajhar West
30. Kokrajhar East
31. Sidli
33. Bijni
40. Sorbhog
41. Bhabanipur
58. Tamulpur
62. Barama
63. Chapaguri

6. BARPETA

Assembly No. & Name

32. Bongaigaon
34. Abhayapuri North
35. Abhayapuri South
42. Patacharkuchi
43. Barpeta
44. Jania
45. Baghbar
46. Sarukhetri
47. Chenga
61. Dharmapur

7. GAUHATI

Assembly No. & Name

36. Dudhnai
48. Boko
49. Chaygaon
50. Palasbari
51. Jalukbari
52. Dispur
53. Gauhati East
54. Gauhati West
55. Hajo
60. Barkhetry

8. MANGALDOI

Assembly No. & Name

56. Kamalpur
57. Rangiya
59. Nalbari
64. Panery
65. Kaliagaon
66. Sipajhar
67. Mangaldoi
68. Dalgaon
69. Udalguri
70. Majbat

9.TEZPUR

Assembly No. & Name

71. Dhekiajuli
72. Barchalla
73. Tezpur
74. Rangpara
75. Sootea
76. Biswanath
77. Behali
78. Gohpur
109. Bihpuria

10. NOWGONG

Assembly No. & Name

79. Jagiroad
80. Marigaon
81. Laharighat
82. Raha
86. Nowgong
87. Barhampur
90. Jamunamukh
91. Hojai
92. Lumding

11. KALIABOR

Assembly No. & Name

83. Dhing
84. Batadroba
85. Rupohihat
88. Samaguri
89. Kaliabor
93. Bokakhat
94. Sarupathar
95. Golaghat
96. Khumtai
97. Dergaon

12. JORHAT

Assembly No. & Name

98. Jorhat
100. Titabar
101. Mariani
102. Teok
103. Amguri
104. Nazira
105. Mahmara
106. Sonari
107. Thowra
108. Sibsagar

13. DIBRUGARH

Assembly No. & Name

115. Moran
116. Dibrugarh
117. Lahowal
118. Dhuliajan
119. Tingkhong
120. Naharkatia
122. Tinsukhia
123. Digboi
124. Margherita

14.LAKHIMPUR

Assembly No. & Name

99. Majuli
110. Naoboicha
111. Lakhimpur
112. Dhakuakhana
113. Dhemaji
114. Jonai
121. Chabua

125. Doom Dooma
126. Sadiya

State: **Bihar**

1. BAGAHA

Assembly No. & Name

1. Dhanaha
2. Bagaha
3. Ramnagar
4. Shikarpur
5. Sikta
6. Lauria

2. BETTIAH

Assembly No. & Name

7. Chenpatia
8. Bettiah
9. Nautan
10. Raxaul
11. Sugauli
13. Adapur

3. MOTIHARI

Assembly No. & Name

12. Motihari
16. Madhuban
17. Pipra
18. Kesariya
19. Harsidhi
20. Gobindganj

4. GOPALGANJ

Assembly No. & Name

21. Kateya
22. Bhore
23. Mirganj
24. Gopalganj
25. Barauli
26. Baikunthpur

5. SIWAN

Assembly No. & Name

28. Goreakothi
29. Siwan
30. Mairwa
31. Darauli
32. Ziradei
34. Raghunathpur

6. MAHARAJGANJ

Assembly No. & Name

27. Basantpur
33. Maharajganj
35. Manjhi
36. Baniapur
37. Masrakh
40. Jalapur

7. CHAPRA

Assembly No. & Name

38. Taraiya
39. Marhaura
41. Chapra
42. Garkha
43. Parsa
44. Sonepur

8. HAJIPUR

Assembly No. & Name

45. Hajipur
46. Raghopur
47. Mahnar
48. Jandaha
49. Patepur
50. Mahua

9. VAISHALI

Assembly No. & Name

51. Lalganj
52. Vaishali
53. Paru
54. Sahebganj
55. Baruraj
56. Kanti

10. MUZAFFARPUR

Assembly No. & Name

57. Kurhani
58. Sakra
59. Muzaffarpur
60. Bochaha
61. Gaighatti
63. Minapur

11.SITAMARHI

Assembly No. & Name

62. Aurai
64. Runisaidpur
67. Sitamarhi
70. Sonbarsa
71. Sursand
72. Pupri

12. SHEOHAR

Assembly No. & Name

14. Dhaka
15. Ghorasahan
65. Belsand
66. Sheohar
68. Bathnaha
69. Majorganj

13. MADHUBANI

Assembly No. & Name

73. Benipatti
74. Bisfi
75. Harlakhi
76. Khajauli
78. Madhubani
91. Jale

14. JHANJHARPUR

Assembly No. & Name

77. Babubarhi
79. Pandaul
80. Jhanjharpur
81. Phulparas
82. Laukaha
83. Madhepur

15. DHARBHANGA

Assembly No. & Name

84. Manigachhi
85. Bahera
88. Dharbhanga Rural
89. Dharbhanga
90. Keoti
92. Hayaghat

16.ROSERA

Assembly No. & Name

86. Ghanshyampur
87. Baheri
94. Warisnagar
100. Rosera
101. Singhia
102. Hasanpur

17. SAMASTIPUR

Assembly No. & Name

93. Kalyanpur
95. Samastipur
96. Sarairanjan
97. Mohiuddin Nagar
98. Dalsinghsarai
99. Bibhutpur

18. BARH

Assembly No. & Name

199. Chandi
200. Harnaut
201. Mokameh
202. Barh
203. Bakhtiarpur
204. Fatwa

19. BALIA

Assembly No. & Name

103. Balia
106. Barauni
107. Bachwara
108. Cheria Bariarpur
109. Bakhri
184. Alauli

20. SAHARSA

Assembly No. & Name

110. Raghopur
111. Kishunpur
112. Supaul
117. Saharsa
118. Mahishi
119. Simri-Bakhtiarpur

21. MADHEPURA

Assembly No. & Name

115. Kumarkhand
116. Singheshwar
120. Madhepura
121. Sonbarsa
122. Kishanganj
123. Alamnagar

22. ARARIA

Assembly No. & Name

113. Tribenganj
114. Chhatapur
127. Raniganj
128. Narpatganj
129. Forbesganj
130. Araria

23. KISHANGANJ

Assembly No. & Name

131. Sikti
132. Jokihat
133. Bahadurganj
134. Thakurganj
135. Kishanganj
136. Amour

24. PURNEA

Assembly No. & Name

124. Rupauli
125. Dhamdaha
126. Banmankhi
137. Baisi
138. Kasba
139. Purnea

25. KATIHAR

Assembly No. & Name

140. Korha
142. Katihar
143. Kadwa
144. Barsoi

145. Pranpur
146. Manihari

26. RAJMAHAL

Assembly No. & Name

147. Rajmahal
148. Borio
149. Barhait
150. Litipara
151. Pakaur
152. Maheshpur

27. DUMKA

Assembly No. & Name

153. Sikaripara
154. Nala
155. Jamtara
156. Sarath
160. Dumka
161. Jama

28. GODDA

Assembly No. & Name

157. Madhupur
159. Jarmundi
162. Poreyahat
163. Godda
173. Dhuraiya
177. Chakai

29. BANKA

Assembly No. & Name

158. Deogarh
172. Amarpur
174. Banka
175. Belhar
176. Katoria
178. Jhajha

30. BHAGALPUR

Assembly No. & Name

164. Mahagama
165. Pirpainti
166. Colgong
167. Nathnagar
168. Bhagalpur
171. Sultanganj

31. KHAGARIA

Assembly No. & Name

141. Barari
169. Gopalpur
170. Bihpur
181. Parbatta
182. Chautham
183. Khagaria

32. MONGHYR

Assembly No. & Name

179. Tarapur
180. Kharagpur
185. Monghyr
186. Jamalpur
187. Surajgarha
188. Jamui

33. BEGUSARAI

Assembly No. & Name

104. Matihani
105. Begusarai
189. Sikandra
190. Lakhisarai
191. Sheikhpura
192. Barbigha

34. NALANDA

Assembly No. & Name

193. Asthawan
194. Bihar
195. Rajgir
196. Nalanda
197. Islampur
198. Hilsa

35. PATNA

Assembly No. & Name

206. Patna West
207. Patna Central
208. Patna East
209. Dinapur
211. Phulwari
212. Bikram

36. ARRAH

Assembly No. & Name

210. Maner
213. Paliganj
214. Sandesh
215. Barhara
216. Arrah
224. Sahar

37.BUXAR

Assembly No. & Name

217. Shahpur
218. Brahmpur
219. Buxar
220. Rajpur
221. Dumraon
222. Jagdishpur

38. SASARAM

Assembly No & Name

228. Ramgarh

229. Mohania
230. Bhabhua
231. Chainpur
232. Sasaram
233. Chenari

39. BIKRAMGANJ

Assembly No. & Name

223. Piro
225. Karakat
226. Bikramganj
227. Dinara
234. Nokha
235. Dehri

40. AURANGABAD

Assembly No. & Name

236. Nabinagar
237. Deo
238. Aurangabad
239. Rafiganj
240. Obra
241. Goh

41. JAHANABAD

Assembly No. & Name

205. Masaurhi
242. Arwal
243. Kurtha
244. Makhdumpur
245. Jahanabad
246. Ghosi

42. NAWADAH

Assembly No. & Name

256. Atri
257. Nawadah
258. Rajauli
259. Gobindpur
260. Warsaliganj
261. Hisua

43. GAYA

Assembly No. & Name

243. Belagunj
248. Konch
249. Gaya Mufassil
250. Gaya Town
252. Gurua
253. Bodh Gaya

44. CHATRA

Assembly No. & Name

251. Imamganj
254. Barachatti
255. Fatehpur
264. Chatra
316. Latehar
318. Panki

45. KODARMA

Assembly No. & Name

262. Kodarma
270. Barkatha
271. Dhanwar
272. Bagodar
273. Jamua
274. Gandey

46. GIRIDIH

Assembly No. & Name

275. Giridih
276. Dhumri
277. Gomia
278. Bermo
280. Tundi
281. Baghmara

47. DHANBAD

Assembly No. & Name

279. Bokaro
282. Sindhri
283. Nirsa
284. Dhanbad
285. Jharia
286. Chandankiyari

48. HAZARIBAGH

Assembly No. & Name

263. Barhi
265. Simaria
266. Barkagaon
267. Ramgarh
268. Mandu
269. Hazaribagh

49. RANCHI

Assembly No. & Name

293. Ichagarh
304. Silli
305. Khijri
306. Ranchi
307. Hatia
308. Kanke

50. JAMSHEDPUR

Assembly No. & Name

287. Baharagora
288. Ghatsila
289. Potka
290. Jugsalai
291. Jamshedpur East
292. Jamshedpur West

51. SINGHBHUM

Assembly No. & Name

294. Seraikella
295. Chaibasa
296. Majhgaon
297. Jaganathpur
298. Manoharpur
299. Chakradharpur

52. KHUNTI

Assembly No. & Name

300. Kharasawan
301. Tamar
302. Torpa
303. Khunti
311. Kolebira
312. Simdega

53. LOHARDAGA

Assembly No. & Name

309. Mandar
310. Sisai
313. Gumla
314. Bishnupur
315. Lohardaga
317. Manika

54. PALAMAU

Assembly No. & Name

319. Daltonganj
320. Garhwa
321. Bhawanathpur
322. Bishrampur
323. Chhatarpur
324. Hussainabad

State: **Goa**

1. PANAJI

Assembly No. & Name

1. Mandrem
2. Pernem
3. Dargalim
4. Tivim
5. Mapusa
6. Siolim
7. Calangute
8. Saligao
9. Aldona
10. Panaji
11. Taleigao
12. Santa Cruz
13. St. Andre
14. Cumbarjua
15. Bicholim
16. Maem
17. Pale
18. Poriem
19. Valpoi

2. MORMUGAO

Assembly No. & Name

20. Ponda
21. Priol
22. Marcaim
23. Siroda
24. Mormugao
25. Vasco Da Gama
26. Cortalim
27. Loutolim
28. Benaulim
29. Fatorda
30. Margao
31. Curtorim
32. Navelim
33. Velim
34. Cuncolim
35. Sanvordem
36. Sanguem
37. Curchorem
38. Quepem
39. Canacona
40. Poinguinim

State: **Gujarat**

1. KUTCH

Assembly No. & Name

1. Abdasa
2. Mandvi
3. Bhuj
4. Mundra
5. Anjar
6. Rapar

2. SURENDRANAGAR

Assembly No. & Name

7. Dasada
8. Wadhwan
9. Limbdi
10. Chotila
11. Halvad
12. Dhrangadhra
15. Wankaner

3. JAMNAGAR

Assembly No. & Name

24. Jodiya
25. Jamnagar
26. Jamnagar Rural

27. Kalawad
29. Bhanvad
30. Khumbalia
31. Dwarka

4. RAJKOT

Assembly No. & Name

13. Morvi
14. Tankara
16. Jasdan
17. Rajkot I
18. Rajkot II
19. Rajkot Rural
20. Gondal
21. Jetpur

5. PORBANDAR

Assembly No. & Name

22. Dhoraji
23. Upleta
28. Jamjodhpur
32. Porbandar
33. Kutiyana
34. Mangrol
35. Manavadar

6. JUNAGADH

Assembly No. & Name

36. Keshod
37. Talala
38. Somnath
39. Una
40. Visavadar
41. Maliya
42. Junagadh

7. AMRELI

Assembly No. & Name

43. Babra
44. Lathi
45. Amreli
46. Dhari
47. Kodinar
48. Rajula
53. Kundla

8. BHAVNAGAR

Assembly No. & Name

51. Palitana
52. Sihor
54. Mahuva
55. Talaja
56. Ghogho
57. Bhavnagar North
58. Bhavnagar South

9. DHANDHUKA

Assembly No. & Name

49. Botad
50. Gadhada
59. Dhandhuka
60. Dholka
61. Bavla
62. Mandal
63. Viramgam

10. AHMDEABAD

Assembly No. & Name

71. Kalupur
73. Rakhial
74. Shaher Kotda
75. Khadia
76. Jamalpur
77. Maninagar
78. Naroda

11. GANDHINAGAR

Assembly No. & Name

64. Sarkhej
67. Sabarmati
68. Ellis Bridge
69. Dariapur-Kazipur
70. Shahpur
72. Asarwa
79. Gandhinagar

12. MEHSANA

Assembly No. & Name

80. Kalol
81. Kadi
82. Jotana
83. Mehsana
84. Mansa
85. Vijapur
86. Visnagar

13. PATAN

Assembly No. & Name

87. Kheralu
88. Unjha
89. Sidhpur
90. Vagdod
91. Patan
92. Chanasma
93. Sami

14. BANASKANTHA

Assembly No. & Name

94. Radhanpur
95. Vav
96. Deodar
97. Kankrej

98. Deesa
99. Dhanera
100. Palanpur

15. SABARKANTHA

Assembly No. & Name

101. Vadgam
102. Danta
103. Khedbrahma
104. Idar
105. Bhiloda
106. Himatnagar
108. Modasa

16. KAPADVANJ

Assembly No. & Name

65. Daskroi
66. Dehgam
107. Prantij
109. Bayad
110. Meghraj
125. Kapadvanj
128. Kathlal

17. DOHAD

Assembly No. & Name

111. Santrampur
112. Jhalod
113. Limdi
114. Dohad
115. Limkheda
116. Devgadh Baria
123. Radhikpur

18. GODHRA

Assembly No. & Name

117. Rajgadh
118. Halol
119. Kalol
120. Godhra
121. Shehra
122. Lunavada
124. Balasinor

19. KAIRA

Assembly No. & Name

126. Thasra
127. Umreth
129. Mehmedabad
130. Mahudha
131. Nadiad
132. Chakalasi
137. Matar

20. ANAND

Assembly No. & Name

133. Anand
134. Sarsa
135. Petlad
136. Sojitra
138. Borsad
139. Bhadran
140. Cambay

21. CHOTA UDAIPUR

Assembly No. & Name

141. Chota Udaipur
142. Jetpur
143. Nasvadi
144. Sankheda
145. Dabhoi
153. Karjan
160. Rajpipla

22. BARODA

Assembly No. & Name

146. Savli
147. Baroda City
148. Sayajiganj
149. Raopura
150. Vaghodia
151. Baroda Rural
152. Padra

23. BROACH

Assembly No. & Name

154. Jambusar
155. Vagra
156. Broach
157. Ankleshwar
158. Jhagadia
159. Dediapada
162. Mangrol

24. SURAT

Assembly No. & Name

168. Olpad
169. Surat City North
170. Surat City East
171. Surat City West
172. Chorasi
173. Jalalpore
174. Navsari

25. MANDVI

Assembly No. & Name

161. Nijhar
163. Songandh
164. Vyara
165. Mahuva
166. Bardoli
167. Kamrej
176. Chikhli

26. BULSAR

Assembly No. & Name

175. Gandevi
177. Dangs-Bansda
178. Bulsar
179. Dharampur
180. Mota Pondha
181. Pardi
182. Umbergaon

State: **Haryana**

1. AMBALA

Assembly No. & Name

1. Kalka
2. Naraingarh
3. Sadhaura
4. Chhachhrauli
6. Jagadhari
7. Mullana
8. Ambala Cantt
9. Ambala City
10. Naggal

2. KURUKSHETRA

Assembly No. & Name

5. Yamunanagar
20. Shahabad
21. Radaur
22. Thanesar
23. Pehowa
24. Guhia
25. Kaithal
26. Pundri
27. Pai

3. KARNAL

Assembly No. & Name

11. Indri
12. Nilokheri
13. Karnal
14. Jundla
15. Gharaunda
16. Assandh
17. Panipat
18. Sambhalka
19. Naultha

4. SONEPAT

Assembly No. & Name

37. Bahadurgarh
38. Baroda
39. Gohana
40. Kailana
41. Sonepat
42. Rai
43. Rohat
49. Julana
50. Safidon

5. ROHTAK

Assembly No. & Name

28. Hassangarh
29. Kiloi
30. Rohtak
31. Meham
32. Kalanaur
33. Beri
34. Salhawas
35. Jhajjar
36. Badli

6. FARIDABAD

Assembly No. & Name

51. Faridabad
52. Mewla Maharajpur
53. Ballabhgarh
54. Palwal
55. Hassanpur
56. Hathin
57. Ferozepur Jhirka
58. Nuh
59. Taoru

7. MAHENDRAGARH

Assembly No. & Name

60. Sohna
61. Gurgaon
62. Pataudi
85. Bawal
86. Rewari
87. Jatusana
88. Mahendragarh
89. Ateli
90. Narnaul

8. BHIWANI

Assembly No. & Name

63. Badhra
64. Dadri
65. Mundal Khurd
66. Bhiwani
67. Tosham
68. Loharu
69. Bawani Khera
72. Hansi
79. Adampur

9. HISSAR

Assembly No. & Name

44. Kalayat

45. Narwana
46. Uchana Kalan
47. Rajond
48. Jind
70. Barwala
71. Narnaund
74. Hissar
75. Ghirai

10. SIRSA

Assembly No. & Name

73. Bhattu Kalan
76. Tohana
77. Ratia
78. Fatehabad
80. Darba Kalan
81. Ellenabad
82. Sirsa
83. Rori
84. Dabwali

State: **Himachal Pradesh**

1. SIMLA

Assembly No. & Name

3. Rohru
4. Jubbal-Kotkhai
5. Chopal
6. Kumarsain
7. Theog
8. Simla
9. Kasumpti
10. Arki
11. Doon
12. Nalagarh
13. Kasauli
14. Solan
15. Pachhad
16. Raindka
17. Shillai
18. Paonta Doon
19. Nahan

2. MANDI

Assembly No. & Name

1. Kinnaur
2. Rampur
54. Bharmour
55. Lahaul & Spiti
56. Kullu
57. Banjar
58. Ani
59. Karsog
60. Chachiot
61. Nachan
62. Sundarnagar
63. Balh
64. Gopalapur
65. Dharampur
66. Joginder Nagar
67. Darang
68. Mandi

3. KANGRA

Assembly No. & Name

34. Nurpur
35. Gangath
36. Jawali
37. Guler
41. Thural
42. Rajgir
43. Baijnath
44. Palampur
45. Sulah
46. Nagrota
47. Shahpur
48. Dharamsala
49. Kangra
50. Bhattiyat
51. Banikhet
52. Rajnagar
53. Chamba

4. HAMIRPUR

Assembly No. & Name

20. Kotkehloor
21. Bilaspur
22. Ghumarwin
23. Geharwin
24. Nadaun
25. Hamirpur
26. Bamsan
27. Mewa
28. Nadaunta
29. Gagret
30. Chintupurni
31. Santokgarh
32. Una
33. Kutlehar
38. Jaswan
39. Pragpur
40. Jwalamukhi

State: **Jammu & Kashmir**

1. BARAMULLA

Assembly No. & Name

1. Karnah

2. Kupwara
3. Lolab
4. Handwara
5. Langate
6. Uri
7. Rafiabad
8. Sopore
9. Gurez
10. Bandipora
11. Sonawari
12. Sangrama
13. Baramulla
14. Gulmarg
15. Pattan

2. SRINAGAR

Assembly No. & Name

16. Kangan
17. Ganderbal
18. Hazratbal
19. Zadibal
20. Idgah
21. Khanyar
22. Habbakadal
23. Amirakadal
24. Sonawar
25. Batamaloo
26. Chadoora
27. Badgam
28. Beerwah
29. Khansahib
30. Chrari Sharief

3. ANANTANAG

Assembly No. & Name

31. Tral
32. Pampore
33. Pulwama
34. Rajpora
35. Wachi
36. Shopian
37. Noorabad
38. Kulgam
39. Homeshalibugh
40. Anantnag
41. Devsar
42. Doru
43. Kokerang
44. Shangus
45. Bijbehara
46. Pahalgam

4. LADAKH

Assembly No. & Name

47. Nobra
48. Leh
49. Kargil
50. Zanskar

5. UDHAMPUR

Assembly No. & Name

51. Kishtwar
52. Inderwal
53. Doda
54. Bhaderwah
55. Ramban
56. Banihal
57. Gulabgarh
58. Reasi
59. Gool Arnas
60. Udhampur
61. Chanani
62. Ramnagar
63. Bani
64. Basohli
65. Kathua
66. Billawar
67. Hiranagar

6. JAMMU

Assembly No. & Name

68. Samba
69. Vijaypur
70. Nagrota
71. Gandhinagar
72. Jammu East
73. Jammu West
74. Bishnah
75. R.S. Pura
76. Suchetgarh
77. Marh
78. Raipur Domana
79. Akhnoor
80. Chhamb
81. Nowshehra
82. Darhal
83. Rajouri
84. Kalakote
85. Surankote
86. Mendhar
87. Poonch Haveli

State: **Karnataka**

1. BIDAR

Assembly No. & Name

1. Aurad
2. Bhalki
3. Hulsoor
4. Bidar
5. Humanabad
6. Basavakalyan
8. Kamalapur
9. Alland

2. GULBARGA

Assembly No. & Name

7. Chincholi
10. Gulbarga
11. Shahabad
12. Afzalpur
13. Chitapur
14. Sedam
15. Jewargi
16. Gurmitkal

3. RAICHUR

Assembly No. & Name

17. Yadgir
18. Shahapur
19. Shorapur
20. Deodurg
21. Raichur
22. Kalmala
23. Manvi
24. Lingsugar

4. KOPPAL

Assembly No. & Name

25. Sindhnoor
26. Kushtagi
27. Yelburga
28. Kanakagiri
29. Gangavathi
30. Koppal
34. Hospet
187. Mundargi

5. BELLARY

Assembly No. & Name

31. Siruguppa
32. Kurugodu
33. Bellary
35. Sandur
36. Kudligi
37. Kottur
38. Hadagali
39. Harpanahalli

6 DAVANAGERE

Assembly No. & Name

40. Harihar
41. Davanagere
42. Mayakonda
43. Bharamasagara
45. Jagalur
49. Holalkere
158. Channagiri
161. Honnali

7. CHITRADURGA

Assembly No. & Name

44. Chitradurga
46. Molakalmuru
47. Challakere
48. Hiriyur
50. Hosadurga
51. Pavagada
52. Sira
53. Kallambella

8. TUMKUR

Assembly No. & Name

54. Bellavi
57. Tumkur
58. Kunigal
59. Huliyadurga
60. Gubbi
61. Turuvekere
62. Tiptur
63. Chiknaikanahalli

9. CHIKBALLAPUR

Assembly No. & Name

55. Madhugiri
56. Koratagere
64. Gowribidanur
65. Chikballapur
66. Sidlaghatta
67. Bagepalli
96. Nelamangala
97. Doddaballapur

10. KOLAR

Assembly No. & Name

68. Chintamani
69. Srinivasapur
70. Mulbagal
71. Kolar Gold Fields
72. Bethamangala
73. Kolar
74. Vemgal
75. Malur

11. KANAKAPURA

Assembly No. & Name

89. Uttarahalli
91. Kanakapura
92. Sathanur
93. Channapatna
94. Ramanagaram
95. Magadi
100. Anekal
104. Malavalli

12. BANGALORE NORTH

Assembly No. & Name

84. Shanthinagar
85. Shivajinagar
86. Bharathinagar
87. Jayamahal
88. Yelahanka
90. Varthur
98. Devanahalli
99. Hosakote

13 BANGALORE SOUTH

Assembly No. & Name

76. Malleswaram
77. Rajajinagar
78. Gandhinagar
79. Chickpet
80. Binnypet
81. Chamarajapet
82. Basavanagudi
83. Jayanagar

14. MANDYA

Assembly No. & Name

101. Nagamangala
102. Maddur
103. Kiragaval
105. Mandya
106. Keragodu
107. Srirangapatna
108. Pandavapura
109. Krishnarajpet

15. CHAMARAJNAGAR

Assembly No. & Name

110. Hanur
111. Kollegal
112. Bannur
113. T. Narasipur
118. Nanjangud
119. Santhemarahalli
120. Chamarajanagar
121. Gundlupet

16. MYSORE

Assembly No. & Name

114. Krishnaraja
115. Chamaraja
116. Narasimharaja
117. Chamundeswari
122. Heggadadevanakote
123. Hunsur
124. Krishnarajanagar
125. Periyapatna

17. MANGALORE

Assembly No. & Name

126. Virajpet
127. Madikeri
128. Somwarpet
137. Sullia
138. Puttur
139. Vittal
142. Mangalore
143. Ullal

18. UDUPI

Assembly No. & Name

141. Bantwal
144. Surathkal
145. Kaup
146. Udupi
147. Brahmavar
148. Coondapur
149. Baindur
151. Moodabidri

19. HASSAN

Assembly No. & Name

129. Belur
130. Arasikere
131. Gandsi
132. Sravanabelagola
133. Holenarasipur
134. Arkalgud
134. Hassan
136. Sakleshpur

20. CHIKMAGALUR

Assembly No. & Name

140. Belthangady
150. Karkal
152. Sringeri
153. Mudigere
154. Chikmagalur
155. Birur
156. Kadur
157. Tarikere

21. SHIMOGA

Assembly No. & Name

159. Holehonnur
160. Bhadravathi
162. Shimoga
163. Tirthahalli
164. Hosanagar
165. Sagar
166. Sorab
167. Shikaripur

22. KANARA

Assembly No. & Name

168. Sirsi
169. Bhatkal
170. Kumta
171. Ankola
172. Karwar
173. Haliyal
195. Kittur
196. Khanapur

23. DHARWAR SOUTH

Assembly No. & Name

179. Kundgol
180. Shiggaon
181. Hanagal
182. Hirekerur
183. Ranibennur
184. Byadgi
185. Haveri
186. Shirhatti

24. DHARWAR NORTH

Assembly No. & Name

174. Dharwar Rural
175. Dharwar
176. Hubli
177. Hubli Rural
178. Kalghatgi
188. Gadag
190. Naragund
191. Navalgund

25. BELGAUM

Assembly No. & Name

192. Ramdurg
193. Parasgad
194. Bailhongal
197. Belgaum
198. Uchagaon
199. Bagewadi
200. Gokak
201. Arabhavi

26. CHIKKODI

Assembly No. & Name

202. Hukkeri
203. Sankeshwar
204. Nippani
205. Sadalga
206. Chikkodi
207. Raibag
208. Kagwad
209. Athani

27. BAGALKOT

Assembly No. & Name

189. Ron
210. Jamakhandi
211. Bilgi
212. Mudhol
213. Bagalkot
214. Badami
215. Guledgud
216. Hungund

28. BIJAPUR

Assembly No. & Name

217. Muddebihal
218. Huvin-Hippargi
219. Basavana Bagewadi
220. Tikota
221. Bijapur
222. Ballolli
223. Indi
224. Sindgi

State: **Kerala**

1. KASARGOD

Assembly No. & Name

1. Manjeswar
2. Kasargod
3. Udma
4. Hosdurg
5. Trikkarpur
7. Payyanur
8. Taliparamba

2. CANNANORE

Assembly No. & Name

6. Irikkur
9. Azhicode
10. Cannanore
11. Edakkad
14. Kuthuparamba
15. Peravoor
16. North Wynad

3. BADAGARA

Assembly No. & Name

12. Tellicherry
13. Peringalam
17. Badagara
18. Nadapuram
19. Meppayur
20. Quilandy
21. Perambra

4. CALICUT

Assembly No. & Name

22. Balusseri
23. Koduvally
24. Calicut I
25. Calicut II
28. Thiruvambadi
29. Kalpetta
30. Sultans Battery

5. MANJERI

Assembly No. & Name

26. Beypore
27. Kunnamangalam
31. Wandoor
32. Nilambur
33. Manjeri
34. Mallappuram
35. Kondotty

6. PONNANI

Assembly No. & Name

36. Tirurangadi
37. Tanur
38. Tirur
39. Ponnani
40. Kuttipuram
41. Mankada
42. Perinthalmanna

7. PALGHAT

Assembly No. & Name

46. Sreekrishnapuram
47. Mannarkkad
48. Malampuzha
49. Palghat
50. Chittur
51. Kollengode
53. Alathur

8. OTTAPALAM

Assembly No. & Name

43. Thirthala
44. Pattambi
45. Ottapalam
52. Coyalmannam
54. Chelakara
55. Wadkkancherry
56. Kunnamkulam

9. TRICHUR

Assembly No. & Name

57. Cherpu
58. Trichur
59. Ollur
60. Kodakara
64. Manalur
65. Guruvayoor
66. Nattika

10. MUKUNDAPURAM

Assembly No. & Name

61. Chalakudi
62. Mala
63. Irinjalakuda
67. Kodungallur
68. Ankamali
69. Vadakkekara
77. Perumbavoor

11. ERNAKULAM

Assembly No. & Name

70. Parur
71. Narakal
72. Ernakulam
73. Mattancherry
74. Palluruthy
75. Thrippunithura
76. Alwaye

12. MUVATTUPUZHA

Assembly No. & Name

78. Kunnathunad
79. Piravom
80. Muvattupuzha
81. Kothamangalam
87. Kanjirappally
93. Poonjar
94. Palai

13. KOTTAYAM

Assembly No. & Name

88. Vazhoor
89. Changanacherry
90. Kottayam
91. Ettumanoor
92. Puthuppally
95. Kaduthuruthy
96. Vaikom

14. IDUKKI

Assembly No. & Name

82. Thodupuzha

55. Tipaimukh
56. Thanlon
57. Henglep
58. Churachandpur
59. Saikot
60. Singhat

State: **Meghalaya**

1. SHILLONG

Assembly No. & Name

1. War-Jaintia
2. Rymbai
3. Sutnga-Shangpung
4. Raliang
5. Nartiang
6. Nongbah-Wahiajer
7. Jowai
8. Mawhati
9. Umroi
10. Nongpoh
11. Jirang
12. Mairang
13. Nongspung
14. Sohiong
15. Mylliem
16. Malki-Nongthymmai
17. Laitumkharah
18. Pynthorumkhrah
19. Jaiaw
20. Mawkhar
21. Mawprem
22. Laban
23. Mawlai
24. Sohryngkham
25. Dienglieng
26. Nongkrem
27. Lyngkyrdem
28. Nongshken
29. Sohra
30. Shella
31. Mawsynram
32. Mawkyrwat
33. Pariong
34. Nongstoin
35. Langrin
36. Mawthengkut

2. TURA

Assembly No. & Name

37. Baghmara
38. Rongrenggiri
39. Rongjeng
40. Kharkutta
41. Mendipathar
42. Resubelpara
43. Songsak
44. Bajengdoba
45. Tikrikilla
46. Dadenggiri
47. Rongchugiri
48. Phulbari
49. Rajabala
50. Selsella
51. Rongram
52. Tura
53. Chopkot
54. Kherapara
55. Dalu
56. Dalamgiri
57. Rangsakona
58. Ampatigiri
59. Salmanpura
60. Mahendraganj

State: **Mizoram**

1. MIZORAM

Assembly No. & Name

1. Tuipang
2. Saiha
3. Sangau
4. Lawngtlai
5. Chawngte
6. Tlabung
7. Buarpui
8. Lunglei South
9. Lunglei North
10. Tawipui
11. Vanva
12. Hnahthial
13. North Vanlaiphai
14. Khawbung
15. Champahai
16. Khawhai
17. Saitual
18. Khawzawl
19. Ngopa
20. Suangpuilawn
21. Ratu
22. Kawnpui
23. Kolasib
24. Bilkhawthlir
25. Lokichera
26. Kawrthah
27. Mamit

28. Phuldungsei
29. Sateek
30. Serchhip
31. Lungpho
32. Tlungvel
33. Aizawl North I
34. Aizawl North II
35. Aizawl East I
36. Aizawl East II
37. Aizawl West I
38. Aizawl West II
39. Aizawl South I
40. Aizawl South II

State: **Nagaland**

1. NAGALAND

Assembly No. & Name

1. Dimapur I
2. Dimapur II
3. Dimapur III
4. Ghaspani I
5. Ghaspani II
6. Tenning
7. Peren
8. Western Angami
9. Kohima Town
10. Northern Angami I
11. Northern Angami II
12. Tseminyu
13. Pughoboto
14. Southern Angami I
15. Southern Angami II
16. Pfutsero
17. Chizami
18. Chazouba
19. Phek
20. Meluri
21. Tuli
22. Arkakong
23. Impur
24. Angetyongpang
25. Monguya
26. Aonglenden
27. Mokokchung Town
28. Kridang
29. Jangpetkong
30. Alungtaki
31. Akuluto
32. Atoizu
33. Suruhuto
34. Aghunato
35. Zunheboto
36. Satakha
37. Tyui
38. Wokha
39. Sanis
40. Bhandari
41. Tizit
42. Wakching
43. Tapi
44. Phomching
45. Tehok
46. Mon Town
47. Aboi
48. Moka
49. Tamlu
50. Longleng
51. Noksen
52. Longkhim Chare
53. Tuensang Sadar I
54. Tuensang Sadar II
55. Tobu
56. Noklak
57. Thonoknyu
58. Shamtorr-Chessore
59. Siyuchong-Sitimi
60. Pungro-Kiphire

State: **Orissa**

1. MAYURBHANJ

Assembly No. & Name

2. Jashipur
3. Bahalda
4. Rairangpur
5. Bangriposi
6. Kuliana
7. Baripada
10. Udala

2. BALASORE

Assembly No. & Name

8. Baisinga
9. Khunta
11. Bhograi
12. Jaleswar
13. Basta
14. Balasore
15. Soro

3. BHADRAK

Assembly No. & Name

16. Simulia
17. Nilgiri
18. Bhandaripokhari

19. Bhadrak
20. Dhamnagar
21. Chandbali
22. Basudevpur

4. JAJPUR

Assembly No. & Name

23. Sukinda
24. Korai
25. Jajpur
26. Dharamsala
27. Barchana
28. Bari-Derabisi
29. Binjharpur

5. KENDRAPARA

Assembly No. & Name

30. Aul
31. Patamundai
32. Rajnagar
33. Kendrapara
34. Patkura
39. Kissannagar
40. Mahanga

6. CUTTACK

Assembly No. & Name

41. Salepur
43. Cuttack Sadar
44. Cuttack City
45. Choudwar
46. Banki
47. Athgarh
48. Baramba

7. JAGATSINGHPUR

Assembly No. & Name

35. Tirtol
36. Ersama
37. Balikuda
38. Jagatsinghpur
42. Gobindpur
53. Nimapara
54. Kakatpur

8. PURI

Assembly No. & Name

49. Balipatna
52. Pipli
55. Satyabadi
56. Puri
57. Brahmagiri
58. Chilka
61. Ranpur

9. BHUBANESWAR

Assembly No. & Name

50. Bhubaneswar
51. Jatni
59. Khurda
60. Begunia
62. Nayagarh
63. Khandapara
64. Daspalla

10. ASKA

Assembly No. & Name

65. Jaganathprasad
67. Suruda
68. Aska
69. Kavisuryanagar
70. Kodala
71. Khallikote
73. Hinjili

11. BERHAMPUR

Assembly No. & Name

72. Chatrapur
74. Gopalpur
75. Berhampur
76. Chikati
77. Mohana
78. Ramagiri
79. Parlakhemundi

12. KORAPUT

Assembly No. & Name

80. Gunupur
81. Bissam-Cuttack
82. Rayagada
83. Lakshmipur
84. Pottangi
85. Koraput
89. Jeypore

13. NOWRANGPUR

Assembly No. & Name

86. Malkangiri
87. Chitrakonda
88. Kotpad
90. Nowrangpur
91. Kodinga
92. Dabugam
93. Umarkote

14. KALAHANDI

Assembly No. & Name

95. Khariar
96. Dharamgarh
97. Koksara
98. Junagarh

99. Bhawanipatna
100. Narla
101. Kesinga

15. PHULBANI

Assembly No. & Name

66. Bhanjanagar
102. Balliguda
103. Udayagiri
104. Phulbani
105. Boudh
112. Sonepur
113. Binka

16. BOLANGIR

Assembly No. & Name

94. Nawapara
106. Titilagarh
107. Kantabanji
108. Patnagarh
109. Saintala
110. Loisingha
111. Bolangir

17. SAMBALPUR

Assembly No. & Name

123. Padampur
124. Melchhamunda
125. Bijepur
126. Bhatli
127. Bargarh
128. Sambalpur
133. Rairakhol

18. DEOGARH

Assembly No. & Name

121. Pallahara
122. Tacher
129. Brajarajnagar
130. Jharsuguda
131. Laikera
132. Kuchinda
134. Deogarh

19. DHENKANAL

Assembly No. & Name

114. Birmaharajpur
115. Athmallik
116. Angul
117. Hindol
118. Dhenkanal
119. Gondia
120. Kamakhyanagar

20. SUNDARGARH

Assembly No. & Name

135. Sundargarh
136. Talsara
137. Rajgangpur
138. Birmitrapur
139. Rourkela
140. Raghunathpali
141. Bonai

21. KEONJHAR

Assembly No. & Name

1. Karanjia
142. Champua
143. Patna
144. Keonjhar
145. Telkoi
146. Ramchandrapur
147. Anandapur

State: **Punjab**

1. GURDASPUR

Assembly No. & Name

1. Fatehgarh
5. Kahnuwan
6. Dhariwal
7. Gurdaspur
8. Dina Nagar
9. Narot Mehra
10. Pathankot
11. Sujanpur
52. Mukerian

2. AMRITSAR

Assembly No. & Name

2. Batala
3. Qadian
13. Majitha
14. Verka
16. Amritsar North
17. Amristar West
18. Amristar Central
19. Amristar South
20. Ajnala

3. TARN TARAN

Assembly No. & Name

12. Beas
15. Jandiala
21. Raja Sansi
22. Attari
23. Tarn Taran
24. Khadoor Sahib
25. Naushahra Panwan
26. Patti
27. Valtoha

4 JULLUNDUR

Assembly No. & Name

29. Jullundur Cantt.
30. Jullundur North
31. Jullundur Central
32. Jullundur South
33. Kartarpur
34. Lohian
35. Nakodar
41. Kapurthala
42. Sultanpur

5. PHILLAUR

Assembly No. & Name

4. Srihargobindpur
28. Adampur
36. Nur Mahal
37. Banga
38. Nawan Shahr
39. Phillaur
40. Bholath
43. Phagwara
48. Sham Chaurasi

6. HOSHIARPUR

Assembly No. & Name

44. Balachaur
45. Garhshankar
46. Mahilpur
47. Hoshiarpur
49. Tanda
50. Garhdiwala
51. Dasuya
65. Nangal
66. Anandpur Sahib-Ropar

7. ROPAR

Assembly No. & Name

63. Samrala
64. Khanna
67. Chamkaur Sahib
68. Morinda
69. Kharar
77. Nabha
78. Amloh
79. Sirhind
80. Dhuri

8. PATIALA

Assembly No. & Name

70. Banur
71. Rajpura
72. Ghanaur
73. Dakala
74. Shutrana
75. Samana
76. Patiala Town
88. Sunam
89. Lehra

9. LUDHIANA

Assembly No. & Name

53. Jagraon
55. Dakha
56. Qila Raipur
57. Ludhiana North
58. Ludhiana West
59. Ludhiana East
60. Ludhiana Rural
61. Payal
62. Kum Kalan

10. SANGRUR

Assembly No. & Name

54. Raikot
81. Malerkotla
82. Sherpur
83. Barnala
84. Bhadaur
85. Dhanaula
86. Sangrur
87. Dirbha
101. Nihal Singh Wala

11. BHATINDA

Assembly No. & Name

109. Talwandi Sabo
110. Pakka Kalan
111. Bhatinda
112. Nathana
113. Rampura Phul
114. Joga
115. Mansa
116. Budhlada
117. Sardulgarh

12. FARIDKOT

Assembly No. & Name

99. Moga
100. Bagha Purana
102. Panjgrain
103. Kot Kapura
104. Faridkot
105. Muktsar
106. Giddar Baha
107. Malout
108. Lambi

13. FIROZEPUR

Assembly No. & Name

90. Balluana

91. Abohar
92. Fazilka
93. Jalalabad
94. Guru Har Sahai
95. Firozepur
96. Firozepur Cantt
97. Zira
98. Dharamkot

State: **Rajasthan**

1. GANGANAGAR

Assembly No. & Name

1. Bhadra
2. Nohar
3. Tibi
4. Hanumangarh
5. Sangaria
6. Ganganagar
7. Kesrisinghpur
8. Karanpur

2. BIKANER

Assembly No. & Name

9. Raisnghnagar
10. Pilibanga
11. Suratgarh
12. Lunkaransar
13. Bikaner
14. Kolayat
15. Nokha
192. Jayal

3. CHURU

Assembly No. & Name

16. Dungargarh
17. Sujangarh
18. Ratangarh
19. Sardarshahr
20. Churu
21. Taranagar
22. Sadulpur
193. Ladnu

4. JHUNJHUNU

Assembly No. & Name

23. Pilani
24. Surajgarh
25. Khetri
26. Gudha
27. Nawalgarh
28. Jhunjhunu
29. Mandawa
30. Fatehpur

5. SIKAR

Assembly No. & Name

31. Lachhmangarh
32. Sikar
33. Dhod
34. Danta-Ramgarh
35. Srimadhopur
36. Khandela
37. Neem-Ka-Thana
38. Chomu

6. JAIPUR

Assembly No. & Name

40. Jaipur Rural
41. Hawamahal
42. Johribazar
43. Kishanpole
44. Bani Park
47. Sanganer
48. Phagi
53. Bassi

7. DAUSA

Assembly No. & Name

39. Amber
49. Lalsot
50. Sikrai
51. Bandikui
52. Dausa
54. Jamwa Ramgarh
55. Bairath
56. Kotputli

8. ALWAR

Assembly No. & Name

57. Bansur
58. Behror
59. Mandawar
60. Tizara
61. Khairthal
63. Alwar
64. Thanagazi
65. Rajgarh

9. BHARATPUR

Assembly No. & Name

62. Ramgarh
66. Lachhmangarh
67. Kathumar
68. Kaman
69. Nagar
70. Deeg
71. Kumher
72. Bharatpur

10. BAYANA

Assembly No. & Name

73. Rupbas
74. Nadbai
75. Weir
76. Bayana
77. Rajakhera
78. Dholpur
79. Bari
87. Mahuwa

11. SAWAI MADHOPUR

Assembly No. & Name

80. Karauli
81. Sapotra
82. Khandar
83. Sawai Madhopur
84. Bamanwas
85. Gangapur
86. Hindaun
88. Toda Bhim

12. AJMER

Assembly No. & Name

94. Kishangarh
95. Ajmer East
96. Ajmer West
97. Pushkar
98. Nasirabad
99. Beawar
100. Masuda
101. Bhinai

13. TONK

Assembly No. & Name

45. Phulera
46. Dudu
89. Niwai
90. Tonk
91. Uniara
92. Todaraisingh
93. Malpura
102. Kekri

14. KOTA

Assembly No. & Name

103. Hindoli
104. Nainwa
105. Patan
106. Bandi
107. Kota
109. Digod
110. Pipalda
111. Baran

15. JHALAWAR

Assembly No. & Name

112. Kishanganj
113. Atru
114. Chhabra
116. Khanpur
117. Manohar Thana
118. Jhalrapatan
119. Pirawa
120. Dag

16. BANSWARA

Assembly No. & Name

128. Kushalgarh
129. Danpur
130. Ghatol
131. Banswara
132. Bagidora
133. Sagwara
134. Chorasi
135. Dungarpur

17. SALUMBER

Assembly No. & Name

127. Pratapgarh
136. Aspur
137. Lasadia
144. Salumber
145. Sarada
146. Kherwara
147. Phalasia
148. Gogunda

18. UDAIPUR

Assembly No. & Name

138. Vallabhnagar
139. Mavli
140. Rajsamand
141. Nathdwara
142. Udaipur
143. Udaipur Rural
149. Kumbhalgarh
150. Bhim

19. CHITTORGARH

Assembly No. & Name

108. Ladpura
115. Ramganjmandi
121. Begun
122. Gangrar
123. Kapasin
124. Chittorgarh
125. Nimbahera
126. Badi Sadri

20. BHILWARA

Assembly No. & Name

151. Mandal
152. Sahada
153. Bhilwara
154. Mandalgarh
155. Jahazpur
156. Shahpura
157. Banera
158. Asind

21. PALI

Assembly No. & Name

159. Jaitaran
160. Raipur
161. Sojat
162. Kharchi
163. Desuri
164. Pali
165. Sumerpur
166. Bali

22. JALORE

Assembly No. & Name

167. Sirohi
168. Pindwara Abu
169. Reodar
170. Sanchore
171. Raniwada
172. Bhinmal
173. Jalore
174. Ahore

23. BARMER

Assembly No. & Name

175. Siwana
176. Pachpadra
177. Barmer
178. Gudamalani
179. Chohtan
180. Sheo
181. Jaisalmer
182. Shergarh

24. JODHPUR

Assembly No. & Name

183. Jodhpur
184. Sardarpura
185. Sursagar
186. Luni
187. Bilara
188. Bhopalgarh
189. Osian
190. Phalodi

25. NAGAUR

Assembly No. & Name

191. Nagaur
194. Deedwana
195. Nawan
196. Mokrana
197. Parbatsar
198. Degana
199. Merta
200. Mundwa

State: **Sikkik**

1. SIKKIM

Assembly No. & Name

1. Yoksam
2. Tashiding
3. Geyzing
4. Dentam
5. Barmiok
6. Rinchenpong
7. Chakung
8. Soreong
9. Daramdin
10. Jorthang-Nayabazar
11. Ralong
12. Wak
13. Damthang
14. Melli
15. Rateypani-West Pendam
16. Temi-Tarku
17. Central Pendam-East Pendam
18. Rhenock
19. Regu
20. Pathing
21. Loosing-Pachekhani
22. Khamdong
23. Djongu
24. LachenMangshila
25. Kabi Tingda
26. Rakdong Tentek
27. Martam
28. Rumtek
29. Assam-Lingjey
30. Ranka
31. Gangtok
32. Sangha

State: **Tamil Nadu**

1. MADRAS NORTH

Assembly No. & Name

1. Royapuram

2. Harbour
3. Dr Radhakrishna Nagar
5. Perambur
17. Thiruvottiyur
18. Villvakkam

2. MADRAS CENTRAL

Assembly No. & Name

4. Park Town
6. Purasawalkam
7. Egmore
8. Anna Nagar
10. Thousand Lights
11. Chepauk

3. MADRAS SOUTH

Assembly No. & Name

9. Theagaraja Nagar
12. Triplicane
13. Mylapore
14. Saidapet
19. Alandur
20. Tambaram

4. SRIPERUMBUDUR

Assembly No. & Name

15. Gummidipundi
16. Ponneri
27. Sriperumbudur
28. Poonamallee
29. Tiruvallur
30. Tiruttani

5. CHENGALPATTU

Assembly No. & Name

21. Tirupporur
22. Chengalpattu
23. Maduranthakam
24. Acharapakkam
25. Uthiramerur
26. Kancheepuram

6. ARAKKONAM

Assembly No. & Name

31. Pallipet
32. Arakkonam
33. Sholinghur
34. Ranipet
35. Arcot
50. Cheyyur

7. VELLORE

Assembly No. & Name

36. Katpadi
37. Gudiyatham
38. Pernambut
47. Anaicut
48. Vellore
49. Arni

8. TIRUPPATTUR

Assembly No. & Name

39. Vaniyambadi
40. Natrampalli
41. Tiruppattur
42. Chengam
43. Thandrambattu
45. Kalasapakkam

9. VANDAVASI

Assembly No. & Name

44. Tiruvannamalai
46. Polur
51. Vandavasi
52. Peranamallur
53. Melmalayanur
54. Gingee

10. TINDIVANAM

Assembly No. & Name

55. Tindivanam
56. Vanur
57. Kandamangalam
58. Villipuram
59. Mugaiyur
60. Thirunavalur

11. CUDDALORE

Assembly No. & Name

61. Ulundurpet
62. Nellikuppam
63. Cuddalore
64. Panruti
71. Rishivandiam
73. Sankarapuram

12. CHIDAMBARAM

Assembly No. & Name

65. Kurinjipadi
66. Bhuvanagiri
67. Kattumannarkoil
68. Chidambaram
69. Vridhachalam
70. Mangalore

13. DHARMAPURI

Assembly No. & Name

79. Harur
80. Morappur
82. Dharmapuri
83. Pennagaram
84. Mettur
85. Tarmangalam

14. KRISHNAGIRI

Assembly No. & Name

74. Hosur
75. Thalli
76. Kaveripattinam
77. Krishnagiri
78. Bargur
81. Palacode

15. RASIPURAM

Assembly No. & Name

72. Chinnaselam
92. Attur
93. Talavasal
94. Rasipuram
95. Sendamangalam
96. Namakkal

16. SALEM

Assembly No. & Name

86. Omalur
87. Yercaud
88. Salem I
89. Salem II
90. Veerapandi
91. Panamarathupatty

17. TIRUCHENGODE

Assembly No. & Name

97. Kapilmalai
98. Tiruchengode
99. Sankari
100. Edapadi
118. Modakurichi
120. Erode

18. NILGIRIS

Assembly No. & Name

101. Mettupalayam
102. Avanashi
103. Thondamuthur
126. Coonoor
127. Ootacamund
128. Gudalur

19. GOBICHETTIPALAYAM

Assembly No. & Name

119. Perundurai
121. Bhavani
122. Andhiyur
123. Gobichettipalayam
124. Bhavanisagar
125. Sathyamangalam

20. COIMBATORE

Assembly No. & Name

104. Singanallur
105. Coimbatore West
106. Coimbatore East
107. Perur
115. Palladam
116. Tiruppur

21. POLLACHI

Assembly No. & Name

108. Kinathukkadavu
109. Pollachi
110. Valparai
111. Udumalpet
112. Dharapuram
114. Pongalur

22. PALANI

Assembly No. & Name

113. Vellakoil
117. Kangayam
129. Palani
130. Oddanchatram
147. Natham
150. Vedasandur

23. DINDIGUL

Assembly No. & Name

137. Thirumangalam
138. Usilampatti
139. Nilakottai
140. Sholavaram
148. Dindigul
149. Athoor

24. MADURAI

Assembly No. & Name

141. Tirupparankundram
142. Madurai West
143. Madurai Central
144. Madurai East
145. Samayanallur
146. Melur

25. PERIYAKULAM

Assembly No. & Name

131. Periyakulam
132. Theni
133. Bodniayakkanur
134. Cumbum
135. Andipatti
136. Sedapatti

26. KARUR

Assembly No. & Name

151. Aravakurichi
152. Karur
153. Krishnarayapuram
154. Marungapuri

155. Kulithalai
156. Thottiam

27. TIRUCHIRAPPALLI

Assembly No. & Name

158. Musiri
159. Lalgudi
165. Srirangam
166. Tiruchirappalli I
167. Tirchirappalli II
168. Thiruverambur

28. PERAMBALUR

Assembly No. & Name

157. Uppiliapuram
160. Perambalur
161. Varahur
162. Ariyalur
163. Andimadam
164. Jayankondam

29. MAYILADATURAI

Assembly No. & Name

169. Sirkali
170. Poompuhar
171. Mayuram
172. Kuttalam
187. Kumbakonam
188. Thiruvidamarudur

30. NAGAPATATTINAM

Assembly No. & Name

173. Nannilam
174. Thiruvarur
175. Nagapattinam
176. Vedaranyam
177. Tiruthuraipundi
178. Mannargudi

31. THANJAVUR

Assembly No. & Name

181. Orathanad
182. Thiruvonam
183. Thanjavur
184. Tirvaiyaru
185. Papanasam
186. Valangiman

32. PUDUKOTTAI

Assembly No. & Name

179. Pudukottai
180. Peruvarani
190. Kolathur
191. Pudukkottai
192. Alangudi
193. Arantangi

33. SIVAGANGA

Assembly No. & Name

189. Thirumayam
194. Thiruppattur
195. Karaikudi
196. Tiruvadanai
197. Ilayangudi
198. Sivaganga

34. RAMANATHAPURAM

Assembly No. & Name

199. Manamadurai
200. Paramakudi
201. Ramanathapuram
202. Kadaladi
203. Mudukulathur
204. Aurppukottai

35. SIVAKASI

Assembly No. & Name

205. Sattur
206. Virudhunagar
207. Sivakasi
208. Srivilliputhur
209. Rajapalayam
212. Koilpatti

36. TIRUNELVELI

Assembly No. & Name

210. Vilathikulam
211. Pottapidaram
218. Tirunlveli
219. Palayamkottai
226. Srivaikuntam
227. Tuticorin

37. TENKASI

Assembly No. & Name

213. Sankaranayarkoil
214. Vasudevanallur
215. Kadayanallur
216. Tenkasi
217. Alangulam
221. Ambasumdram

38. TIRUCHENDUR

Assembly No. & Name

220. Cheranmahadevi
222. Nanguneri
223. Radhapuram
224. Sattangulam
225. Tiruchendur
228. Kanniyakumari

39. NAGERCOIL

Assembly No. & Name

229. Nagercoil

230. Colachel
231. Padmanabhapuram
232. Thiruvattar
233. Vilavancode
234. Killiyoor

State: **Tripura**

1. TRIPURA WEST

Assembly No. & Name

1. Simna
2. Mohanpur
3. Bamutia
4. Barjala
5. Khayerpur
6. Agartala
7. Ramnagar
8. Town Bordowali
9. Banamalipur
10. Majlishpur
11. Mandaibazar
12. Takarjala
13. Pratapgarh
14. Badharghat
15. Kamalasagar
16. Bishalgarh
17. Golaghati
18. Charilam
19. Boxanagar
20. Nalchar
21. Sonamura
22. Dhanpur
30. Bagma
31. Salgarh
32. Radhakishorepur
33. Matarbari
34. Kakraban
35. Rajnagar
36. Belonia
37. Santirbazar

2. TRIPURA EAST

Assembly No. & Name

23. Ramachandraghat
24. Khowai
25. Asharambari
26. Pramodenagar
27. Kalyanpur
28. Krishnapur
29. Teliamura
38. Hrishyamukh
39. Jolaibari
40. Manu
41. Sabroom
42. Ampinagar
43. Birganj
44. Raima Valley
45. kamalpur
46. Surma
47. Salema
48. Kulai
49. Chawmanu
50. Pabiachhara
51. Fatikroy
52. Chandipur
53. Kailasahar
54. Kurti
55. Kadamtala
56. Dharmanagar
57. Jubarajnagar
58. Pencharthal
59. Panisagar
60. Kanchanpur

State: **Uttar Pradesh**

1. TEHRI GARHWAL

Assembly No. & Name

1. Uttarkashi
2. Tehri
3. Deoprayag
423. Mussorie
425. Chakrata

2. GARHWAL

Assembly No. & Name

4. Lansdowne
5. Pauri
6. Karanprayag
7. Badrikedar
424. Dehradun

3. ALMORA

Assembly No. & Name

8. Didihat
9. Pithoragarh
10. Almora
11. Bageshwar
12. Ranikhet

4. NAINTAL

Assembly No. & Name

13. Nainital
14. Khatima
15. Haldwani
16. Kashipur
56. Baheri

5. BIJNOR

Assembly No. & Name

19. Afzalgarh
20. Nagina
21. Nazibabad
22. Bijnor
23. Chandpur

6. AMROHA

Assembly No. & Name

17. Seohara
18. Dhampur
24. Kanth
25. Amroha
26. Hasanpur

7. MORADABAD

Assembly No. & Name

30. Chandausi
31. Kundarki
32. Moradabad West
33. Moradabad
34. Moradabad Rural

8. RAMPUR

Assembly No. & Name

35. Thakurdwara
36. Suartanda
37. Rampur
38. Bilaspur
39. Shahabad

9. SAMBHAL

Assembly No. & Name

27. Gangeshwari
28. Sambhal
29. Bahjoi
40. Bisauli
41. Gunnour

10. BUDAUN

Assembly No. & Name

42. Sahaswan
43. Bilsi
44. Budaun
45. Usehat
347. Kasganj

11. AONLA

Assembly No. & Name

46. Binawar
47. Dataganj
48. Aonla
49. Sunha
50. Faridpur

12. BAREILLY

Assembly No. & Name

51. Bareilly Cantt
52. Bareilly City
53. Nawabganj
54. Bhojipura
55. Kawar

13. PILIBHIT

Assembly No. & Name

57. Pilibhit
58. Barkhera
59. Bisalpur
60. Puranpur
61. Powayan

14. SHAHJAHANPUR

Assembly No. & Name

62. Nigohi
63. Tilhar
64. Jalalabad
65. Dadraul
66. Shahjahanpur

15. KHERI

Assembly No. & Name

69. Paila
70. Lakhimpur
71. Srinagar
72. Nighasan
73. Dhaurehara

16. SHAHABAD

Assembly No. & Name

67. Mohammadi
68. Haiderabad
87. Bawan
88. Pihani
89. Shahabad

17. SITAPUR

Assembly No. & Name

74. Behta
75. Biswan
78. Laharpur
79. Sitapur
80. Hargaon

18. MISRIKH

Assembly No. & Name

76. Mahmoodabad
77. Sidhauli
81. Misrikh
82. Machhrehta
83. Beniganj

19. HARDOI

Assembly No. & Name

84. Sandila
85. Ahirori
86. Hardoi
90. Bilgram
91. Mallawan

20. LUCKNOW

Assembly No. & Name

100. Mohana
101. Lucknow East
102. Lucknow West
103. Lucknow Central
104. Lucknow Cantt

21. MOHANLALGANJ

Assembly No. & Name

97. Purva
98. Hasanganj
99. Malihabad
105. Sarojini Nagar
106. Mohanlalganj

22. UNNAO

Assembly No. & Name

92. Bangarmau
93. Safipur
94. Unnao
95. Hadha
96. Bhagwant Nagar

23. RAE BARELI

Assembly No. & Name

107. Bachhhrawan
109. Rae Bareli
110. Sataon
111. Sareni
112. Dalmau

24. PRATAPGARH

Assembly No. & Name

114. Kunda
115. Bihar
116. Rampurkhas
117. Garwara
118. Pratapgarh

25. AMETHI

Assembly No. & Name

108. Tiloi
113. Salon
121. Amethi
122. Gauriganj
123. Jagdishpur

26. SULTANPUR

Assembly No. & Name

124. Isauli
125. Sultanpur
126. Jaisingpur
127. Chanda
128. Kadipur

27. AKBARPUR

Assembly No. & Name

129. Katehari
130. Akbarpur
131. Jalalpur
132. Jahangirganj
133. Tanda

28. FAIZABAD

Assembly No. & Name

134. Ayodhya
135. Bikapur
136. Milkipur
137. Sohawal
138. Rudauli

29. BARA BANKI

Assembly No. & Name

140. Siddhaur
141. Haidergarh
142. Masauli
143. Nawabganj
144. Fatehpur

30. KAISERGANJ

Assembly No. & Name

139. Dariyabad
145. Ramnagar
146. Kaiserganj
147. Fakharpur
148. Mahsi

31. BAHRAICH

Assembly No. & Name

149. Nanpara
150. Charda
151. Bhinga
152. Bahraich
153. Ikauna

32. BALRAMPUR

Assembly No. & Name

154. Gainsari
155. Tulsipur
156. Balrampur
157. Utraula
158. Sadullah Nagar

33. GONDA

Assembly No. & Name

159. Mankapur
160. Mujehna
161. Gonda
162. Katra Bazar
163. Colonelganj

34. BASTI

Assembly No. & Name

164. Dixir
165. Harraiya
166. Captainganj
167. Nagar East
168. Basti

35. DOMARIAGANJ

Assembly No. & Name

170. Domariaganj
171. Itwa
172. Shohratgarh
173. Naugarh
174. Bansi

36. KHALILABAD

Assembly No. & Name

169. Ramnagar
175. Khesraha
176. Menhdawal
177. Khalilabad
178. Hainsarbazar

37. BANSGAON

Assembly No. & Name

179. Bansgaon
180. Dhuriapur
181. Chillupar
182. Kauriram
183. Mundera Bazar

38. GORAKHPUR

Assembly No. & Name

184. Pipraich
185. Gorakhpur
186. Maniram
187. Sahjanwa
183. Shyamdeurawa

39. MAHARAJGUNJ

Assembly No. & Name

188. Paniara
189. Pharenda
190. Luxmipur
191. Siswa
192. Maharajganj

40. PADRAUNA

Assembly No. & Name

194. Naurangia
195. Ramkola
196. Hata
197. Padrauna
198. Seorahi

41. DEORIA

Assembly No. & Name

199. Fazilnagar
200. Kasia
201. Gauri Bazar
202. Rudrapur
203. Deoria

42. SALEMPUR

Assembly No. & Name

204. Bhatpar Rani
205. Salempur
206. Barhaj
222. Siar
224. Sikanderpur

43. BALLIA

Assembly No. & Name

223. Chilkahar
225. Bansdih
226. Doaba
227. Ballia
228. Kopachit

44. GHOSI

Assembly No. & Name

207. Nathupur
208. Ghosi
209. Sagri
220. Mau
221. Rasra

45. AZAMGARH

Assembly No. & Name

210. Gopalpur
211. Azamgarh
213. Atraulia
214. Phulpur
215. Saraimir

46. LALGANJ

Assembly No. & Name

212. Nizamabad
216. Mehnagar
217. Lalganj
218. Mubarakpur
219. Muhammadabad Gohna

47. MACHHLISHAHR

Assembly No. & Name

119. Birapur
120. Patti
257. Khutahan
258. Garwara
259. Machhlishahr

48. JAUNPUR

Assembly No. & Name

250. Barsathi
251. Mariahu
254. Jaunpur
255. Rari
256. Shahganj

49. SAIDPUR

Assembly No. & Name

234. Jakhania
235. Sadat
236. Saidpur
252. Kerakat
253. Bayalsi

50. GHAZIPUR

Assembly No. & Name

229. Zahoorabad
230. Mohammadabad
231. Dildarnagar
232. Zamania
233. Ghazipur

51. CHANDAULI

Assembly No. & Name

237. Dhanapur
238. Chandauli
239. Chakiya
240. Mughalsarai
244. Chiraigaon

52. VARANASI

Assembly No. & Name

241. Varanasi Cantt
242. Varanasi South
243. Varanasi North
245. Kolasia
246. Gangapur

53. ROBERTSGANJ

Assembly No. & Name

260. Dudhi
261. Robertsganj
262. Rajgarh
263. Chunar
264. Majhwa

54. MIRZAPUR

Assembly No. & Name

247. Aurai
248. Gyanpur
249. Bhadohi
265. Mirzapur
266. Chhnabey

55. PHULPUR

Assembly No. & Name

270. Jhusi
271. Handia
272. Pratappur
273. Soraon
274. Nawabganj

56. ALLAHABAD

Assembly No. & Name

267. Meja
268. Karchana
269. Bara
275. Allahabad North
276. Allahabad South

57. CHAIL

Assembly No. & Name

277. Allahabad West
278. Chail
279d. Manjhanpur
280. Sirathu
281. Khaga

58. FATEHPUR

Assembly No. & Name

282. Kishunpur
283. Haswa
284. Fatehpur
286. Bindki
318. Tindwari

59. BANDA

Assembly No. & Name

315. Manikpur
316. Karwi
317. Baberu
319. Banda
320. Naraini

60. HAMIRPUR

Assembly No. & Name

321. Hamirpur
322. Maudaha
323. Rath
324. Charkhari
325. Mahoba

61. JHANSI

Assembly No. & Name

326. Mehroni
327. Lalitpur
328. Jhansi
329. Babina
330. Mauranipur

362. JALAUN

Assembly No. & Name

331. Garautha
332. Konch
333. Orai
334. Kalpi
335. Madhogarh

63. GHATAMPUR

Assembly No. & Name

285. Jahanabad
294. Ghatampur
295. Bhognipur
296. Rajpur
300. Derapur

64. BILHAUR

Assembly No. & Name

292. Kalyanpur
293. Sarsaul
295. Sarvankhera
298. Chaubepur
299. Bilhaur

65. KANPUR

Assembly No. & Name

287. Ayanagar
288. Sisamau
289. Generalganj
290. Kanpur Cantt
291. Gobindnagar

66. ETAWAH

Assembly No. & Name

301. Auraiya
302. Ajitmal
303. Lakhna
304. Etawah
305. jaswantnagar

67. KANNAUJ

Assembly No. & Name

306. Bhartana
307. Bidhuna
308. Kannauj
309. Umarda
310. Chibramau

68. FARRUKHABAD

Assembly No. & Name

311. Kamalganj
312. Farrukhabad
313. Kaimganj
314. Mohammadabad
336. Bhongara

69. MAINPURI

Assembly No. & Name

337. Kishni
338. Karhal
340. Jasrana
341. Ghiror
342. Mainpuri

70. JALESAR

Assembly No. & Name

349. Nidhauni Kalan
350. Jalesar
354. Tundla
355. Etmadpur
367. Sadabad

71. ETAH

Assembly No. & Name

343. Aliganj
344. Patiyali
345. Sakeet
346. Soron
348. Etah

72. FIROZABAD

Assembly No. & Name

339. Shikohabad
351. Firozabad
352. Bah
353. Fatehabad
360. Kheragarh

73. AGRA

Assembly No. & Name

356. Dayalbagh
357. Agra Cantt
358. Agra East
359. Agra West
361. Fatehpur Sikri

74. MATHURA

Assembly No. & Name

362. Goverdhan
363. Mathura
364. Chhata
365. Mat
366. Gokul

75. HATHRAS

Assembly No. & Name

368. Hathras
369. Sasni
370. Sikandara Rao
371. Gangiri
372. Atrauli

76. ALIGARH

Assembly No. & Name

373. Aligarh
374. Koil
375. Iglas
376. Barauli
377. Khair

77. KHURJA

Assembly No. & Name

378. Jewar
379. Khurja
380. Debai
386. Sikandrabad
387. Dadri

78. BULANDSHAHR

Assembly No. & Name

381. Anupshahr
382. Siana
383. Agota
384. Bulandshahr
385. Shikarpur

79. HAPUR

Assembly No. & Name

388. Ghaziabad
389. Muradnagar
390. Modinagar
391. Hapur
392. Garhmukteshwar

80. MEERUT

Assembly No. & Name

393. Kithore
394. Hastinapur
396. Meerut Cantt
397. Meerut
398. Kharkhadua

81. BAGHPAT

Assembly No. & Name

399. Siwalkhas
400. Khekra
401. Baghpat
402. Barnawa
403. Chhaprauli

82. MUZAFFARNAGAR

Assembly No. & Name

395. Sardhana
405. Khatauli
406. Jansath
407. Morna
408. Muzaffarnagar

83. KAIRANA

Assembly No. & Name

404. Kandhia
409. Charthawal
410. Baghra
411. Kairana
412. Thana Bhawan

84. SAHARANPUR

Assembly No. & Name

413. Nakur
414. Sarsawa
417. Harora
418. Saharanpur
419. Muzaffarabad

85. HARDWAR

Assembly No. & Name

415. Nagal
416. Deoband
420. Roorkee
421. Lhaksar
422. Hardwar

State: **West Bengal**

1. COOCH BEHAR

Assembly No. & Name

2. Sitalkuchi
3. Mathabhanga
4. Cooch Behar North
5. Cooch Behar West
6. Sitai
7. Dinhata
8. Natabari

2. ALIPURDUARS

Assembly No. & Name

9. Tufanganj
10. Kumargram
11. Kalchini
12. Alipurduars
13. Falakata
14. Madarihat
16. Nagrakata

3. JALPAIGURI

Assembly No. & Name

1. Mekliaganj

15. Dhupgiri
17. Mainaguri
18. Mal
19. Kranti
20. Jalpaiguri
21. Rajganj

4. DARJEELING

Assembly No. & Name

22. Kalimpong
23. Darjeeling
24. Kurseong
25. Siliguri
26. Phansidewa
27. Chopra
28. Islampur

5. RAIGANJ

Assembly No. & Name

29. Goalpokhar
30. Karandighi
31. Raiganj
34. Itahar
41. Kharba
42. Harishchandrapur
43. Ratua

6. BALURGHAT

Assembly No. & Name

32. Kaliaganj
33. Kushmandi
35. Gangarampur
36. Tapan
37. Kumarganj
38. Balurghat
40. Gajol

7. MALDA

Assembly No. & Name

39. Habibpur
44. Araidanga
45. Malda
46. English Bazar
47. Manikchak
48. Suzapur
49. Kaliachak

8. JANGIPUR

Assembly No. & Name

50. Farakka
51. Aurangabad
52. Suti
53. Sagardighi
54. Jangipur
57. Nabagram
66. Khargram

9. MURSHIDABAD

Assembly No. & Name

55. Lalgola
56. Bhagabangola
58. Murshidabad
59. Jalangi
60. Domkal
62. Hariharpara
69. Karimpur

10. BERHAMPORE

Assembly No. & Name

61. Naoda
63. Berhampore
64. Beldanga
65. Kandi
67. Barwan
68. Bharatpur
282. Ketugram

11. KRISHNAGAR

Assembly No. & Name

70. Palashipara
71. Nakashipara
72. Kaliganj
73. Chapra
74. Krishnaganj
75. Krishnagar East
76. Krishnagar West

12. NABADWIP

Assembly No. & Name

77. Nabadwip
78. Santipur
79. Hanskhali
80. Ranaghat East
81. Ranaghat West
82. Chakdaha
83. Haringhata

13. BARASAT

Assembly No. & Name

84. Bagdaha
85. Bongaon
86. Gaighata
87. Habra
88. Ashokenagar
90. Barasat
92. Deganga

14. BASIRHAT

Assembly No. & Name

93. Swarupnagar
94. Baduria
95. Basirhat
96. Hasnabad

97. Haroa
99. Hingalganj
107. Bhangar

15. JOYNAGAR

Assembly No. & Name

98. Sandeshkhali
100. Gosaba
101. Basanti
102. Kultali
103. Joynagar
105. Canning West
106. Canning East

16. MATHURAPUR

Assembly No. & Name

121. Magrahat East
122. Mandirbazar
123. Mathurapur
124. Kulpi
125. Patharpratima
126. Kakdwip
127. Sagar

17. DIAMOND HARBOUR

Assembly No. & Name

111. Bishnupur West
114. Garden Reach
115. Maheshtala
116. Budge Budge
117. Satgachia
118. Falta
119. Diamond Harbour

18. JADAVPUR

Assembly No. & Name

104. Baruipur
108. Jadavpur
110. Bishnupur East
112. Behala East
113. Behala West
120. Magrahat West
147. Kabitirtha

19. BARRACKPORE

Assembly No. & Name

89. Amdanga
128. Bijpur
129. Naihati
130. Bhatpara
131. Jagatdal
132. Noapara
133. Titagarh

20. DUM DUM

Assembly No. & Name

91. Rajarhat
134. Khardah
135. Panihati
136. Kamarhati
137. Baranagar
138. Dum Dum
139. Belgachia East

21. CALCUTTA NORTH WEST

Assembly No. & Name

140. Cossipur
141. Shyampukar
142. Jorabagan
143. Jorasanko
144. Bara Bazar
145. Bow Bazar
154. Taltola

22. CALCUTTA NORTH EAST

Assembly No. & Name

153. Entally
154. Beliaghata
156. Sealdah
157. Vidyasagar
158. Burtola
159. Manicktola
160. Belgachia West

23. CALCUTTA SOUTH

Assembly No. & Name

109. Sonarpur
146. Chowringhee
148. Alipore
149. Rashbehari Avenue
150. Tollygunge
151. Dhakuria
152. Ballygunge

24. HOWRAH

Assembly No. & Name

161. Bally
162. Howrah North
163. Howrah Central
164. Howrah South
165. Shibpur
166. Domjur
169. Sankrail

25. ULUBERIA

Assembly No. & Name

170. Uluberia North
171. Uluberia South
172. Shyampur
173. Bagnan
174. Kalyanpur
175. Amta
176. Udaynarayanpur

26. SERAMPORE

Assembly No. & Name

167. Jagatballavpur
168. Panchla
177. Jangipara
178. Chanditala
179. Uttarpara
180. Serampore
181. Champdani

27. HOOGLY

Assembly No. & Name

182. Chandernagore
183. Singur
184. Haripal
186. Chinsurah
187. Bansberia
190. Polba
191. Dhaniakhali

28. ARAMBAGH

Assembly No. & Name

185. Tarakeswar
192. Pursurah
193. Khanakul
194. Arambagh
195. Goghat
196. Chandrakona
197. Ghatal

29. PANSKURA

Assembly No. & Name

198. Daspur
199. Nandanpur
200. Panskura West
216. Sabang
217. Pingla
218. Debra
219. Keshpur

30. TAMLUK

Assembly No. & Name

201. Panskura East
202. Tamluk
203. Moyna
204. Mahishadal
205. Sutahata
206. Nandigram
207. Narghat

31. CONTAI

Assembly No. & Name

208. Bhagabanpur
209. Khajuri
210. Contai North
211. Contai South
212. Ramnagar
213. Egra
214. Mugberia

32. MIDNAPORE

Assembly No. & Name

215. Pataspur
223. Midnapore
224. Kharagpur Town
225. Kharagpur Rural
226. Keshiari
227. Narayangarh
228. Dantan

33. JHARGRAM

Assembly No. & Name

220. Garhbeta East
221. Garhbeta West
222. Salbani
229. Nayagram
230. Gopiballavpur
231. Jhargram
232. Binpur

34. PURULIA

Assembly No. & Name

233. Banduan
234. Manbazar
235. Balrampur
236. Arsa
237. Jhalda
238. Jaipur
239. Purulia

35. BANKURA

Assembly No. & Name

240. Para
241. Raghunathpur
242. Kashipur
243. Hura
248. Chhatna
251. Bankura
252. Onda

36. VISHNUPUR

Assembly No. & Name

244. Taldangra
245. Raipur
246. Ranibandh
247. Indpur
253. Vishnupur
254. Kotulpur
255. Indas

37. DURGAPUR

Assembly No. & Name

249. Gangajalghati

250. Barjora
256. Sonamukhi
264. Durgapur I
265. Durgapur I
266. Kanksa
269. Galsi

38. ASANSOL

Assembly No. & Name

257. Kulti
258. Barabani
259. Hirapur
260. Asansol
261. Raniganj
262. Jamuria
263. Ukhra

39. BURDWAN

Assembly No. & Name

268. Bhatar
270. Burdwan North
271. Burdwan South
272. Khandaghosh
273. Raina
274. Jamalpur
275. Memari

40. KATWA

Assembly No. & Name

188. Balagarh
189. Pandua
276. Kalna
277. Nandanghat
278. Manteswar
279. Purbasthali
280. Katwa

41. BOLPUR

Assembly No. & Name

267. Ausgram
281. Mangalkot
283. Nanur
284. Bolpur
285. Labhpur
286. Dubrajpur
290. Mayureswar

42. BIRBHUM

Assembly No. & Name

287. Rajnagar
288. Suri
289. Mahammad Bazar
291. Rampurhat
292. Hansan
293. Nalhati
294. Murarai

UT: **A&N Islands**

1. A&N ISLANDS

UT: **Chandigarh**

CHANDIGARH

UT: **Dadra & Nagar Haveli**

1. DADRA & NAGAR HAVELI

UT: **Daman & Diu**

1. DAMAN & DIU

UT: **NCT of Delhi**

1. NEW DELHI

Assembly No. & Name

1. Sarojini Nagar (Part)
2. Gole Market (Part)
3. Minto Road (Part)
4. Kasturba Nagar (Part)
5. Jangpura
58. Matia Mahal (Part)

2. SOUTH DELHI

Assembly No. & Name

1. Sarojini Nagar (Part)
2. Gole Market (Part)
4. Kasturba Nagar (Part)
6. Okhla
7. Kalkaji
8. Malviya Nagar (Part)
9. Haus Khas
10. R.K. Puram
11. Delhi Cantt
12. Janak Puri (Part)
13. Hari Nagar
14. Tilak Nagar
15. Rajouri Garden

3. OUTER DELHI

Assembly No. & Name

8. Malviya Nagar (Part)
12. Janak Puri (Part)
16. Madipur
17. Tri Nagar
18. Shakurbasti
19. Shalimar Bagh
20. Badli
21. Sahibabad Daulatpur
22. Bawana
23. Sultanpur Majra
24. Mangolpuri
25. Nangloi Jat
26. Vishnu Garden

27. Hastsal
28. Najafgarh
29. Nasirpur
30. Palam
31. Mahipalpur
32. Mehrauli
33. Saket
34. Dr Ambedkar Nagar
35. Tughlakabad
36. Badarpur
54. Narela (Part)
55. Bhalswa Jahangirpur (Part)

4. EAST DELHI

Assembly No. & Name

37. Trilok Puri
38. Patpar Ganj
39. Mandawali
40. Geeta Colony
41. Gandhi Nagar
42. Krishna Nagar
43. Vishwas Nagar
44. Shahdara
45. Seemapuri
46. Nand Nagari
47. Rohtas Nagar
48. Babarpur
49. Seelampur
50. Ghonda
51. Yamuna Vihar
52. Qarawal Nagar
53. Wazirpur
54. Narela (Part)
55. Bhalswa Jahangirpur (Part)
56. Adarsh Nagar
61. Timarpur (Part)
62. Model Town (Part)

5. CHANDNI CHOWK

Assembly No. & Name

3. Minto Road (Part)
57. Pahar Ganj
58. Matia Mahal (Part)
59. Balli Maran
60. Chandni Chowk
69. Ram Nagar (Part)

6. DELHI SADAR

Assembly No. & Name

61. Timarpur (Part)
62. Model Town (Part)
63. Kamla Nagar
64. Sadar Bazar
65. Moti Nagar (Part)

7. KAROL BAGH

Assembly No. & Name

65. Moti Nagar (Part)
66. Patel Nagar
67. Rajinder Nagar
68. Karol Bagh
69. Ram Nagar (Part)
70. Baljit Nagar

UT: Lakshadweep

1. LAKSHADWEEP

UT: Pondicherry

1. PONDICHERRY

Assembly No. & Name

1. Muthialpet
2. Cassicade
3. Raj Bhavan
4. Bussy
5. Oupalam
6. Orleampeth
7. Nellithope
8. Modeliarpeth
9. Ariankuppam
10. Embalom
11. Nettapakkam
12. Kuruvinatham
13. Bahour
14. Thirubuvanai
15. Mannadipeth
16. Ossudu
17. Villenour
18. Ozhukarai
19. Thattanchavady
20. Reddiarpalyam
21. Lawspet
22. Cotchery
23. Karaikal
24. Karaikal South
25. Neravee-Grand Aldee
26. Tirunallar
27. Neduncadu
28. Mahe
29. Palloor
30. Yanam

Index